Performing Motherhood

•

The Sévigné Correspondence

Michèle Longino Farrell

•

PERFORMING MOTHERHOOD

The Sévigné Correspondence

UNIVERSITY PRESS OF NEW ENGLAND

Hanover and London

•

© 1991 by University Press of New England, Hanover, NH 03755
All rights reserved
Printed in the United States of America   5   4   3   2   1
CIP data appear at the end of the book

FOR NICHOLAS WITH LOVE

Contents

Acknowledgments

This book has been the proverbial long time in the making. Hence I am thankful to many people and to three institutions in particular for encouragement, support, and good counsel over the years of its maturation. I am indebted to members of the Romance Languages Department at the University of Michigan—to Floyd Gray, to Ross Chambers, and to Domna Stanton for their contributions at the inception of this project. I thank my former colleagues at Rice University for their interest in my work. I am grateful to Michael Fischer, Jane Gallop, and Elizabeth Long for their advice on thinking through and shaping the book. Elizabeth was an especially important critic and friend; her careful readings of chapters, her helpful comments, and our back porch consultations were invaluable. And I owe many thanks to my colleagues in the Department of Romance Studies at Duke University for their enthusiasm and encouragement. Philip Stewart asked pertinent questions that caused me to rethink certain points. Alice Kaplan deserves a very special thanks for helping me see the manuscript through the final throes and for helping see me through them as well. I am also grateful to Naomi Schor for her generous readiness to share her wisdom and talk through the travails of the writing and publishing process.

In addition, I thank Susan Weiner and Margaret Spires for their assistance with the translations and the final manuscript preparation. Faith Beasley and English Showalter provided most sensitive and useful readings of the manuscript; they made excellent suggestions for revisions. Irma Garlick is to be thanked for her superb copyediting of the manuscript. Many other friends and colleagues read portions of the book in earlier versions or discussed some of the ideas with me. I have particularly benefited from conversations or correspondences with Odette de Mourgues, Roger Duchêne, Marie-Odile Sweetser, Joan DeJean, Virginia Carmichael, Melanic Hawthorne, Patsy Baudoin, Helen Longino, Deborah Brown, Joan Stewart, and Harriet Allentuch. The book is the better for the advice of these people.

Warm thanks go to my mother and to my sisters for their support of this project; I particularly want to thank my sister Helen Longino for her steady belief in me and my work through the years.

Some of the chapters are based on previously published materials. Part of chapter 1 was first published as "Praise, in Theory . . . and in Practice: The Case of La Bruyère and Sévigné," *Cahiers du dix-septième: An Interdisciplinary Journal* 1, 1 (Spring 1987): 203–11. Portions of chapter 6 first appeared as "Sévigné: The Art of Vicarious Living," in *Women in French Literature*, ed. Michel Guggenheim (*Stanford French and Italian Studies* 58, 1988), 65–75; "Measuring Maternity," in *Competition: A Feminist Taboo?* ed. Valerie Miner and Helen Longino (New York: The City University of New York, The Feminist Press, 1987), 141–51; and "Patterns of Excellence: Sévigné in the Classical Maternal Tradition," *Papers on French Seventeenth-Century Literature* 13, no. 25 (1986): 27–38. A version of chapter 8 appeared as "Grandmother Sévigné: Shaping Relationships," *Stanford French Review* 11 (Fall 1987): 279–96. I am grateful to the editors for permission to use this material.

April 1991   M.L.F.

Performing Motherhood

·

The Sévigné Correspondence

Introduction

In recent years, feminist critics have been intent on establishing a history of women's writing that would ground current discourses of feminism. They would consider, while locating and rereading women's texts, the coherences, contradictions, and shifts of the constituent concerns of those discourses as informed by a social system that has, for all its mutations, persisted over time in maintaining a fixed set of gender relations. But such an archaeological project runs the risk of any such systematizing endeavor—that of articulating a canon that will in its turn privilege certain authors and texts at the expense of others.[1]

Works by women that cannot be readily cited or recovered as exemplary feminist texts tend to be disregarded, and, as a consequence, the complexities of the history of women's coming to writing are discreetly repressed. The story of women and writing is a complicated one, and it is perhaps through attention to that very complication, to those troubling writings that cannot be easily claimed, that a more enabling construction of the relationship between women and writing can be imagined.

This study of Mme de Sévigné's writing aims to complement the ongoing project of discovering and revalorizing forgotten and obscured women's texts by interrogating the conditions of the ready integration and celebration of her letters in the traditional canon. It problematizes the writing of a woman so readily received and discusses the political frames or "contingencies of literary values"[2] that have assigned her her position of prominence and constructed our understanding of who she is and what her writing represents. My reading of Mme de Sévigné's correspondence calls into question the ideological functions of her canonization, primarily through investigation of her complex enactment of maternity, or motherhood, and through tracings of her position in relation to the prevailing literary culture as well as to the dominant cultural authority of her time.[3]

Feminist revision of the French seventeenth-century canon has to date addressed the need to rediscover women's texts that were relegated to obscurity, to reassess women's texts that were misunderstood, or to reclaim those that were misattributed, as well as to celebrate those that have been identified as significant models of a distinctive female plot.[4] A complementary task entails reviewing those women's works that have known great success—that have been easily integrated into the normative canon— and examining how these writings have passed so readily into the official domain of "Literature." The Sévigné *Correspondance* is a case in point. Indicative of the popularity this work has enjoyed through the centuries is the proliferation of editions, anthologies, thematic collections, articles, and studies derived from and devoted to it. That this text was selected to inaugurate the prestigious series Les Grands Ecrivains de la France, launched by the publishing house Hachette in the mid-nineteenth century, and that, in the twentieth century, Gallimard's distinguished Bibliothèque de la Pléiade should trouble to publish not one but two editions of the *Correspondance*, and this within only fifteen years of each other, attests to the status it enjoys as a classic in the French world of writing.[5] However, the interest and enthusiasm Mme de Sévigné's writing enduringly inspires in the official, normative domain of letters has not been readily shared by feminist scholars, and this fact alone invites investigation.

I suggest that Mme de Sévigné's superb talent as writer, demonstrated in her correspondence, was undisputed because she absorbed and represented the code governing appropriate generic behavior for women in her time. As a consequence, her letters were readily accepted and assimilated by the male corpus. Her contemporary peers perceived her as intent upon enacting her assigned role and propagating her own acceptable attitudes particularly in her exchange with her daughter. And they saw the correspondence as an appropriate mode of expression for women's sentiment and, unlike the grand world-defining genres (history, drama, poetry, philosophy), as a writerly medium where women might claim pride of place.

Mme de Sévigné inscribed herself within the bounds of propriety by restricting her writing to the appropriately marginal domain of the epistolary, and by positing her authority within the plausible sphere of her maternity.[6] The acceptability of her passion for writing was thus ensured and its immediate and enduring success guaranteed. But these same delimitations of ambition appear to have produced discord within the domestic realm they privileged. This alienation is particularly evident in the female generational continuum of mother/daughter/granddaughter and appears necessary to the workings of the patriarchal body politic that the family microcosmically enfigures and supports.[7]

The study that follows traces the absorption of the dominant social code in Mme de Sévigné's project of epistolary self-representation and focuses on the process of its transmission. It helps to explain how it is that Mme de Sévigné has been so enthusiastically claimed by the guardians of the traditional canon. She has successfully represented to them and for them their own tacit vision of women's "proper" place in the world and in writing.

The Sévigné *Correspondance* has traditionally been received not only as an outstanding example of fine style, or as a rich source of journalistic information on daily life and particular events in seventeenth-century France, but also as a rare expression of maternal sentiment and exquisite testimony to maternal devotion. Convention has accorded to Mme de Sévigné the maternal niche in the typology of literary figures.[8] Today, however, the term *maternal* no longer functions as an automatic accolade. In recent years, a certain number of critics have given special attention to the maternal dimension of Mme de Sévigné's self-portrayal and interpreted her profile variously.[9] None of them has claimed her for a pantheon of maternity or one of feminism, but they have all worked toward developing an understanding of the relationship between her writing and her maternity. What is needed is a study that neither forces current theories of the maternal on this seventeenth-century text nor renounces the possibility of understanding a mother-daughter relation inscribed in a distant past, but which respects and explores the tensions between these two positions in an effort to map out distances traveled and yet to be charted in the project of locating, historicizing, and theorizing "the maternal."

Current historical analyses maintain that the institution of motherhood (as opposed to the "experience," to borrow Adrienne Rich's distinction) represents a social construct elaborated within the framework of patriarchal society: definitions and prescriptions for maternal behavior fluctuate in accordance with the needs of that organizing system.[10] In the light of such investigations, close reading of the Sévigné letters, attentive to the historical, social, cultural, and literary context of their writing, reveals a more complex and intricately constructed image of the "maternal" than has been previously described. The choice of epistolary writing and the generic privileging of the maternal role are mutually motivated by the patriarchal context that informed Mme de Sévigné's world and which significantly continues to shape our own.

A brief glance at some facts of Mme de Sévigné's biography reads the familiar pattern of a female life shaped by the lives of the men surrounding her, with the marked exception of her eventual enthusiastic commitment to the status of widowhood. Marie de Rabutin-Chantal, Mme de Sévigné (1626–96) lived a life constrained by the fact that her father and her husband, Henri, were both of the minor nobility, and by the chance of the early death of her husband (1651), killed in a duel over his mistress. She had two children, Françoise-Marguerite (1646–1705) and Charles (1648–1713). Her own parents had died while she was still very young: she was only one year old when her father Celse-Bénigne de Rabutin, baron of Chantal, was killed at the siege of the island of Ré (1627); and her mother, Marie de Coulanges, died when she was seven (1633). She was brought up mainly by the maternal side of her family, the Coulanges, with supervision from the paternal Rabutins. From what can be known of her childhood through her own letters and other documents, she enjoyed no special relation with any older female relative but was fondly looked after by her maternal uncles, Philippe (1595–1659), who was appointed her official guardian in 1637, and Christophe, the abbé of Livry (1607–87), in particular; and she developed lasting friendships with her first cousins Philippe-Emmanuel de Coulanges (1633–1716) and Roger de Rabutin, count of Bussy (1618–93).[11] In this complex of relationships with males—nurturing matrilineal father figures, more distant patrilineal relatives, brotherly cousins, flighty husband, and, eventually, fatherless son, Sévigné's tie to her daughter stood apart. Françoise-Marguerite, married to the count of Grignan, became a crucial element in the process of self-definition her mother's letters constitute.

Mme de Sévigné's *Correspondance* represents the totality of this woman's writings. The first letter in the most complete collection available today, Roger Duchêne's edition, is dated 1648; the last one, 1696. Forty-eight years are spanned in this writing; but for the most part, the letters, in their chronology and focus, coincide with and are profoundly informed by the early and middle years of the reign of Louis XIV (1661–1715). Mme de Sévigné corresponded with her cousins Coulanges and Bussy, and with a number of friends, but her most intense epistolary relationship was with her married daughter. Over a period of twenty-three years, from the moment of her daughter's departure from Paris to Provence in 1671 until their final reunion there, Mme de Sévigné wrote copiously to her at least twice a week. The only interruptions in the exchange of letters occurred when the two women found themselves together. She produced no other sorts of texts, nor is her life distinguished by any other so-called accomplishment or significant activity. What can be known of Mme de Sévigné, except for minor references here and there in writings of her contemporaries, is available only through her letters. However, unlike Virginia Woolf's Elizabethan woman, whose entire self-inscription consisted only of "a handful of . . . letters,"[12] the Sévigné epistolary corpus is enormous and offers a wealth of auto-graphical material to the reader interested in studying how a seventeenth-century woman assigned meaning to her life through writing. In order to understand the place of her maternal writing in the *his*-story of motherhood, it is necessary to understand the *her*-story of her coming to writing. A sociohistorical contextualizing of the scene of her relational writing allows at least a speculative perspective on that story.

The year 1661 marked the end of a turbulent era in France, a period remarkable for the degree of influence aristocratic women enjoyed, and for the amount of power they wielded. In that year, Mazarin, the prime minister who had represented the interests of the queen mother, Anne of Austria, during her regency, died, and her son Louis XIV assumed absolute control of the government. To summarize briefly, the Fronde (1648–53) had divided the nobility into royalist and antiroyalist camps, and women (particularly the duchess of Longueville) had played an active role in the politics of that split. Upon his accession, the young king was determined not to allow such a threat to the monarchy to recur. He gradually removed the seat of power from Paris to Versailles, redistributed favor, and established a system of privilege and authority based on merit rather than title. He thereby forced the nobility into a posture of dependence. Earlier, in the 1640s, the more dispersed salon society of Paris had provided cultural and political leadership. Distinguished women, such as Mme de Rambouillet, had healed the wounds of the Civil Wars and refined the rough manners of a generation bred to bloodshed. This society had cultivated an ethos of *préciosité* that valorized women. It was now displaced in the 1670s and 1680s by a centralized court society that was organized exclusively around the king. The social spectacle of life at Versailles, with its closely monitored rituals and its carefully orchestrated displays, constituted the visible expression of absolute power.[13] Etiquette functioned as a discreet instrument of coercion: its articulation of hierarchy conservatively ensured the preeminence of the monarch. This concentration of power fostered both compliance and competition among the courtiers in efforts to secure royal favor. The status that women had earlier enjoyed among the salon elite in a plurality of centers of influence was diminished and reduced to supportive and ornamental obligation at court, absorbed in the monolithic cult of the king.[14]

Mme de Sévigné occupied an interstitial position in this society. She had access to the court, visited it occasionally, and like all of France she had her eye constantly on that arena. But she and her friends were primarily Parisian. Many of them, either directly (Retz, La Rochefoucauld) or indirectly (Mme de Lafayette), had been implicated in plottings against the monarchy during the Fronde. Or they were products of an earlier period and held to the values of their salons (Mlle de Scudéry). And one good friend in particular, Fouquet—an ambitious minister of finance and distinguished patron of the arts—fell from grace as the king assumed power. Mme de Sévigné's own paternal cousin Bussy was exiled to his estate, and neither the Sévigné household nor the Coulanges family enjoyed particular favor with the king. Although Mme de Sévigné followed with avid attention all the court intrigues and acted whenever possible to advance her family's interests, she herself played only a minor role on the periphery of that centralized circle of influence.

Mme de Sévigné divided her time between her native Paris, Livry—the country seat of her maternal uncle "le bien bon" abbé de Coulanges—and her husband's estate of Les Rochers in Brittany. She made occasional visits as well to various properties inherited in Burgundy from the Rabutin side of her family. Upon her daughter's marriage and move to Grignan in Provence, she began also to visit the south of France; and it is there that she died in 1696.[15] Unlike most of her peers, while she was an eminently social creature and thoroughly enjoyed city life, she did not feel deprived or unhappy when she had to spend time in the provinces. She did not mind looking after her estates and protecting her revenue. Rather, she often claimed to enjoy country life, and when she was forced to spend prolonged periods away from Paris in efforts to economize by living a simpler country life and by taking personal interest in her property, she made the best of it through her writing.

Mme de Sévigné cultivated and privileged her public maternal identity, performing her chosen role in keeping with the demands for display of her milieu. She thus asserted purpose and assured visibility for herself in a society that was intent on categorizing and thereby stratifying itself, organizing itself in relation to the king. The circumstances of her situation in the world help to explain this choice. Orphaned at a tender age, of only moderate means, of the lesser nobility, and widowed early on, she could expect neither distinction nor support from family, fortune, or marriage. She sought a certain stability and continuity through the network of her family relations and identified the meaning of her own life in her daughter's, as *mater*.

Like many of her social standing, Mme de Sévigné often found her finances in a precarious state, despite her constant attention to them. Her means just met her needs; they barely permitted her to establish her two children in society. Only regular retreats to the country, a careful watch on expenses, the administrative assistance of her uncle enabled her to maintain the appearances requisite to her station. Although, as a Rabutin, she had roots in the aristocracy, she was raised by the less distinguished Coulanges and absorbed their more bourgeois code regarding expenditure. She did not spend money she did not have, she paid her debts, and she abhorred prodigality. Her social standing was also somewhat precarious: Henri, her husband and the father of her two children, did not hold a real claim to the title of baron; she herself was known as "marquise" simply as a courtesy.[16]

Her status as a widow from 1652 on limited her potential role in court society. Deprived early of the more socially integrated role of wife, she was relegated to the margins of a patriarchically organized world. However, Mme de Sévigné did not seek to remedy her situation and to reinstate herself through remarriage (a common practice at that time). Instead she actively embraced her widowhood and continued to enjoy circulation in the less male-dominated, socially eclipsed, but ever lively salon society of Paris. While she regularly acknowledged the troubling state of her finances, she preferred independence to security. Although she did not comment directly on her own widowhood, she recognized indirectly that this was one of the few social identities that allowed some autonomy to women. She celebrated it in her remarks on the death of her niece's husband: "le nom de veuve emporte avec lui celui de *liberté*" (II, L. 781, p. 999) [the name of widow carries with it the name of liberty]. She listed all the advantages to be enjoyed by her widowed niece, not the least of which was her niece's own pleasure at her new status, clouded only by the continuing demands of yet another man, or still the first one—her father;[17] and she claimed the death of a child to be greater cause for grief than that of a spouse.[18]

The disparagement of marriage and the commitment instead to motherhood is consonant with Mme de Sévigné's own biography. Indeed, widows did enjoy a degree of autonomy unusual for women in the seventeenth century. As Ian Maclean points out, during the Renaissance, "only the widow enjoys any real privileges, for she has the wardship of her children and the dispensation of her husband's goods and property," and she retains this advantage in the next century: "as widows, women keep their husband's place in society, they are assured the protection of both God and man, they are exempt from the trials of marriage." [19] Widows commonly assumed the paternal role both within and without the family. Mme de Sévigné's good friend, Mme de Lafayette, in fact, elaborated the phallic function of the widowed mother in *La Princesse de Clèves*.[20] Indeed her pivotal character, Mme de Chartres, is often said to have been modeled on Mme de Sévigné.[21] As Mme de La Fayette's fiction suggests, there were profound implications for relations in the dynamic obtaining between a widowed mother and her daughter. This fiction is substantiated in the charged relation Mme de Sévigné and her daughter, Françoise-Marguerite, both enjoyed and endured.

Mme de Sévigné was known among her contemporaries as the *caméléon*.[22] While this label was ostensibly intended to epitomize her inconstancy, it suggests also, on the part of those who thus named her, a certain discomfort with the fact that she moved fairly freely in the world, unconstrained by conjugal loyalties and obligations. She elaborated her own politics and behaved in her own interest. And, in contrast to the implied criticism, the record shows that she was markedly faithful to her friends even as they fell from power, among them Fouquet, Retz, and Bussy. But she needed to and did seek footing in the world, both for her own sake and for her children's: she sought to adapt to various situations by shaping herself conservatively according to others' visions of her. She was thereby able to conform to the demands and expectations of a full range of social situations and different personalities and to establish a broad base of friends and allies. This talent of Mme de Sévigné for accommodating self-presentation points up the performed aspect of her social behavior, and the fact that it was not visibly harnessed to any immediately male interests probably explains the distrust it engendered.

Her cousin Bussy described her caustically on more than one occasion, and although the nastiness was gratuitous, there was often a grain of truth in his words. He said of her in his satirical *Histoire amoureuse des Gaules*: "Elle aime l'encens, elle aime d'être aimée, et pour cela elle sème afin de recueillir, elle donne de la louange pour en recevoir"[23] [She loves flattery, she loves to be loved, and for that she sows in order to reap, she gives praise in order to receive it].[24] Bussy's remark finds more than a clinical echo in Freud's description of narcissistic women as those who "n'aiment à strictement parler, qu'elles-mêmes, à peu près aussi intensément que l'homme les aime. Leur besoin ne les fait pas tendre à aimer, mais à être aimées" [strictly speaking, love only themselves, more or less as intensely as man loves them. Their need does not make them tend to love, but to be loved]. This narcissistic case is further theorized as related to the woman's attempt to reproduce the founding relationship of herself as nursing child to her mother.[25] To categorize Mme de Sévigné as a "narcissistic chameleon" is indeed a markedly judgmental diagnosis, but to consider the personality structure and implied behavior that portrayal suggests is useful in understanding the social profile she elaborated as writing mother. It is equally helpful in situating the perspective of her portrait artists. Mme de Sévigné lived in a sense through the assimilative and protective image she succeeded in eliciting for herself (like a chameleon) from her environment, and in projecting (like Narcissus) onto others, and she recognized that image most clearly in her own daughter. In this mirroring activity, she turned to her daughter for nurturing.[26] In so doing, she was enacting and inscribing the maternal figure and the relational posture prescribed for women by male authorities in manuals on "feminine" comportment and "feminine" writing during her time. Successors of these experts who insisted on the relational nature as proper to women would, once they succeeded in eliciting that behavior in them, diagnose it as pathological.

Before considering further Mme de Sévigné's actualization of the maternal role through correspondence with her daughter, an obvious question demands attention. There were two children. Why did the mother favor a writing relationship with the daughter rather than with her son, Charles? Françoise-Marguerite's younger brother led a fairly effaced life, and he plays little role in his mother's letters: he provides amusing material or happens to be in the vicinity and is therefore included as his mother writes. A fragmented portrait, composed of anecdotes, scraps of information, and a few lines of his own added to his mother's letters is almost all that remains of Charles. Mme de Sévigné did not count on him as she did on his sister: he was a welcome diversion when she had him with her, he was always a trial when it was a question of money, and he was an embarrassment to her when his lack of ambition surfaced.

His own potential future was restricted, paradoxically, in this rigidly patriarchal system, by his patrimonial entitlement. He inherited his father's rank and fortune, but since these were both unexceptional, they provided no assurance of a brilliant career. Further, Charles was deprived, from the age of three, of the father who might have been able to introduce him into the male spheres of influence and favor at court; nor, because of his limited finances, could he hope to build a great reputation in the military. It must be added, in fairness to this dubious system of advancement, that Charles was reputed to be lacking in ambition as well. He led a somewhat dissolute life in his youth, had a brief and undistinguished career in the army, and then settled into a discreet life of religious devotion. He married beneath his station in order to secure his finances, and he and his wife produced no children. His situation did not augur well for a brilliant social ascendancy. As a man in a man's world, but without a father, it was both his prerogative and his fate to determine his own life, to forge his own destiny, alone.

The widowed Mme de Sévigné assumed the paternal role with regard to her children and did what she could to advance their interests, but she did not have access to a system of patronage that could benefit her son. The paternal authority that devolved on her as widow allowed for the familial stability that would preserve the honor of the patronym, but it did not extend to entitle her to actual participation in the world of men on behalf of her son. Social mobility paradoxically favored women: men were both cursed and blessed in bearing the patronym. It appears that Sévigné saw in her adult daughter a fascinating mirror of herself that would explain why it was to her that she chose to write. But it must also be remembered that she was not socially invested in Charles as she was in Françoise-Marguerite. It may have been less likely that she could bind her more convention- ally autonomous son to a writing contract in the way that she could her daughter.

The patriarchal system was arranged so that, whereas ambitious men could rise socially by certain skills, women could rise by marriage. If a woman were reasonably presentable and her family in a position to offer an attractive dowry, she was free to ascend in the social hierarchy. She would take the name and title of her husband and thus in one stroke efface and extend the limits of her own familial heritage, attaching herself to his. It was the duty and the privilege of Mme de Sévigné to choose and secure a son-in-law. Françoise-Marguerite was presented at court at age seven- teen: beautiful and poised, she was a gifted and enthusiastic dancer. She performed in several ballets and was honored partner to the king. She and her mother sat at his table in 1668. La Fontaine celebrated in his poetry the king's fancy for her.[27] Mlle de Sévigné was twenty-three when she mar- ried; this was, by the standards of her day, a fairly advanced age. Her mother had been eighteen at the time of her own marriage. Why Françoise- Marguerite married late is not clear; there were rumors of a few other engagements prior to the arrangement her mother settled on, but there is no ready explanation for its delay.

Mme de Sévigné negotiated for her daughter an excellent match, ex- changing, as was commonly done at that time, money for rank. She was obliged to go into debt and commit herself to a fairly austere life in order to raise the requisite dowry and to settle her daughter well. But, this done, her daughter was a countess, and Mme de Sévigné had a count from a distin- guished family for a son-in-law.[28] The count of Grignan was already twice widowed when he married Mlle de Sévigné, and father of two daughters. Aged thirty-seven, he was only six years younger than his mother-in-law. Although he was reputed to be charming, he was also, from all accounts, of unattractive appearance, and syphilitic—a condition he was to transmit to his wife and their children. He was of a great but impoverished family, in need both of a dowry and a male heir. Mme de Sévigné, who opted not to remarry herself, and who had little good to say about marriage, committed her daughter to conjugal life nonetheless and settled her well according to the criteria of the period.

By virtue of their gender, Mme de Sévigné's children, Charles and Françoise-Marguerite, were marked respectively for divergence and repetition in relation to their mother's life story. However, within a social system that sought to perpetuate itself by shoring up existing claims to entitlement (through the practice of matching well-endowed and reasonably well-born women and impoverished noblemen), the reverse obtained. Charles played out his father's minor name in relative obscurity, attaching to his interest through marriage a modest dowry from a less distinguished family than his own. The collective Sévigné ambitions were vested in the more socially mobile daughter. Françoise-Marguerite both diverged from and repeated her mother's life. She moved into another social stratum as she became countess, and into another social definition as she adopted her husband's perspective on the world, as his wife. She took social precedence over her mother by reason of her prestigious marriage. But she, with her husband, remained financially indebted to Mme de Sévigné as a consequence of that marriage, and she was cast as filially subordinate to her insofar as her earlier social definition as daughter continued to be invoked. And, most saliently, she herself became mother and, in her turn, reproduced the social role that had been her mother's.

Her new husband, the Count of Grignan, was honored by the king shortly after their marriage. He was sent back to govern his native Provence as lieutenant general in May 1670. Although it was a singular distinction to be named the personal representative of the king, to figure as a veritable extension of the monarchical reach, the role entailed not only a great deal of expense but, even worse, absence from the court and, for Mme de Sévigné, her daughter's departure. Françoise-Marguerite followed her husband to the family seat eight months later, two and a half months after the birth of their first child in Paris, on 4 February 1671, and from that date, Mme de Sévigné corresponded intensely with her daughter.

We can only speculate as to the tenor of the mother-daughter relationship prior to Françoise-Marguerite's marriage and departure for Provence. Little is known of it. From the moment of this separation, however, the maternal voice found its vehicle in writing. Mme de Sévigné's epistolary writing gave to her life a direction, rhythm, logic, and comportment that shaped for her a distinct social role. Her proclaimed reason for being, her daughter, shaped her own identity, as mother. This role (and eventually that of grandmother) most effectively countered her peripheral social status as widow and ensured her continued integration in the social order.

Her options as widow were limited: she was more drawn to a position of relative salon independence with a functioning maternal role than to a life of self-effacing devotion or one of self-compromising dissolution. These few encoded postures—maternal, devout, dissolute—point up the narrow spectrum of potential roles for the widow in seventeenth-century society. In settling on the maternal role, the widow Sévigné reserved for herself the advantages of respectability and a continued investment in the interests of family affairs in the world. She aspired to an active and participatory life. But she continually had to assert herself against the notion of superfluity that threatened her in her maternal designation. With her daughter grown, married, mother herself, and departed, the widow Sévigné was reduced to ceaselessly justifying her existence as mother in order to integrate herself socially, to maintain a place for herself in the world.

This drive to maintain herself as socially necessary generated whole sets of behaviors for Mme de Sévigné: the acts of writing the letters, especially when among (and occasionally with the collaboration of) her friends, of waiting anxiously and publicly for the responses, of sharing them with her circle, of panicking when they were not promptly forthcoming, of collecting news and compliments for daughter and family, of attracting these by projecting herself socially as the devoted and afflicted mother. All of these cues gave purpose and visibility to Mme de Sévigné's life.

It was common in seventeenth-century salon circles to share letters with one's friends, to circulate them, and to join in collective appreciation of their merits not only as conveyors of news, but as works of art in themselves. Mme de Sévigné's letters became famous in their own time, finding publics at both their point of inception and their point of reception. She frequently penned her letters in salons among friends who participated in her writing activity, adding postscripts and messages to her text not only for the addressee's pleasure, but also for their own immediate amusement. Upon their reception, the letters would be shared by the daughter-addressee with her entourage in turn. The letters were savored not only for the abundance of information, gossip, and court politics they offered from the capital, but also for the easy and entertaining style Mme de Sévigné affected as she wrote on anything that struck her fancy. Her letters emulated the art of conversation and seemed to extend her salon and those she frequented to embrace and include absent friends, and her daughter in particular, within a privileged circle of communication and understanding. Her letters were copied, circulated, even offered to the king. Her writing talent and her attachment to her daughter, harnessed together, furnished her with a discreet public identity.

Her performance of her role through corresponding constituted a constant and predictable point of view on the world for her. And it offered society a constantly operative perspective on her as well. Mme de Sévigné filtered her world—properties, assets, debts, travels, readings, friendships —through a maternal lens focused on her daughter, and those who wished to please her appealed to this image. Her friends and acquaintances were of consequence in her life to the extent that they played to and addressed Mme de Sévigné in her chosen role. In her salon circles, often enough, the pastimes of conversation and reading evoked the presence of the absent daughter. Those who sought to please Mme de Sévigné would speculate as to the daughter's likely opinions and reactions to topics at hand. They thus supported the maternal project and actively participated in Mme de Sévigné's performance. At moments of retreat in this eminently social world, when friends pursued their own interests—reading, writing, embroidering, ruminating—they would frequently remain together in one room. Mme de Sévigné's letters attest to this practice of intermittent intense sociability and peopled solitude typical of the enjoyment of collective leisure in the world of the salons.

At moments of individual activity, Mme de Sévigné represents herself in her letters, seated at her desk, just as she must appear to her circle of friends. She inscribes the image they have before them of the mother writing devotedly to, or if not, probably about her daughter. Thus she projects and publicizes her preferred identity. The company of friendly witnesses can participate in the written scene as well, by adding a word or sending a message in the mother's letter. Thus Mme de Sévigné plays her maternal role as she writes it and sends it.

She attempts to control the reception and replay of the performance as well. She addresses not only her daughter in writing, but also those surrounding her—the count, the children, the visitors in residence at Grignan, and the servants and friends. In this way the letter demands its own circulation, and thus does the implied message as well. It is not sufficient that the countess be cast in the role of daughter only within the confines of the letters, solely at the moment of receiving or writing letters, in the exclusivity of her relationship with her mother. In order that Mme de Sévigné's role function effectively, it is necessary not only that Françoise-Marguerite confirm the maternal role by accepting her filial one, but also that the countess be perceived by her own coterie principally as the mother's daughter. Thus the success of the mother's project requires not only the daughter's cooperation but also, just as importantly, the confirmation and complicity of the daughter's entourage.

While Mme de Sévigné did entertain aspirations to the status of author, her ambitions were focused as intensely on social recognition and a fulfilled life in her own time. She wrote her way into the world. The creation of a novel, or even a volume of letters, composed, collected, and preserved for posterity, would never have served so well the immediate needs of this potentially marginalized widow, intent on claiming her place in the world, who becomes through this maternal construct her own author. Mme de Sévigné's inscribed performance of the maternal role not only secured recognition of her public existence and thereby confirmation of a private sense of self; it also served as tautological testimony to her virtuous nature and generous character. For in so doing, she was acting out a role that had already been scripted for her, described and prescribed by male authorities. Her exaltation of what is defined as the quintessentially feminine paradoxically operates as cover for and entrée to the male domain of writing.

There is, then, to be found in the *Correspondance* a public performance of the maternal role. The epistolary act figures as the development, representation, and projection of a maternal persona, addressed to a generalized audience, intended for general consumption. The letters have an intimate character in that they express the emotional relationship between the mother and her daughter; they also testify to a public dimension as they bear witness to the mother extolling, publicizing, and exploiting the relationship, thereby inventing her relationship to the world. The complicated motivation behind this correspondence accounts for its paradoxical character: it is at once an intimate confession and a public display. The examination of the *Correspondance* as performance takes into consideration and attempts to explicate this paradox.[29]

Mme de Sévigné's inscribed self-representations underscore the problematic nature of performance—at once act and enactment of—and signal the crucial role played by both the anticipated and the actual reception of behavioral and inscribed messages in assigning meaning to them. The ambiance of theatricality pervaded daily life in the higher echelons of French society during the latter half of the seventeenth century. A self-conscious view of life as spectacle and of the individual as performer favors and informs the interpretation of the most commonplace activities and routines as performances:[30] the performative character of social intercourse sets the tone of the letters. An undertaking of the duration and the magnitude of the *Correspondance* represents not merely the discrete repetition of a private ritual over a period of years but the invention of a role and the enactment of a drama played to a public inscribed, in its turn, in the text.

The tendency to confuse life and theatre (*être* and *paraître* in the useful jargon of French literary criticism) is a common phenomenon, perhaps particularly marked in the world of Louis XIV, but not necessarily restricted to any particular historical period or literary enterprise. "All the world's a stage" applies across the board. Everyone involved with others is to some degree a performer: the "performed self" is "seen as some kind of image, usually creditable, which the individual on stage and in character attempts to induce others to hold in regard to [her]."[31] The reader of the *Correspondance* is enjoined, then, not so much to get to know a Mme de Sévigné of "behind the scenes," as if there could be such a place, as to deal with the projected linguistic persona of the text, which will inevitably be, in significant part, a construct of the addressee's reception of the inscribed performance. The goal of the persona's performance meanwhile is to "sustain a particular definition of the situation, this representing, as it were, [her] claim as to what reality really is."[32] Mme de Sévigné's goal, as she defines her project, is to express her great love for her daughter, and the world of this love through writing—equating "je vivrai pour vous aimer" [I will live to love you] and "je vivrai pour vous écrire" [I will live to write to you][33]—and thereby to ratify through its inscription her role as maternal paragon. In order to determine the veracity of impressions imparted, the audience (read: reader) has recourse to the less controllable aspects of the performer's (read: writer's) behavior. The performer, not unfamiliar with the role of audience herself from her dealings with others, will anticipate this search for discrepancies and may even exploit it in turn. When Mme de Sévigné insists on the spontaneity of her style as she constantly claims affection for her daughter, she identifies her style as reliable alibi of the sincerity of her feeling. The crafting of writing would suggest the calculation of expressed sentiment as well. In order to persuade both her daughter and the greater public of her genuine affection, she must affect a spontaneous and ungovernable nature in her writing:

Vous savez que je n'ai qu'un trait de plume; ainsi mes lettres sont fort négligées, mais c'est mon style, et peut-être qu'il fera autant d'effet qu'un autre plus ajusté. (I, L. 204, p. 355)

You know that I have only one pen stroke; thus my letters are quite loose, but that's my style, and perhaps it will have as much of an effect as a more fitted one.

Thus she might be seen as attempting to make of her own style adequate evidence of her sincerity and to serve as her own witness to the authenticity of her affective life. Paradoxically, this self-consciousness is evidence itself that her style cannot be entirely spontaneous. At the very least, she has chosen not to correct it.

Mme de Sévigné's claims to spontaneous style indicate as well a rigorous adherence to the tenets of the epistolary art, first set forth by Aristotle, and reiterated in the manuals of her own time, with particular pertinence for women writing. It cannot be said that Mme de Sévigné's letters offer an example of unprecedented improvisation any more than her maternal figura is an original invention. Both her style and her role embody the confluence of male prescriptions for women's place in writing and in the world. Even as she claims to write against the epistolary tradition, she inscribes herself within it, and discernible in her strategy is evidence that she has internalized those lessons, the most important being to admit to no imitation.

Mme de Sévigné consistently and emphatically denied acquaintance with any texts setting forth the rules of epistolary writing. Along with her generation, she professed admiration for specific practitioners of the genre, for some of her actual correspondents, as well as for her immediate published predecessors, Voiture in particular. She had particular fondness for Pascal's *Lettres provinciales* and for the *Portugaises*, and she submitted tactfully to the tutelage of her cousin Bussy-Rabutin, who styled himself a writer of no little talent. However, she admits to no model for her own letters; her only stated guidelines are her nature and her maternal devotion; all else is subordinated to expressing them and absorbed in the project of persuasion to that effect. Her success is dependent on the world—her audience's reception of that message: "The orator persuades by means of his hearers," says Aristotle, and so will his seventeenth-century followers.[34] Traditionally, the rules for public speaking were encoded as obtaining equally for letter writing. In Aristotle's world, "oratory and epistolary composition were considered branches of a single art: students were encouraged to follow a literary discipline which demanded practice in imitative declamation and composition from models."[35]

Yet, fundamental to that apprenticeship in these arts was the denial of imitation, a careful erasure of the model, paradoxically contained in the overriding recommendation of the imitation of the natural: "Wherefore those who practice this artifice . . . must conceal it and avoid the appearance of speaking artifically instead of naturally; for that which is natural persuades, but the artificial does not," states the expert. The same fundamental contradiction is repeated again and again as the classical art of representation is assigned its necessary guise of "naturalness": "Art is cleverly concealed when the speaker chooses his words from ordinary language."[36]

Mme de Sévigné rejected scornfully the rhetoric of the letter as practiced by many of her contemporaries, detecting in their writings clumsy effort, pedantry, ill-concealed artifice, affectation. In order to succeed in her epistolary project, she recognized the need to obscure and mystify her own writing origins and models. If to persuade required conveying a convincing impression of naturalness, then there could be from her no admission of imitation whatsoever. Mme de Sévigné's metacommentary evinces strict adherence, witting or unwitting, to the tenets set forth by Aristotle for the "art" of rhetoric and restated again and again in the epistolary manuals that abounded at the time of her writing.

Just as Mme de Sévigné admitted to no models for her writing, she denied models for her behavior. But, in the same vein, so also was there a proliferation around her of instructional literature prescribing proper behavior and fitting activities for women. And, in the same way that "art" was intent on presenting itself as "nature," so gender politics were most effectively represented as merely descriptive of the relations already operative among individuals—"natural." Although Mme de Sévigné may not have consulted any of this literature per se (and there is no sure indication that she did), if she did, she would have had no more reason to acknowledge it than she did the epistolary manuals. Whether she read them or not, the tenets articulated in them merely reflected those already governing the world in which she lived. The elaboration of her chosen role as *mater* indicates that she had internalized social expectations for her, and that she was merely successfully reflecting back to the world the vision it preferred to entertain of her:

L'honneste femme étant le miroir de sa fille . . . celle-ci ne peut recevoir de plus utiles leçons que de celle qui la précède, et qui joint l'exercice aux enseignements.[37]

The virtuous woman being the mirror of her daughter . . . the latter cannot receive lessons more useful than those from the one who precedes her and who combines practice with teachings.

In spite of the fact that Mme de Sévigné and her daughter did not get along well when together, she attempted through her writing to realize an ideal mother-daughter relationship; she subscribed to a desire that was prescribed for her by the society to which she belonged. She embraced her role and aspired to distinction in performing her maternity as would a model student. The daughter was necessarily implicated in the mother's project of social definition, and the difficulties in their relationship may be attributable to the oppressive shaping, the forcing of whatever feelings actually obtained between them into sanctioned behaviors.

Guidelines for mothers and for daughters held up the mirror as paradigm for their relations: the mother was to serve as exemplary mirror to her daughter; the daughter was to be a reflection of her mother's behavior; and thus the mother in her daughter was to see an image of herself. Little wonder that identity confusion and separation anxiety should plague their relationship. This trauma was further aggravated by the complementary tenet that the wife was to serve as mirror to her husband. The mother-daughter relationship was then a training ground for the conjugal one, and once Françoise-Marguerite was wife, but still retained as daughter—and, further, mother herself—she necessarily experienced profound conflict of identity. That such fraught relations should be the consequence of applied lessons suggests that it was to the advantage of the prevailing social organization of those times as articulated in those lessons (not so distant or different from our own) that women be divided within themselves and against one another. That scission was to take place at the very core of women's relations—between mother and daughter. Encoding the relationship in the mirror metaphor ensures the fracturing of that bond as it moves into the realm of the symbolic.

Mme de Sévigné defined herself in an androcentrically imposed relational mode: the epistolary figures the generic form into which the markedly other-oriented self-image of woman translates textually. Writing letters corresponds to the mirroring function assigned to women that comes to inform their own notion of self. It also represents the sort of writing activity assimilable within the constraints of other-oriented daily life. It does not require long stretches of time or total concentration; it tolerates interruption, distraction, discontinuity.

For Mme de Sévigné, the projects of self-invention, self-assessment, and communication are one. To read her letters is to read the self and life she invented for herself, to have at hand the project, the process, and the product. In the act of corresponding with her daughter ("je vivrai pour vous écrire"), Mme de Sévigné came to appreciate the virtues and pleasures of yet another specular activity—the mirror of writing now between them. She discovered the joys of committing herself to paper, of organizing her world, and of staging her self-presentation in words—"je vivrai pour écrire." [38]

However, in the process of constituting herself linguistically, Mme de Sévigné entered into a language that was not of her making and did not take her into account. As she sought words to articulate her relation to the world, to her daughter, she borrowed from the discourses available to her. She applied her readings and lessons in order to translate herself into writing. But these, men's words and models, filtering her own experience of the world, produced an alienation from the very self she was attempting to render, whatever that might be. The passage into the symbolic, the verbalization of maternity, is a linguistic process of masculinization. It is impossible to know maternity through the mother's text—there is no unmediated mother's text. It is equally impossible to locate it in the daughter's, who has herself internalized the mirror-mother. The mirror game refers back incessantly to the interested party proffering it. As one feminist theorist quoting another puts it, in a gesture that reclaims the mirror as an instrument of identification for women to proffer among themselves: "Narcissism [an element of the female gender stereotype] ensures that woman identifies with that image of herself that man holds up: 'Hold still, we are going to do your portrait so that you can begin looking like it right away.' "[39]

Mme de Sévigné, through her writing, cultivated the notion of a culture and language specific to women, thus subscribing to a program of domestication through the assignment of distinct spheres and competences for women. She thus both represented and reinforced conservative tradition while breaking into the scene of writing. Increasingly, during her own time, the epistolary genre was elided with the feminine and epitomized the relational activity that was woman's social assignment. While other women during that same period, friends even, embarked on more oppositional projects—rewriting history from a feminine perspective through the novel, rewriting gender relations through fiction—Mme de Sévigné embraced her assigned marginal status and proceeded from that periphery to write herself into the center of French letters.

The difference that is claimed for women, celebrated even, is a difference constructed and mobilized through language. The verbal performance of motherhood enacted in the *Correspondance* displays the borrowed and cobbled nature of its discourse, and its reception, to the extent that it is acknowledged and reinscribed in the mother's letters, attests also to the tensions between women consequent upon its articulation. Motherhood, which has been understood as the key experience for grounding the specificity of women, is itself encoded into a construct elaborated in the interest of prevailing patriarchal order and is disseminated by a mother in a troubling feat of ventriloquism. This scriptoral performance of motherhood, premised on a condition of absence, is paradoxical when considered against the prevalent theoretical stance positing the maternal as the strongest presence—the major influence, positive or negative, in the shaping of the individual and the consequent structuring of gender relations.[40]

This inscription of presence in absence is emblematic of the activity of correspondence at various levels: the letter itself operates as a simulacrum of presence; within it and through it, the mother constructs a simulacrum of her self as *mater* and encodes the daughter as mirror in which, through which, her own confirming image must be reflected back to her. It calls into question the accessibility of the mother-daughter relationship as mediated by language. As Marianne Hirsch states, "the story of mother-daughter relationships has been written even if it has not been read . . . [for] it constitutes the hidden subtext of many texts."[41] What transpires in the process of encoding that relationship through available discourse precludes its articulation and allows only for a performance of its simulacrum. The "hidden subtext" remains just that and persists in eluding the reader in search of that story, only to come up against, again and again, women's faithful transcriptions of their portraits, in the artist's language—always absent, even in their own texts.

This reading of the *Correspondance* endeavors to take into account the problematic of deciphering letters written three centuries ago, in a specific sociohistorical context, to named individuals. Fundamental to such writing is a shared world and the absence of the correspondents to each other. Tacit understanding between the writing partners frequently obviates the need among them of explicitation, leaving the external twentieth-century reader in the lurch of puzzling voids. Extra-referentiality is ingrained in the nature of the genre itself and is particularly marked in the case of this predominantly familial exchange.[42] Impressions of elusion interfere persistently with the latter-day reader's attempts at decoding the text of the letters. The signature convention constantly at play in the epistolary act serves as a regular reminder of the inadequacy of any reading of these letters. Nevertheless, the ambition in this study of the performance of maternity is to examine the *Correspondance* as text; to concentrate on the discernible structuring of its rhetoric and the dynamic of its discourse. I aim to consider Mme de Sévigné not exclusively as overdetermined historicizer of her own fiction, nor as self-structured fiction of her own history, but as both author and textual persona.

The *je*/I persona corresponding to the signature of the author Mme de Sévigné is grounded iteratively at its repeated inception in time, in letter after letter, aspiring to the eventual domain of literature, but is also more immediately purposeful. It thus represents a constant tension between reality and fiction. The status of the subject marker as autonomous textual signifier is ceaselessly challenged by its own history. The tension between the historical and the scriptoral subject is reinvoked regularly for the reader by the very issue of epistolarity that constitutes their context. Henceforth in this study, I refer to Mme de Sévigné not as such, although I keep in mind the implications of her full name—Marie de Rabutin-Chantal, Mme de Sévigné; I endeavor instead to highlight the tension of her double identity, as author of and principal figure in her letters—Sévigné.

As for her correspondents, they too enjoy status both as historical subjects and as fictional figures, as actual addressees and respondents, and as inventions of her discourse in the text of the letters. In this reading,

I draw from letters written by Sévigné to various individuals, and occasionally from their answers to her, included in the Duchêne edition of the *Correspondance*. I take into account the centrality of the addressees to the texts penned for them. Since they are multiple, my shifting perspective as interceptor of these letters is often necessarily aligned to that of an external reader as I move between Sévigné's letters to them and theirs to her. However, my focus is primarily on the mother-daughter relationship, and in that exchange, or lack thereof, my focus tends to collapse the internal-external/intended-accidental distinction. I tend to read as the daughter the maternally encoded *vous* whose *je* is missing.

Sévigné's letters passed easily into the canon of French literature. To the feminist reader today, though, in search of a past as well as a future—both historically and politically motivated—a question occurs, the answer to which opens the text for a revision of the traditional Sévigné profile: Since this was indeed an epistolary exchange, where are the daughter's letters? Sévigné's good literary fortune and her place as maternal paragon become suspect as the answer is considered. The daughter's letters, so vital to the exchange, and, as evidenced within the text of the mother's letters, so faithfully penned, were eliminated (I, p. 765). Mme de Simiane, granddaughter and editor of Mme de Sévigné and daughter of Mme de Grignan, destroyed them. As she completed the direction of the publication of her grandmother's letters, she suppressed her own mother's half of the exchange. The mother-daughter tensions discernible in the Sévigné letters were reproduced in the next generation. Mme de Simiane silenced her mother, creating thereby a troubling lacuna in her grandmother's text. Only recently have readers ventured to peer into that seeming void.

My reading of Sévigné's performance of maternity—and *maternity*, as a cognate of the French *maternité*, can be used interchangeably with *motherhood*—depends frequently for its perspective on that of the textless daughter, Françoise-Marguerite, Mme de Grignan. It features attempts to restitute the daughter's voice, to hypothesize her role in the epistolary exchange, and to understand the relationship from her point of view. In the repeated absence of her contribution to the exchange, the external reader is easily drawn into inferring and inventing the internal intended addressee's viewpoint. Indeed, this is the proclivity for any reader of published correspondences.[43]

Sévigné's letters offer ample material from which to reconstruct a profile of the addressee. The dynamic of the relationship is deciphered through speculative contextualizing of reverberations in the mother's letters on the part of the external reader. Such a reading is aided by the testimony of the few daughter texts still extant.[44] In the light of such an approach, the conventional Sévigné profile as maternal paragon recedes, as does that of a cold, ungrateful daughter. In their place emerges a picture more familiar to the contemporary reader: a more complex and less romanticized vision of mother-daughter relations.

What sets this example apart from more recent variations on the same tale is that here the daughter's voice has been stifled and must be reconstructed. Women who write in twentieth-century France of relationships between mothers and daughters from their own experience tend to write from the position of daughter. Simone de Beauvoir, Marie Cardinal, Marguerite Duras, Luce Irigaray, Violette Leduc, Nathalie Sarraute are just some of those who come to mind.[45] In the Sévigné *Correspondance*, we have the opportunity to examine a mother's discourse and to gain historical perspective on our "maternal" heritage as well as to listen for resonances of our own experience. But here too, this reading of the letters produces a daughter's view of a writing mother. A maternal perspective on the writing mother remains unavailable except, ironically, to the extent that it is reproduced in the daughter's.

In occupying the inviting void of the *vous*, and inventing dialogue with the inscribed *je*, it is inevitable that the reader bring into play her or his own history, or *hystorics*, as James Joyce would say.[46] A remembrance and projection of one's own founding relation is inscribed in interpretations of the letters and is significantly gender-marked. The *hystorics* of a female reader (daughter herself, by definition, and occasionally mother as well) and those of a male reader (excluded by definition from personal experience of this particularizing bond, but marked by his own filial relationship to his mother) produce different readings.[47] This is an argument not for essentializing difference, but merely for recognizing reading subjects to be sociocultural artifacts bringing different imprints to the text. Nor is it to claim a superior vantage for a daughter's reading of a daughter (as opposed to a mother's, a son's, a brother's, a father's); it is merely to highlight the specificity of the reading position, and to suggest a greater possibility of slippage between the writing daughter and the missing written one.[48]

Mme de Grignan's letters might have balanced a radically subjective view of the relationship, but the reading daughter is met with silence, the silence of burned, destroyed, missing letters. This situation invites speculation and invention—invention controlled, however, by the half of the correspondence that remains, the mother's letters—and speculation cognizant of the *différance* that always already precludes apprehension.[49] One might expect that symmetry would order a correspondence, that the reader's viewpoint would shift regularly from one correspondent to the other as the correspondents become addressees in turn.[50] In the case of Sévigné's letters to her daughter, that symmetry must be supplied by the reader and is ceaselessly undone by the reader's knowledge of those missing letters.

The following study attempts to weight the balance, deriving its subjectivity from the presumed one of the voiceless daughter, while acknowledging the fiction it is. My concern is not simply to study the rhetorical code of the maternal inscription or the project of maternal identity; it is to examine the perlocutionary force that makes of these letters a performative field wherein the writing subject figures as agent and the addressee as "acted upon."[51] Which is not to say that in the dynamics of the relation the one necessarily dominates the other; the agent is as dependent on the inscribed daughter as she in turn is on the agent her mother. A relation of interdependence, one of many in the social network of Sévigné's world, and by far the most prominent in her writing, informs the dynamic of the correspondence.

The performance, then, takes place between the text (the mother's letters) and the reader (the hypothetical daughter). The textual *vous*, the schematic addressee, is animated by the external reader's interception of the maternal message and consequent incitement to response. The external reader invents the daughter's text by measuring the gaps between explicit intention and perceived effect, and by examining contradictions, by drawing implications. The reading of the mother's text produces the daughter's. Hence, as I address the performance of maternity, my subject is just as importantly the institutionalizing of daughterhood, engendered and genealogized reading. I recognize that the dynamic of the relationship played out between the maternal *je* and the filial *vous* as apprehended in my reading of the *Correspondance* is ultimately my own fiction. My interpretation rests on an assumption of epistolary dimensionality that, while it is inscribed in the letters, eludes them.

Part I

·

Installing the Mirror

Women and the Epistolary Domain in Seventeenth-Century France

Ce sexe va plus loin que le nôtre dans ce genre d'écrire.   LA BRUYÈRE[1]

This sex goes further than ours in this kind of writing.

We can speak only about a structure observed in a sociohistorical context, which is that of Christian, Western civilization and its lay ramifications. In this sense of psychosymbolic structure, women . . . seem to feel that they are the casualties, that they have been left out of the sociosymbolic contract, of language as the fundamental social bond.   JULIA KRISTEVA[2]

The following discussion presents an overview of the seventeenth-century epistolary writing scene as it is reflected in Sévigné's letters and as it can be construed to impinge on the scene of her own writing. This framing of Sévigné's writing focuses on the ways in which the canon is taking shape as she writes, and on the published letter writers she recognizes as canonical in her own texts. These authors figure as her own designated potential precursors, since it is in relation to their writing that she explicitly positions her own by deigning to name them. The two writers most frequently invoked by Sévigné as she reflects on the epistolary art are Guez de Balzac and Vincent Voiture. They were both widely accepted as distinguished practitioners of the art, and their names together summed up for seventeenth-century epistolary enthusiasts the achievement of the period in that generic domain. Although the *Lettres provinciales* and the *Lettres portugaises* are often cited as well, it is clear that they are considered to fall into a category of more deliberate authorship and writing endeavor. The epistolary flirts along the less explicitly delineated boundaries of the realm of literature.

It is not surprising that Sévigné should allude to Voiture and Balzac in her own writing; they are part of her received canon; it is telling, however, that they should surface as often as they do in her discourse. Their frequent figuration in her letters attests to her awareness that she was participating in a genre with its conventions, etiquettes, and models—that this ostensibly private act of corresponding with friends and family was susceptible of being transmuted into literature. It is equally telling that not once does Sévigné refer explicitly to any of the numerous manuals, illustrative collections, and *secrétaires* that were produced, especially between 1645 and 1690, as she herself was writing letters. The double gesture of regularly referencing Voiture and Balzac while pointedly ignoring the instructional literature on the epistolary suggests that Sévigné was positioning herself vis-à-vis the world of letters. Evidence both of a pronounced class bias against effort and of subscription to a compatible esthetics of *"négligence"* ("Les gens de qualité savent tout sans avoir jamais rien appris"[3] [People of quality know everything without ever having learned anything]) helps to explain Sévigné's distancing from such texts. This, coupled with her frequent mention of the canonical epistolary authors of her time, implies that she was discreetly situating herself, and it argues for seeing in this double gesture the implicit willed insertion of herself into the authored rather than the merely signed epistolary domain.

Guidelines for appropriate epistolary style and content abounded at this time, and this phenomenon corresponds to a more general social concern. Just as seventeenth-century society was developing into rapidly proliferating competitive strata, sifting into increasingly diverse occupational groups, and intent on setting and marking boundaries between them through visible codes of dress and behavior, so the question of address was taken up prescriptively. The preoccupation with codifying relations generated by a pronounced movement toward more complex differentiation and stratification, encouraged under Louis XIV, and of particular concern to the traditional elite as well as to the newly aspirant meritocracy, is reflected in these texts devoted to letter writing.[4]

Here, and among the practicing literati generally, it was agreed that this genre was one in which women could and did distinguish themselves as writers. In 1673, François Poullain de la Barre included this point in his treatise *De l'égalité des deux sexes*. He claimed for women in this domain not mere equality, in keeping with his thesis, but superiority, as was his wont. In his panegyric, intended as a philosophical, rational demonstration of equality between the sexes, he himself waxes eloquent on the subject of feminine epistolary eloquence:

Se peut-il rien de plus fort et de plus éloquent que les lettres de plusieurs Dames sur tous les sujets qui entrent dans le commerce ordinairement, et principalement sur les passions, dont le ressort fait toute la beauté et tout le secret de l'éloquence. Elles les touchent d'une manière si délicate, et les expriment si naïvement, qu'on est obligé d'avouer qu'on ne les sent pas autrement, et que toutes les rhétoriques du Monde ne peuvent donner aux hommes ce qui ne coûte rien aux femmes.[5]

Can there be anything stronger and more eloquent than the letters of many Ladies about all the subjects that ordinarily enter into discussion, and principally the passions, whose energy makes for all the beauty and the entire secret of eloquence. The Ladies feel them in such a delicate way, and express them so naïvely, that one is obliged to admit that one does not feel them otherwise, and that all the rhetorics of the World cannot give to men what costs women nothing.

His mode of establishing the excellence of women as writers of letters reflects the edge granted to women by the manuals and *secrétaires* of the period—an edge allotted perhaps in calculating cognizance of the composition of their primary targeted readership—an increasingly literate population of women intent on self-expression and in search of improving instruction. At the same time, Poullain explains away that excellence as a natural and effortless consequence of women's special relationship to the passions—thus excluding women from the challenges and rewards of producing crafted writing, of participating fully in the profession of writing. This problematic comment foreshadows Jean de La Bruyère's complicated position on the subject of women and letters.

Admission to the Canon: Theory and Practice

In the chapter "Des Ouvrages de l'esprit" in his book *Les Caractères* (1687), La Bruyère intervened actively as a self-appointed agent and contributed significantly to the formal shaping of the classical French literary canon. He pronounced his own sure judgment on authors, works, and genres and inscribed as universal truth his personal (albeit quite conventional) taste, with an occasional nod to general consensus. La Bruyère granted status to the epistolary genre while, at the same time, encoding it, like Poullain, as a sort of writing at which female practitioners excelled. It is worth pausing to consider closely the complexity of his statement as it is indicative not only of his own stance but of a more generally pervasive opinion regarding women and the epistolary domain in particular, women and writing in general.

Paradoxically, in his discussion, La Bruyère evinces sensitive appreciation of the exigencies of the form itself and concedes stylistic achievement in this art to women letter writers, but names not one. Rather, he names and thereby immortalizes in his text two male letter writers, Balzac and Voiture, the same two Sévigné also acknowledges.[6] Such onomastic politics are symptomatic of a deeper bias: he presumes in his text to address an exclusively male readership and, in a display of solidarity with that group, claims for it exclusive possession of language itself. How is a woman to read a text that suppresses her literary heritage and excludes her as reader, praising all the while some abstraction entitled "les femmes"?

Je ne sais si l'on pourra jamais mettre dans les lettres plus d'esprit, plus de tour, plus d'agrément et plus de style que l'on en voit dans celles de Balzac et de Voiture; elles sont vides de sentiments qui n'ont régné que depuis leur temps, et qui doivent aux femmes leur naissance. Ce sexe va plus loin que le nôtre dans ce genre d'écrire. Elles trouvent sous leur plume des tours et des expressions qui souvent en nous ne sont l'effet que d'un long travail et d'une pénible recherche; elles sont heureuses dans le choix des termes, qu'elles placent si juste, que tous connus qu'ils sont, ils ont le charme de la nouveauté, et semblent être faits seulement pour l'usage où elles les mettent; il n'appartient qu'à elles de faire lire dans un seul mot tout un sentiment, et de rendre délicatement une pensée qui est délicate; elles ont un enchaînement de discours inimitable, qui se suit naturellement, et qui n'est lié que par le sens. Si les femmes étaient toujours correctes, j'oserais dire que les lettres de quelques-unes d'entre elles seraient peut-être ce que nous avons dans notre langue de mieux écrit.[7]

I do not know if one will ever be able to put into letters more wit, more turns, more pleasure and more style than what one sees in Balzac and Voiture; theirs are void of sentiments that have reigned only since their time, and which owe their birth to women. This sex goes further than ours in this sort of writing. They find beneath their pen turns of phrase and expressions which often in us are only the effect of long work and tiresome research; they are fortunate in their choice of terms, which they place so well that, as familiar as they are, they have the charm of novelty, and seem to be made exclusively for the purpose to which they are put; only they have the ability to render an entire feeling through one word, and to express delicately a thought that is delicate; they have an inimitable mode of association, which follows naturally, and which is linked only by meaning. If women were always correct, I would dare say that the letters of some of them would perhaps be what is best written in our language.

This condescending but complimentary statement on women's epistolary writing opens with a hypothetical proposition ("Je ne sais si l'on pourra . . .") and closes with yet another ("Si les femmes étaient . . ."). Such rhetorical uncertainty frames some firm opinions, however, and even the wavering opening and the reluctant and inconclusive conclusion contribute to the actual pronouncement. While exhibiting extreme deference toward the two *épistoliers,* the critic maintains that *épistolières* excel in this particular genre.[8] However, the praises are grudging; even the epistolary art itself is somewhat mystified by a general vagueness ("ce genre d'écrire"), and the final compliment, couched in a seemingly impossible and irreparable conditional ("Si les femmes étaient toujours correctes . . .") is suspended even as it is bestowed. Such a paradoxical statement provokes two questions: 1) to what extent does the inscribed readership (and the critic's claims to solidarity with that group by use of the first person plural) account for the ambivalent stance; and 2) are women's letters or women themselves the issue of the pronouncement?

The opening statement, focusing on the male writer, suggests a promising future of challenge, grounded in a superlative past of performance, and confers specific immortality in naming Balzac and Voiture. In a disjointed way, the second half of the sentence introduces a qualification to the first, but it produces an ambivalent statement that takes nothing away from the two named authors and gives nothing to the new group of practitioners. The critic withholds value judgment by refusing to weight the observation, to grammaticize it in relation to the first half of the sentence. If compliment this be, it is of the most discreet sort. In any event, Balzac and Voiture are exonerated from the ensuing discussion; their status is unthreatened because their letters antedate the vogue of "sentiments" and therefore cannot be assessed according to the new standard. They are not to be displaced in La Bruyère's canon.

The specificity of compliments attaching to Balzac and Voiture ("esprit," "tours," "agrément," "style") is replicated in association with the writing of women ("tours," "expressions," "choix des termes"). In the latter case, however, there seems to be, rather than acknowledgment of actual talent, speculation that such writing is the result of mere coincidence ("Elles trouvent sous leur plume") and luck ("elles sont heureuses"). The gender-oriented opposition continues implicitly through the text in familiar nature-versus-culture terms once it has been initiated by this contrast of intuitive luck with "travail" and "recherche." [9] La Bruyère has claimed not that women write better letters, but simply that they go further, and even this dubious compliment is undermined by the derogation of applied talent to casual chance. In the same vein, other stereotypical observations seem to prevail: *épistolières*, as befits their nature as women ("il n'appartient qu'à elles"), are calculating ("elles placent si juste"), and their terms are seductive ("ont le charme") and even perhaps dissembling ("semblent être faits"). The logic of their discourse is not grounded in grammar or rhetoric; rather, it is peculiar to them, somehow "natural" for them and concerned only for the exigencies of "sens." The superiority of women as practitioners of the epistolary genre is argued, then, from an entrenched gender-differentiated position. While La Bruyère is clearly celebrating the new fluidity of women's epistolary writing, approving its—and, by extension, their—liberation from the constraints of an outmoded rhetoric, he appears to be caught in a major contradiction. He wants to affirm the epistolary genre and credit the practitioners responsible for its revitalization, but at the same time he wants to preserve the gender hierarchy in place in his world. Hence the tension between praise and repression and the ultimately ambivalent nature of his pronouncement.

The evaluating critic has already aligned himself with male letter writers and posited their solidarity with his intended readership by indicating that they all belong to the same gender, "le nôtre." The elision between the generic and the masculine in this simple phrase indicates his strong yet unacknowledged elocutionary position. The solidarity of the male world of male literature is summed up in the use of the possessive pronoun. Voiture, Balzac, the readership of *Les Caractères*, and the critic-author himself belong to a realm to which women are not privy, except insofar as they figure collectively, anonymously, and even then, only at the instance of "nous" as "*l'autre*" ("Ce sexe"). Even more fundamentally, the critic claims for his male world "notre langue" as well. To the extent that La Bruyère is writing this under his earlier expressed conviction that women are "other," they are, then, encroaching, trespassing, usurping in their very presumption to use language.[10]

For both genders there is implied a confusion of the conventional conditions of creativity that seems, in this case, to favor the female. The term "naissance," in the first sentence, introduces a subtext wherein considerations of writing and giving birth converge. A natural disposition for and ease in epistolary writing, albeit calculating, characterizes the women practitioners. The men, on the other hand, suffer "un long travail" and "une pénible recherche." Their common writing experience, characterized by long and painful labor, resembles that typically assigned to childbirth. It is implied that they inhabit an impossible domain of the figurative, where texts are recuperated metaphorically as children with great difficulty, while women, having a privileged relationship to the new standard of "sentiment,"[11] enjoy access to immediate and literal experience and facility in its expression. If indeed seventeenth-century women's letters are marked by a consistently different esthetic, would it not seem more plausible to conclude that they had simply learned to inscribe an imitation of the "natural" stereotyping they had been assigned?

It is no wonder, given such an atmosphere of at once presumptuous and defensive territoriality as that of the male world of language and writing, of "notre langue," that women should excel in those assigned unassuming, marginal domains where they threaten male hegemony the least.

What more proper, what safer place than in the contingent and relational mode of the epistolary genre? Writing a letter can be understood as simply another gesture of domestic sociability, proper to the concerns of the burgeoning private sphere—woman's place. As such, therefore, feminine incursions into writing through the practice of letters might be tolerated.

The concluding sentence of La Bruyère's remark builds up conditionally ("Si"), hesitantly ("j'oserais"), timidly ("quelques-unes"), and uncertainly ("peut-être") to a final judgment conceding excellence in the practice of the epistolary genre to women. But the compliment never quite materializes because of the initial reservation or bias, which has to do not with women's letters but with women themselves. The praise is suspended arbitrarily; the pretext is that of "correctes." The quality of the letters is not in question; the failing appears to attach directly to women as a category, or a subspecies, and includes them all, not only those who pen letters: "Si les femmes étaient toujours correctes." It might be assumed, since the context of the discussion is that of writing, that correctness has to do with the grammatical sort, "dans les règles." But "correctes" here, depending on "femmes" as it grammatically does, suggests just as plausibly instead an equivalence of *correct* and *male*.

La Bruyère's judgment is at once controversial and ambivalent. Even as the critic sings the praises of women letter writers, he ascribes the excellence of their letters to their fundamental femininity and reaffirms his allegiance to the other camp. In this way he undermines his own affirmation and covers for any possible disloyalty. Before even approaching his considerations on *épistolières*, the ostensible subject of his praise, the critic has celebrated their male predecessors. He has honored Balzac and Voiture by naming them. This specific inclusion in his text already constitutes in itself another step toward authorial immortality for them. The inscription in his text of their possibly eternal incomparability serves as a further tautological guarantee of that incomparability.

As for the women letter writers, no names are given; authorship is not developed, and anonymity characterizes (or fails to characterize) the subject of the uncertain praise. "Correctes" points to the sole reservation. La Bruyère weighs "femmes" against "correctes," but leaves the verdict suspended, the terms enigmatically related. The term "correctes" and its problematic relation to "les femmes" constitutes a fixed tease in the text.

La Bruyère cannot bring himself to assume a more affirmative stance in favor of women letter writers either because they are not men, or because he considers himself already radical enough in the praise he does accord them. Does he fear alienating his readership, isolating himself from his own group, by taking a firmer stand for women? He does set up an "elles" versus "nous" tension that defies satisfactory resolution, and that, while acknowledging the incursion of *épistolières* into the margins of the world of writing, and even their significant talent, holds them, resolutely, just there.

It is against this background of discreet recognition that the production and publication of Sévigné's *Correspondance* might be considered. La Bruyère's pronouncement offers insights on the context for the production of the letters: Sévigné passed for an occasional writer, as an amateur writing in a marginal albeit both popular and distinguished genre that was enjoying increasing status in the prevailing hierarchy of literary forms and that was being explicitly associated with women's writing. Her license for permission to do so as obsessively as she did was ostensible devotion to her daughter (a properly domestic fixation and associated certainly with some of the connotative aspects of the term *sentiments*[12]), and she could only excel in her writing to a certain degree without alienating society and risking the loss of that passport.[13] Therefore she herself had to insist on the imperfection of her writing, and she had to renounce repeatedly and publicly any attempts at correcting herself. This marginal status in itself contributes a great deal to her rhetoric of the letter, both facilitating and circumscribing her expression. Sévigné's notions of what constitutes a felicitous letter coincide neatly with La Bruyère's. She appears to have successfully internalized the prescriptions and descriptions of feminine epistolary writing circulating in the manuals and among the gatekeepers of the Republic of Letters, and it is generally retrospectively accepted that, if La Bruyère had ventured generously to name any of the *épistolières* (these "quelques unes") to whom he alludes, Sévigné would figure prominently among them.[14] Instead, France's premiere correspondent goes unnamed in the literary pantheon her contemporary was inscribing.

In the course of his pronouncement, La Bruyère posits an esthetic of the letter that relates in a telling way both to that articulated and practiced by Sévigné in the *Correspondance* and to that evidenced by the practices of its eighteenth-century editors. Various pirate editions were published before Sévigné's granddaughter Mme de Simiane appointed the chevalier Perrin official editor of the family documents (I, "Note sur le texte," pp. 755–70). As Perrin was prompt to point out, in matters of grammar and spelling, of "correctness," the letters are consistently "incorrectes." This is not entirely obvious to the twentieth-century reader using the most recent Pléiade edition of the *Correspondance*. Punctuation, paragraphing, and regularized spelling have been introduced by Roger Duchêne into a text of already questionable authenticity, pieced together from varying manuscripts of uneven reliability, each having different quirks and reflecting different criteria of propriety and style. Duchêne has succeeded in producing a soundly documented and highly readable edition.[15]

At the same time, Duchêne deplores "enlightened" tampering by his predecessors: "Mme de Sévigné n'a pas été défigurée par paresse, mais au nom du goût" (I, p. 800) [Mme de Sévigné has been defaced not out of laziness, but in the name of taste]. A blatant example of this is in the selection of letters first published. As Janet Gurkin Altman points out, the early editors of Sévigné's letters focused primarily on those featuring "narratives of major historical events from 1670 to 1676, appropriately titled to anchor these events in court life," and thus effectively obviating the need to come to terms with Sévigné's "excessive maternal love." [16] If we examine the "improvements" introduced by Perrin, Sévigné's first official editor, we see that the very qualities signaled by La Bruyère as distinguishing women's letters and contributing to their excellence are those suppressed in the name of "taste" in the eighteenth century, in particular, that of the "enchaînement inimitable."

Once the letters were to take their place in the official literary canon, traces of the very imperfections that had enabled their coming into existence and eased their initial acceptance had to be erased. Manuscripts that did not surface until the nineteenth century attest to the extent that those dealt with in the eighteenth century were expunged of "irregularities" (I, p. 796). As Duchêne points out, although Perrin did not radically suppress and misrepresent expressions of feelings that pointed to the fraught relationship between mother and daughter, he did correct grammar, spelling, and vocabulary. He substituted clichés for novel expression, and he shortened the letters so that they might conform to a more currently fashionable length (I, p. 796–801). Further, he attempted to replace what La Bruyère refers to as the "enchaînement inimitable" of the discourse with what Duchêne terms an "armature logique" (I, p. 798) [framework of logic]. In Duchêne's notes on the text, he emphatically reproaches Perrin for having significantly deformed the letters by dint of his various corrections: "Elle cesse d'être confidence parlée pour devenir discours écrit" (I, p. 799) [It ceases to be spoken confidence and becomes instead written discourse]. The extent of the modifications undergone by the text at the hands of Perrin corroborates La Bruyère's sole reservation concerning the excellence of women's letters (that is, that they are not *correctes*—if we correct *his* grammar) and his praise as well. But if we are to deplore in a credible manner the tampering done by Sévigné's editors, we cannot subscribe to a correction of La Bruyère's text either.

The fact that Perrin and, even more so, his unauthorized predecessors, suppress particularly what La Bruyère seems to suggest are typically feminine epistolary traits in order to prepare the letters for their official reception into the world of "notre langue" suggests that La Bruyère's praise of women's letters is genuine and even, for its time, generous. If it is not more forthright, this might be because the *je* is addressing a male readership that accepts only with difficulty the notion of women writing and that is ill at ease with the notion of being bettered by women in any area of literary endeavor, even one as relatively marginal and minor as the epistolary genre. La Bruyère's rhetorical equivocation allows his possibly disloyal and conceivably subversive praise of women's writing to get past his male readership, but perhaps not much further.[17]

Traces of Lessons

As La Bruyère's comments attest, the letter was firmly instated as a recognized genre in the seventeenth century. This sums up a web of meanings: not only did the letter have its place and function in the practical domain of the communicatory circuit (this was increasingly so as the organization of the mails was refined under Louis XIV),[18] but it became an increasingly accepted literary form, with efforts made to renew acquaintance with its history, to celebrate illustrious exemplary precursors, and to further legitimate its status with the deliberate production of collections for publication.[19] From a minor, marginal literary form, the letter was emerging, in the process of codifying relations through analytical and erudite practices of salon sociability, as an important instrument of positioning. At the crossroads of life and fiction, it functioned as a means of describing and prescribing the self in relation to others. It also offered possibilities for positioning the self vis-à-vis literature. It was a genre practiced by virtually all who wielded pens. And as Poullain's and La Bruyère's praise corroborate, the letter was also becoming an increasingly gender-identified genre. As Sévigné practiced the art, it can be seen both as serving the purpose of communicating and as the vehicle for the insertion of her voice into literary discourse. Ordinary and "high" culture converge in her correspondence.

In the mid-seventeenth century, a plenitude of instructive collections and manuals provided guidance for those amateurs of letter writing unsure of voice or even thoughts.[20] These books offered advice on appropriate address according to the social stations and familial relations of addresser and addressee, ready-made phrases, reactions, sentiments, even advice on appropriate stationery and handwriting.[21] In theory, then, any literate person was potentially a writer of letters and, given a little guidance, could produce a correspondence. Special allowance was made, in some of the guidelines of these texts, specifically for women writing. Indeed, examples of their writing were ostensibly furnished as proof of their eligibility for serious consideration in the elaboration of this genre. Charles Du Boscq, in the introduction to his collection of women's letters, specifically applauds the literary quality of women's literacy:

Je diray seulement, que s'il y en a eu jusques icy qui n'ayent pu consentir que les Dames se meslent d'escrire, je m'asseure qu'ils changeront leur sentiment en lisant ce livre.

I will only say that, if there have been up to now some who have not been able to consent that Ladies get involved in writing, I am assured that they will change their minds upon reading this book.

He projects a skeptical male reader as the intended narratee of his discourse but takes the stance of an impartial critic, distancing himself from both male readers and female writers by referring to both groups in the third person and arguing from above on behalf of women writers. This positioning may be a strategy for winning an unspoken audience, the female reader-would-be-writer. That women should be capable of producing fine letters is not surprising, he claims, since they are distinguishing themselves in even more "serious" writing enterprises:

Si l'on en voit plusieurs en ce siecle qui escrivent avec approbation de tout le monde, sur les matieres les plus importantes, et de religion et de la morale; on ne doit pas s'estonner si elles scavent faire de bonnes lettres, puisque mesme elles peuvent faire de bons livres.[22]

If one sees in this century many of them who write with the approval of everyone on the most important subjects, on religion and morality, one must not be surprised if they know how to write good letters, since they can even write good books.

The project of affirming the epistolary as a distinguished art form is elided with legitimizing women as capable practitioners, making room for both genre and gender at once. The "on" stands in for that normative anonymity, the patriarchal jury, to whom Du Boscq's polemic is obliquely addressed. The collection of letters that follows is equally anonymous, this, claims Du Boscq, as a delicate gesture to respect the privacy of the letter writers. Propriety demands that these women remain anonymous.

But, lest Du Boscq be suspected of himself authoring these letters, given their obscured origins, he goes to great if not necessarily convincing lengths to insist on their authenticity: "Personne ne doit douter que ce ne soit leur ouvrage"[23] [No one should doubt that this is their work]. The letters themselves share certain characteristics that arouse suspicion regarding their purported multiple authorship: unity of tone, only one subject addressed in each letter, uniformity of length, and a steady rhythm of exchange with each letter neatly succeeded by a response. Even more suspect are some of the sentiments represented as expressed by writing women:

J'advoue librement que je ne sçay pas faire de bonnes lettres mais je pense qu'il vaut mieux avoir de l'affection pour rendre du service, que de l'éloquence pour l'offrir. Et qu'importe-t-il en cette occasion de violer les loix de la Rethorique [sic], pour veû qu'on observe celles de l'Amitié? J'ayme mieux passer pour fidelle, que pour Scavante.[24]

I freely confess that I do not know how to write good letters, but I think it is better to have affection in order to be of service than to have eloquence with which to offer it. And of what importance on this occasion to violate the laws of Rhetoric, as long as one observes those of Friendship? I prefer to be known as faithful rather than as learned.

I have to wonder if these letters are not in fact Du Boscq's fictions, and if, in the guise of presenting outstanding examples of women's writing, he was not circulating his own lessons for women's behavior, as they presumed to write. The above message tacitly prescribes affection, friendship, and faithfulness for writing women and encodes eloquence, rhetoric, and wisdom as unseemly qualities in their letters. Even if Du Boscq's letters are authentic (which seems highly doubtful), they contain not merely pointed lessons on penning letters but maxims reflecting and reinforcing standard seventeenth-century ideology on women and their place.

Once again, women are included as practitioners of the genre but excluded as writing subjects and represented as preferring to be "of service" rather than aspiring to serious writing, relational rather than professional. Du Boscq's scruples may cover for a powerful act of subversion: the manufacturing of anonymous "women's" letters by a man articulating in the guise of women's voices a male code of comportment for women. Women readers who believe themselves to be modeling themselves on women writers through consultation of such collections may find themselves absorbing a code that undermines the motivations of their reading activity and that neatly circumscribes the scope of their personal writing ambition.

Another self-appointed authority on the subject, Pierre d'Ortigue de Vaumorière, offered advice on women's writing of love letters (the sort of letter they were most authorized to write) and explicitly prescribed their allowed feelings:

Mais je ne voudrais pas qu'un sexe, qui doit avoir la modestie en partage, témoignât de l'emportement. J'aimerais, au contraire, qu'une femme enveloppât les marques de son amour, qu'elle se contentât de les laisser entrevoir, et qu'un caractère de retenue et de pudeur fût mêlé à sa tendresse."[25]

But I would not want that sex, which must have its allotment of modesty, to display passion. I would like, instead, that a woman conceal the signs of her love, that she be content to have them glimpsed, and that a character of restraint and modesty be combined with her tenderness.

Affective behavior was being shaped just as surely as its expression was being guided. Fundamental lessons on comportment are embedded in the didactic instructions for appropriate feminine language. These manuals, then, were powerful instruments for the covert containment of feminine scriptoral identity and the subtle manipulation of a feminine ethos.

Lessons were also offered to men on writing to women. Du Plaisir's manual concerns itself mainly with this facet of epistolary etiquette.[26] Charles Sorel, as well, prescribed appropriate tones for men's letters to women and contributed thus to keeping gender distinctions, already threatened by the incursion of women into writing, clearly articulated in the epistolary realm:

On sait que pour écrire à des Dames, hors des sujets de dévotion et de Morale, ou d'affaires du Monde, il ne faut rien que douceur, civilité et galanterie, et que les Sujets de divertissement y ont meilleure grace que tous les autres.[27]

One knows that for writing to Ladies, beyond the subjects of devotion and Morality, or of the business of the World, one must use only sweetness, civility, and gallantry, and that subjects of amusement are better received than all the others.

And Vaumorière, in his professed concern to cater to the delicate nature of women, advocated a veiled discourse proper for epistolary conversation with them:

Il est certain qu'il ne leur [aux dames] faut rien représenter, qui puisse choquer leur délicatesse. Envelopons ce que la bienséance nous défend d'expliquer: contentons nous de faire entendre ce qu'il ne nous est pas permis de dire.[28]

It is certain that one must not represent anything to them [ladies] which might upset their delicacy. Let us conceal what decorum forbids us to explain; let us be satisfied with making understood what we are not permitted to say.

As relations between correspondents were spelled out in directives for appropriate address, so were social relations in general crystallized. Through the act of catering considerately to women's "delicate" nature, women were reinscribed as sensitive and at the mercy of powerful men who needed to agree (in the solidarity proposed above) to curb their own strong tongues, ostensibly in order not to cause offense, but, just as pertinently, to uphold the gender conventions governing the identities of the sexes in relation to each other, conventions over which men had the greater control and which worked to their advantage.

As well as offering guidelines on the epistolary art, Vaumorière wrote on the art of conversation, in theory the behavior model for all letter writing. His precepts for seemly conversation often reduced to a formulaic respect for the coherence of gender signals:

Je voudrais aussi que l'on suivit exactement ce qu'approuverait la bienséance, selon le sexe, l'âge, et la profession, et que l'on observa même les temps et les lieux. En effet, une dame serait-elle charmante, si elle avait les emportements d'un Gendarme? un Officier général d'Armée aurait-il bonne grâce, s'il affectait de parler gras comme une petite coquette?[29]

I would also like everyone to follow exactly what decorum would allow, by sex, age, and profession, and that everyone be attentive even to time and place. In effect, would a lady be charming if she had the outbursts of a Soldier? Would a General of the Army be in favor if he affected to speak coyly like a little flirt?

Although age, profession, time, and place are cited as just as important as sex in setting appropriate conversational tone, the examples given— "dame"/"gendarme" and "général"/"coquette"—and their resurfacing in Vaumorière's discourse on letters indicate to what extent the real issue is a fear of gender confusion—of mixed signals. The code that applied in conversation was just as pertinent for the letter: he reworked his own text and included it in his epistolary manual, reaffirming in that generic domain the principle of separate spheres and essentialist behaviors:

Une dame qui aurait l'air déterminé d'un gendarme pourrait faire peur, mais je ne sais si elle donnerait de l'amour, comme je doute que beaucoup de monde approuvât qu'un vieux guerrier eût les petites affectations d'une coquette.[30]

A lady who seemed like a determined soldier might inspire fear, but I do not know if she would inspire love, just as I doubt that many people would approve of an old warrior who had the little affectations of a flirt.

Women were to inspire affection while men were to command respect. Separate and distinct roles were assigned them, and to the extent that they flouted the code, that they did not conform to the generic conventions prescribed for them, they risked social ostracism—tantamount to loss of identity. Vaumorière underscored his concern for propriety, repeating the same criteria, in a self-admitted obsessive reformulation of his earlier message:

Il est nécessaire, comme je l'ai déjà dit, et comme on ne le saurait trop dire, que l'on considère la condition, le sexe, l'humeur, l'âge et la profession de la personne à qui l'on est obligé d'écrire.[31]

It is necessary, as I have already said, and as cannot be repeated too often, that one take into consideration the condition, the sex, the humor, the age, and the profession of the person to whom one is obliged to write.

This resurfacing of tenets on conversation in a manual on letter writing illustrates to what extent the two activities were elided. Letter writing was understood to be a conversation *entre absents*. It was completely assimilated to protocols of dialogic exchange, and, in keeping with the classical esthetic of transparency, or belief in the efficacity of the act of representation, great faith was expressed in the ability to compensate for the absence of a person with the presence of a letter. This confidence was grounded through a mythicizing of the history of the letter, encapsulating a complete theory of perception and representation:

L'invention de la lettre est presque aussi ancienne que celle de la parole, dont elle est l'image: car elle est l'image du discours, comme le discours l'est de la pensée, et comme la pensée l'est de la chose. Les premiers hommes trouvèrent le secret de se rendre présents les uns aux autres dans leur absence même, en s'écrivant sur des tablettes de bois.[32]

The invention of the letter is almost as old as that of the word, of which it is the image: for the letter is the image of speech, as speech is of thought, and as thought is of the actual thing. The first men found the secret of being present to each other even in their absence, by writing to each other on tablets of wood.

The terms "discours," "pensée," and "chose" operate on an uninterrupted continuum and make of the letter, according to this belief, an exact "image" of the "parole." This very concept of transparency seems compromised by its association with that of propriety in the general discussion unless it is intent upon acting on the central term "pensée" in such a way as to ensure its propriety, and vice versa. Any discontinuity between perception, reflection, and projection is denied and, at the same time, implied in the apprehension of a need for lessons on what, and what not, how and how not to write.

Vaumorière offers his own slightly less complacent definition of the letter, acknowledging a fundamental difference between the written and the spoken word, and suggesting preference for the latter. He points to the letter's function of compensatory adequation of a more desirable situation where the interlocutors would be in direct communion rather than in mediated correspondence:

Un écrit que nous envoyons à une personne absente pour lui faire savoir ce que nous lui dirions, si nous étions en état de lui parler.[33]

A piece of writing we send to an absent person to let him know what we would say to him, if we could speak to him.

Here the letter is encoded as an only proximate substitute for conversation.[34] The standard seventeenth-century conceptualization of the relationship between subject and object and its implications for the double project of perception and self-representation propose a fairly uncomplicated faith in the ability to communicate by letter and at the same time are embedded in discourses that imply a nagging doubt of the veracity of that metaphysical system.

The need to reflect accurately the hierarchical relations of the correspondents in written exchanges was a frequently elaborated topic. Just as, in conversational situations, the interlocutors needed to project, establish, and recognize status in order to know how to relate, relying on costume, voice, accent, manners, and context, so social stratification was often sorted out in the letter exchange process. The mode of address being the first consideration in the composition of any letter, it also figured foremost in the manuals. Vaumorière spelled out the general rule: "Il faut examiner, sans préoccupation, qui l'on est et à qui l'on écrit"[35] [One must examine, without distraction, who one is and to whom one is writing]. This seems to recapitulate Socrates' dictum "Know thyself" but suggests that essential to that is knowing who one is in relation to others, and that this knowledge of relationship amounts to an understanding of one's place in the social hierarchy. It appears crucial to apply this knowledge of the social station and the relative positions of the correspondents in the choice of appropriate style. Vaumorière went on to elaborate the way this knowledge was to be reflected in the style of address:

On est obligé d'accommoder ses expressions à la nature des sujets et au rang des personnes. Il faut qu'on s'élève noblement quand on écrit à des personnes d'une grande considération et que l'on descende à des façons de parler plus familières . . .[36]

One is obliged to adapt one's expressions to the nature of the subjects and to people's rank. One must rise up nobly when one writes to people of great consideration and descend to more familiar ways of speaking . . .

Jean Puget de La Serre, in developing his typology of letters, distinguishing between content and form, points out that there are certain kinds of messages that can be addressed only to people to whom one is superior. For instance, he says of letters of command that they are to be written only "à ceux sur lesquels on a du pouvoir, comme sont ses enfants, serviteurs et semblables"[37] [to those over whom one has power, like one's children, servants, and the like]. This convergence of servants and children as common subjects of the power of others will be of particular interest further along in this study, when we consider Sévigné's writing relationship to her daughter and her advice to that daughter on raising her children.[38]

Vaumorière was equally concerned with appropriate modes of address for one's superiors: "Evitons aussi l'extrémité opposée, ne traitons jamais trop familièrement les personnes qui sont au-dessus de nous"[39] [Let us also avoid the opposite extreme; let us never treat too familiarly the people who are above us]. This entire activity of codifying, classifying, and modeling— identifying types of letters, types of sentiments, types of relations, types of writing, types of address—was symptomatic of the drive to work out the complexities of the social fabric in a world that had left feudalism behind but had not quite developed a bourgeois class, that was straining nonetheless with obsolete categories and unsure of the hierarchy of new ones, and that for the moment was organized under an absolute monarchy intent on maintaining and cultivating the order that privileged it and guaranteed its continuance.

But at the heart of this concern for social order appears to be an anxiety about a more profound destabilization, the emergence of women as writing subjects. These purportedly helpful manuals were perhaps more nefarious than they appear. While granting women a place in the domain of writing, citing them as models, and even offering them assistance, they were carefully prescribing their limited place in the world of writing and, by implication, in the world at large.

In these manuals as elsewhere, Balzac and Voiture were cited regularly as paired examples of fine epistolary writing. Of Balzac, Vaumorière says: "Nous en avons un fameux, qui aime de telle sorte tout ce qui sent le sublime" [We have a first-rate one, who likes everything that smacks of the sublime]; and of Voiture, in characteristic tandem if not wholehearted praise:

L'autre auteur célèbre . . . manque rarement à dire les choses d'une manière galante et enjouée: mais il tombe quelquefois de ce caractère charmant, dans des expressions populaires, sans parler de celles qui peuvent faire mal au coeur, comme quand il dit que l'on trouva trois poux sur une dame.[40]

The other famous author . . . rarely misses the chance to say things in a gallant and playful way: but he sometimes falls out of this charming character into popular expressions, not to speak of the ones that can physically offend, as when he says that three lice were found on a lady.

The two writers are cited frequently as standards of epistolary excellence. Pierre Richelet furnished examples of their letters in his instructive collection,[41] and Vaumorière returns to them later in his treatise:

Voyons les deux plus fameux Ecrivains que nous ayons en matière de lettres. Il y en a un qui ne cherche qu'à plaire en se jouant, l'autre fait tous ses efforts pour attirer une admiration continuelle.[42]

Let us see the two most famous Writers we have in the way of letters. There is the one who seeks only to please by dallying, the other does all he can to attract continuous admiration.

Although they are equally cited, they obviously produced different re-actions and appealed to different readerships. Their writing profiles appear to fall into gender-inflected categories. As was seen earlier, women were to inspire affection, men to command respect. In seeking "to please," Voi-ture aligned himself with the masculine prescription of a feminine ethos, whereas Balzac, in seeking admiration, upheld the masculine ethos. This difference in the intentionality of their writing is indicated in two distinct attitudes toward the inscribed addressee, the intended reader—the other: Balzac appears consistently self-absorbed and sufficient—autonomous; and Voiture encodes himself as other-directed and engaged—relational.

If Sévigné first encountered Balzac and Voiture in this instructional lit-erature, she certainly did not admit to it. She held all of it in great contempt. She dismissed any writing that smacked of formulaic imitation as the "style à cinq sols" (I, L. 167, p. 258) [five-cent style], suggesting haughtily that money, the price of a manual, could not buy quality—quality was not for sale. She mentions not one manual or collection in her own letters, ad-mitting only to reading published correspondences of confirmed renown and savoring letters of her friends. It is highly unlikely, however, that they were totally unknown to her, as witness her name for such writing, above. The rate at which they proliferated and circulated as she herself was writ-ing suggests that she must minimally have been aware of them even if she preferred not to acknowledge it. The manuals were subject to class bias: admitting to reading them was tantamount to admitting of effort, inadmis-sible under the reign of *négligence*. In refusing to acknowledge them (if, indeed, she had ever consulted them),[43] Sévigné was, however, also being faithful to one of their most fundamental tenets, expressed so succinctly by Vaumorière: "Tout doit paraître naturel dans une lettre, et il faut ab-solument que l'art s'y cache"[44] [All must appear natural in a letter, and it is absolutely necessary that the art be hidden]. Certainly, to acknowledge resorting to any sort of guidance in writing would have smacked of ped-antry, of artifice, and of application. Sévigné can be said to have followed the dictates of the manuals in their strictest interpretation in refusing to acknowledge them in her writing. She was faithful to the basic esthetic les-son propounded by encoders of the genre such as Vaumorière in her very unfaithfulness to their text:

Rien ne doit sentir la contrainte ni l'affectation dans une lettre. Tout y doit avoir l'air de liberté qui règne dans l'entretien ordinaire.[45]

Nothing must suggest constraint or affectation in a letter. Everything must seem to have the freedom that reigns in ordinary conversation.

How to appear free, unconstrained, unaffected and at the same time admit to following conscientiously the lessons of all of these would-be masters?

Sévigné's Canon: Balzac and Voiture

Sévigné herself contributed to the sure status of Balzac and Voiture by alluding to them in her own letters. She as much as La Bruyère is responsible for their authorial immortality. They have since been frequently cited by literary historians as Sévigné's canonical precursors in the developing art of correspondence. This, one must conclude, is how Sévigné would have wanted it. It is interesting indeed to consider certain parallels: La Bruyère, in a text on women letter writers, names not one but privileges two male writers; Sévigné, in her letters, distances herself from manuals and pedagogical tools of the sort and privileges those same two male writers. These two moves can be read as representing similar gestures. Both attach themselves to the dominant, the conventional, the authorized literary wisdom and thus position their own writing securely in the mainstream.

Nevertheless, the manuals and, in turn, Sévigné, while regularly pairing Balzac and Voiture, just as significantly distinguished between them. Just as they aligned along distinct gender-coded writing positions, so did they by class. Although reservations were often expressed regarding Balzac's pomposity and pretentiousness, his letters were generally regarded as un controversial and emblematic of fine writing. He was viewed as a solid citizen of the "République des lettres," and if he also happened to be of a noble family, that was merely incidental. Voiture, on the other hand, could not escape judgments that appear to reflect class bias as much as any esthetic appraisal, as witness the above statement by Vaumorière. Is it seemly to write of lice? Voiture, it is suggested, in his eagerness to please, occasionally forgets himself and lapses verbally into the vulgarity of his social origins.

Voiture's assimilation into the elite through writing parallels in interesting ways Sévigné's assimilation into the canon. Both wrote their way conservatively from positions of marginality into the worlds to which they aspired. Voiture came from the trading class, the son of a wealthy wine merchant, and made his way into the select circle of the Hôtel de Rambouillet by dint of his wit and charm. *Roturier* (plebeian), he participated in, and benefited from, the *précieuses'* valorizing of merit over title. He gained entry to the circle of the salon elite, which was, at this time, defying traditional titular stratification and favoring social mobility.[46] In a sense his exclusion by birth from the aristocratic pact of good taste explained his popularity there. His later critics were to see his journey through life primarily as one of escape from his bourgeois background ("Il se hâte de fuir la boutique empuantie," and again, "Il aurait maintes luttes à soutenir pour se décrasser de sa roture," and more positively, "Il n'y avait rien en lui qui sentit le cabaret de son père"[47] [He hurries to escape the stinking shop . . . He would have many a struggle to wage to rid himself of his commonness . . . There was nothing in him that smacked of his father's tavern). Actually, one of his appealing charms was the very fact that, as an outsider, he could say things that others could not, and a great part of his talent lay in doing so gracefully and in getting away with it, this thanks to the condescending permissiveness of his well-bred friends.

He saw things through a prism different from that of the refined vision of Mme de Rambouillet's circle. He valorized his own life experience as he inserted himself into the world of polite discourse. His moderate lack of inhibition or failure to adhere faithfully to the code of the speakable guaranteed a *succès de scandale* as he judiciously imported an invigorating bourgeois realism into the effete salons and brought some fresh air into a rarefied environment that welcomed revitalization. He was appreciated in large part because he was at once an outsider and a conformist. He knew both how much "otherness" the salon could tolerate and how much conformity it required of him. He met unfailingly the expectations of his patrons for someone of his background, thus confirming them in their prejudices, and at the same time he demonstrated an exquisite sensibility that made him one of them. His social acceptance was mirrored in his literary acceptance. He came to occupy a position of distinction in both worlds.

Sévigné repeatedly expressed admiration for Voiture. In her letters she invents amusing typologies of letters and refers to "voitures," "petites lettres" (III, L. 1186, p. 810), and "portugaises" (III, L. 844, p. 80) as if they constituted subgenres of the mode, indicating thus her awareness of the impact that a particular style might have on a form in general.[48] Balzac, however, figures in her letters only when paired with Voiture, in a sort of received formulaic summary of the epitome of fine writing. For example, in praise of her friend Pomponne's epistolary talent, she writes:

Il [M. de Pomponne] a écrit aussi . . . une lettre à M. de Vivonne bien plus jolie que Voiture et Balzac; les louanges n'en sont point fades. (II, L. 524, p. 331)

He [M. de Pomponne] also wrote . . . a letter to M. de Vivonne much finer than Voiture and Balzac; the praises are not insipid.

And Jean Corbinelli, a frequent writing partner, in a joint letter to Bussy, takes up Sévigné's pen and names the same two writers to indicate a standard he claims Bussy and Sévigné surpass:

Le P. Bouhours aurait peut-être aussi bien fait de rapporter des fragments de vos lettres et de celles de Mme de Sévigné que de celles de Balzac et Voiture pour donner des exemples de la justesse, de la délicatesse, ou de la noble simplicité des pensées. (III, L. 990, p. 340)

Father Bouhours would perhaps have done just as well to refer to fragments of your letters and Mme de Sévigné's as to Balzac's and Voiture's to give examples of soundness, of delicacy, or of the noble simplicity of thoughts.

Sévigné had prepared the way for such a comparison by privileging the Balzac-Voiture standard in her own writing. She contextualized her work as she wrote.

Balzac receives no particular attention from Sévigné, aside from the obligatory nod when named in conjunction with Voiture. A consideration of their respective voices does much to explain her preference, as well as providing a context for a more precise understanding of Sévigné's own tones.

The epistolary art, as practiced by Balzac, represents the grand Latin tradition, revered, preserved, and imported to France by repatriated humanists. Balzac's first collection of letters, published in 1624, established his reputation in literary France as "l'unico eloquente" [the single most eloquent individual]. He had been strongly influenced during his stay in Rome by the popularity of the epistolary form in Italy, as practiced by Aretino, for example. He resorted to the letter as a way of participating in and influencing intellectual life in Paris after his self-imposed exile, upon his falling out with Richelieu. His letters represent an attempt not so much to communicate with individuals as to impose himself in the forum of ideas. He states of his own work: "Il n'a tenu qu'à la fortune . . . que ce qu'on appelle lettres n'ait été harangues ou Discours d'état"[49] [It was only the result of fortune . . . that what one calls letters was not harangues or Discourses of State]. Politics, ethics, philosophy are the sorts of topics addressed in Balzac's letters; the addressees are only of secondary concern.

The model of Roman classicism determines Balzac's style: it is marked by a concern for unity, concentration, and subordination of detail to the whole.[50] The esthetic of writing "naturally" or (as his own words, read by the literary historian Antoine Adam, suggest) "like a woman" is totally alien to him. Without reflecting on the gender coding to which he thus unwittingly subscribes, Adam points out: "Il n'essaie pas . . . d'être naturel et de parler 'comme il faut que parle une honnête femme,' car il prétend travailler 'pour l'éternité' "[51] [He doesn't try . . . to be natural and to speak "as an honest woman should," for he claims to work "for eternity"]. Balzac's aspiration then, to a grandiose and monumental permanence in his style is, interestingly if not surprisingly, elided with the masculine. Sévigné, on the other hand, will obligingly and perhaps not so coincidentally meet the implicit gendered prescriptions set by Balzac for women writing—naturally and conversationally, and, by implication, if he were to have his way, transitorily.

An analysis of what Balzac offers as a model of the personal love letter points up the distance between his esthetic, Voiture's, and Sévigné's, as seen in comparable letters to her daughter. Balzac wrote a series of letters purporting to court a country neighbor by name of Clorinde, but circulated in Paris rather than sent next door. Inventing a situation of disappointment that his suit has not been favorably received, he displays his writing talent in the composition of a reproachful, not to say spiteful letter, the tone of which is summarized in his final threatening appeal: "Laissez-vous gaigner à la raison, puis que vous ne pouvez y résister qu'à vostre désadvantage"[52] [Let yourself be won over by reason, since you can resist only to your disadvantage].

This series of letters, with its menacing conclusion, is a set piece working out a conventional literary theme for display purposes. The general strategy of the closing argument is reminiscent of Ronsard's sonnets for Hélène. Balzac repeats the usual dire threats of age and ugliness, deploying the standard strategy for gallantly bullying women; by emphasizing her ornamental qualities, by objectifying her, he reminds Clorinde of her marginal, incidental, ephemeral, and replaceable status. She serves at once as muse and as victim—his immortality as writer is contingent on her mortality as woman. Balzac appeals to Clorinde's reasoning faculties (which, according to him, she doesn't even possess) in order to display his own brilliant powers, and while he constructs a sound argument, the letter certainly does not constitute a convincing expression of "love." In fact, it is informed by a strong dose of misogyny evidenced by the zest with which Balzac describes precisely and at length how Clorinde will age and wither, and how her loss of beauty will spell her end—she existing, then, solely in and according to the eyes of the masculine beholder, and only as long as he holds his gaze on her.

His letter is not an impassioned attempt to persuade an actual individual of love but a calculated argument designed to impress a sympathetic readership with his fine intellect and sharp wit. The closest Balzac comes to personalizing this love letter is in suggesting that it is the season for love, and that even philosophers (by implication, himself) are susceptible to the passions, in spite of their ferocity (suggested by the contiguity with lions and tigers): "Nous sommes au mois, où tout fait l'amour, sans excepter les Lyons, les Tigres, et les Philosophes" [53] [This is the month where everything makes love, without excepting Lions, Tigers, and Philosophers].

It hardly matters whether this letter is written with a Clorinde actually in mind or is addressed to the Parisian public. It is manifestly clear that Balzac's immortality, insofar as this particular letter contributes to securing his enduring reputation, is at the expense of Clorinde's: he strives for immortality by insisting on her mortality. If she endures, it will be in his text, as does Hélène in Ronsard's. Such wooing tactics bear no resemblance to the sort to be found in the Sévigné letters, even if possible parallels in the subtextual dynamics are not to be dismissed. The extent to which both writers fictionalize their addressees through projections of their own needs and at the expense of the addressees can be understood as a constant tension between the temptation to objectify and the capacity for intersubjectivity in literary as well as human relations.

Balzac's rhetorical celebration of tradition and explicit aspiration to immortality earned him a place in the "République des lettres" but did not endear him to all of his seventeenth-century readers. Although his style was admired, he was considered pedantic and pompous,[54] and his letters to Clorinde in particular were found offensive. Although he was firmly instated in the canon, as witness La Bruyère's praise (1687), he fell out of fashion as women increasingly set the style, and his writing was outmoded by 1690, when the Abé *** passed the following judgment:

Je ne puis souffrir les Lettres de Balzac à sa prétendue maîtresse; et le nom de Clorinde me choque presqu'autant dans ce grave avocat; que le tour guindé de ses poulets.

I cannot stand Balzac's Letters to his supposed mistress; and the name of Clorinde shocks me almost as much coming from this grave lawyer as the affected manner of his love notes.

Voiture fared much better with the same critic:

Voiture s'y prend d'une autre sorte. Il n'apartient qu'à lui de badiner agréablement comme il n'apartient qu'au seul Balzac de pousser la métaphore aussi loin qu'elle pouvait aller.[55]

Voiture sets about it differently. He alone can banter agreeably just as Balzac alone can push a metaphor as far as it will go.

Sévigné must have appreciated that even with the esteemed Balzac there was risk in taking oneself too seriously, and she obviously did not experience a personal attraction to his writing. Nevertheless, faithful as she was to the received notions of her day, she did not fail to invoke his name dutifully as signal of excellence, nor did she trouble to investigate the contradiction of her predilection for his constant companion in the canon and her marked indifference to him.

On the other hand, Sévigné's quotations of Voiture are frequent; she borrows his expressions freely to convey her own sentiments. There can be no stronger praise or greater subscription to another's writing than such easy intertextuality: "Du reste, il faut que je dise comme Voiture: Personne n'est encore mort de votre absence hormis moi" (I, L. 136, p. 161) [Moreover, I must say as Voiture does: No one has yet died from your absence but me]. She appreciates his humor and borrows his *bons mots* regularly to translate her own amusement:

Tout le monde se moque de lui [Saint-Aoust], quoique Voiture nous ait appris que c'est très mal fait de se moquer des trépassés. (II, L. 422, p. 94)

Everyone makes fun of him [Saint-Aoust], although Voiture has taught us that it is not proper to make fun of the dead.

The ease with which she cites verses of his poetry and offers them to serve as accurate expressions of her own thoughts further confirms the general compatibility of the two (II, L. 713, pp. 747–48). Sévigné upholds the defense of Voiture when he is criticized and applauds others who share in her enthusiasm for his writing:

Corbinelli abandonne Méré et son chien de style et le ridicule critique qu'il fait, en collet monté, d'un esprit libre, badin et charmant comme Voiture. (II, L. 712, p. 745)

Corbinelli is abandoning Méré and his awful style and the ridiculous criticism he produces, straitlaced, of a free, bantering, and charming spirit like Voiture.

Appreciation of Voiture serves as a criterion of good taste, that is, of compatibility with Sévigné's own.[56] She enjoys the role of literary arbiter and passes judgment on her contemporaries and their proclivities in her letters, just as La Bruyère does in his *Caractères*. The degree of popularity he enjoys in her immediate circle translates into a self-congratulatory measure of her own influence; she was pleased to learn that her granddaughter Pauline shared her taste:

Montgobert me mandait l'autre jour que Pauline lisait auprès d'elle les lettres de Voiture et qu'elle les entendait comme nous. (III, L. 806, p. 11)

Montgobert wrote to me the other day that Pauline was reading Voiture's letters near her, and that she appreciated them as we do.

The term "voiture" comes to serve in the *Correspondance* as a password for a flirtatious and contentious bantering tone (*badinage*) that is often put to use to divert, deflect, defuse in a lightly humorous way a situation that is facetiously represented as potentially explosive (e.g., III, L. 1016, p. 380). The entire drama is invented within the letter but grounded in the relations between writer and addressee. It is this at once irreverent and sensitive pleasure that Sévigné savored and reproduced in her own writing.

Sévigné remained a faithful admirer of Voiture's writing; even as late as 1690, she repeats:

Voiture nous divertit aussi quelquefois, aussi bien que vous. Pour moi, je ne m'accoutume point à l'agrément de son style. Vous me faites rire quand vous croyez que quelqu'un puisse écrire comme lui. (III, L. 1209, p. 883)

Voiture also amuses us sometimes, as well as you. As for me, I do not cease to be taken with the charm of his style. You make me laugh when you believe that someone else might be able to write like him.

Voiture serves as ultimate model, measure, and password in the Sévigné rating code for quality in letters. The fact that others flattered her by claiming similarities between their writing styles can only have further endeared him to her.

The affinity Sévigné obviously felt with Voiture can be explained perhaps by similarities of the social intersections they occupied as they wrote. Sympathies between the two writing profiles are quite evident. Elegance, charm, grace, and humor of a flexible, conversational sort, and above all, a desire to please, a constant concern for the addressee and the reception of the letter—these are some of the characteristics of their shared esthetic. Adam sees a direct relationship between Voiture's tone and the character of Sévigné's early letters: "Ses lettres des débuts ont de la finesse, de la désinvolture, mais aussi, comme son modèle, une certaine affectation. On la sent qui s'applique à badiner."[57] [Her first letters have finesse, ease, but also, like her model, a certain affectation. One senses that she is straining to be clever.] The critic reproaches Sévigné not at all her choice of model but that hint of effort which belies the "naturalness" of her developing style and explains its slightly stilted quality. Voiture is cited as the liberator of poetry from rhetoric and Petrarchan tradition, and as the first purveyor of "véritable galanterie" [genuine gallantry] in French literature.[58] At the same time, he was often reproached both for an overly common and an overly precious style. There appears to be a delicate balance between vulgarity and overrefinement, constantly invoked with reference to Voiture, that points as much to concern for his tenuous social position as to any esthetic issue. The aristocracy enjoys impeccable taste as a birthright and discerns unfailingly the presence or lack thereof in others.

Voiture may have been admitted to the elite, but he was always on trial there. His unsure status was reflected in contemporary appreciations of his work and has continued to be an issue in the institution of literary history.[59] This class reservation, translated into literary assessment concerning Voiture's writing, finds resonance with the gender-permeated criticism that shaped or failed to shape Sévigné's early literary reputation ("Si les femmes étaient toujours correctes . . ."). Both inserted themselves in the margins of class and gender-organized society and literature and remain incompletely assimilated there.

Voiture's addressee, unlike Balzac's, did not function solely as pretext; and further, Voiture wrote with a more immediate purpose in mind than that of immortality. He sought to charm particular individuals, for the most part distinguished and erudite ladies of leisure—powerful organizers of society and letters in their time—to keep a hold on their affections in his absence, and to maintain his reputation at the Hôtel de Rambouillet as a *bel esprit*. He offers letters as substitutes for his presence and engages his addressees directly and personally. It is not writing alone that interests him but sociability and a continued welcome in the privileged society of the *hôtel*.

He is not totally innocent, however, of writerly aspirations. Publication is not foremost among his articulated ambitions; he does not appear as driven as Balzac. But, just as the thought of publishing, or being published, would eventually cross Sévigné's mind and find its way into her letters, so it also occurred to Voiture that his letters might someday appear in print. He is cited as having confided to Mme de Rambouillet:

Vous verrez . . . qu'il y aura quelque jour d'assez sottes gens pour chercher ça et là ce que j'ai fait, et après, le faire imprimer; cela me fait venir quelque envie de le corriger.[60]

You will see . . . that some day there will be people silly enough to seek out what I have written, and afterward, to print it; this gives me something of a desire to correct it.

The disparaging way in which he alludes to those who might think to publish him rings of false modesty. In deriding his admirers, he affects a self-effacing attitude (although one in contradiction with the boastfulness of his prediction to his confidante) that stands in marked contrast with Balzac's proferred self-image of "philosophe." Voiture as a *parvenu* knows better than to take and present himself seriously in the same way. He cannot plausibly and coherently confess literary ambition as his erudite

counterpart professes it without admitting to the craft applied in constructing the social and literary profile that has secured his access to high culture,
and thereby revealing his fundamental inadmissibility to that circle.

Although there may be just as much ambition behind his epistolary activity as behind Balzac's, his tactics are radically different; they generally
resemble Sévigné's aims to please and charm correspondents more than
Balzac's quest to construct and win arguments. The difference between
Balzac and Voiture, the similarity between Sévigné and Voiture, is located
in the complicated interrelationship between these writers and their audiences. Their different social positions, their different status in the writing
community, their different readership contribute to the production of their
different styles. Both Voiture and Sévigné will play on the worlds they
come from and exploit them as source material for tributary contributions to the domains they seek to enter. They write resolutely as outsiders,
claiming no explicit ambitions for publication. They know their place.
And they write to individuals rather than for more generalized publics,
but these individual readers constitute an influential readership capable of
immortalizing them if they so choose. That the readers enjoy social and
censorial power over them is reflected in the messages produced. From the
precariousness of Voiture's writing position flow certain stylistic tactics
that Sévigné will reproduce in her letters.

A comparison of Voiture's letter to Mlle de Rambouillet with that of
Balzac to Clorinde offers a measure of the greater intimacy expressed in
Voiture's writing and, in spite of its stilted self-consciousness, an indication
of the easy and witty banter Sévigné will emulate:

Mademoiselle, quand je vous aurois présenté autant de perles que les poètes en
font pleurer à l'Aurore. et qu'au lieu que je vous ai donné qu'un peu de terre je
vous l'aurois donnée tout entière, vous n'auriez pu me faire un plus magnifique
remerciement . . .
Voilà, mademoiselle, un commencement fort brillant, et ceux qui, à quelque prix
que ce soit, veulent écrire de beaux mots, seroient bien aises de commencer par
là ce qu'ils appellent une belle lettre. Mais le courrier ne m'en donne pas le loisir.
Et, de plus, après avoir bien lu celle de Madame votre mère et les vôtres, je suis
résolu de ne m'en plus mêler. Sans mentir, il ne se peut rien voir de plus galant ni
de plus beau que celle que j'ai reçu d'elle, et cela est merveilleux, qu'une personne
qui n'écrit qu'en quatre ans une fois, le fasse de sorte, quand elle l'entreprend, qu'il
semble qu'elle y ait toujours étudié, et que durant tout ce temps elle n'ait pensé à
autre chose. Je devrais être tantôt accoutumé aux miracles de votre maison, mais
j'avoue que je ne puis pas m'empêcher de m'en étonner. J'admire de vous particu-
lièrement, mademoiselle, que, sachant si bien danser, vous sachiez si bien écrire, et
que vous emportiez le prix en même temps de trois choses qui ne marchent guère
ensemble, étant comme vous êtes, la meilleure danseuse, la meilleure dormeuse, et
la plus éloquente fille du monde.[61]

Mademoiselle, if I had presented you with as many pearls as the poets make Dawn shed tears, and if instead of giving to you a bit of earth I had given it to you whole, you could not have given me a more magnificent thanks . . .
Here, mademoiselle, is a quite brilliant beginning, and those who, at any cost, want to write beautiful words would be very glad to begin thus what they call a fine letter. But the courier doesn't give me the leisure to do so. And, further, after having properly read Madame your mother's and yours, I am resolved not to try any longer. Truthfully, there can be nothing more gallant nor more beautiful than the one I received from her, and it is marvelous that a person who only writes once every four years can write so that, when she undertakes it, it seems that she has always studied, and that during all this time she has thought of nothing else. I should by now be accustomed to the miracles of your family, but I declare that I cannot prevent myself from being surprised. I particularly admire in you, made-moiselle, that, knowing how to dance so well, you know how to write so well, and that you carry away the prize at the same time for three things that hardly go together, being as you are, the best dancer, the best sleeper, and the most eloquent girl in the world.

Voiture evinces a flirtatious writerly awareness as he rereads himself and deems his opening epistolary flourish emblematic of a "belle lettre." At the same time, this move establishes a defensive distance between Voiture's missive and the ornamentation common to a conventional *belle lettre,* lest his be found wanting. Voiture facetiously proposes his text (by extension, himself) as model to those in need of one, thus rising above those who need and desire instruction. He positions himself as a member of the class and aligns himself with the gender to which such things come "naturally." In the same letter he takes great pains to honor Madame de Rambouillet's and her daughter's writing, bestowing upon it the ultimate compliment of its obvious effortlessness—deferring thus to their social superiority. As a humored outsider, he both projects a sense of his own entitlement and indicates that he knows his place in relation to his distinguished corre-spondents. This putative interest in the process of writing well intersects with Voiture's project of social positioning vis-à-vis his correspondent. His divergence from the social norm of his correspondent is veiled by the de-flection of attention to the epistolary norm of the *belle lettre.* One set of conventions stands in for another; by making light of one set, he challenges the sanctity of the other.

Balzac admits of no such self-evaluation in process, since he produces only finished and polished letters. Nor need he. Member of the nobility, secure in his world, he has only to pronounce and prescribe for others. On the other hand, Sévigné, like Voiture, will reflect regularly on her writing and its relationship to the generic norm as she claims to strive toward a mirror relationship with her epistolary expression in her articulation of an esthetic of sincerity. The activity of constantly positioning herself in her world through her text produces many of the same sorts of reflections on writing and on letters as those found in Voiture. Deliberate nonconformity to the generic norm signals both acknowledgment and refusal of social and gender-related norms.

Immediate constraints (a waiting messenger) enter into Voiture's repertory of epistolary strategies, bearing witness to the materiality of the writing and sending process, and also evincing sensitivity to the function of others in the corresponding activity. This awareness of the work involved for some in the transmitting of letters suggests an identification with another class, those who serve the elite, and is offered as justification for a change in style. The fact of the courier's waiting is incorporated into the text of the letter as a pretext for a more familiar, less poetic tone of address than that of the grandiose opening, replete with "perles que les poètes en font pleurer à l'Aurore." Voiture's exploitation of the circumstances of the epistolary situation as subject matter for the letter prefigures Sévigné's preoccupations with such contingent concerns in her letters; she as well is in touch with other worlds, the exigencies of which influence the writing she produces.

The hyperbolic compliment on the letters of the Rambouillet ménage is followed by gestures of renouncement and of teasing; Voiture shifts mercurially from one stance to another, eschewing any seriousness on the part of sender or receiver, refusing to light. Frivolous logic, devised for the sole purpose of entertaining, often characterizes Sévigné's writing as well, as she seeks to seduce her correspondents. Voiture did want to please; he knew exactly whom he wanted to please and how to do it, and he can be said to have served himself well by the kind of writing he did. As much as Sévigné's, his letters are oriented toward his own *réalité vécue* [lived experience]. He established a ludic space of relation in which considerations of class and etiquette were suspended or made light of, and thus he made room for himself in a domain that was otherwise closed to him. And Sévigné established a maternal space of relation in which gender could not interfere with but only abet her writing drive, and thus she eased her way into literature. Voiture's discreet entry into the world of the lettered elite parallels Sévigné's entry into the world of the elite lettered.

Voiture came to embody and to be acknowledged as the precursor of an increasingly popular standard of writing. André-Louis Personne wrote in 1662, in a surprising admission of emulation:

S'il était vrai ce que l'on vous a dit, que je valusse mieux que Voiture, je lui en aurais l'obligation, puisque ce serait lui qui m'aurait appris à le surpasser lui-même.[62]

If what they told you was true, that I am better than Voiture, I would owe it to him, since it would be he himself who would have taught me to surpass him.

The communicative contract, the epistolary pact between sender (narrator) and receiver (narratee) determines the sort of message that will be encoded. The contract is grounded in the social relations that structure the spectrum of speech acts possible between the two correspondents. The codification of social relations evident in the lessons of the manuals points to the anxiety generated in the seventeenth century around the increasing complexity of the social network and to particular concern for the place of women writing. The social relations that obtained between Voiture and his correspondents generated a sort of writing that became the preferred standard among the elite, but that was also devalorized in the hierarchy of genres as it became increasingly gender-identified, as it was feminized. As the prestige- and birth-grounded economy of the aristocracy was increasingly subjected to the pleasure of the king and threatened by the rise of a new money- and merit-based system of valuation, the entire elite felt threatened with superfluity and was, as a class, (re)constructed as feminine, emasculated. It is interesting to consider the extent to which Voiture's writing, addressed in the main to aristocratic women whose company he appeared genuinely to enjoy, set a new, more gynophilic standard, flattering thus an entire group in particular need of specular reaffirmation at this historical juncture, and to what extent, correlatively, Balzac's, blatantly misogynous as it was, fell into disfavor and was channeled into more subtle forms of repression of the feminine. It is in this general context that the production of Sévigné's letters can be considered.

TWO

Sévigné's Apprenticeship

Je veux toujours de la justesse dans les pensées, mais quelquefois de la négligence dans les expressions, et surtout dans les lettres qu'écrivent les dames.
BUSSY-RABUTIN

I always want accuracy in thoughts, but sometimes carelessness in expressions, and especially in the letters that ladies write.

Manuals and published letters featured discreetly in Sévigné's epistolary articulation, but one actual correspondence significantly shaped her education in writing. From 1646 until 1692, with sporadic gaps, she and her cousin Bussy-Rabutin corresponded, and she served an epistolary apprenticeship with him. His example, his influence, and his interest contributed to shape her self-image as a writer. Bussy bore the family title and enjoyed dominion of the family property. In the configuration of Sévigné's genealogy, he represented the surviving scion of the noble patriarchal lineage and consequently commanded a certain respect from his cousin. Eight years her senior and worldly-wise, he also functioned in her affective life as a responsible older brother. In the absence of a husband, the widow Sévigné conferred with him, at least formally, on familial responsibilities that devolved upon her. While the maternal and bourgeois side of her family, the Coulanges, in particular the "bien bon" abbé, provided guidance in practical and financial matters, Bussy was consulted and kept abreast of titular matters and family rituals—marriages, alliances, issues bearing on the family name and status. He assumed the prerogatives of his gender, estate, age, and experience, and obligingly included her in his life. Gender, class, and seniority converged in the familial nexus to produce the power dynamics that would determine the cousins' respective writing voices.

The uneven footing of the relationship, Bussy's condescension and Sévigné's amenability, is reflected in the dynamic of their exchange. Although a good deal of friendly, even flirtatious banter, as well as some serious disagreement, takes place between the two cousins, Sévigné generally deferred to the patronizing Bussy and graciously accepted the subordinate role in their relationship. Their correspondence offered valuable lessons and insights on the virtuosities inherent to the epistolary praxis and brought her writing as close to publication as it would come during her lifetime.

All that she learned from her cousin she passed on to her daughter when they began to exchange letters in 1671. Not only the lessons in writing, but the hierarchically charged dynamic itself, are repeated in the correspondence Sévigné cultivates with her daughter, with the difference that, in this instance of mother-daughter relating, Sévigné enjoys the position of privilege and authority monopolized by Bussy in the other. As he had been the instigator, arbiter, and prime beneficiary in the exchange with his amenable cousin, so Sévigné assumes and enjoys the lead in the epistolary relationship with her daughter.

Certain moments in the history of the Bussy-Sévigné exchange strike me as particularly revealing of the way the two cousins related to each other. Focus on them illuminates the way in which that relationship informed Sévigné's writing and attitude toward writing, as well as contributing to shape her epistolary relationship with her daughter.

Certainly the Sévigné-Bussy writing relationship was not the only context in which Sévigné developed her writing identity. The earliest letters of the *Correspondance* are addressed to a variety of admirers, relatives, friends. They merely begin to suggest the importance that epistolary communication would assume in Sévigné's life. They are for the most part short, polite, and occasionally flirtatious exchanges, but they contain the seeds of her later concerns.[1] The subject is feeling her way here, learning to write as she does so, incorporating into her letters reflections on her writing and on the epistolary situation, developing a metacriticism on her activity. Each of the exchanges will eventuate in a markedly different voice—the gazette-like missives to Pomponne, the breezy and affectionate exchanges with Coulanges—structured to render scriptorally the relationships in play. Sévigné was assured early on in these correspondences of her friends' appreciation of her letters, and as a consequence an easy tone of confidence sealed the epistolary pact.

In Sévigné's early letters to Bussy, however, we find her reflecting in a more precise and wary way on her style: "le mien n'est pas laconique" (I, L. 34, p. 32) [mine isn't laconic]; and assigning value to her letters: "elle me paraissait assez badine" (I, L. 33, p. 30) [it seemed bantering enough to me]; and "elle était assez jolie" (I, L. 34, p. 31) [it was pretty enough]; as well as: "Ce n'est point ici une belle lettre" (I, L. 34, p. 32) [This is not at all a beautiful letter]. Her own judgment, sure as it is, appeals to his tolerance: "il faut que vous supportiez mes défauts" (I, L. 34, p. 32) [you must put up with my flaws]; and defers to his superiority in matters epistolary: "Ce n'est point ici une réponse digne de la vôtre" (I, L. 34, p. 32) [This is not at all a response worthy of yours]. A mixture of confidence and modesty colors her voice. She incorporates her own self-appraisal into her text, anticipating and thus perhaps preempting the critical reading she knows to expect from her cousin.

Her expectation of a judgmental reception is borne out by evidence of Bussy's critical eye. His response confirms the wisdom of her tactic of modesty, as he offers a systematic critique of the various letters he has recently had from her:

J'ai reçu vos trois lettres, Madame . . . Celle de Livry est effectivement fort plaisante; mais, comme vous dites, elle n'est pas la plus tendre du monde . . . Pour votre lettre du 14 juillet, il n'y a rien de plus obligeant ni de plus flatteur que ce que vous me dites . . . Pour votre troisième lettre du 19 juillet, je vous dirai que, pour n'être pas d'un style laconique, elle ne laisse pas d'être fort agréable. (I, L. 35, p. 33)

I received your three letters, Madame . . . The one from Livry is really quite pleasant; but, as you say, it is not the most tender in the world . . . As for your letter of 14 July, there is nothing kinder or more flattering than what you tell me . . . As for your third letter of 19 July, I will tell you that, for a style that is not laconic, it is all the same quite agreeable.

Bussy does not hesitate to issue pronouncements as the arbiter of good taste, and Sévigné, in appealing to his tolerance and in offering her own self-deprecating remarks, contributes to setting him up as such. Although Bussy's response seems to be full of compliments, there is a slight edge of real appraisal in the specific ordering and characterizing of each of the letters that must have recommended to his correspondent care, self-consciousness, and a constant eye to reception.

Early on in their correspondence, Bussy exercises the prerogative of his familial ascendancy and extends it to establish his epistolary authority over his cousin in an expansive critique of her letter:

Votre lettre est fort agréable, ma belle cousine; elle m'a fort réjoui. Qu'on est heureux d'avoir une bonne amie qui ait autant d'esprit que vous. Je ne vois rien de si juste que ce que vous écrivez, et l'on ne peut pas vous dire: "Ce mot-là serait plus à propos que celui que vous avez mis." Quelque complaisance que je vous doive, Madame, vous savez bien que je vous parle assez franchement pour ne pas vous dire ceci si je ne le pensais, et vous ne doutez pas que je m'y connaisse un peu, puisque j'ose bien juger des ouvrages de Chapelain, et que je censure quelquefois assez justement ses pensées et ses paroles. (I, L. 45, p. 43)

Your letter is most agreeable, my fair cousin; it cheered me up a great deal. How lucky one is to have a good friend who has as much wit as you. I see nothing as true as what you write, and one cannot say to you: "This word would be more appropriate than the one you used." Whatever kindness I may owe you, Madame, you know well that I speak to you frankly enough that I would not say this if I were not thinking it, and you should not doubt that I am something of an expert, since I venture to judge Chapelain's works, and I sometimes find fault quite rightly with his thoughts and his words.

He inscribes his critical distance by addressing Sévigné first as "cousine," then as "amie," and finally as "Madame." He legitimizes his right to pronounce on her writing by mentioning that he criticizes—and well—even an author as respected and published as Chapelain. The affection he owes Sévigné as a relative does not enter in, he insists, to his appraisal of her writing. He addresses his "objective" assessment to a stranger, "Madame." His offering of hypothetical criticism, inventing a citation of himself in order to show her what he is not saying, serves as a reminder of the critical stance of which he is capable, if not an outright threat.

To entertain, over a period of years, a correspondence with a writer as hypercritical, censorious, and contentious as Bussy is to develop, in the interest of self-preservation, a self-conscious epistolary manner. Whereas Sévigné developed and practiced her writing skills primarily in her exchange with her daughter, she learned and refined them under Bussy's tutelage. If the student surpassed her master eventually, he did not notice or certainly did not admit to it. Nor did Sévigné flaunt her success. Rather, she loyally and subserviently humored her irascible cousin over the years.

But there was a period of marked estrangement between the two cousins, signaled in the text of Sévigné's correspondence by an eloquent absence of Bussy-related letters. Bussy's writing, in which he took such pride, was to cause him serious trouble both with the king and with his cousin. If he succeeded in mending affairs with Sévigné, he never, in spite of repeated efforts, regained favor with the king. In 1665, he published the satirical and scandalous *Histoire amoureuse des Gaules*, slandering easily identifiable members of the court and Paris society. Imprisoned by order of the king in the Bastille, and then exiled to his estate in 1666, he found himself disgraced and isolated. Since 1658, he and his cousin had quarrelled, over money that she could not—would not—lend him, and he had not spared her in his literary attack on society. So he found himself estranged as well from the one person from whom he might have sought solace.

He undertook to make amends to his cousin and to reestablish the epistolary relationship, which he now needed more than ever. If Sévigné's initial responses to his overtures were kind and solicitous, the score remained to be settled. Sévigné alluded obliquely to the imbalance, displacing it onto the turn taking that had gone awry in their correspondence, accusing her already guilty cousin of further offense: "Chi offende, non perdona" (I, L. 78, p. 88) [He who offends is not the one who pardons].

In response to Bussy's inadequate apologies for the unkind portrait of his cousin in the *Histoire*, Sévigné vented her spleen. She focused on the irreparable damage that the printed word can do to a reputation:

Etre dans les mains de tout le monde, se trouver imprimée, être le livre de divertissement de toutes les provinces, où ces choses-là font un tort irréparable, se rencontrer dans les bibliothèques, et recevoir cette douleur, par qui? (I, L. 81, p. 93)

To be in everyone's hands, to find oneself in print, to be the recreational book of all the provinces, where those things do irreparable damage, to find oneself in the libraries, and to be given this pain, by whom?

And she threatened him with death by her own verbosity if his admission of guilt was not forthcoming:

Au lieu d'écrire en deux mots, comme je vous l'avais promis, j'écrirai en deux mille, et enfin j'en ferai tant, par des lettres d'une longueur cruelle et d'un ennui mortel, que je vous obligerai malgré vous à me demander pardon, c'est-à-dire à me demander la vie. (I, L. 81, p. 94)

Instead of writing in two words, as I had promised you, I will write in two thousand, and finally I will push so far, with letters of a cruel length and of a deadly boredom, that I will oblige you in spite of yourself to beg my pardon, that is to say to beg me for your life.

The two cousins devoted a good deal of text to clearing the way for the possibility of resuming their correspondence. The wronged Sévigné enjoyed in this instance the power of righteousness and magnanimity. She proceeded to play out her advantage, to impose her own closure on the dispute, to claim the last word: "Encore un petit mot, et puis plus; c'est pour commencer une manière de duplique à votre réplique" (I, L. 85, p. 100) [One last brief word, and then no more; it's to start a sort of duplicate to your reply]. The letter thus begun is a firm analysis of the ways in which Bussy has wronged and maligned her. She declares at the outset the purpose of this communication and then sets about her own defense in lawyerly fashion. She takes up the points of the quarrel one by one and justifies her own position. While the sparring tone is somewhat flirtatious, there is always an element of qui vive in the exchange. There can be no hope for the friendship unless her cousin acknowledges his wrongs. Bussy responds to this defense that he is incapable of formulating a "triplique"

(I, L. 86, p. 102); he playfully accuses her, the "petite brutale," of unfairness and cruelty: "vous me voulez tuer à terre" [you want to kill me when I'm down] When she has received this sufficiently humble and penitent letter from him, she pardons him, and in her next missive replies:

Levez-vous, Comte, je ne veux point vous tuer à terre, ou reprenez votre épée pour recommencer notre combat. Mais il vaut mieux que je vous donne la vie et que nous vivions en paix. Vous avouerez seulement la chose comme elle s'est passée; c'est tout ce que je veux. (I, L. 87, p. 103)

Rise, Count. I certainly do not want to kill you when you're down, or take up your sword again to recommence our combat. But it is better that I grant you life and that we live in peace. Only you will acknowledge the incident as it actually happened; that's all I want.

Sévigné held her ground. She wants both an apology and a renewal of friendship, not an easy request. The tone here is combative, offensive and defensive. The conflict can be resolved only by the surrender of the one correspondent and the generosity of the other. The sword in question can be read as a synonym for pen; Sévigné learned the power of the written word and the parrying gesture of the letter as the two cousins resolved the quarrel through this stichomythic sequence of exchanges. The sorting out of facts, feelings, and relationships is a frequent occupation in the Sévigné letters; nowhere else, though, is this type of relational preoccupation as evident as in the exchange with Bussy and, even more intensely, with Françoise-Marguerite, the daughter. The fact that Sévigné firmly asserted her position of wronged innocence and insisted on Bussy's recognition of his error is what allowed that correspondence to regain a healthy footing and continue. Sévigné's insistence on the correctness of her version of the affair, the assuredness of her point of view, saved her from being totally bullied by her cousin. Her daughter was not to be so able to stand up for herself to her mother. Sévigné's confidence and her daughter's timidity were to shape a less balanced, a more profoundly troubled epistolary relationship.

Bussy did insist, in spite of the resolution of this quarrel, on asserting his authority over Sévigné. Shortly after one of their little feuds, Bussy reports with a veritable appreciation:

Vous me remettez en goût de vos lettres, Madame. Je n'ai pas encore bien démêlé si c'est parce que vous ne m'offensez plus, ou parce que il y a toujours un petit air naturel et brillant qui me réjouit. En attendant cette décision, je crois pouvoir vous dire qu'il y entre un peu de tout cela. (I, L. 268, p. 497)

You restore my taste for your letters, Madame. I have not quite figured out yet if this is because you no longer offend me, or because there is always a natural and brilliant little air to them that delights me. While contemplating this decision, I think I can tell you that a little of all this enters in.

His critical stance, with precise comments on specific reactions to the letter, is deliberately obfuscated and suspended. His claim that any judgment would be premature serves as a reminder that he continues to posit himself as arbiter and knows what to expect of a good letter. He reasserts his authority to criticize and, in suspending judgment, exercises it most effectively, baring its structural form of dominance.

From this early incident, Sévigné acquired a healthy skepticism concerning printed texts and vengeful cousins. She learned to use the pen as a weapon, and to understand the epistolary space not merely as a salon for flirtatious exchanges, or as a garden for more intimate conversation, but as an arena for contests of will. Bussy's disgrace with the king altered the relationship between the two cousins in significant ways. Although Bussy continued to insist on his right to evaluate Sévigné's letters, he became increasingly dependent on them for news and entertainment from his position of banishment and eventually sought to exploit them as a means of reingratiating himself with the king. While Sévigné continued to defer to Bussy, she retained the lesson learned and took her self-obsessed cousin less seriously.

Under her cousin's guidance and in the process of stabilizing their relationship by letter, Sévigné invented her own voice, discovered the efficacy of letters, and was encouraged to take her writing seriously. In the Bussy-Sévigné exchanges are to be found some of the most explicit reflections on the nature of the epistolary. Basic to a felicitous letter relationship, according to these partners, is a prior state of total presence. Words are already superfluous to communication when two compatible souls are together. Sévigné claims this perfect understanding—*homoousia*—between herself and Bussy:

Il faudrait que je fusse bien changée pour ne pas entendre vos turlupinades, et tous les bons endroits de vos lettres. Vous savez bien, Monsieur le Comte, qu'autrefois nous avions le don de nous entendre avant que d'avoir parlé. L'un de nous répondait fort bien à ce que l'autre avait envie de dire; et si nous n'eussions point voulu nous donner le plaisir de prononcer assez facilement des paroles, notre intelligence aurait quasi fait tous les frais de la conversation. Quand on s'est si bien entendu, on ne peut jamais devenir pesant. C'est une jolie chose à mon gré, que d'entendre vite; cela fait voir une vivacité qui plaît, et dont l'amour-propre sait un gré nonpareil. M. de La Rochefoucauld dit vrai dans ses *Maximes*: "Nous aimons mieux ceux qui nous entendent bien que ceux qui se font écouter." Nous devons nous aimer à la pareille pour nous être toujours si bien entendus. (I, L. 272, p. 508)

I would have to have changed not to understand your jokes, and all the good parts of your letters. You know well, Monsieur le Comte, that in the past we had the gift of understanding each other even before having spoken. One of us responded quite well to what the other felt like saying; and if we had not wanted to give ourselves the pleasure of pronouncing words easily enough, our intelligence alone would have sufficed to keep the conversation going. When people have understood each other so well, they can never become burdensome. It's a wonderful thing, in my opinion, to understand quickly; it shows a vivacity that pleases, and for which self-esteem is incomparably grateful. M. de la Rochefoucauld speaks the truth in his *Maxims*: "We prefer those who understand us well to those who make themselves heard." We must love each other similarly to have always understood each other so well.

The cousins' satisfying relationship is not so much a result of as a condition for the rewarding epistolary exchange. The epistolary style thus is merely a transposition of transparency from the context of presence into that of absence—the deferred, the invisible, the inaudible. Such a mimesis is an impossible contradiction in terms, as is its simulacrum—the "conversational letter." Behind the style lies the elaborate ideological construction of an idealized conception of interpersonal relations grounded in the assumption of the complete efficacy of presence and intuition.

Bussy responded to Sévigné's formulation, pronouncing more analytically and impersonally on the ingredients necessary for a felicitous letter:

Je sais qu'il faut avoir de l'esprit pour bien écrire, qu'il faut être en bonne humeur, et que les matières soient heureuses. Mais il faut surtout qu'on croie que les agréments qu'on aura ne seront point perdus, et sans cela on se néglige. En vérité, rien n'est plus beau ni plus joli que votre lettre, car il y a bien des choses du meilleur sens du monde, écrites le plus agréablement. (I, L. 275, p. 515)

I know one needs wit to write well, that one has to be in a good mood, and that the subjects must be good. But above all, one must believe that the pleasure one takes in writing will not go unappreciated, and without that one neglects oneself. In truth, nothing is more beautiful or more charming than your letter, for in it there are many comments of the greatest sense in the world, written the most agreeably.

Wit, mood, and good material are elemental, but, as does Sévigné, Bussy recognizes the necessity of a prior understanding between the correspondents indicated in the crucial role played by the addressee in inspiring the writer to work toward that moment of reception, of assured appreciation. As if to cement their writing relationship, he demonstrates his own prowess as addressee by marking his appreciation of her letter with praise.

Bussy's analytical tone and offer of praise in the above passage are emblematic of his consistently condescending attitude toward his writing cousin. His stance repeatedly conveys the impression that he is making room for his cousin in the realm of literary and social preeminence that he inhabits. He knows the rules since he is of those who make them, and he can offer praise because he is in a position to judge. Sévigné is frequently to be seen tactfully deferring to him.

Sévigné's style was submitted by letter to her cousin's taste. She often claims lack of control in her writing ("je n'ai qu'un trait de plume" [I have but one pen stroke]), and, through such gestures of self-caricaturing, performs acts of self-protective dissociation. These punctuate her letters regularly. This divorce of writer and pen renders implausible any accusation of calculation or intentionality:

Je suis tellement libertine quand j'écris, que le premier tour que je prends règne tout du long de ma lettre. Il serait à souhaiter que ma pauvre plume, galopant comme elle fait, galopât au moins sur le bon pied. (II, L. 676, p. 660)

I am such a libertine when I write that the first turn of phrase I make reigns throughout my letter. It would be desirable that my poor pen, galloping as it does, gallop at least on the right foot.

By asserting the willfulness of her at once unruly and pathetic pen (i.e., her style), she frees herself of accountability for what she produces in writing and attests thereby to the inevitable, since uncontrollable, sincerity of her writing. Such insistence on lack of control implies just the contrary, so that spontaneity and sincerity become suspect claims in her letters. Indeed, it would be suspicious that she should label herself "libertine" here were it not that she is addressing Bussy, playing *to* him by playing *on* his reputation as a prominent *libertin*, identifying with her correspondent, and thus shaping herself ingratiatingly in his image, dealing in the coin of the realm, using the local currency.[2]

By-products—and, perhaps, a price as well—of her insistence on sincerity are her stance of helplessness vis-à-vis her pen and her generally apologetic attitude. While such self-effacement can be read as merely the dose of requisite modesty, inviting reassuring compliments, it also places her at the mercy of her correspondent: "Je ne sais comment vous pouvez aimer mes lettres; elles sont d'une négligence que je sens, sans y pouvoir remédier" (II, L. 638, p. 602) [I don't know how you can like my letters; they have a carelessness I can sense, without being able to remedy]. Bussy does not hesitate to occupy the position of knower, of broker of value, especially when it is so explicitly offered to him by Sévigné, and to assert his taste and his will in matters epistolary. The *négligence* Sévigné has bemoaned as her incorrigible fault Bussy allows, sometimes, and specifically to women:

Je veux toujours de la justesse dans les pensées, mais quelquefois de la négligence dans les expressions, et surtout dans les lettres qu'écrivent les dames. (II, L. 646, p. 612)

I always want accuracy in thought, but sometimes carelessness in expressions, and especially in the letters that ladies write.

His prescriptive pronouncement points to the formulation of a double standard distinguishing between two writing communities, implicitly positing a dominant male rule, and encouraging an unthreatening imperfection in the other, a stance that will be abetted by compliant women writers. Rather than set a single rule of measure, allowance is made for difference on the basis of gender—valorizing for women writing a rhetoric of *négligence* to which they are expected to adhere. The extent to which they deviate from that and write more carefully will determine the degree of presumption they are assigned, the extent to which they will be judged pretentious and pedantic.[3] As Sévigné writes herself self-disparagingly into prominence, Bussy seizes on her self-criticism, encourages it, and uses it to map out a second class of writers.

There can thus be seen a certain complicity between the two cousins in the formulation of a double standard through complementary acts of description (on her part) and prescription (on his) which allows women writers to flourish without threatening their male counterparts. Women cannot and must not take themselves seriously. They must cultivate *négligence* not only as a sign of class, but as reassurance to their correspondents that they do not aspire to unseat them. Tenets about how one ought to behave, acknowledgments of how one does behave are always bound up with issues of stratification. In this instance, concerns of both social and gender organization are displaced onto considerations of style.

Certainly the esthetic of *négligence* is neither Sévigné's nor Bussy's invention. It is a complete social attitude reflected in an elitist literary tradition that has been traced from the Latin Classics, through Castiglione, Rabelais, Montaigne, by John C. Lapp, among others, in his study of Sévigné's contemporary, La Fontaine. Lapp documents and emphasizes the relationship between *négligence* and conversation, the model of deliberately purposeless discourse the letter aspires to replicate.[4] *Négligence* represents the estheticization of a prerogative of class: the valorization of the idle life as the idyllic life. The leisured class sets the style in participatory solidarity.

In the letter, this haphazard but always felicitous and never pedantic approach to communication is mainly exemplified by chancy, arbitrary, and inventive transitions from one subject to another. It is, more often than not, such free associative organization that, when particularly pronounced in the epistolary text, causes Sévigné to note, at once proudly and apologetically, her *négligence*.[5]

The seventeenth-century cult of *négligence* is also a reaction to the rigidly codified court life that enslaves the elite in relations dictated by, and mobilized through, elaborate etiquette designed to protect the authority of the king. Fritz Nies interprets the appeal of the esthetic of *négligence* to the aristocracy sociohistorically. He emphasizes the distinction between the hereditary *noblesse d'épée* [nobility of the sword], domesticated by the king, and displaced in favor by the purchased *noblesse de robe* [nobility of the robe] following the Fronde. He concludes that the *noblesse d'épée* espoused an esthetic of *négligence* in the wake of their loss of political power and their relegation to the margins of decision making; they were driven to cultivate an exclusive and impenetrable social milieu of seeming freedom and independence. Therein, this group wielded arbitrary social power in spite of, and in compensation for, its fall from grace with the king. Entree to its circle was decided not only by the criterion of birth, but, beyond that, by a more elusive standard: that of the *je ne sais quoi*, which only the standing membership could recognize.[6]

Within this ideological domain, refracted in the world of writing, women might be seen to occupy a position comparable to that of the *noblesse d'épée*, marginal and powerless, if distinguished, with the further similarity that they did not arrogate to themselves their place but were assigned it and embraced it faute de mieux, and challenged it at the risk of ridicule and ostracism. The strictures of *négligence* would be particularly intensified for women writing who were also members of this elite. They were doubly bound to accept the definition imposed on them, to meet the expectations set for them, and to hypersignify, as customary, for their male counterparts. Hence, perhaps, another motivation for Bussy's recommendations of *négligence* to his cousin.

Bussy pursued the formation of two different writing communities in a later letter praising Sévigné's style:

Votre manière d'écrire, libre et aisée, me plaît bien davantage que la régularité de Messieurs de l'Académie; c'est le style d'une femme de qualité, qui a bien de l'esprit, qui soutient les matières enjouées et qui égaye les sérieuses. (II, L. 677, p. 662)

Your way of writing, free and easy, pleases me much more than the regularity of the Masters of the Academy; it's the style of a woman of quality, who has plenty of wit, who dignifies lively subjects and brightens up the serious ones.

In opposing the "Messieurs de l'Académie" and "une femme de qualité," he claims his personal preference for the style of the particular amateurish latter while reinforcing the normative and therefore dominant position of the collective professional former. Is it because women have been excluded de facto from the rigorous exigencies of "academic regularity" that they have been free to develop a more relaxed and spontaneous style? And is it because of this exclusion that even favorable assessments of their writing convey a tone of "generous" tolerance? Or is this simply what is allowed them, an imposed standard of *négligence* that they must meet at the risk of writing out of gender? Here can be glimpsed the shaping of a feminine writing style by a masculine writing authority. The tendency to essentialize women and their writing taking place during the same general period (in the writings of Poullain de la Barre and La Bruyère, among others mentioned in chapter 1) is seen here in the very process of transmitting and validating itself. Further, is it perhaps because Bussy himself had not been consecrated as writer, was not himself a member of the "Académie" despite, if not because of, his own publications, that he professes here to embrace another standard, valorizing the "femme de qualité" through feelings invested in his own marginality? Be that as it may, Bussy did compliment and encourage his cousin's writing, and his suggestive reflections surely contributed to a crystallization of her style. The two cousins were definitely engaged in a writing pact, if not necessarily one of equals.

When *La Princesse de Clèves* first appeared, Sévigné wrote to Bussy, lavishing praise on it, but made the tactical mistake of asking his opinion of the novel:

C'est un petit livre que Barbin nous a donné depuis deux jours, qui me paraît une des plus charmantes choses que j'aie jamais lues . . . Je vous en demanderai votre avis, quand vous l'aurez lu. (II, L. 638, p. 602)

It is a little book Barbin has just brought out to us in the past two days, which strikes me as one of the most charming pieces I have ever read . . . I want your opinion when you have read it.

Bussy delivered his thorough critique four months later and was anxious to know Sévigné's reaction. He took his cousin's writing seriously enough to propose a collaborative effort on their part to improve on the novel:

J'attends votre sentiment sur le jugement que j'ai fait de La *Princesse de Clèves*; si nous nous melions, vous et moi, de corriger une petite histoire, je suis assuré que nous ferions penser et dire aux principaux personnages des choses plus naturelles que ne pensent et disent ceux de *La Princesse de Clèves*. (II, L. 649, p. 618)

I'm awaiting your opinion on the judgment I have pronounced on *La Princesse de Clèves*; if we were to engage, you and I, in correcting a little story, I am assured we would make the principal characters think and say more natural things than do those of *La Princesse de Clèves*.

In showing concern for Sévigné's reception of his analysis, and indicating an interest in writing with her—co-authoring—Bussy paid her the ultimate compliment, on this occasion, of treating her as a peer. He is evidently concerned with the textual construction of plausibility in the novel in his comments above. Unconvinced by the plot, he appeals to Sévigné's vanity—her writing talent—as well as to her general sensibility, which he assumes to be more in tune with his own. *La Princesse de Clèves* has enjoyed an enduring reputation as an exceptional instance of the articulation of an enigmatic feminine ethos. It seems likely that Bussy's proposed revision would have been an attempt to masculinize that text, to write out that unfamiliar perspective. By engaging Sévigné, even hypothetically, in the project, he attempts to bind her to his "more natural" point of view or assumes that she already shares it.

To his critique, Sévigné responded with an apparently complete capitulation:

Votre critique de *La Princesse de Clèves* est admirable, mon cousin. Je m'y reconnais, et j'y aurais même ajouté deux ou trois petites bagatelles qui vous ont échappé . . . J'ai été fort aise de savoir votre avis, et encore plus de ce qu'il se rencontre justement comme le mien; l'amour-propre est content de ces heureuses rencontres. (II, L. 650, p. 618–19)

Your critique of *La Princesse de Clèves* is admirable, cousin. I can see myself in it, and I would even have added two or three little details that escaped you . . . I was quite pleased to learn your opinion, and even more so since it is just like my own; self-esteem is gratified by these felicitous instances.

On the surface, a consensus of opinion between the two cousins has been reached; it is reaffirmed in Sévigné's next letter:

Je suis encore d'accord de ce que vous dites de *La Princesse de Clèves*; votre critique et la mienne étaient jetées dans le même moule. (II, L. 651, p. 619)

I still agree with what you say about *La Princesse de Clèves*; your critique and my own were cast in the same mold.

But these words are unconvincing given the lack of further critical references to *La Princesse de Clèves* in her letters. Sévigné never specifies the "deux ou trois bagatelles" of her own view that she had hinted at. She has subordinated whatever particular differences she had to his judgment. The "mold" of family casts for her the "mold" of critique. Bussy, for his part, classed their now joint opinion as: "de gens de qualité qui ont de l'esprit" (II, L. 652, p. 621) [of witty people of quality], echoing his pronouncement cited earlier on Sévigné's writing—"le style d'une femme de qualité qui a bien de l'esprit" (II, L. 677, p. 662) [the style of a woman of quality who has plenty of wit]—insisting here on their shared social status, their classy writing.

In what might be understood as a gesture of noblesse oblige, Bussy actually deferred to the printed word and favored over theirs the official critique that was circulating, attributed to "messieurs" Bouhours and Valincour, more attuned perhaps to the exigencies of the "Académie:" "Celle qui est imprimée est plus exacte et plaisante en beaucoup d'endroits" (II, L. 652, p. 621) [The one that is in print is more exact and more pleasing in many regards]. By withholding their own comments from print, Bussy and Sévigné together maintained their social status, conforming to what Alain Viala terms "the image of the amateur writer."[7]

But there is a difference: if Bussy did not rush to see his critique into print, it did circulate. By virtue of his gender, he was authorized participation in literary debate. Again, I cite Viala:

Les gentilshommes peuvent se mêler au débat littéraire sans déroger à l'idéal d'honnêteté: ainsi Bussy intervenant comme critique au même titre que Bouhours et Rapin.[8]

Gentlemen can get involved in literary debate without transgressing against the ideal of propriety: thus Bussy intervening as critic in the same way as do Bouhours and Rapin.

And in effect, his comments on *La Princesse de Clèves* are among those most regularly cited to this day. Thus his position represents a tension between the social and the material economy, the position of the overly gifted amateur who cannot be neatly accommodated in the organizational framework of the literary world as it takes critical shape. For her part, by completely suppressing her "bagatelles," Sévigné not only preserved family solidarity and remained loyal to her friend Lafayette; she also respected the preserve of criticism staked out for "gentlemen." Nothing more was said by Sévigné and Bussy directly regarding *La Princesse de Clèves*; epistolary focus was diverted instead to the criticism the novel had generated. Ultimately then, despite the evidence of her own words, it is impossible to know to what extent Sévigné was merely flattering her cousin in subscribing enthusiastically to his opinion of the novel, to what extent she genuinely shared it, and specifically, just what those "bagatelles" of hers were.

When the first edition of Sévigné's correspondence was published in 1725, Sévigné entered officially, if posthumously, into the marketplace. The capital that had accrued to her socially made possible for her letters their transfer into the world of the material economy. Her success can be construed to have cost her only her own opinion. Sévigné invested in the social economy, she cultivated her friends and family through writing, shaping her thoughts and her writing accordingly, and was consequently readily integrated into the institution of literature. Her friend Mme de Lafayette, who gave manuscripts to Barbin, who played the material market, was not. Viala offers a "top-ten" list of the early eighteenth-century classics (defining classics literally as those works which are taught in class) in which Sévigné figures as the eleventh: "Même Mme de Sévigné prend place parmi les classiques dès 1740"[9] [Even Mme de Sévigné takes her place among the classics from 1740 on]. That Mme de Lafayette does not figure in that list at all strongly suggests that, if the salon was a fluid milieu, the institution of literature taking shape at that time was not. Popularity and canonization were not to be confused, and women's writing had a greater chance of being officially appropriated as exemplum if it knew and kept its prescribed place—that world of privacy which was being invented for the very purpose of containing women and their writing, away from the material market.[10]

Within that social frame, Sévigné and Bussy corresponded in circles where writing was taken seriously, and Sévigné negotiated her way modestly and cautiously toward prominence. She was surrounded by people, even within her own letters, who considered the epistolary art a grave enterprise. An occasional third party to her exchanges with Bussy contributed to set a tone of self-importance to their correspondence. Corbinelli, in an addition to a letter from Sévigné to Bussy, discusses with regret the merits of a letter of his sent and lost:

Ma lettre perdue était fort ample, et du style sublime, les sujets traités plus que superficiellement, et moins qu'à fond, tels qu'on les soutient dans les lettres qu'on veut garder. (III, L. 853, p. 92)

My lost letter was quite ample, and in a sublime style, the subjects treated more than superficially, and less than thoroughly, just as one does in the letters one wants to keep.

The concern expressed here is not so much for messages lost as for style gone unappreciated. This is the lament of an author without an audience for want of a text that has disappeared. The passage represents the author's attempt to recapture his readership, and to recuperate the value of the text by offering, in its place, an evaluation of it. The reader's right to judge has been expropriated; she or he is called upon to corroborate, as reader-witness of its praise (emanating somewhat suspiciously from the same pen that produced the original text), its excellence. Personal opinion is rendered superfluous. Bussy and Corbinelli did indeed enjoy such a relationship in their epistolary pact that such hubris, perhaps mildly tempered with some self-mockery, encountered in the context of their exchange, does not shock. Surrounded by pen wielders of such self-consciousness and self-importance as these two, it was inevitable that Sévigné would assume some of that seriousness, that she also should consider herself, at least occasionally, a writer, and consequently that she should speculate on the eventual fate of her writings.

But on the whole, the well-indoctrinated Sévigné insisted on her flair for a lighter vein of writing and cultivated just that her entire life. While she exhibited knowledge of the epistolary conventions, more often than not she flouted the constricting rules and professed little real concern to conform to them:

Nous disions que la dernière lettre que je vous écrivis était toute terre à terre. Celle-ci commence de la même façon . . . mais elle finit d'une manière si relevée, en vous souhaitant les biens éternels, que j'ai peur qu'on ne puisse m'accuser d'avoir donné dans le sublime. (III, L. 1260, p. 983)

We were saying that the last letter I wrote you was completely pedestrian. This one starts in the same way . . . but it concludes in such an inspired manner, by wishing you eternal well-being that I fear one might accuse me of entering into the sublime.

Making light of the codified levels of style is a way of letting Bussy know that she is aware of the rules, that sometimes her writing happens to fit one or another of the categories, and not necessarily that prescribed (*le moyen*) for letter writing, and that it does not matter. She is writing outside the "Académie," but within the law, in her prescribed place, safe from accusations of ambition or pedantry.

The etiquette that most rigorously governed the Bussy-Sévigné correspondence was that of the conversational model, particularly to the extent that it insisted on turn taking and thus ensured a predictable and prompt regularity for the rhythm of the exchange. The interval between letters could not be long without causing the train of thought to be lost. More often than not, though, it was Bussy who would accuse his cousin of dallying and jeopardizing the exchange:

Je vous conseille en ami, ma chère cousine, de vous corriger à l'avenir et de ne plus remettre à Livry les réponses que vous avez à me faire, car, outre qu'en répondant si tard, vous ne sauriez plus imiter les conversations, qui est la chose la plus agréable dans un commerce de lettres, c'est que vous me faites voir que vous ne m'entretenez que quand vous n'avez plus personne à qui parler, et cela n'est pas si tendre que vous dites. (II, L. 671, p. 650)

I advise you as a friend, my dear cousin, to correct yourself in the future and no longer to put off until Livry the responses you owe me, for, besides the fact that, in answering so late, you would no longer be imitating conversation, which is the most agreeable thing in an exchange of letters, you make me see that you only correspond with me when you no longer have anyone to speak to, and that is not as tender as you claim it to be.

Sévigné frequently found herself in a position of having to apologize to her cousin for not complying more readily with his need for letters:

Je reçus votre lettre du 10e décembre au mois de février. Elle était si vieille que je ne crus pas y devoir faire réponse; je vous en demande pardon, et je ne vous en aime pas moins. Voici donc une lettre toute propre à nous remettre sur les voies, et à reprendre le fil interrompu de notre commerce. (III, L. 1250, p. 970)

I received your letter of 10 December in February. It was so old that I didn't think I had to answer it; I beg your pardon for this, and I don't love you less for it. Here, then, is an appropriate letter to put us back on track, and to pick up the interrupted thread of our exchange.

Sévigné, rather than scrupulously respect and adhere to the conversation paradigm, as did her more rigid and exacting, her more needy cousin, would passively resist the demands of the relationship and at once acknowledge and flout the convention: "Je ne m'amuserai point, mon cousin, à répondre à vos réponses; quoique ce soit la suite d'une conversation" (III, L. 967, p. 299) [I will not amuse myself at all, cousin, by responding to your responses; even if this is the proper sequence for a conversation]. Sévigné took control of what could have been an imprisoning pact by letting Bussy know that she was well aware of the rules but would not be enslaved to them. She exercised thereby an informal power within a situation that was repeatedly presented to her as codified and inflexible, deciding the degree and extent of her participation. Her cousin had come to depend increasingly on her faithfulness to the exchange for his own entertainment and promoted his pupil to peerage by flattery in efforts to keep the correspondence going:

L'absence de ses bons amis est un grand mal, Madame, surtout quand elle dure longtemps, mais quand avec cela le commerce est difficile, c'est ce qui fait enrager. Je vous écris le 20e mai, vous me faites réponse le 12e juillet, et je la reçois le 8e août; voilà qui est bien languissant pour des gens aussi vifs que nous sommes. (III, L. 1254, p. 975)

The absence of one's good friends is a great affliction, Madame, especially when it lasts a long time, but when the exchange of letters is difficult as well, this makes one fume. I write you on 20 May, you answer me on 12 July, and I receive the letter on 8 August; this is pretty slow for people as lively as we are.

Sévigné developed a self-conscious attitude toward her writing under the tutelage of her cousin. Although she was to surpass him in the epistolary art by refusing to bow to the exacting rules that had been made by a writing community from which she was tacitly excluded, and by excelling in the practice of *négligence,* which she was explicitly assigned, she never directly challenged Bussy. Rather, she loyally humored him.

A good deal of Bussy's epistolary activity was devoted to attempts to reingratiate himself with the king. He seized on every opportunity to undo the past and to write himself back into favor. When Louis XIV honored his son, he sought to exploit the occasion by asserting himself in the role of the father, on whom the honor "naturally" redounded, and thus fabricated a pretext for writing to the king. He sent a copy of his letter to Sévigné:

Il faut que je vous entretienne de mes prospérités, Madame; ce discours ne sera pas long. Le Roi vient de donner une compagnie de cavalerie toute faite à mon fils, dans le régiment de Sibourg . . . tout cela étant, je prétends avoir été agréablement distingué en cette rencontre, et je viens d'en faire un remerciement au Roi dont je vous envoie la copie. (II, L. 629, p. 589)

I must speak to you of my good fortune, Madame; this speech will not be long. The King has just given a complete cavalry company to my son, in the Sibourg regiment . . . this being the case, I claim to have been agreeably honored in this instance, and I have just written my thanks to the King, of which I send you the copy.

The relational structuring in the letter to Sévigné, although addressed to "Madame," divides preeminence equally between "je" and "le Roi." As the son is assigned a filial extension role, the "vous" is strictly relegated to the witness function. Sévigné is invited to share Bussy's pleasure at his vicarious stroke of fortune, to read and admire his response, but certainly not to evaluate his writing in any way. Bussy, in his exile, yearned desperately for a return to favor and persistently turned to the letter as the only vehicle available to capture royal attention and elicit forgiveness. Sustained correspondence with such a dedicated and ambitious writer as he certainly must have contributed to develop in Sévigné a sense of the political use to which letters might be put as well as a writerly attitude toward communication by mail.

Sévigné had already learned one lesson about the dangers of corresponding at the moment of Fouquet's arrest.[11] Letters from her were found in his safe. Although they were said to be innocent, the mere fact of their existence and preservation exposed the Sévigné-Fouquet relationship to interpretation and gossip and threatened to compromise Sévigné's reputation as an *honnête femme*. She mustered her friendships and alliances to support her through this period and was acutely aware henceforth that her letters were no longer under her control once they left her hands, but that she was permanently accountable for them. Experience with her cousin caused this lesson to be repeated.

Not only did Bussy educate Sévigné in the betrayals possible through the printed word, not only did he give her constant encouragement to write, but he also, in a spectacularly self-serving and insensitive way, committed the ultimate violation of the epistolary pact: in 1680 he announced to Sévigné that he was forwarding to the king copies of letters they had exchanged between 1673 and 1675. Once again, the hope of improving his standing with Louis XIV motivated Bussy's behavior:

Madame, vous ne savez pas que je vais associer le Roi à ce commerce (le Roi ne vous déplaise). Vous avez su que je lui avais envoyé un manuscrit au mois de juin dernier. Il y a pris tel goût qu'il l'a gardé et m'en a fait demander un autre. Celui donc que je vais lui envoyer à ce jour de l'an prochain est depuis 1673 jusqu'à la fin de 1675, qui sont les trois ans de votre vie où vous m'avez le plus et le mieux écrit. Comme il a bien de l'esprit, il sera charmé de vos lettres. Il en verra aussi quelques unes de Mme de Grignan qui ne lui déplairont pas. Je vous montrerai cela à ce printemps que j'irai à Paris, et je vous étonnerai que je vous ferai voir que, tout exilé que je suis, je parle aussi franchement et aussi hardiment au Roi que si j'étais son favori. (III, L. 823, p. 58)

Madame, you do not know that I am going to make the King a party to this correspondence (the King, no less). You knew that I had sent him a manuscript last June. He liked it so much that he kept it and requested another. This one, then, that I'm going to send him a year from today goes from 1673 to the end of 1675, which are the three years of your life when you wrote me the most and the best. Since he has much wit, he will be charmed by your letters. He will also see some of Madame de Grignan's, which will not displease him. I will show you all this in the spring when I go to Paris, and I will surprise you in showing you that, although I am exiled, I speak as frankly and as boldly to the King as if I were his favorite.

The assurance to Sévigné that the letters selected are excellent, that they will be well received, and that he has even been so thoughtful as to include texts by Mme de Grignan in this good deed—these points are obviously offered as recompense and justification for his presumptuous act.

Such a gesture might be understood and minimized as a mere extension of the prevalent practice of sharing letters in salon circles, but in fact it deviates from that pattern significantly. As a rule, there was some degree of awareness on the part of the letter writer that the addressee normally kept company with a particular, predictable, and somewhat restricted group of people, and that, if a letter was shared, it would be with members of that group. This knowledge was reflected in the messages sent. The king had not figured in Sévigné's implicitly intended extended readership as she wrote to her cousin.

Sévigné's inscribed reaction to Bussy's announcement is either surprisingly naïve or exceedingly sophisticated; evidence from her past suggests the latter. She is familiar with Bussy's arrogance and has shown great aptitude for countering it successfully in earlier epistolary exchanges with him; the following represents a culmination of that wisdom:

Mais, mon cousin, vous me mandez une chose étrange; je n'eusse jamais deviné le tiers qui est entre nous. Pensez-vous que l'on puisse estimer les lettres que vous avez mises dans ce que vous avez envoyé. Toute mon espérance, c'est que vous les avez raccommodées. Croyez-vous aussi que mon style qui est toujours plein d'amitié ne se puisse mal interpréter? Je n'ai jamais vu de lettres entre les mains d'un tiers qu'on ne put tourner sur un méchant ton, et ce serait faire une grande injustice à la naiveté et à l'innocence de notre ancienne amitié. Je suis assurée (quoi que je die) que vous n'avez rien fait que de bien, et c'en est un fort grand de pouvoir divertir un tel homme, et d'être en commerce avec lui. Pour moi, je crois qu'une dame de mes anciennes amies, qui passe réglément deux heures dans son cabinet, pourrait bien lire avec lui vos mémoires, et vous seriez en assez bonne main. Que sait-on ce que la Providence nous garde? (III, L. 826, pp. 60–61)

But, cousin, you send me strange news; I would never have guessed the third party who is between us. Do you think one can appreciate the letters you included with what you sent? My sole hope is that you corrected them. Also, don't you believe that my style, always full of friendship, could be misinterpreted? I have never seen letters in the hands of a third party that couldn't be transformed maliciously, and this would be a great injustice to the naïveté and innocence of our long-standing friendship. I am assured (no matter what I say) that you have done nothing but good, and it is a great virtue to be able to amuse such a man, and to be in correspondence with him. As for me, I believe that a lady [Mme de Maintenon], one of my old friends, who regularly spends two hours in his study, might read your memoirs with him, and you would be in good enough hands. What can one know of what Providence holds for us?

The first movement in the passage is one of shock, followed by gestures of dissociation and embarrassment: Sévigné posits herself as inferior to Bussy and deferent to his wisdom. In expressing hope that he has corrected her letters before sending them on, she places Bussy in not only a position of superiority but one of responsibility as well. She wishes to be held in no way liable for the consequences of such an arrogant act. Should the project misfire, she reminds him that her unwitting participation had been inspired by friendship, always open to misinterpretation in the hands of a third party. Having exculpated herself, having affirmed Bussy's responsibility, having renewed her oath of friendship, having reminded him of the risks at hand, she then congratulates him with praise and admiration and joins with him, as it were, in their shared venture. What more ingenious tactic could Sévigné have devised in order to cover all of the exigencies of such a delicate situation? In any case, here she has, not without misgivings (though she has little choice), thrown in her lot with a writer, taking her chances with the king for a reader.

Her inscribed reaction is not one of consternation or anger at the violation of the epistolary pact (or at least at the taking of the letters' potential for social circulation to the extreme), as might be expected, but more authorial and complicitous in its concern as to whether the letters will be well received. She wonders whether her friend Mme de Maintenon's presence as the king reads them will help assure a favorable reception. It is significant that Sévigné here claims to have an ally close to the king who might be useful to Bussy, and that she expresses concern not so much for reception of her own letters as for Bussy's: she knows he has far greater need of favor in this instance than she. She knows she counts less than he in the monarchic mind; she knows that she has less at risk as well. Both she and her friend Mme de Maintenon are encoded as facilitators and wield their "feminine" power more discreetly and indirectly in the form of influence. Sévigné must have realized at some level that her own talent and solid reputation were being exploited by her cousin, just as he had earlier taken advantage of his son's good fortune to try to insinuate himself into Louis' good graces. Nevertheless, her final flourish ("Que sait-on") confirms the unison of their fate and consequent acceptance of their de facto complicity.

Another fifteen years of correspondence follow this event. Surely Sévigné wrote letters in order to communicate with her correspondents, but increasingly, with the years and with a steadily accumulating stream of recognition and praise, she wrote letters because she wrote, because she wrote well, because she enjoyed writing. After this incident of unwitting publication, Sévigné must always have written with an eye to the possibility of her writing being transformed into text.[12] This is borne out in exchanges with her daughter on the same subject.

In spite of Bussy's assiduous efforts, he was unsuccessful in changing the tide of his fortune with the king:

Le Roi a bon esprit et juge bien de toutes choses, cependant les *bonnes* lettres que je lui écris ne m'attirent rien de bon de sa part. (III, L. 955, p. 281)

The King has a good mind and judges everything well; nevertheless the *good* letters I write him gain me nothing good from him.

In the face of this wounded pride, Sévigné affects a constant modesty. As if to atone to her socially marginalized cousin for the fact that she was able to be present at Bossuet's and Bourdaloue's funeral orations for M. Le Prince in 1687, she concludes her reports of these elocutionary events with self-deprecating remarks: "Voilà, mon cher cousin, fort grossièrement, le sujet de la pièce" (III, L. 957, p. 284) [Here, my dear cousin, quite roughly, is the subject of the play], and then:

De vous dire de quels traits tout cela était orné, il est impossible, et je gâte même cette pièce par la grossièreté dont je la croque. C'est comme si un barbouilleur voulait toucher à un tableau de Raphaël. (III, L. 962, p. 293)

To tell you how all of this was ornamented is impossible, and I am ruining even this version by the clumsiness with which I render it. It is as if a dauber presumed to touch up one of Raphael's paintings.

The self-effacing attitude is not so coy as it is self-protective; she is not so much using false modesty to invite compliments as she is consoling Bussy for his exclusion from society by deferring to his superiority as writer and critic. The self-denigration here also takes the form of clumsy paraphrasing: she is not the great Titian of Bussy's compliment, discussed in the following section, but a mere dauber. She catered to his vanity in order to insure herself against the already proven viciousness of his pen. Self-conscious concern for representation, translated through a code borrowed from the lexicon of painting, is at once veiled and revealed by the two writing cousins. While the project of transmitting messages is ostensibly the purpose of the correspondence, concern for the mode of communication, style, the art of writing, permeates the exchange.

Bussy fell back, in his exiled solitude, on a form of occupation perfectly suited to comfort his offended ego. He took it upon himself to reconstruct his family genealogy. Since he occupied the prominent position extant in that construction of patriarchal lineage, he took pleasure in the pastime of ordering his relatives in subordinate relation to himself, and in featuring himself as the legitimate head of the hierarchized family. In 1685, Bussy completed the document and sent a copy to his cousin. Appropriately, her response was one of thanks, praise, and critical appreciation. She states that she feels he rather overdoes it in his praises of her, perhaps (she speculates) to compensate for some of his past unkind remarks. She feels he does justice to her daughter, but not at all to her son: Charles is not represented in sufficient glory in the text. She sees as an explanation for such uneven treatment the degree of obsequiousness her children themselves have manifested toward Bussy, along with their own apparent worldly status. Her son, having been less deferent than his sister toward his distinguished cousin, has been dismissed peremptorily in Bussy's text, demoted to a rank lower than the one he actually held. Sévigné points out these problems candidly to Bussy as she evaluates the genealogy, but her final remarks are unmistakably laudatory:

C'est une histoire en abrégé qui pourrait plaire même à ceux qui n'y ont point d'intérêt . . . Enfin je ne puis assez vous remercier de cette peine que vous avez prise . . . Je garderai soigneusement ce livre. (III, L. 917, p. 216)

It's an abridged history which could please even those who have no interest in it at all . . . Really, I cannot thank you enough for the trouble you have taken . . . I will treasure this book.

On the very same day, 22 July 1685, she comments on this same genealogy in a letter to her daughter. While her specific comments in the two letters echo one another, the concluding tone and the final judgment are markedly different:

Si Bussy avait un peu moins parlé de lui et de son heroïne de fille, le reste étant vrai, on peut le trouver assez bon pour être jeté dans le fond d'un cabinet, sans en être plus glorieuse. (III, L. 918, p. 219)

If Bussy had spoken a little less of himself and his heroine daughter, the rest being true, one might find it good enough to toss in the back of a closet, without taking any greater pride in it.

This dismissal, in the suggestion of a fitting disposal for this text, contrasts vividly with her words to Bussy professing her intention to keep and to cherish the manuscript.[13] The discrepancy between the two statements allows a rare view into the actual nature of Sévigné's feelings for Bussy and points up the tenuousness of the cousins' relationship. The complexities of self-representation and the crucial function of the addressee (narratee) in determining the posture and message of the sender are epitomized in these two contradictory statements. This comparison serves as a reminder that the letter writer is negotiating a complicated network of relationships in the writing process, that it is not so much the truth value of any one of the individual statements that can be confirmed as telling as the weaving of positional identity through the cultivation of these different ties.

Underlying the master-apprentice relationship, the courteous bantering and teasing, the mutual and self-congratulatory posturing that characterizes this epistolary exchange in the years following the reconciliation after the falling out over the slanderous *Histoire*, there is an unmistakable current of dislike in Sévigné's tone. She appears to have chafed under the yoke of the relationship. While she dutifully kept her part of the epistolary pact with Bussy, she was not as fond of him as she professed to be when writing to him. While she catered to it out of necessity, she was fully cognizant of his inflated notion of himself. She respected the hierarchy of family but did not subscribe blindly to her cousin's self-image, so dependent on patriarchal structures and institutions for his own sense of worth in the world.

Sévigné enjoyed the same familial privilege over her daughter as Bussy had exercised over her, and, in turn, she obligated Mme de Grignan in much the same way to keep up her end of their correspondence. The actual modeling of the mother-daughter exchange on the cousins' is suggested by the intertextuality of some of their letters. For example, when Bussy sought to mitigate the admission that he had edited Sévigné's letters to him in preparation for their presentation to the king, he couched the fact in a flattering compliment:

Je n'ai pas touché à vos lettres, Madame: Le Brun ne toucherait pas à un original du Titien, où ce grand homme aurait eu quelque négligence . . . J'ai supprimé seulement de certaines choses qui, quoique belles, ne seraient peut-être pas du goût du maître. (III, L. 827, p. 61).

I haven't touched your letters, Madame: Le Brun would not touch an original of Titian's in which this great man might have shown some carelessness . . . I left out only certain things which, although beautiful, would perhaps not be to the master's liking.

Sévigné's appropriately humble concern had been whether he had managed to correct all of her carelessness. She consistently assumed the role of the unruly, incorrigible student in relation to him. However, when corresponding with her daughter, she occupied his place of authority, set herself up as the arbiter of style, and pronounced on her daughter's writing. It is telling in this regard to note that she passes on to her daughter the very compliment Bussy had recently paid her:

Corbinelli a été charmé de la peinture au naturel de votre savantas. Vous parlez de peinture; celle que vous faites de cet homme pris et possédé de son savoir, qui ne se donne pas le temps de respirer ni aux autres, qui veut rentrer à toute force dans la conversation, et qui est toujours au guet pour prendre l'occasion de se remettre en danse, ma chère enfant, cela est du Titien. (III, L. 1061, p. 484)

Corbinelli was charmed by the natural depiction of your intellectual. You speak of painting; the one you do of this man taken and possessed by his knowledge, who does not give himself nor others the time to breathe, who wants at any cost to enter into the conversation, and who is always eager for the occasion to get back into the dance, my dear child, that is like Titian.

The choice of the term "peinture" introduces the echo of Bussy's compliment, "Titien," and prepares the way for its transfer. Sévigné had obviously been flattered by the comparison, since she exploits it herself in turn. Unfortunately, Mme de Grignan's original "painting" is no longer in existence, since her letter did not survive, and so it cannot be subjected to scrutiny. If it were, a comparison of her textual painting and its rewriting by her mother in the guise of appreciation would reveal the extent to which Sévigné assumed the LeBrun-Bussy corrective touch-up role, in turn, in relation to her daughter's writing. There is a certain ambivalence in the pertinence of the Titian compliment: does it in fact attach to the daughter's portrait of the "savantas," or is Sévigné commenting specularly, with no little satisfaction, on the version she has just produced?

The transmission of the compliment suggests a transference of the writing relationship as well. While it cannot be said that Bussy served as Sévigné's model, it can be said that their epistolary relationship suggested to Sévigné a similar pact with her daughter. Bussy's constantly critical gaze encouraged Sévigné to take her writing seriously, as "art," with actual concern for the act of representation. He guided her by defining principles of women's writing as well as by approbation of her accommodating formulation for her own epistolary rhetoric. While Sévigné was somewhat skeptical of her cousin because of his pride and his inflated opinion of himself, she did value his word on matters of writing. It is in her exchanges with him, since she is constantly reminded that he sits in judgment of her letters, that she develops a conscious and critical position toward her own writing and that of others.

Bussy would be called upon in his capacity as family elder to mediate between the mother and daughter, to pronounce on the familial dilemma in which Mme de Grignan was to find herself—divided between mother and husband, retained by the one in Paris, anxious to join the other in Provence. In a letter from Sévigné to Bussy, Mme de Grignan took advantage of the situation to communicate her feelings as much to the co-writer, her mother, as to the addressee, Bussy:

Si je vous écrivais ailleurs que dans une lettre de ma mère, je vous dirais que c'est même beaucoup retarder mes devoirs qui m'appellent en Provence, mais elle trouverait mauvais de n'être pas comptée au nombre de ceux qui doivent régler ma conduite. Elle en est présentement la maîtresse; et j'ai le chagrin de n'éprouver son autorité qu'en des choses où ma complaisance et mon obéissance seront soupçonnées d'être d'intelligence avec elle. Je ne sais pas pourquoi je m'embarque à tout ce discours. Il ne me paraît pas que j'aie besoin d'apologie auprès de vous. C'est donc par le seul plaisir de parler à quelqu'un qui écoute avec plus d'attention, et qui répond plus juste que tout ce qui est ici. (I, L. 378, p. 705)

If I wrote to you other than in one of my mother's letters, I would tell you that I have already significantly put off my duties which summon me to Provence, but she would find it wrong not to be counted among those who must order my conduct. She is the mistress of it at present; and I have the chagrin to be subject to her authority only in matters where my compliance and my obedience will be suspected to be in league with her. I don't know why I am launching into all this. It does not seem to me that I need apologize with you. It is, then, for the sole pleasure of speaking to someone who listens with more attention, and who responds more justly than all who are here.

Grignan's appeal to Bussy's attentive ear and sense of justice situates him as arbiter and administrator of family justice. She reaches over her mother and seeks the verdict of this higher, less partial court. She alludes to her awareness of the context of her writing ("dans une lettre de ma mère") and therefore to her prismatic readership, and flaunts that awareness by making a statement that she claims violates the code dictated by that sharing context ("Si je vous écrivais ailleurs . . . je vous dirais que . . ."). In fact, what she is doing here is exploiting this very context, this familial triangle, to transmit a message of ambivalence and passive resentment to her mother, "la maîtresse." She appeals to the greater authority, Bussy, "plus juste que tout ce qui est ici," to arbitrate the conflict. He is called upon to serve as witness and judge to the varying dimensions of Mme de Grignan's plight as she endeavors to reconcile filial and marital duty as well as to please herself. The fact that she articulates her dilemma to the patriarchal head of family suggests that she seeks his official blessing to leave her mother and to join her husband. Perhaps it is because of her implicit recognition of his authority over the family, and specifically over her mother, that Mme de Grignan always enjoyed favor with Bussy. He was continually solicitous of her in letters to Sévigné. While his concern showed that he recognized and thereby further validated Sévigné's attachment to her daughter, it also suggests that he kept a watchful and interested eye on the mother-daughter couple to ensure that the bounds of familial propriety were observed, that, in the absence of her own father, Mme de Grignan remained the father's daughter.

As Bussy played an important role in Sévigné's development as a letter writer, so he figured as an important force in the regulation of her affective life. As a widow, Sévigné had assumed the functions of both father and mother in administering her family. While, as a consequence, she enjoyed greater authority than that normally enjoyed by mothers in families where the father is present, there were still certain paternal prerogatives that were relayed out of the immediate family unit and visited on the male head in the extended family. The place Bussy occupied in her world she attempted to claim and fill in her daughter's.

T H R E E

The Moment of Separation

Mme de Sévigné

Les signes de cette passion risquent d'étouffer l'autre. Ne faut-il pas alors, *précisément parce que je l'aime,* lui cacher combien je l'aime? Je vois l'autre d'un double regard: tantôt je le vois comme objet, tantôt comme sujet; j'hésite entre la tyrannie et l'oblation. Je me prends ainsi moi-même dans un chantage: si j'aime l'autre, je suis tenu de vouloir son bien; mais je ne puis alors que me faire mal: piège: je suis condamné à être un saint ou un monstre: saint ne puis, monstre ne veux: donc je tergiverse: je montre *un peu* ma passion.   ROLAND BARTHES [1]

The signs of this passion risk smothering the other. Don't I, then, *precisely because I love,* have to hide how much I love? I see the other doubly: sometimes as object, sometimes as subject; I hesitate between tyranny and oblation. I thus trap myself in a blackmail: if I love the other, I am obliged to wish her well; but then I can only harm myself: a trap: I am condemned to be a saint or a monster: a saint I cannot be, a monster I do not want to be: therefore I equivocate: I show my passion *a little.*

Under a series of concatenated rubrics: the first, "Cacher" [Hide]; the second, "Les lunettes noires" [The dark glasses]; and the third, "Deux discours" [Two discourses]; Barthes sets up a countergloss between his text and the simple mention of Mme de Sévigné in the margin, leaving it up to the reader to decide how the two sides of the page speak to each other. The interception of Sévigné's initial letters to her departing daughter that follows here can be understood as emblematic of a will to weave meaning between the juxtaposed name and the fragment, to explore the tease of calculation suggested in the Barthesian fantasy of "showing one's passion *a little,*" discreetly encoded from behind protective "shades" as relating to the literary figure that is Mme de Sévigné.

The occasion for Sévigné's total absorption in epistolary writing arises with the daughter's departure to join her husband in Provence and the call to bridge the separation by letter. Henceforth Sévigné's life was to be structured around, by and within this correspondence. Both the act of writing and the person of her daughter became the determinant factors in the organization of her life, in her construction of identity. They converged in the form of the relational letter that was to constitute Sévigné's ceaseless activity over a period of twenty-three years.

All that Sévigné gleaned from her incessant and varied reading, from her exquisite social sensibilities, from her writing with Bussy (as well as others), she concentrated in the cultivation of correspondence with her daughter. The sheer volume of the collection of letters to the daughter extant as well as the regularity of their dating attests to a sense of urgent intensity that colors the correspondence with an almost fictional quality. The problematic relationship between art and life, between fiction and reality, is epitomized in this epistolary writing. The question of whether Sévigné lived her life in order to write it or wrote her life in order to live it appears unanswerable from her letters. Those two moments are seamlessly related in her text. In any case, it is clear that she focused her life and her writing on her daughter, that the mother-daughter scriptoral relationship becomes fundamental to her way of being in the world.

In this chapter, I examine closely the writing inspired during the first moments of the two women's separation. Many of the themes that will develop, recur, and ultimately characterize the mother's writing persona are announced in three inaugural letters (the first letters penned to the daughter: I, L. 95; L. 130; and L. 131). Further, it is useful to study the early letters to learn how Sévigné encouraged and trained her daughter to write in order to ensure the sustenance of the exchange. Since reciprocity is essential to correspondence, and since Sévigné is clearly the initiator of the project, her major aim, in the early phase of the exchange, must be to shape her daughter's will, habits, and writing, to secure her cooperation in establishing the writing relationship.

The very first letter addressed by Sévigné to her daughter precedes Françoise-Marguerite's departure for Provence by a little over a year. It marks a separation of minor consequence: Sévigné is in the country at Livry, and her daughter, recently married and pregnant, has stayed with her husband in Paris. Sévigné responds to a letter she has just received from her:

Il faut, ma bonne, que je sois persuadée de votre fond pour moi, puisque je vis encore. C'est une chose bien étrange que la tendresse que j'ai pour vous; je ne sais si contre mon dessein j'en témoigne beaucoup, mais je sais bien que j'en cache encore davantage. Je ne veux point vous dire l'émotion et la joie que m'a donnée votre laquais et votre lettre. J'ai eu même le plaisir de ne point croire que vous fussiez malade; j'ai été assez heureuse pour croire ce que c'était. Il y a longtemps que je l'ai dit, quand vous voulez, vous êtes adorable; rien ne manque à ce que vous faites. (I, L. 95, p. 112)

I must, *ma bonne*, be persuaded of your affection for me, since I am still alive. It's quite a strange thing, the tenderness I have for you; I don't know if I show it much despite my intentions, but I know quite well that I hide even more of it. I cannot tell you of the emotion and joy that your lackey and your letter gave me. I even had the pleasure of not believing you were sick; I was happy enough to believe I knew what it was. I have said this for a long time: when you want to be, you are adorable; there is nothing lacking in what you do.

Some of the major themes that traverse the twenty-three years of the correspondence and the formalization of the mother-daughter relationship are introduced through writing in this opening passage.[2] There is the immediate avowal of the mother's dependence, for her well-being, indeed for her very life, on assurance of her daughter's affection for her. This is followed, appropriately, by a profession of the mother's love for her daughter, in accordance with the need to establish affective reciprocity that will translate later into epistolary reciprocity.

Sévigné's comment on the singularity of her feeling ("une chose bien étrange") prefigures the notion of exceptionality and distinction she will later entertain and cultivate with regard to her writing and affective relationship with Françoise-Marguerite, one that will feed on comparison and aspire to excellence, that will culminate in the formulation of a paradigm of a maternal paragon. Sévigné's puzzlement here at her own feelings can also be appreciated as genuine, for there existed at the time of her writing few prior models of mother-daughter affection through which to situate and understand her own feelings.[3] As will be seen later, a search for models and an incorporation of available discourses become important aspects of her inscribed self-quest and maternal self-textualization.

An indication of the difficulty she has in knowing how to conceptualize and articulate her own feelings is the fact that, in this same letter, she borrows from a repertoire of masculine heterosexual amorous discourse in order to convey her feelings for her daughter. She resorts to quoting from Malherbe's poetry addressed to Mme d'Auchy:[4]

> "Mais quoi que vous ayez, vous n'avez point Caliste,
> Et moi, je ne vois rien quand je ne la vois pas."
> (I, L. 95, p. 113)

> "But whatever you have, you do not have Caliste,
> And I see nothing when I do not see her."

The rhetorics in circulation have not yet formalized the relationship she is attempting to express in writing. Consequently, that relationship will be rendered in borrowings from other codes of address, while being framed in the organization of a letter exchange already familiar to her from her epistolary relationship with Bussy. Her own maternal discourse will have some of its identifiable roots in the prevalent courting rhetoric of her period.

The ambivalence that regards professing or hiding the as yet culturally unassimilated or repressed feeling of a mother for her daughter also raises an issue that resonates throughout the correspondence. Sévigné opts eventually and emphatically for overt display of affection while the daughter consistently prefers discreet attestation; this difference in attitude correlates with the fact that Sévigné is constructing a social identity as mother, while Françoise-Marguerite seeks a more autonomous identity than that of the mother's daughter.

Further, the stated importance of reception of a letter to determining the happiness of the mother will recur with predictable regularity, although often preceded, unlike in this seemingly gratuitous instance, by a period of agonizing wait. Thus responsibility devolves upon the daughter to ensure the mother's happiness by remaining faithful to the correspondence.

In addition, the issue of the daughter's health, merely touched on here, will persistently trouble the exchange as the daughter moves through her difficult childbearing years, and as she increasingly exploits the self-defeating excuse of illness in attempts to protect herself from her mother's invasive concern.

Finally, Sévigné asserts herself in the position of longtime knower of and over her daughter by turning her compliment in the shape of self-confirming dogma ("Il y a longtemps que je l'ai dit") that she has decreed and reiterated over the years. While she points out that her daughter is "adorable," she couches it in such a way as to suggest that this is not an essential trait in Françoise-Marguerite but a calculated effect that the daughter can produce when she wants to. The underlying message ("quand vous voulez") is that the daughter is capricious and willful. The final compliment ("rien ne manque") is curiously empty and negative. The general tone of the letter, as well as demonstrating the recourse to a borrowed rhetoric to gloss the relationship, attests to the centrality of the relationship to Sévigné's sense of identity, with telling hints at the arbitrary nature of the daughter's charm for the mother as well as the daughter's conditional responsiveness to the mother—indications of tensions already in play between the two women.

Two days before the separation, an exchange took place between mother and daughter that I read to reflect and announce the struggle of wills between the two women evidenced throughout the letters. The daughter reclaimed a case of hers that had been in her mother's keeping, and the mother returned it with, inside the case, a gift of a diamond ring for her daughter. Gifts are traditionally symbolic markers in western culture; in this instance, the exchange occurs at a moment of separation and articulates, in the face of that prospect, both the daughter's desire to take her leave and the mother's will to bond. The epistolary accompaniment to the transaction underscores the imbalance in the relationship and spells out the attempt at redressing it through the mediation of object exchange. The transaction appears markedly one-sided as it figures in the *Correspondance*: Sévigné returns to her daughter, at the latter's insistence, a case: "Puisque vous voulez absolument qu'on vous rende votre petite boîte, la voilà" (I, L. 130, p. 149) [Since you absolutely want your little case returned to you, here it is].

Françoise-Marguerite's reclaiming of her case can be interpreted as an effort to repossess herself, to free herself of claims on the mother as well as to end the mother's obligations toward her. She attempts to undo the bond represented in the mother's keeping of the case, symbolic perhaps of a more profound keeping that is ending with the daughter's departure to join her husband and pass into his keeping. While Sévigné acquiesces, it is clearly only in response to her daughter's willfulness, and, while it might be literally true that the case is small, its symbolic significance—the daughter's claim to self—is trivialized by the adjective.[5]

Sévigné's desire to secure and strengthen the bond between them at this moment of separation is represented in the contents of the case. Inside is the gift of a diamond ring. She explicitly states the purpose of her offering:

Qu'il vous fasse souvenir de moi et de l'excessive tendresse que j'ai pour vous, et par combien de choses je voudrais vous la pouvoir témoigner en toutes occasions, quoi que vous puissiez croire là-dessus. (I, L. 130, p. 149)

Let it remind you of me and of the excessive tenderness I have for you, and of how many ways I would like to be able to show it to you all the time, no matter what you might believe.

Various conjectures converge to explain, at least partially, why Sévigné is making this present: 1) it is because the diamond has been recut, set, and just happens to be ready at this critical juncture; 2) it is in response to the daughter's request for her case and the need to replace this retracted exchange with another equally binding one; and 3) it is because the daughter is about to leave and the mother seeks to send something of herself along with her daughter as a material reminder of her presence and of her affection, and, not least, of her power. The symbolic power of gift giving is played out in the overdetermined gesture and its accompanying epistolary directives for interpretation. The daughter claims merely what appears to be rightfully hers but receives as well a superfluity that is the mother's.

Because the jewel is "excessive" in this exchange economy and specifically designated to function as a reminder of "excessive tenderness" (in excess of what? what is the normative standard of "tenderness" that makes this excessive?), the daughter is thereby indebted to a materially and emotionally patronizing mother. Further, the gift of the diamond serves to occasion somewhat menacing explicit wishes for loyalty, prosperity, and a long life as the daughter takes her leave and joins her husband, her other and perhaps less sure patron: "que jamais je ne le voie en d'autres mains que les vôtres" (I, L. 130, p. 149) [let me never see it in hands other than yours].

The mother's ostensible affection is obviously questioned by the daughter as refracted in the mother's words: "quoi que vous puissiez croire là-dessus." The mother exhibits awareness that the daughter entertains doubts concerning her professed attachment, and she dismissively offers in her own defense a categorical denial of the daughter's feelings. Such a gesture cannot be expected to bridge the gap between the two women, and to seal the pact Sévigné appears desirous of contracting.

The return of the daughter's case and the giving of the mother's diamond represent a mediation that, as it claims acquiescence and affection, produces maternal excess and filial indebtedness. It rights the earlier imbalance of the mother's keeping of the daughter's case, only to cause yet another in the relationship, one that will be regularly reinstated by the mother's production of excess in the correspondence, the new medium of exchange (exemplified most tellingly in the "lettres de provision" discussed in chapter 4), and a constant posture of apologetic inadequacy in the indebted daughter's letters.[6] In fact, by a week later, with her daughter en route to Provence, Sévigné was realizing a return on her diamond: her daughter's first letters arrived:

Je reçois vos lettres, ma bonne, comme vous avez reçu ma bague. Je fonds en larmes en les lisant; il semble que mon coeur veuille se fendre par la moitié. (I, L. 132, p. 151)

I receive your letters, *ma bonne,* as you received my ring. I burst into tears while reading them; it seems that my heart wants to break in two.

Although the focus is on the comparability of two moments because of their shared lachrymose character, behind that pairing appears to lurk a perception of the ring as cause and the letters as effect, suggesting the deliberate if unconscious basis of the correspondence contract.

On 4 February 1671, Françoise-Marguerite finally left her mother and followed her husband to Grignan. Twenty years before, to the day, on 4 February 1651, Sévigné's husband had received the fatal wound (in a duel over his mistress) that was to spell his death two days later. Although the marriage was reported as far from idyllic and is hardly mentioned by Sévigné herself in any of her writings, surely it must have been a blow, minimally to her sense of security, coming as it did in the wake of her earlier orphaning.

And her own birthday was 5 February (1626). Although it generally went uncelebrated, Sévigné occasionally mentioned it in her letters, so that it was not altogether unmarked. For example, in 1672, a year after her daughter's departure, apparently heavy with feelings of sorrow stirred up by the anniversary of the separation, she glossed the date of her letter with: "Il y a aujourd'hui mille ans que je suis née" (I, L. 243, p. 431)[7] [I was born a thousand years ago today]. And in 1674, she again inscribed her birthdate, here in the form of a contrived riddle, situating her exclusive reason for living in her love for her daughter:

Il y a aujourd'hui bien des années, *ma chère bonne,* qu'il vint au monde une créature destinée à vous aimer préférablement à toutes choses; je prie votre imagination de n'aller ni à droite ni à gauche: *Ce monsieur-là, Sire, c'était moi-même.* (I, L. 368, p. 690)

Many years ago today, *ma chère bonne,* a creature destined to love you above all else came into the world; I beg your imagination to go neither to the left nor the right: *That man, Sire, was myself.*

She projects a persona committed by fate to a sole purpose in life. She borrows her key line from Marot's "Epitre au Roi pour avoir été dérobé" [Missive to the King on the Occasion of Having Been Robbed]; she recycles the verse intact, recognizable, apparently ignoring the gender difference between her implied self and the textual "monsieur" as well as the misfit between "Sire" and her addressed daughter. The borrowing of the quotation points to a more profound borrowing: it is in a male-engendered body of literature (her only readily available store of expressions) that Sévigné seeks and finds formulas to translate her own experience. Filtering her self through this "other" construction of the world produces a grammatically enforced self-alienation ("il vint au monde une créature") and works against the intimacy she ostensibly seeks to cultivate with her daughter. Although such intertextuality will anchor and ornament her writing, it will repeatedly vitiate attempts at self-apprehension and expression and point to the constructed nature of her assumed identity. At the same time, it represents an attempt at another sort of bonding, through cultural commonality. The redirected citation gestures now beyond a king to her daughter, and, in its new context, the familiar verse highlights a new story.

She specifically contextualized her birthday as of significance because it coincided yearly with the anniversary of her daughter's departure. All of the feelings of abandonment that a widow (a husbandless woman) and orphan (a parentless child) might have on the anniversary of the spouse's death and on her birthday are stirred up by the new blow of her daughter's departure as she experiences for the first time being a childless mother. Early February must have been a regularly charged mourning season for Sévigné. Bereft of parents and husband, she relied on her relations the Coulanges and on Bussy, as well as on her friends, for a sense of belonging and invested emotionally in her children, particularly her daughter and her daughter's eventual family, as the primary source of her familial identity.

Upon Françoise-Marguerite's departure to join her husband in Provence, Sévigné followed her through letters that caught up with her at the various places where she stopped on her journey south. As Sévigné initially contemplated the void created by her daughter's absence, she recognized it to be both external and internal and sought expression for the inner feeling of loss in the articulation of the daughter's physical absence: "Ma douleur serait bien médiocre si je pouvais vous la dépeindre; je ne l'entreprendrai pas aussi" (I, L. 131, p. 149) [My grief would be quite mediocre if I could depict it to you; I will thus not attempt it]. These are the initial words of the twenty-three-year correspondence. Here, at the very outset, the writing mother's concern is with representation. She renounces any attempt at depicting her sorrow, not, as she puts it, because it is too painful, but because of concern for its possible devaluation through verbalization. Language is viewed as fundamentally inadequate to expression; emotion articulated is, by that logic, emptied of its force. The proof of great feeling, then, is the degree to which it resists or eludes expression. The project of maternal expression opens thus both on a modest note of renunciation and with a strong claim to powerful feeling.

Paradoxically, having stated what she will not do in this first letter, she proceeds to attempt just that. She sets about depicting the very grief that she claims defies expression. She uses concrete images and actual fact to illuminate the void; what is present points relentlessly to what is missing. She renders the abstraction through a palpable account of her first day alone. Rather than translating her feelings into concepts and interpreting her reactions as general truths, she lets her various activities speak for her. The language that proliferates in the letter that follows is assigned no distinct function; it is governed only by the disclaimer, perhaps merely a rhetorical device to underscore the difficulty of the enterprise ahead, but premised on a powerful assumption concerning the relationship between being and representation. The body of the letter stands in clear contrast to its introduction of negative intent:

> A Paris, vendredi 6 février [1671]
>
> Ma douleur serait bien médiocre si je pouvais vous la dépeindre; je ne l'entreprendrai pas aussi. J'ai beau chercher ma chère fille, je ne la trouve plus, et tous les pas qu'elle fait l'éloignent de moi. Je m'en allai donc à Sainte-Marie, toujours pleurant et toujours mourant. Il me semblait qu'on m'arrachait le coeur et l'âme, et en effet, quelle rude séparation! Je demandai la liberté d'être seule. On me mena dans la chambre de Mme du Housset, on me fit du feu. Agnès me regardait sans me parler; c'était notre marché. J'y passai jusqu'à cinq heures sans cesser de sangloter; toutes mes pensées me faisaient mourir. J'écrivis à M. de Grignan; vous pouvez penser sur quel ton. J'allai ensuite chez Mme de La Fayette, qui redoubla mes douleurs par la part qu'elle y prit. Elle était seule, et malade, et triste de la mort d'une soeur religieuse; elle était comme je la pouvais désirer. M. de La Rochefoucauld y vint. On ne parla que de vous, de la raison que j'avais d'être touchée, et du dessein de parler comme il faut à *Mélusine*. Je vous réponds qu'elle sera bien relancée. D'Hacqueville vous rendra un bon compte de cette affaire. Je revins enfin à huit heures de chez Mme de La Fayette. Mais en entrant ici, bon Dieu! comprenez-vous bien ce que je sentis en montant ce degré? Cette chambre où j'entrai toujours, hélas! j'en trouvai les portes ouvertes, mais je vis tout démeublé, tout dérangé, et votre pauvre petite fille qui représentait la mienne. Comprenez-vous bien tout ce que je souffris? Les réveils de la nuit ont été noirs, et le matin je n'étais point avancée d'un pas pour le repos de mon esprit. L'après-dîner se passa avec Mme de la Troche à l'Arsenal. Le soir je reçus votre lettre qui me remit dans les premiers transports, et ce soir j'achèverai celle-ci chez M. de Coulanges, où j'apprendrai des nouvelles. Car pour moi, voilà ce que je sais, avec les douleurs de tous ceux que vous avez laissés ici. Toute ma lettre serait pleine de compliments si je voulais.
>
> Vendredi au soir,
>
> J'appris chez Mme de Lavardin les nouvelles que je vous mande; et j'ai su par Mme de La Fayette qu'ils eurent hier une conversation avec Mélusine dont le détail n'est pas aisé à écrire, mais enfin . . . (I, L. 131, pp. 149–50)

> Paris, Friday, 6 February [1671]
>
> My grief would be quite mediocre if I could depict it to you; I will thus not attempt it. It is useless to search for my dear daughter, I cannot find her, and each step she takes distances her further from me. So I went off to Sainte-Marie, still crying and still dying. It seemed to me that my heart and soul were being torn from me, and in effect, what a difficult separation! I asked for the liberty to be alone. I was taken into Mme du Housset's bedroom; a fire was made for me. Agnes watched me without speaking; this was our pact. I was there until five o'clock, sobbing unceasingly; all my thoughts were killing me. I wrote to M. de Grignan; you can imagine the tone. Then I went to Mme de La Fayette's, which doubled my sufferings by the interest she took in my state. She was alone, and sick, and sad from the death of a sister who is a nun, she was in just the state that suited mine. M. de La Rochefoucauld arrived. We spoke only of you, of the reason I had for being upset, and of the intention of speaking as one should to Mélusine. I guarantee you that she will be put in her place. D'Hacqueville will take care of this affair for you. I finally

returned from Mme de La Fayette's at eight o'clock. But upon entering, good God! Can you actually understand what I felt upon climbing this stair? This bedroom I always entered, alas! I found all its doors open, but I saw all the furniture moved, everything disarranged, and your poor little daughter who represented my own. Can you really understand all I suffered? The wakings of the night were dark, and in the morning I had not progressed at all toward peace of mind. The after dinner hours were spent with Mme de la Troche at the Arsenal. In the evening I received your letter which put me back into my first state, and tonight I will finish this one at M. de Coulanges's where I will find out what is new. As for me, this is my news, along with the sufferings of all those here you have left behind. My whole letter would be full of compliments if I wanted it so.

Friday evening

I learned the news I send on to you at Mme de Lavardin's; and I found out through Mme de La Fayette that they had a conversation with Mélusine yesterday which is not easy to write about in detail, but after all . . .

The writing subject's inaugural gesture is to represent two movements in order to evoke the physical reality of the daughter's absence from the mother's world and to invest it with meaning: she inscribes her own active and futile search for the departed daughter there where she is no longer to be found, and she points accusingly to the daughter's simultaneous and purposeful movement of distancing from the mother: "J'ai beau chercher ma fille, je ne la trouve plus, et tous les pas qu'elle fait l'éloignent de moi" (I, L. 131, p. 149). It is striking that in this letter addressed to the daughter, the vous appropriate to simulating the intersubjective mode in epistolary writing is suppressed in favor of third-person forms (ma fille, la, elle). Such a writing tactic may be summoned to translate the difficulty the subject has in accepting the painful fact that the other subject is indeed no longer present to her, and in acknowledging that henceforth vous can only be inscribed on paper, with all the contrivance that implies. But it has other consequences as well. The object of the search, the daughter, is transformed into the object of the mother's discourse and is denied, by this withholding of recognition (vous) her own place of center as subject. The writing mother invents a textual daughter in the letter, often at the expense of the real one, and the subject of the mother's discourse is most often je.

This je reorganizes the dimension of space around the separation of the two women. The central point of this spatial dimension is nothing so general as Paris, so imprecise as the hôtel they have shared; the focal point is persistently the narcissistic moi, accompanied henceforth by the experience of a void—a wounded moi, since the daughter is no longer available to serve as mirror to the mother. Attempts to compensate for the loss, to rejoin, to replace, and to recreate the mirror, thereby reaffirming the identity of the moi, constitute the motivation and provide the drive that sustains the epistolary endeavor.

The issue of sociability, the search for mirrors, is raised immediately thereafter. Sévigné expresses a characteristic ambivalence concerning the desire for company in this her depiction of dolor. Although she does circulate promptly after her daughter's departure, seeking an audience for her sorrow, in paradoxical fashion, she conveys her suffering by excusing herself from the very company she has taken the trouble to seek out: "Je m'en allai donc à Sainte-Marie . . . Je demandai la liberté d'être seule" (I, L. 131, p. 149). It is not at all solitude that she seeks, nor is it actual company, but rather a simple witness to her grief. The paradox of the need she expresses to be at once both alone and with others plays off the tension between being and representation, the need to represent oneself in order to experience being, the experience of being through its projection to another: "Agnès me regardait sans me parler; c'était notre marché" (I, L. 131, p. 150). Solitude can only be experienced by Sévigné with the aid of mirrors through whom to perceive herself.[8] Here another exchange is taking place as well: Agnès receives company in the convent in return for being company to her visitor, and thus her own cloistered existence is acknowledged. The project of self-confirmation through representation functions reciprocally to benefit both parties to the scene.

The attempts at breaking through the solitude take the form of writing and visiting, markedly specular activities: "J'écrivis à M. de Grignan . . . J'allai ensuite chez Mme de La Fayette" (I, L. 131, p. 150). Indeed, letters and conversation comprise the major activities discussed and represented in the *Correspondance*. These are eminently social but self-confirming activities, and they subsume and eclipse other featured pastimes such as reading, politicking, managing finances, reverie, and occasional religious meditation. Indeed, many of these inscribed reportings figure in the letters as maternal offerings proffered to spin out connectedness to a daughter in retreat. Relating is Sévigné's way of being in the world.

The mourning mother will always prefer the company of those who join with her in adulation of and grieving for the lost daughter, those who reflect back to her and confirm her own moods and preoccupations.[9] Rather than concern herself with consoling her friend, who is "seule, et malade, et triste," Sévigné takes a certain pleasure in La Fayette's depressed state, so in keeping with her own miserable mood: "elle était comme je la pouvais désirer." The cause of La Fayette's grief is not at all the same as that of Sévigné, nor does it appear to be of particular interest to her since she passes over it so quickly. Whereas the one mourns the departure of a daughter, the other mourns the death of her sister, a nun.[10] The comparability of effect is what matters here; causes are irrelevant. What counts is surface manifestation, effect, the mirror. What seems to be sought here by Sévigné is not relief from sorrow but the reflection—and thereby, the intensification and illustration—of sorrow. Sévigné appears to earn recognition among her friends by emoting in their presence; she establishes her maternal social profile on the grounds of her mourning persona—the *mater dolorosa*.

Sévigné manages to monopolize attention indirectly by focusing it on her daughter: "On ne parla que de vous." It is a tribute to her, and not necessarily to her daughter, that these friends take an interest in what is so dear to her heart, which is, in this case and more often than not, her daughter. Even absent, the daughter continues to function as an enabling mirror agent for the mother in her social construction of self.

Sévigné's return home after her rounds prompts another burst of realization and reappraisal of spatial dimensions that signify to her the daughter's departure. Yawning doors, rooms stripped, order disturbed constitute the visible signs of absence. The lonely presence of the child Marie-Blanche (two and a half months old) serves only as a further reminder: "et votre pauvre petite fille qui me représentait la mienne" (I, L. 131, p. 150). If the child were referred to as "my granddaughter," there might be a suggestion that the grandmother could be consoled through this compensating and bonding presence. Perhaps too young, perhaps too distraught herself, the child does not comfort the grandmother but only further heightens her sense of loss. Nor does Sévigné think to reassure her daughter that the child is well and in good hands; she uses the child as an instrument for representation of her own feelings. The opposition of "your child" and "mine" posits parallel experiences of motherhood for Sévigné and her daughter but introduces a troubling comparison: the seemingly innocent insertion of "pauvre" in "votre pauvre petite fille" can be read as well to impute Mme de Grignan's cruelty as a mother in abandoning her unhappy child, as opposed to Sévigné's consuming maternal devotion attested to by this very letter. It indicates, even more tellingly, an emotional identification of Sévigné not with the mother, but with the child. She assumes the plight of the child not in order to dispel it but to intensify her own feelings of distress—she is twice abandoned.

The rhetorical question that follows, "Comprenez-vous bien tout ce que je souffris?" echoes an earlier and equally urgent refrain, "Comprenez-vous bien ce que je sentis . . . ?" The concern for effect can be seen as a contradiction of the initial negatively stated aim of the letter and a betrayal of the profound concern of the writer: she does intently wish to know if she has succeeded in depicting her sorrow, in translating the invisible through the visible, the abstract via the concrete, and her own absence from her daughter into presence via the letter. She admits through these questions to her ambition in writing such a letter, and she invites evaluation of her epistolary performance, displacing responsibility for its success onto the daughter's ability to comprehend, all the while suggesting, as a provisional defense, that her expression cannot (indeed, must not) adequately represent her state.

While Sévigné might find comfort in the act of writing, it is clear here that, at least initially, her aim is not merely to console herself. She seeks to produce certain effects in her daughter and in a more immediately available public. While firmly centered on the *moi* of the sender, the discourse seeks to act on the addressee, to persuade her of her devotion and suffering, and perhaps not so incidentally, of her ability to express and convey her sorrow, even if it is at the expense of the peace of mind of the object of this devotion.

The letter itself and its production become a public display since Sévigné announces her intention to finish writing it at the Coulanges's. In the last section, written there, she dwells on the fact that she is receiving attention for her grieving:

Je ne vois que des gens qui vous aiment et vous estiment, et qui entrent bien aisément dans ma douleur . . . On s'empresse fort de me chercher et de me vouloir prendre.

I see only people who love and esteem you, and who share my grief easily . . . I am eagerly sought out and looked after.

Sévigné is easily the center of attention; she prefers the company of those who enter into her interests and seems to take pleasure in the way her obsession operates socially. It is difficult to see here the conventional demeanor of proverbial selfless "maternal" love. Rather, there appears to be a filtering whereby the public enters into and shares the mother's concerns through profession of interest in the daughter and reciprocally, Sévigné is socially incorporated as mother. The *moi* is reflected, affirmed, and even magnified by this group mirroring, and on its way to inventing a social role of maternity.

FOUR

The Daughter's Apprenticeship

L'honnête fille est l'image et le chef d'oeuvre de l'honnête femme.

The virtuous daughter is the image and the masterpiece of the virtuous woman.

•

Une mère voyant son image et son trésor dans celle qu'elle a produite, conserve l'un avec soin, et tâche de polir l'autre.

A mother seeing her image and her treasure in the one she has produced, conserves the one with care, and tries to polish the other.

•

Il n'y aurait point d'honnêtes femmes s'il n'y avait d'honnêtes filles.
FRANÇOIS DE GRENAILLE [1]

There would be no virtuous women if there were no virtuous daughters.

Following the separation, Sévigné promptly set about exploring the potential of the newly framed epistolary situation. Simultaneously, she worked at subtly shaping her correspondent and defining the nature of their correspondence. As she was textually extending the training of her now writing daughter by providing advice, compliments, and models, she was developing and exercising her own authority and thus coming to her own voice as well. The lessons imparted to the daughter reflect the position she was mapping out for herself in the epistolary domain. In her capacity as mentor, she elaborated her own stylistics and illustrated her art through exemplary writing.

In cultivating her writing primarily in relation to her daughter, Sévigné established a writing position of maternal authority. But that traditional authority which devolved on her in her role as mother did not necessarily extend to validate her in her own view as writer. While serving as mirror to her daughter, she made of her a writing mirror, retaining all the while for herself the advantage of maternal preeminence. In doing so, she was merely reflecting common *doxa* that confounded mother-daughter relations. Just as epistolary manuals circulated surreptitiously, as powerful but inadmissible shapers of writing relations, so did there exist manuals on childrearing that contained in their own message prohibition against explicit reference to them. Both cultural and social relations, constructed in the interest of a particular political order, were to be understood as "natural," and therefore in no need of explicitation.

François de Grenaille outlined a program of mother-daughter relations in *L'Honneste fille* (1639–40), featuring the mirror as metaphor for the mother-daughter tie. The mother was to serve as mirror to the daughter, presenting an image that she was to strive to match: "Or il me semble que l'honnête fille voyant sa mère a une parfaite description de ce qu'elle doit être un jour"[2] [Now it seems to me that the virtuous daughter seeing her mother has a perfect description of what she must one day be]. Thus the mother's responsibility is to display herself to her daughter, and to elicit from her the desired reflection of herself. Hence she, the mother, apprehends herself in the image she succeeds in projecting onto the daughter, her mirror. Social identity of both mother and daughter, then, is reciprocally deferred onto the other and leaves them equally dependent on each other for their senses of self. This problematic intrasubjectivity is generalized and legitimated in de Grenaille's treatise by allusion to such classic authorities as Seneca: "Nous nous servons de théâtre l'un à l'autre, ainsi que parle Sénèque . . . nous sommes des images les uns des autres"[3] [We serve as theatre for one another, as Seneca says . . . we are images of one another]. The mirror image, constantly in flux as it both reflects and projects the other, highlights the instability of the two subjects ever in process as they seek their respective identities in relation to each other.

Exercising both the prerogative and the responsibility of mother, Sévigné played off the daughter and situated herself as at once superior to and dependent on her. This tended to produce a paradoxical role reversal in her discourse, the modulation of a self-indulgent voice not dissimilar to that of a confident, affectionate, and slightly patronizing child toward a nanny; it is encapsulated in the mother's preferred form of address for her daughter, "ma bonne," and the enabling function of that specular relationship is realized for Sévigné in her maternal writing.

Before exploring in detail the epistolary lessons imparted to the daughter and the benefits of these to the writing mother, it is useful to examine Sévigné's general understanding of the genre she was practicing as she communicated it to her daughter. Already a seasoned correspondent, she was well aware that the letter was an encoded form with its conventions and formulas, and that it was produced within the context of a particular set of constraints. She became acutely sensitive to the formal features of the letter upon her daughter's departure. Deprived of her company, she sought to replicate it and attempted to reconstitute what she apparently most missed: the intense mirroring activity of conversation with her daughter. In so doing, she was reinventing the already conventionalized encodement that governed the theory and practice of the epistolary genre in her day, but coming to personal terms with the underlying rationale. She reflected ceaselessly on the elements of conversation as they were inadequately reproduced in writing, and in so doing, she articulated certain tenets that were to function as her basic assumptions, to determine her epistolary stylistics, and to govern the exchange over the years.

Operative throughout the *Correspondance* is the basic premise that words are inadequate to the sentiment they purport to convey. Vision (hence presence), not language, offers the only adequate access to the other. But this privileging of the ocular spells its own limitations also, since feeling, lodged in the heart, and inexpressible, is invisible to the eye as well:

Il me semble que je fais tort à mes sentiments, de vouloir les expliquer avec des paroles; il faudrait voir ce qui se passe dans mon coeur à votre sujet. (I, L. 139, p. 169)

It seems to me that I do wrong to my sentiments, in wanting to explain them with words; one should see what is going on in my heart about you.

The purported goal of "intelligence," dependent on a situation of mutual presence, is basic to the esthetics of conversation and hence of the letter.[4] The difficulty of its attainment, through written communication, causes the mother's correspondence with her daughter to take on the character of an enormously absorbing, only fleetingly gratifying, and frequently disappointing Sisyphean task.

The already frustrating state of incomplete identity for the two women, even together, is further aggravated by the distance now between them. The implied opacity at once contradicts and confirms the notion of mother-daughter symbiosis circulating in seventeenth-century prescriptive and descriptive lore, as evidenced by de Grenaille's formula:

Une Dame et sa fille ne semblant avoir qu'un corps qui néanmoins se trouve à même temps mis en deux lieux, ou divisé en deux parties, elles n'auront aussi qu'une âme.[5]

A Lady and her daughter seeming to have but one body which is nevertheless in two places at the same time, or divided in two parts, they will as well have only one soul.

Sévigné's epistolary rhetoric derives, then, in large part, from an acknowledgment of the impossibility of complete symbiosis, and, at the same time, a commitment to strive toward this idealized relation; it engenders repetition and multiplication, innovation and ceaseless attempts to translate the invisible, articulate the unspeakable, encode the uninscribable—to represent the maternal as invisible, unspeakable, instinctive.

Many of Sévigné's remarks in the formative period of the mother-daughter exchange concentrate on situating identity and locating the source of meaning in the "heart." While she laments the lack of direct access to the other and continually upholds mutual presence as the preferable state, since that brings the "heart" into physical proximity, she must accept for herself and accommodate her daughter to the only available alternative. She must make her letters function as mirror and write out her heart. She laments the limitations of the epistolary situation, the time and context gap that impede the immediacy of the exchange, that stand in the way of contact, but resolves not to let knowledge of the complications introduced by the deferral of reception inhibit the production of communication:[6]

C'est le malheur des commerces si éloignés: toutes les réponses paraissent rentrées de pique noire. Il faut s'y résoudre, et ne pas même se révolter contre cette coûtume; cela est naturel, et la contrainte serait trop grande d'étouffer toutes ses pensées. Il faut entrer dans l'état naturel où l'on est, en répondant à une chose qui vous tient au coeur. Résolvez-vous donc à m'excuser souvent. (I, L. 141, p. 176)

It's the misfortune of such long-distance communications: all the responses come up spades. One must accept this, and not even rebel against this custom; it is natural, and it would be too great a constraint to stifle all one's thoughts. One must enter into one's immediate natural state, by responding to something of actual concern. Resolve yourself, then, to excuse me often.

She formalizes the requisite attitude of the sender ("il faut . . ." "il faut . . .") so that, while in theory merely explaining her own position, she is in fact offering a lesson to her daughter on the proper attitude to assume when she herself is writing to her mother, along with a strong implicit message exhorting pure resolve—an act of will.

When Sévigné's attention shifts to focus on the receiver, she must acknowledge that the message might not succeed in reaching its destination. She is acutely aware that she relinquishes control over the text once she sends it, and that the addressee's reading of the letter can be tantamount to a radical rewrite:

Je ne sais en quelle disposition vous serez en lisant cette lettre. Le hasard peut faire qu'elle viendra mal à propos, et qu'elle ne sera peut-être pas lue de la manière qu'elle est écrite. A cela je ne sais point de remède. (I, L. 149, p. 200)

I do not know what mood you will be in when reading this letter. Chance may be that it will come at a bad moment, and that it will perhaps not be read in the way it is written. For this I know no cure.

This possibility of misapprehension must be posited as a given early on in the exchange in order to contend with it, by incorporating it explicitly in the formative rhetoric of the letter. The problem of deferred communication constitutes one of the major underlying themes of the entire collection of letters. Its constant invocation attests to Sévigné's recognition of the inadequacy of the letter as simulacrum of presence and at the same time confirms her project to render it such.

On the occasion of an early felicitous exchange of letters, Sévigné celebrated her gratification. The difficulties of communication spelled out earlier had been surmounted in this happy instance:

Je pleurais amèrement en vous écrivant à Livry, et je pleure encore en voyant de quelle manière tendre vous avez reçu ma lettre, et l'effet qu'elle a fait dans votre coeur. Les petits esprits se sont bien communiqués, et sont passés bien fidèlement de Livry en Provence. (I, L. 156, p. 221)

I wept bitterly while writing to you in Livry, and I weep again seeing in what a tender manner you received my letter, and the effect it had in your heart. The little thoughts communicated themselves well, and have faithfully passed between Livry and Provence.

The obstacles of absence, distance, time were overcome here, but apparently not by words alone. If Sévigné's letter reached her daughter's heart, it is thanks to the cooperation of Cartesian "petits esprits," harnessed by her to express an impression of perfect intuition.[7] This mutually congratulatory passage marks an early moment of success in the enterprise, bearing a message of encouragement for future endeavors as well. Dwelling constantly on the impossibility of the enterprise would have doomed the project to failure and would have hastened its end. Glimmers of success punctuate and sustain the exchange.

Nevertheless, presence continues to be touted as a state that the letter can only approximate. Intimacy is necessarily compromised by distance, the distance imposed even by the constraining company of others, since the garden—"le mail"—affording surer privacy, is cited as the ideal place for conversation:

Il y a peu de choses dont on puisse parler à coeur ouvert de trois cents lieues. Une conversation dans le mail me serait bien nécessaire; c'est un lieu admirable pour discourir, quand on a le coeur comme je l'ai. (I, L. 176, p. 279)

There are few things of which one can speak openly from three hundred leagues away. A conversation in the garden would be really necessary for me; it's an admirable place in which to discourse, when one has a heart like mine.

Correspondence with the daughter is regarded as a last resort, an inadequate substitute for her company. The motif of the "coeur ouvert" articulates the mother's need to expose herself to the daughter in order to relieve herself of what she is repressing. It is not clear whether it is her emotional constitution, the singular condition of having a "heart" such as hers, or the three hundred leagues between the correspondents that inspires the invention of such a thing as a "coeur ouvert." The distance stipulates writing as the only mediation possible and thus sets the conditions for epistolary self-display.

On the other hand, Sévigné does not ignore, and comes to appreciate, that there are moments when, in spite of the actual availability of the interlocutor, the letter is preferred to talking as the mode of communication. Sévigné addresses letters to her daughter from the next room during reunions when the two women are not getting along. She resorted to this strategy in 1678, venting her spleen and citing her "heart" as alibi for her choice of pen over presence: "Mes lettres sont plus heureuses que moi-même; je m'explique mal de bouche, quand mon coeur est si touché" (II, L. 642, p. 607) [My letters are more felicitous than myself; I explain myself badly by word, when my heart is so affected]. This choice underscores the difference between the letter and the conversation: the letter is one-sided, of a more permanent, inscribed nature, and uninterrupted—at least as far as the writer/sender is concerned. The person writing enjoys a position of dominance at least during the penning of the letter: "Je vous tiens à mon avantage quand je vous écris, vous ne me répondez point, et je pousse mes discours tant que je veux" (II, L. 579, p. 464) [I have the advantage over you when I write to you: you do not answer back, and I extend my lectures as much as I please]. This preclusion of interruption, denial, and contradiction distinguishes the epistolary from the conversational situation. As long as Sévigné is actually writing, she can entertain the illusion that she holds her daughter's attention. While the mother-daughter relation is, in theory, a double mirror, when the ostensible reflecting image is recalcitrant and uncooperative, it is preferable simply to emit messages.

But although this one-sidedness might serve as an advantage in the one instance, when Sévigné is writing, it is a real hindrance in the other: as Sévigné receives messages from her daughter, she is forced to admit to the fundamental doubt fostered in her by the knowledge that she cannot verify her daughter's messages by her own observations. To her daughter, in response to a lively and pleasing but perhaps misleading letter, she writes: "Vous êtes plus gaie dans vos lettres que vous ne l'êtes ailleurs" (II, L. 459, p. 194) [You are gayer in your letters than you are elsewhere]. The unilateral nature of the letter can spell deception. Sévigné recognizes the potential for misrepresentation in the written communication when there is no recourse to other modes of verification. This acknowledgment seems to recognize the conversational esthetic as a wishful illusion rather than an accurate model for letter writing.

Sévigné turns this knowledge to her advantage and enjoys controlling her epistolary output accordingly, reveling in extending herself for her daughter, and meeting only her obligations in letters to others:

Je fais à peu près ce que je dois, et jamais que des réponses; j'en suis encore là. Je vous donne avec plaisir le dessus de tous les paniers, c'est-à-dire la fleur de mon esprit, de ma tête, de mes yeux, de ma plume, de mon écritoire, et puis le reste va comme il peut. Je me divertis autant à causer avec vous que je laboure avec les autres. (II, L. 453, p. 174)

I do only what I have to do, and never more than responses; I am still at it. I give you with pleasure the cream of the crop, I mean the flower of my wit, my mind, my eyes, my pen, my desk, and the rest goes as it will. I amuse myself as much chatting with you as I struggle with the others.

She can choose and design her self-presentation; she can shape it according to its destination and regulate her own degree of investment because of those same constraints that elsewhere are viewed less positively. Whereas they create a certain atmosphere of suspicion in Sévigné's mode of receiving a letter, these checks also invite inventive exploitations of themselves. The mother claims to do her finest and most effortless writing in her letters to her daughter. Such a statement functions to flatter the daughter, to assure her that she enjoys a privileged relationship with her mother; it also suggests a confidence Sévigné might experience in writing to her daughter that actually does make it easier for her to write to her than to others, a confidence grounded in the socially sanctioned power relationship between the two women that works to the mother's advantage. Sévigné contrasts with this pleasurable correspondence other epistolary obligations as so many tasks undertaken not at her own initiative but only strictly in response to letters received, and so she discloses the deliberate modulation of her writing voice.

Conversation with her daughter, then, is sincere and spontaneous on the one hand, but also the "fleur," and so selected and calculated. Such contradictions abound in the letters as Sévigné persists in measuring them against the conversation paradigm. The notion that conversation is itself natural is highly improbable, as attested by the plenitude of available manuals codifying that form of social exchange as well.[8] The project of valorizing the category of "natural" is subject to scrutiny, just as Sévigné's metaphor "coeur" invites analysis. Both terms pass as self-evident, especially to the extent that usage continues to accept them as such, but they operate as key terms in the implementation of an organization of social relations to which Sévigné, in her role as writing mother, unwittingly subscribes.

By 1675, four years after the daughter's departure, the routine of exchanging letters was well established and Sévigné could congratulate her daughter on the epistolary conversation they had succeeded in establishing and could rejoice in the pleasure to be had from it: "Ma bonne, votre commerce est divin. Ce sont des conversations que vos lettres; je vous parle, et vous me répondez" (II, L. 410, p. 39) [*Ma bonne,* communication with you is divine. Your letters are like conversations; I speak to you, and you answer me]. Her preferred position in the exchange as expressed here appears to be that of speaker, with her daughter in that of respondent. Then again, she may simply be expressing sheer amazement at being able to put something on paper, send it off subject to the myriad vagaries of the post, and receive eventually a message that contains echos of her own. Indeed the notion of echo, confirming the initial enunciation in returning it to the sender, correlates with the notion of the letter as narcissistic mode of self-confirmation and suggests the correspondence as an ideal vehicle for the articulation of the mother-daughter imaging relation.[9]

The illusion of coherence in epistolary "conversation," of correspondence, depends both on the exchange flow between letters and on the organization of material within them. Sometimes the direction of the conversation is from letter to letter, at others from idea to idea—on the one hand passing between correspondents, on the other representing one correspondent's train of thought. The mirroring activity takes place within letters as well as between them.

Allusion to the direction of a conversation in a letter written by Sévigné alone often serves to convey the illusion of irrepressible spontaneity. The letter offers itself as a faithful transcription of the thoughts that come to the writer's mind and therefore as a reliable witness to its own sincerity. When the letter is not inspired by the playful whimsy of a collective social effort, with several correspondents participating, the solitary writer endeavors to give that same impression of casual and immediate representation. Sévigné prides herself in her inability to espouse a more proper and coherent, and therefore less trustworthy, style and thus valorizes the fidelity of her writing to the self it is representing:

Mais où suis-je, ma fille? Voici un étrange égarement, car je veux dire simplement que la poste me retient vos lettres un ordinaire, parce qu'elle arrive trop tard à Paris, et qu'elle me les rend au double le courrier d'après; c'est donc pour cela que je me suis extravaguée, comme vous voyez. Qu'importe? En vérité, il faut un peu, entre bons amis, laisser trotter les plumes comme elles veulent; la mienne a toujours la bride sur le cou. (II, L. 451, p. 170)

But where am I, my daughter? This is a strange digression, for I simply want to say that the post usually retains one of your letters for me, because it arrives in Paris too late, and delivers twice as many letters in the next mail; that's why I extravagated, as you see. What does it matter? Truthfully, one must, a bit, between good friends, let pens trot along as they wish; mine always has free rein.

The luxury of extravagance suggested in the passage relates to the excess of text and affect that Sévigné is able to produce, given the leisure time she enjoys as a member of the privileged class. That same class code rigorously precludes more explicitly purposeful activity and hence necessarily valorizes the spontaneous display of self. It intersects powerfully with yet another code, that of gender, which enjoins women to eschew overt profession of specific ambition, which casts them particularly in mirroring roles, and which, at the same time, locates superfluity in them. As a consequence of her class, her gender, her widowed status, Sévigné is constantly available to herself and to her daughter as mirror.

As the years passed, having successfully imposed her will to correspond, and having exercised her maternal authority in the choice of her correspondent, Sévigné acknowledged more readily the limitations of her power. She recognized increasingly that conversation took place between letters, between individuals, that it could not be generated or sustained autonomously, just as her relationship with her daughter could not be simply a product of her own will but was necessarily one of interdependence, of reciprocity.[10]

But she also discovered and experienced the joy of writing as a self-fulfilling activity, and she became less dependent on the notion of exchange to justify her compulsion to write. She had secured her daughter as a reliable correspondent and had established a reputation among her contemporaries as a gifted writer. Her letters were prized as objets d'art. And so she continued to write to her daughter as always, but with a greater sufficiency and a stronger sense of her own place. It was increasingly in the writing rather than in the daughter that she mirrored herself.

Conversation, as it is generally understood, implies both language and behavior, as generated, commentated, and observed among and by a select group of engaged interlocutors. It takes place in a context that contributes to determine its scope and tenor, and it takes shape according to what the participants have to share with one other, this modulated by their knowledge of one another, the entire activity being inflected by awareness of the individuals' general social standing and hierarchical relationships to one another.[11] Sévigné reiterated over the years her understanding of the ways in which letters and conversation were comparable and regularly aired her frustration at the ways in which they were not.

Within the constraints of this mode of contact, she was attentive to all of the dimensions of conversation and devoted herself to shaping not only her daughter's writing but her epistolary behavior as well. She did this both by example and by less subtle methods, but always indirectly, exercising discreetly her maternal authority over her daughter. She took the task of shaping her daughter's epistolary persona seriously since, according to the wisdom of her day (never of course explicitly acknowledged by her), it constituted a direct image of her own. François de Grenaille indeed prescribed the shaping of the daughter as a mother's obligation and grounded maternal power over the daughter in the accomplishment of this duty:

Les femmes ne servent pas seulement à les [les honnêtes filles] former, mais comme elles en prennent le dessein sur elles-mêmes, et que pour produire une fille la mère fait son image; on peut encore dire qu'elles ont le même droit sur leur ouvrage, qu'a un Peintre sur son portrait.[12]

Women serve not only in forming them [virtuous daughters], but since they use themselves as models, and since in order to produce a daughter the mother makes her own image; one can further say that they have the same right over their work as a painter over his self-portrait.

The daughter, then, was understood to be an artifact of the mother's making that served to display the mother's talent, and to which the mother held title. Sévigné's task was not to be easy. She had to persuade an insecure daughter of her competence, gain her confidence, establish conditions conducive to intimacy, and strive for smooth communication within a system that did not guarantee privacy, so as to negotiate successfully the transfer of her imprint.

A week after their separation in 1671, she commented that she had received to date only three of the four letters her daughter had already sent to her as she traveled south, but she offered forceful compliments on the style of those. They are "très bien écrites," "tendres," "naturelles" [very well written, tender, natural], and imbued with a "caractère de vérité" and a "noble simplicité" [character of truth and a noble simplicity] (I, L. 133, p. 154–55). These are the qualities that will be invoked time and again as basic to the felicitous letter. Sévigné's compliments serve not merely to analyze the elements of a good letter, but to encourage the daughter in feeling good about her style, to continue to write, in the same style preferably, but above all, to continue to write.

Again, a week later, Sévigné showers Françoise-Marguerite with compliments on her style, this time voiced in a more directive and insistent fashion:

Vous écrivez extrèmement bien; personne n'écrit mieux. Ne quittez jamais le naturel: votre tour s'y est formé, et cela compose un style parfait. (I, L. 136, p. 161)

You write extremely well; no one writes better. Never give up the natural: your turn of phrase was formed in it, and that composes a perfect style.

These flattering remarks might be understood as just that, were it not for evidence of serious doubt in the daughter of her own writing abilities. Insecurity appears to plague Françoise-Marguerite early on as she attempts to uphold her end of the correspondence. Her mother sought to bolster her daughter's frail ego by insisting on the fine quality of her writing: "Mais d'où vient, ma bonne, que vous craignez qu'une autre lettre efface la vôtre?" (I, L. 149, p. 201) [But from where comes the fear, *ma bonne*, that another letter might efface your own?]. She expresses bewilderment at the daughter's sense of inferiority as a writer/correspondent and seeks to reassure her of her prowess as a storyteller: "Je ne sais pourquoi vous nous dites que vous ne contez pas bien; je ne connais personne qui attache plus que vous" (I, L. 149, p. 201) [I do not know why you tell us that you do not tell stories well; I know no one more engaging than you]. The daughter's self-doubts were potentially inhibiting to the correspondence, so the mother had to work constantly against them, showering her with compliments on her writing at every opportunity merely to ensure the continuance of the exchange. Tacitus was frequently cited as a model of superb writing; Sévigné would liken her daughter's writing to his, formalizing an observation that might also be understood as a subtle directive on appropriate style for Françoise-Marguerite to emulate:

Il y a quelquefois des endroits dans vos lettres qui sont très plaisants, mais il vous échappe des périodes comme dans Tacite. J'ai trouvé cette comparaison; il n'y a rien de plus vrai. (I, L. 270, p. 505)

Sometimes there are parts of your letters which are quite pleasing, but full sentences escape you just as in Tacitus. I found this comparison; there is nothing truer.

While Sévigné was intent upon securing the epistolary exchange by instilling her correspondent with confidence, she was at the same time concerned to form her daughter's prose style, and since she sees fit to comment on sporadic brilliance, it can only be concluded that the daughter's style is not, in her judgment, of consistent quality. This Sévigné associates with apparent effort on the daughter's part; ironically, good writing escapes her in spite of her control. Contrivance produces mediocre writing and is responsible for the unevenness of the daughter's style. This lesson on style is a variation on the theme of the mirror: spontaneity alone can render faithful self-representation and foster the intimacy sought by Sévigné in the exchange.

Sévigné introduced outside corroboration to further validate her own advice to her daughter. Another critical eye, strategically joined to her own, presented a more impartial, and therefore more authoritative, perspective:

> Il [l'abbé Arnauld] me pria l'autre jour de lui montrer un morceau de votre style; son frère lui en dit du bien. En lui montrant, je fus surprise moi-même de la justesse de vos périodes, elles sont quelquefois harmonieuses. Votre style est devenu comme on le peut souhaiter; il est fait et parfait. Vous n'avez qu'à continuer, et vous bien garder de vouloir le rendre meilleur. (I, L. 277, p. 518)

> He [the abbé Arnauld] asked me the other day to show him a sample of your style; his brother spoke well of it to him. In showing him, I was surprised myself by the accuracy of your sentences, they are sometimes harmonious. Your style has become as one might wish it; it is finished and perfect. You have only to continue, and to guard against wanting to improve it further.

Her praise begins on a fairly ambiguous note ("je fus surprise"), as if to deny the vigilance of her own ever alert critical eye, and is couched in guarded ("quelquefois"), anonymously authoritative ("comme *on* peut le souhaiter"), and provisional ("vous n'avez qu'à continuer") terms. Such remarks do not amount to wholehearted endorsement as much as they suggest cautious approval. One can only speculate to what extent Sévigné genuinely applauds Mme de Grignan's style. For herself she eschews any sentences contrived as "périodes" [full sentences] that "sentent l'huile" [are painstaking]. She herself does not aspire to a style "fait et parfait," and the supposed perfection of the daughter's style is ironically called into question by the mother's insistence that the daughter not attempt to improve it further. Since there is nothing "better" than "perfect," the advice is empty and transforms "perfect" into a possibly pejorative term. Sévigné counters, in the effortless rhyme of "fait" and "parfait," the calculated striving for perfection she detects in her daughter's style. That forced effort, with its inhibitions and worries, represses spontaneity and compromises the desired transparency of the epistolary relationship. But the mother's very act of drawing attention to the issue of style implicates the daughter in a self-conscious state as she writes.

Sévigné's daughter appears to have readily absorbed her mother's lessons on writing, and to have dutifully reflected them back to her. In the cultivation of epistolary intimacy between mother and daughter, eloquence had no place:

Vous me dites plaisamment que vous croiriez m'ôter quelque chose en polissant vos lettres. Gardez-vous bien d'y toucher; vous en feriez des pièces d'éloquence. Cette pure nature, dont vous parlez, est précisément ce qui est bon et ce qui plaît uniquement. (I, L. 280, p. 531)

You tell me amusingly that you believe you would be taking something away from me by polishing your letters. Beware of tampering with them; you would make eloquent documents of them. This pure nature you speak of is precisely what is good and what alone pleases.

Sévigné approved her daughter's stance, this echo of her own, and reinforced the valorizing of "nature" over "art" as effecting a more accurate and therefore more pleasing, more satisfying letter.

Sévigné slid easily into the role of teacher and critic in relationship to her daughter, as Bussy did with her. She expressed an easy confidence in herself as writer, evidenced by her sure pronouncements on her daughter's writing. She guided her daughter and contended again and again with Mme de Grignan's greatest block, her lack of confidence:

Ne me dites point de mal de vos lettres. On croit quelquefois que les lettres qu'on écrit ne valent rien, parce qu'on est embarrassé de mille pensées différentes, mais cette confusion se passe dans la tête, pendant que la lettre est nette et naturelle. Voilà comme sont les vôtres. Il y a des endroits si plaisants que ceux à qui je fais l'honneur de les montrer en sont ravis. (I, L. 349, p. 636)

Don't speak badly of your letters. Sometimes one believes that the letters one writes are worth nothing, because one is encumbered by a thousand different thoughts, but this confusion occurs in the mind, while the letter is clear and natural. This is how yours are. There are parts so pleasing that those to whom I do the honor of showing them are delighted by them.

Mme de Grignan may use the tactic of false modesty, as does her mother sometimes, in order to elicit praise, but responses to protestations such as Sévigné's here occur frequently enough to point to a habitual self-deprecating posture on the part of the daughter at least as she relates to her writing mother. The mother failed to see that she herself constituted her daughter's block, that her own confidence occasioned the daughter's lack thereof. To the extent that she occupied the position of authority in the relationship, she dominated it, and the daughter was reduced to seeking footing for herself, alternating between submission and rebellion, locked specularly either way, into a pattern of reaction.

In 1680, after and in spite of nine years of writing, Sévigné continued to counter the daughter's sense of inferiority:

Je n'aime point, ma bonne, que vous disiez que vos lettres sont insipides et sottes; voilà deux mots qui n'ont jamais été faits pour vous. Vous n'avez qu'à penser et à dire, je vous défie de ne pas bien faire; tout est nouveau, tout est brillant, et d'un tour noble et agréable. Reprenez sur moi le trop de louanges que vous me donnez; mettez-les de votre côté. (II, L. 788, p. 1020)

I don't at all like it, *ma bonne,* that you say your letters are insipid and silly; these are two words never meant for you. You have only to think and to speak, I challenge you to not do well; all is new, all is brilliant, and of a noble and agreeable kind. Take back the surfeit of compliments you have paid me, and credit them to your own account.

Evidently this was not merely a writing issue but a problem that permeated the whole of their relationship. The last sentence, a directive seeking to redress the equilibrium of the exchange of compliments, tellingly suggests that Mme de Grignan needs to improve her self-esteem, her self-image, paradoxically, by being less obsequious toward her mother. However, it is not clear that the mother's words really serve to enable this coming to confidence. Sévigné chooses the tactic of negating emphatically rather than erasing discreetly the daughter's self-criticism, thus retextualizing and re-mobilizing, perhaps renewing the trauma of doubt for the daughter, rather than producing the comfort and reassurance ostensibly offered. "Sottes" and "insipides," the daughter's self-disparaging words, are materially mirrored back to her and assume a reality in their echoing that other words and contexts cannot silence. The writing mother knew that, if the imbalance were to become too great between them, the continuation of the epistolary exchange would be threatened. Not merely for the sake of her daughter's feelings, but, just as importantly, for the sake of the *Correspondance,* Mme de Grignan's fragile opinion of herself had to be held together, if not improved. Whether Sévigné's tactics for doing so were the most tactful remains a question in this reading.

There were occasions when Sévigné sharply rebuked her daughter concerning her epistolary comportment. In the following instance, Françoise-Marguerite had apparently committed an indiscretion implicating the family friend Pomponne, and the mother promptly chastised her.[13] Sévigné's strategy on this occasion is complex: she harnesses a male voice of authority to her own, appeals to a sense of devoted obligation in the daughter, solicitously expresses concern for her health in this charged issue, and proceeds, through a subdued imperative to remind Mme de Grignan of her proper place:

J'ai lu votre lettre avec notre cher d'Hacqueville que vous ne sauriez trop aimer et qui gronde de vous voir si emportée; il voudrait que vous imitassiez vos ennemis qui disent des douceurs et donnent des coups de poignard, ou que, du moins, si vous ne voulez pas suivre cette parfaite trahison, vous sussiez mesurer vos paroles et vos ressentiments, que vous allâssiez votre chemin sans vous consumer ni vous faire malade, que vous n'eûssiez point approuvé la guerre déclarée, et surtout que jamais vous ne missiez en jeu M. de Pomponne dans les choses qui vous sont écrites en particulier et dont la source peut aisément se découvrir. (I, L. 341, p. 617)

I read your letter with our dear d'Hacqueville, whom you couldn't love too much and who grumbles to see you so upset; he wishes you would imitate your enemies who say sweet things and then stab people in the back, or that, at least, if you did not want to go along with this perfect betrayal, you would be able to measure your words and your reactions, that you had proceeded without exhausting yourself or making yourself ill, that you had not approved the declaration of war, and above all that you never compromise and risk M. de Pomponne in the things that are written to you in particular and whose source can easily be discovered.

The daughter's letter has been shared with d'Hacqueville, and the exhortation that follows, although penned by Sévigné, is entirely in his name ("il voudrait que . . . ou que . . . que . . . que . . . et surtout que"). An extended imperative reported in the guise of indirect discourse implies at the very least a strong interest in the matter on the part of the reporter, and probably her complete concurrence and complicity. Sévigné must have been as anxious as d'Hacqueville to curb her daughter's outspoken and tempestuous writing behavior—behavior both self-destructive and threatening to others—which threatens to compromise a family ally such as Pomponne, while not at all advancing her cause. It is not clear whether d'Hacqueville or Sévigné is responsible for the precise wording of the injunction. The line "vos ennemis qui disent des douceurs et donnent des coups de poignard" is a masterful aural and scriptoral representation of the discreet sort of betrayal being described and advocated. The breach (k)—reversing d into p, of the literally encoded pact of fidelity (d/d/d/d/d) figures on the level of signifier as well as signified. The felicitous phrasing of the aphorism contributes to the forcefulness of the admonishment. But interestingly, here is a maternal lesson for the daughter in marked contrast to the more usual pleas for sincerity when she is corresponding with the mother. Here Sévigné, in ventriloquist style, exhorts her to repress her anger, to control her spontaneity, to measure her words. It is, however, a call to the daughter to produce a mirror response, recommending that, in this case, she imitate her enemies and turn on them their own tactics.

The detailed way in which this advice is transmitted, suggesting a quotation as nearly verbatim as possible, might be read as an indication of the extent to which Sévigné subscribes to the counsel she is passing on to her daughter. It seems equally plausible, however, that d'Hacqueville's name might serve as a foil to deflect attention from the fact that the advice is actually the mother's. Mme de Grignan may be less likely to react negatively and reject the advice if she thinks it emanates from someone other than her mother, and so Sévigné exploits a third party in order to introduce criticism without jeopardizing the writing relationship. This adjuration also suggests to what extent the mother is held responsible to acculturate her daughter, to integrate her socially, to ensure that her behavior is irreproachable.

Sévigné found fault with her daughter's style again on another occasion when in fact what she was objecting to was her behavior.[14] She attempted to mediate between her friend Retz and Grignan; she found her daughter's haughty dismissal of Retz reprehensible, and threatening to herself as well:[15] "Cela ne vaut pas, en vérité, les tons que vous avez pris" (II, L. 682, p. 667) [It does not warrant, truthfully, the tones you have taken]. Apparently, when the message is to Sévigné's liking, the style in which it is phrased receives praise; in contrast, when the message is displeasing, the style is faulted. The displacement of evaluation of signified— manners—onto that of signifier—manner—functions as a way of conveying positive and negative messages indirectly, a frequent tactic of Sévigné's as she pursued the delicate task of polishing her daughter. Circuitousness, an oblique approach both to shaping her daughter and to contemplating authorship, is the strategy of the writing mother.

The instance of Sévigné's indirect rebuking of Mme de Grignan's indiscreet and potentially damaging inscribed remarks was prompted by a fact that constituted a significant constraint for correspondence by letter during her time. Censorship was actively practiced under Louis XIV. The king's couriers answered to a program of surveillance and containment devised to support the royal system of absolutism.[16] From her early brush with Fouquet's disgrace, Sévigné was already well acquainted with the dangers of correspondence. Although not all of Sévigné's letters were entrusted to the mails (some were carried by friends traveling, others were delivered by servants), various forms and degrees of censorship are evidenced and practiced in her writing.[17]

Sévigné expresses concern for the confidentiality of her letters in transit as they pass through possibly inquisitive and unreliable hands. The letter, as prima facie material, is released to all sorts of interpretive possibilities as it makes its way to its destination, and so Sévigné explictly censors her own writing, inscribing the act by direct allusion to it; and she censors her daughter's letters by controlling the access of third parties to letters received. These are all acts of protecting and ensuring the continuance of the correspondence by seeing to it that the bounds of royal law and personal confidence are respected. In a sense, this awareness of censorship, the specter of the eavesdropper, frames the epistolary conversation, delimiting the bounds of the communicable field.

The relationship of the individual to the state as articulated through the practice of government censorship resonated in the ways individuals related to one another within the system of the postal network. Lack of faith in the confidentiality of letters promoted a practice of self-censorship and encoding. Spelled-out acts of self-restraint at once create an area of deliberate obscurity and call for interpretation, thus reinforcing a relationship of complicitous intimacy that transcends the bounds of the letter while protecting both correspondents from the watchful eye of the state. For example, reporting court gossip to her daughter, Sévigné says of Mme de Monaco and her behavior toward Elisabeth Charlotte de Bavière, Philippe d'Orléans's second wife:

On est seulement un peu fâché de lui voir faire quelquefois à cette Madame-ci les mêmes petites mines et les mêmes petites façons qu'elle faisait à l'autre. Il y a encore eu quelque petite chose; *mais cela ne s'écrit point.* (I, L. 333, p. 602)

One is simply a little annoyed to see her sometimes make the same little faces and little fusses for this Madame as she did for the other. There was another little detail as well; *but that cannot be written.*

Sévigné censors herself here, carefully omitting the source of this bit of commentary, and not telling all, but she can count on her correspondent to enter into the game, to bring a certain prior knowledge to the letter and draw appropriate conclusions from the hints given her. Sévigné's allusion to propriety as she refuses to write explicitly operates both as a cover and as an invitation. She demonstrates respect for the code while she flouts it by making it the explicit agent prohibiting the divulging of "quelque petite chose." Thus she has given enough information to her daughter to suggest the scandalous nature of "chose" and to point without transgressing in the direction of meaning. Her self-censorship serves as an instructive example to her daughter while creating ties of covert understanding between the two women.

Often it is in the simple juxtaposing of key clues that Sévigné transmits risky gossip to her daughter:

Madame de Coulanges a été à Saint-Germain. Elle m'a dit mille bagatelles qui ne s'écrivent point, et qui me font bien entrer dans votre sentiment sur ce que vous me disiez l'autre jour de l'horreur de voir une infidélité. (I, L. 262, p. 480)

Madame de Coulanges has been to Saint-Germain. She reported to me a thousand trifles which cannot be written, and which make me quite agree with your feeling about what you were telling me the other day of the horror of witnessing an infidelity.

She does not address her subject directly here; rather, she sets up contiguities: the testimony of Mme de Coulanges, the location of Saint-Germain, the issue of infidelity, and the allusion to a prior exchange on the subject; and thus transmits a message that, while it eludes possible censors and the latter-day reader as well, can be decoded by her daughter. Prior understanding is reaffirmed by the addressee's participation in the process of making sense of these clues. Censorship, rather than repress communication, breeds intimacy.

Later in the *Correspondance*, a collection of code names proliferates, permitting an at least oblique passage of court gossip from Paris to Provence. Mme de Montespan will be referred to as "Quantova," Mme de Maintenon will be "Maintenant," Mme de Ludres is "Io." While these appelations hardly disguise their referents, they ease the passage of news through unsure territory, at least in the minds of the writers.

Sévigné also used the idea of censorship to emphasize the private nature of her correspondence with her daughter, her judicious control over letters received, thereby encouraging her daughter's confidence:

Parlez-moi de vous, de vos affaires, de ce que vous dites à ceux que vous aimez; tout est sûr, rien ne se voit, rien ne retourne, et c'est justement cela qui me touche, et qui fait ma curiosité et mon attention. (III, L. 896, p. 163)

Speak to me of yourself, of your concerns, of what you say to those you love; everything is safe, nothing is seen, nothing returns, and that's what affects me, what engages my curiosity and my attention.

Sévigné assures her daughter of absolute discretion and invites total confidence. Her great love is the ostensible reason for her insatiable appetite for information about her daughter. She does not trust her daughter to select the salient details that might warrant sending. What is or is not important shall be hers to decide. She will process *vous* confidentially into *moi*. In positing herself as guarantor of the daughter's letters, she also instates herself as censor and the daughter as censored, producing a mimesis of the power relation already in place in the state's mail system.

The brother-sister relationship between Françoise-Marguerite and Charles was mediated by their mother in the same way. Charles, more frequently than not, communicated with his sister only through messages added to his mother's letters to her, so Sévigné was privy to his exchanges. Since she controlled the reception of the daughter's letters, she shared with Charles only the news from his sister that she deemed appropriate for him. The daughter and mother enjoyed a certain complicity in the knowledge of the mother's control over letters from Provence:

Votre frère ne voit de vos lettres que les endroits que je veux bien lui montrer. Je n'ai qu'à lui dire: "Il n'y a rien qui vous puisse divertir." (III, L. 1187, p. 816)

Your brother sees only the parts of your letters that I want to show him. I have only to tell him: "There's nothing here that would amuse you."

Thus censorship can be seen to operate on many levels in the epistolary relationship, both inhibiting and enabling a flow of information between the correspondents, revealing most interestingly the resourceful ways in which Sévigné incorporates and exploits a supposed limitation to further her own interests and secure her writing relationship with her daughter.

What could not be written but only hinted at marks the outer bounds of the permissible. While Sévigné recognized the necessity of self-restraint and resourceful encoding in order to avoid the king's extended eye and professed to practice censorship of her daughter's letters in order to encourage her confidence, she could not bear to think that her daughter might censor family news from her end, and, although she discouraged Françoise-Marguerite's indiscreet and potentially dangerous outbursts of feeling about others, she insisted that she needed to know all that was on her daughter's mind:

Je n'aime point, ma très chère, que vous soyez fâchée de m'avoir mandé l'état de votre fils quand il était mal. Et le moyen de cacher une telle chose? Je haïrais cette dissimulation extrême, et la plume me tomberait des mains. Et le moyen de parler d'autre chose que de ce qui tient au coeur à ce point-là? Pour moi, j'en serais incapable, et j'honore tant la communication des sentiments à ceux que l'on aime que je ne penserais jamais à épargner une inquiétude au préjudice de la consolation que je trouverais à faire part de ma peine à quelqu'un que j'aimerais. Voilà mes manières, voilà *l'humeur de ma mère;* je vous prie que ce soit *l'humeur de ma fille,* et de ne vous point repentir de m'avoir fait sentir vos douleurs, puisque vous m'avez aussi fait sentir votre joie. Et n'est-ce pas là le vrai commerce de l'amitié? Ah! oui, ce l'est, et je n'en connais point d'autre. (II, L. 714, p. 754)

I do not like it at all, my dearest, that you are sorry to have sent me news of the state of your son when he was ill. And the way to hide such a thing? I would hate this extreme dissimulation, and the pen would fall from my hands. And how to speak of things other than what hurts most at the moment? As for me, I would be incapable of doing so, and I so honor the communication of sentiments to those one loves that I would never think of sparing a concern at the cost of the consolation I would find in sharing my pain with someone I loved. Here are my manners, here is *the humor of my mother,* I beg you that it be *the humor of my daughter,* and that you not repent at all for having made me feel your sorrow, since you have also made me feel your joy. And is this not the true conversation of friendship? Ah! yes, this it is, and I know no other.

Anything that preoccupies the daughter at the time of writing, according to the mother, constitutes ipso facto not only appropriate but necessary subject matter for the letter: not to share that would compromise the transparency of the correspondence and cloud the exchange. Intimacy resides in the perfect harmony of the two *humeurs* and is postulated as that much more to be expected in writing relations between the already mutually correlated mother and daughter. Total confidentiality is both a requisite and a consequence of the mirroring relationship.

But, at the other extreme, is the problem of the dearth of news. In Brittany, writing from Les Rochers, Sévigné regularly apologizes for the lack of news or for the triviality of what news there is. Implied in this stance is the notion that she suffers just as much from the dullness of her life as will the correspondent to whom she conveys her impressions of her routine existence. Having transcribed the local gossip, Sévigné comments:

Voilà ce qui s'appelle, ma bonne, des contes à dormir debout. Mais ils viennent au bout de la plume, quand on est en Bretagne et qu'on n'a pas autre chose à dire. (I, L. 189, p. 314)

Here are what are called, *ma bonne*, stories to put you to sleep standing up. But they come to the pen when one is in Brittany and has nothing else to say.

Ultimately, Sévigné acknowledges that, for lack of other topics, she is herself most conspicuously the subject in these country letters. Stripped of the distractions of Paris life that so often furnished the necessary circumlocutions for her maternal lessons, she falls back more often on readings, nature, and self-portraiture as vehicles for projecting her maternal self and performing her mirroring duty.

As the rhythm of exchange established itself, Sévigné distinguished between letters of response, news letters, and those that simply kept the flow going:[18]

Cette lettre du vendredi est sur la pointe d'une aiguille, car il n'y a point de réponse à faire et, pour moi, je ne sais point de nouvelles. (I, L. 157, p. 223)

This Friday letter could fit on the head of a pin, for there is no response to make, and, as for me, I don't know any news.

This was to be an ongoing theme throughout the *Correspondance*; as late as 1694 she would still be inventively lamenting a dearth of news:

Ma bonne, je suis honteuse des pauvretés que je vous mande. Je ne sais point nourrir notre commerce. Je n'ai
> Pas un seul petit morceau
> De mouche ou de vermisseau.
> (III, L. 1295, p. 1028)

Ma bonne, I am ashamed of the scraps I send you. I do not know how to nourish our exchange. I have

Not one little morsel
Of a fly or an earthworm

As if to compensate for meager news offerings and to ornament her apologies, Sévigné deploys a few verses from La Fontaine. She thus shows that she knows how to "nourish" her letter and demonstrates her trust that any text is better than no text at all. The association of the exchange of information with nourishment—of the letter, of the relationship—figuratively reproduces the originary symbol of the relation, the umbilical cord. As with salon conversation, the letter often serves a purely phatic function, keeping open the lines of communication by making them function, even when empty. So, more urgently, the maternal letter insists on the primacy of the exchange, maintaining the relation of the cord, news or no news.

The mother seeks to nourish her letter with news to pass on to the daughter, thus ceaselessly activating the umbilical relation, and affirming her maternal role: "Je laisse là ma lettre; je m'en vais faire un tour de ville pour voir si je n'apprendrai rien qui vous puisse divertir" (II, L. 527, p. 341) [I am breaking my letter off here; I am going to take a walk in town to see if I can't learn of anything that might amuse you]. She acknowledges her reliance on extraneous material to secure and hold the epistolary devotion of her daughter. Her bits of news and gossip function as placating and seductive offerings; her own creative prose, on the other hand, she often treats as a form of self-indulgence. She probably had to pay social calls in any case, but rather than separate or oppose the two activities, she associates them, and rather than give the social calls priority, she makes them accessory to the letter and thus turns ordinary life into maternal devotion.

As intent as Sévigné was on inculcating in her daughter certain attitudes toward epistolary writing, eschewing the guidelines and models of the *manuels* and *secrétaires*—those false mirrors—she came to recognize the origins and purposes behind formulaic conventions. The actual experience of distance and waiting brought home to her the full meaning of such pat phrases: "Quand on est fort éloignés, on ne se moque plus des lettres qui commencent par 'J'ai reçu la vôtre'" (I, L. 133, pp. 155–56) [When one is quite far away, one no longer mocks letters that begin with "I received yours"]. The commonplace of acknowledgment, motivated by the material constraints of the correspondence situation, provides an ideal showplace for Sévigné's virtuosity. She exploits the conventional as pretext for innovation: she personalizes and thus reinvents, while reinscribing and reinforcing tradition:

Me revoilà dans les lamentations du prophète Jérémie. Je n'ai reçu qu'un paquet cette semaine, et voilà l'autre perdu. (I, L. 212, p. 368)

Here I am again in the lamentations of the prophet Jeremiah. I received only one package this week, and now the other one is lost.

The novel comparison of her own inscribed complaints with those of a sacred text, the Book of Lamentations, recuperates the drabness of her common plight; it elevates both her suffering and her text to dramatic heights. It is tempered nicely, however, with just a hint of irony, since this is evidently not the first ("me revoilà") nor, most likely, the last of such moments of crisis in the epistolary relationship. Sévigné articulates a rhetoric of the letter that is grounded in the contingency of the communicatory purpose and moment, but which follows certain general guidelines that derive from the esthetics and practice of her social milieu. The cult of the *naturel* reigns among the elite as they claim and exercise a privileged relationship to the world, and social ease sets the standards according to which texts and behavior alike are assessed. Nevertheless, fixed epistolary conventions develop in response to the realities of the corresponding situation. In acknowledging these structural limitations while improvising on them, Sévigné at once mocks the prevailing etiquette, admits to its necessity, and prescribes a more authentic manner to her daughter.

She repeatedly disdains the "style à cinq sols"; empty formulas subvert the purpose of corresponding, substituting cliché for truth.[19] Conventions alienate correspondents or falsify their relations rather than bring them together. When Françoise-Marguerite is not well enough to write herself, her secretary, "la petite Deville," must be reminded not to fall into platitudes:

Faites écrire la petite Deville et empêchez-la de donner dans *la justice de croire* et dans *les respectueux attachements*. Qu'elle me parle de vous, et quoi encore? de vous et toujours de vous. (I, L. 162, p. 247)

Make the little Deville write, and prevent her from going into *the justice of believing* and *the respectful affections*. She should speak to me of you, and what else? of you and always you.

While this guideline is directed to Mme de Grignan's companion, it applies just as forcefully to her, when she is well enough to wield her own pen.

Sévigné objected early on in the correspondence to the formal way in which her daughter addressed her, resenting the impersonal tone set by such formulas:

Je hais les dessus de vos lettres où il y a: *Madame la marquise de Sévigné;* appelle-moi *Pierrot*. Les autres sont aimables, et donnent une disposition tendre à lire le reste. (I, L. 230, p. 407)[20]

I hate the envelopes of your letters where there is written: *Madame la marquise de Sévigné;* call me *Pierrot*. The others are agreeable and tenderly dispose one to read the rest.

What Sévigné finds objectionable in her daughter's formal posturing is that their supposedly already intimate relationship is misrepresented and thereby actually threatened with deterioration by its epistolary formulation. As if to underscore her concern with maintaining the intimacy of the relationship, she words her jesting command in the more familiar *tu* form; the message comes across as that much more urgent since it is a unique aberration from the *vous* form of address consistently used throughout all of the other letters. It also points up the inherent contradiction of her desire: that one person should be in a position to order the other signals an uneven footing that precludes the possibility of intimacy and underscores instead the power relationship that obtains between the two parties.

Sévigné adapted her attitude toward epistolary conventions to situations as they presented themselves. She recognized the need to play to audiences when her letters had specific pragmatic goals, and she was well aware of the role that epistolary conventions play in strategies of address. She knows that certain protocols can be useful in eliciting a positive reception. She compliments her daughter on her success in composing such a letter:

C'est un chef d'oeuvre en sa manière que la lettre que vous avez écrite à l'abbé Charrier; elle était vraiment difficile car le sujet vous manquait un peu, mais vous avez si bien employé *l'abbé de Guimperle, Mme de Sévigné, le fils de M. Charrier*, et *Mme de Grignan*, qu'il n'y a pas un mot qui ne porte et qui ne soit nécessaire. (III, L. 1198, p. 844)

It's a masterpiece in its own way, the letter you wrote to the abbé Charrier; it was really difficult for you didn't have much of a topic, but you deployed *the abbé de Guimperle, Mme de Sévigné, the son of M. Charrier*, and *Mme de Grignan* so well that there is not a word which does not matter and is not necessary.

The letter in question is Mme de Grignan's response to a communication from Charrier; its tone is presumably in keeping with that set by his (see III, L. 1187, p. 816). If the convention of obsequious naming plays such an important role, it serves no doubt as a reflection of Charrier's predilection for such. Mme de Grignan astutely perceives the need in this instance to cater to his taste, to set a certain social dynamic in action by the careful juxtaposing of the names cited, to mirror back to him the world organized as he wants to see it. The ultimate requirement is that a letter be well received, and so the convention of naming, and any other that might ensure this, meets with Sévigné's approval. Such strategies of writing are invoked and explicitly encouraged for purposes of social maneuvering with others, but categorically banned from exchanges between the mother and daughter.

However, within that writing relationship, Sévigné herself attempted to innovate and establish certain conventions that would operate as a sort of shorthand: she makes use of marks of emphasis to draw attention to and indicate her desire for a response on a particular issue in her letter. In attempting to initiate this practice, she is obliged to explain the function of these marks, to cue her daughter in on their significance and purpose:

Il est vrai que j'aime mes *petites raies*. Elles donnent de l'attention. Elles font faire des réflexions, des réponses. Ce sont quelquefois des épigrammes, des satires. Enfin, on en fait ce qu'on veut. (III, L. 1050, p. 457)

It's true that I like my *little underlinings*. They draw attention. They call for reflections to be made, they prompt answers. They are sometimes epigrams, satires. In the end, one makes of them what one will.

These marks attest to Sévigné's uncertainty about the power of written language to convey adequately the greater weight and importance of certain words among others. The "petites raies" do duty for intonation and reproduce the tone and circumstances of oral communication or conversation. Sévigné's resort to this secondary system of signifying indicates her lack of trust in the written word alone. It also indicates the extent to which she endeavors to control the reception of her letter and structure its response— her daughter's letter.

The passage quoted above seems to indicate a casual attitude. Sévigné merely speculates as to how her underlined remarks might be interpreted. She suggests discreetly that they prompt answers ("font faire des réponses"); and in so doing, she offers them as gentle imperatives. She then recognizes that people make of them what they will. First comes the suggestion that the little underlinings function self-evidently, followed then by the observation that they do not since people react to them as they please. This juxtaposition can be read as Sévigné's attempt to give an order without seeming to do so, to make her wishes clear by treating them as if they were autonomous fact, minimizing her dependence on the addressee as the agent necessary to actualize her wishes. This presentation is both an expression of wishful thinking and another instance of indirectly exercised authority.

It is followed and intensified a few letters later when Sévigné assigns an explicit function to the underlining: "Mes *petites raies* font trouver les endroits où il faut que vous répondiez" (III, L. 1077, p. 523) [My *little underlinings* call attention to the passages to which you must respond]. Her earlier, more oblique comments have obviously not succeeded in eliciting the informative responses she had in mind, and she finds herself obliged to spell out her strategy. A few months later, she gives a direct order: "Répondez à mes *petites raies*" (III, L. 1120, p. 623) [Respond to my *little underlinings*]. We have gone from wishful thinking to direct imperative. Her project for discreetly controlling the production of particular responses to her letter has failed.

The "petites raies" are ostensibly meant to clarify and enhance the message of the text, but the text has to be engaged and their meaning spelled out, in order to decode them. The failure is attributable to the one element of the *Correspondance* over which Sévigné has the least and wants the most control: her addressee-daughter-mirror. The early statement, "on en fait ce qu'on veut," proves to have been accurate and even prophetic. Sévigné endeavors to control and shape her world in writing, by refusing, reinventing, exploiting, and initiating conventions, but that world, in the person of her daughter, persists in eluding her.

Sévigné's disdain for received conventions appears to stem not only from her sensibilities as a self-conscious writer or her attempts to forge a reliable channel of genuine information between herself and her daughter, but also from an acute awareness of the correlations between styles of comportment and styles of writing—manners and manner. Affectation or insincerity in the one translate directly into the other. Mlle du Plessis, with her contrived airs and ways, was a regular target of Sévigné's sharp wit. Since Mme de Grignan also had known her, Sévigné could evoke an appreciation of her relational antics by applying just a few brush strokes in a letter:

Mlle du Plessis laisse périr toutes les affaires qu'elle a à Vitré, et ne veut pas y mettre le pied, de peur de me donner de la jalousie de sa nouvelle amie; et même l'autre jour, pour me donner un entier repos, elle m'en dit beaucoup de mal. (I, L. 172, p. 269)

Mlle du Plessis is neglecting all the business she has in Vitry, and does not want to set foot there, for fear of making me jealous of her new friend; and just the other day, to give me complete reassurance, she spoke very badly of her.

That writing mirrors behavior, that one style governs both manifestations of the individual, is particularly emphasized in Sévigné's remarks on Mme de Bagnols, sister of the wife of her cousin Coulanges, and sometime object of her son Charles's affections. Mme de Bagnols's writing situation, faithful to and regulated by the rhythms of the mails, was uncomfortably similar to Sévigné's own, and Sévigné took pains to distance herself from this caricatural image of herself (II, L. 592, n. 4, p. 1337). Sévigné reacted violently to Mme de Bagnols' extreme affectation and incorporated her critique as a salutary corrective for her own tendencies to excess:

Le voyage de La Bagnols est assuré. Vous serez témoin de ses langueurs, de ses rêveries, qui sont des applications à rêver. Elle se redresse comme en sursaut, et Mme de Coulanges lui dit: "Ma pauvre soeur, vous ne revez point du tout." Pour son style, il m'est insupportable, et me jette dans des grossièretés, de peur d'être comme elle. Elle me fait renoncer à la délicatesse, à la politesse, crainte de donner dans ses tours de passe-passe. Comme vous dites, cela est triste de devenir paysanne. *On sent qu'on serait digne de ne pas vous déplaire, par l'envie qu'on en a,* et cent autres babioles que je sais quelquefois par coeur, et que j'oublie tout d'un coup. Nous appelons cela des *chiens du Bassan;* ils sont enragés à force d'être devenus méchants. (II, L. 598, p. 522)

The voyage of La Bagnols is assured. You will be witness to her languors, to her reveries, which are attempts at dreaming. She sits up with a start, and Mme de Coulanges says to her: "My dear sister, you aren't dreaming at all." As for her style, it's unbearable to me, and sends me into vulgarities, for fear of being like her. She makes me renounce delicacy, politeness, for fear of falling into her conjuring tricks. As you say, it is unfortunate to become a peasant. *One feels one would be worthy of not displeasing you, by the desire one has to do so,* and a hundred other baubles that I sometimes know by heart, and all of a sudden forget. We call this *the Bassan's dogs;* they are rabid as a result of having become nasty.

The sharpness of Sévigné's scorn for such behavior and writing suggests a tacit recognition of distressing parallels and affirms a determination to avoid such a simultaneously calculated and enslaved, and consequently ridiculous demeanor. Mme de Bagnols (along with a few other recurring figures, Mme de Ludres, for example) will be the object of Sévigné's relentless and distancing attack on pretention. Her coiffures, her sentiments, her gestures, her words, her slavish subscription to fashion, will be a constant pretext for cautionary derision in Sévigné's writing to her daughter: "La Bagnols m'écrit aussi mille douceurs tortillonnées" (II, L. 605, p. 543) [La Bagnols writes me a thousand twisted sweetnesses as well].

When Sévigné makes excuses for her own unpolished letters, it is almost with pride, indicating that they are vastly preferable, in their accidental and therefore reliable nature, to deliberate and obfuscating attempts at elegant self-presentation: "Si vous trouvez mille fautes dans cette lettre, excusez-les; car le moyen de la relire?" (II, L. 415, p. 63) [If you find a thousand mistakes in this letter, excuse them; for how to find a way to reread it?]. Her critique of others' writings and behavior, as well as being self-corrective, served as forceful reminders to the daughter of the bounds of comportmental and epistolary propriety.

Sévigné entertained a double standard with regard to the question of prolixity in letters. On the one hand, the specific act of story-telling recommended brevity and rigorous pertinence;[21] on the other, the act of communicating among friends, and particularly with her daughter, demanded and offered a proliferation of detail. While such expansiveness was a nuisance in letters from others and labeled a mark of inferior story-telling, it was treasured coming from her daughter and friends close to her. The double standard is ultimately resolved in favor of prolixity, longer letters to Mme de Grignan englobing tight and well-told stories. Occasionally one floats relatively free—for example, the double recounting of Vatel's suicide (I, L. 159, p. 234; L. 160, p. 235)—but, for the most part Sévigné simply writes incessantly and ornaments her extravagantly long letters with anecdotes within which the economy of narration is respected. She thus signals parts of letters that call for sharing and collective appreciation. These fragments of Paris gossip or entertaining banter can be socially exploited by her daughter and bartered in her circle for attention and prestige.

Sévigné slowly builds permission to write expansively and, as she does so, establishes an imbalance of volume in her exchange with her daughter that will reflect and further aggravate an imbalance in the relationship. The mother's availability to the exchange is enormous, whereas the daughter's (wife, mother, mistress of the château de Grignan) is only partial. That availability, measurable in time, also translates into emotional availability. The mother's affection is excessive in relation to the economy of patriarchal family feelings. In fact, the widowed maternal mother-in-law, once the marriage is transacted—the father's daughter and goods transferred to the next holder—is in danger of becoming altogether superfluous and excessive. Sévigné will actively work at maintaining a place for herself by insisting on her claims to her daughter's affection and will be continually financially indispensable to her daughter's new household as well. The economy of family affect and its workings will be reflected in the elaboration of an economy of narrative.

Early on, Sévigné articulated an esthetics of brevity in narration. She ended one of her informative letters to Pomponne on the progress of Fouquet's trial thus:

Adieu, je sens que l'envie de causer me prend. Je ne veux pas m'y abandonner; il faut que le style des relations soit court. (I, L. 59, p. 56)

Goodbye, I feel the desire to chat taking hold of me. I do not want to abandon myself to it; the style of narration must be short.

Although she already acknowledges that her personal inclination is toward prolixity, and that it requires an effort on her part to resist the temptation, she breaks off, with an impersonal dictum ("il faut que"). It is not altogether clear whether she has conveniently summoned up this rule to provide an appropriate closure to the letter, or whether there is actual conviction behind it. She later complacently reinvokes the same rule in a concluding self-critique of a tidy story presented in the guise of a letter of recommendation for Picard, an overseer leaving her employ in disgrace (commonly known to Sévigné scholars as her "lettre des foins"). To Coulanges she writes:

> Voilà l'histoire en peu de mots. Pour moi, j'aime les narrations où l'on ne dit que ce qui est nécessaire, où l'on ne s'écarte point ni à droite, ni à gauche, où l'on ne reprend point les choses de si loin; enfin, je crois que c'est ici, sans vanité, le modèle des narrations agréables. (I, L. 185, p. 304)

> Here is the story in few words. As for me, I like narrations in which one says only what is necessary, in which one strays neither to the right, nor the left, where one does not take up the story too far from the point; in short, I think that here, without vanity, is the model of agreeable narrations.

In the first instance, she refuses her own pleasure and gives as her reason a tenet of good writing. To judge by the prevalent literary style of her day (exemplified in the writings of Racine, La Rochefoucauld, La Fontaine), succinctness is indeed prized. But Sévigné, writing news and telling stories, must also be convinced that her correspondents are eager to receive as much as she can give. Thus, while Sévigné nods and adheres in certain instances to principles of good style, she admits the difficulty she has in doing so. Such a strategy can be read to work toward ensuring that her correspondent will encourage her tendency toward prolixity rather than approve her orthodoxy. She is building public permission to write in her own style: that is, as much as she likes, and as she likes.

In the second instance, the letter about the uncooperative Picard, Sévigné, with no little satisfaction, preempts the addressee/reader's right to evaluate her just-told story. She proffers her own *art poétique* in a final pirouette as valorizing standard for the preceding narration. The generation of both performance and evaluation of that performance by the same pen underscores the self-sufficiency of the textual artifact and its maker. However, this is narrative with a purpose: it is a damning letter of recommendation for the uncooperative Picard as he leaves her employ. Rather than end her letter on the negative albeit humorous note ("Si vous le voyez, ne le recevez point, ne le protégez point" [I, L. 185, p. 304] [If you see him, do not receive him, do not protect him], Sévigné draws attention away from the unpleasant purpose of the letter and to its winning way. Her claims for the exemplary nature of her narrative here have as much to do with the purpose to which it is put as with principles of writing.

Nonetheless, be they tactical or sincere, her statements on good writing stand in contrast to her own usual practice, which is emphatically and by her own admission not laconic, and the writing pact she establishes with her daughter.

Leisure and pleasure appear to be the sole principles regulating that exchange and set the only limit for the amount of detail in their letters. Here again, Sévigné evokes a double standard: showering her daughter with news, she reminds her of their particular agreement to tell all and signals the distinction of their correspondence, as she reiterates the nuisance of prolixity from other less intimate friends:

Vous savez que nous avons réglé que l'on hait autant les détails des gens que l'on n'aime guère qu'on les aime de ceux que l'on aime beaucoup. (I, L. 140, p. 173)

You know we have agreed that one hates details from people one scarcely likes just as much as one loves those from people one likes very much.

She adds, a few letters later, already conscious of the imbalance developing in their exchange, barely a month into the separation:

Voilà bien des lanternes, et je ne sais rien de vous . . . Les moindres circonstances sont chères de ceux qu'on aime parfaitement, autant qu'elles sont ennuyeuses des autres; nous l'avons dit mille fois, et cela est vrai. (I, L. 144, p. 184)

Here is a lot of nonsense, and I know nothing of you . . . The least news is cherished from those one loves perfectly, just as it is boring from others; we have said it a thousand times, and it is true.

There is a strong note of insistence on the contractual nature of their agreement to this truth, already well established between them in an evidentiary past, reinscribed and marked here by the use of the first person plural pronoun. Moreover, it is implied that this is a universal truth, shared with that collective authority, *on*.

Throughout the correspondence, Sévigné reminds her daughter how she prizes details and continually solicits them: "Parlez-moi beaucoup de vous. Tous les détails sont admirables quand l'amitié est à un certain point" (II, L. 423, p. 96) [Speak to me a great deal of yourself. All details are admirable when affection is at a certain point]. The terms "détail" and "amitié" recur frequently and point to a third term, intimacy. Sévigné continues to question the propriety of minutiae, and to apologize for excess when she considers her letters in the context of writing as opposed to that of communication, but she never renounces her own or her daughter's right, indeed obligation, to share as much as possible of themselves in their writing. Details serve to render friends as present to each other as possible. Just as a letter represents an attempt to compensate for an absence, to fill a void, so the detailed letter goes further in the same vein and suggests a commitment to representation as compensation. Mother and daughter must hold up as much as possible of themselves to the mirror.

In order to conjure up her daughter, Sévigné needs detail as grist for her imagination, the only faculty, coupled with memory, that can render her daughter in absentia to her:

Je trouve de la commodité de connaître tous les lieux où sont les gens à qui on pense toujours; ne savoir où les prendre fait une obscurité qui blesse l'imagination. (I, L. 398, p. 750)

I take comfort in knowing all the places where the people are who are always on one's mind; not knowing where to find them creates a dimness which offends the imagination.

What details allow her to do, as well as envision her daughter, is to write and thereby perform her reflecting function. She can recreate not only her own but her daughter's universe textually, appropriate the daughter's world in detail, and write herself into it. An example of such appropriation occurs when Sévigné comments at length on an event about which her daughter has just written to her. Mme de Grignan's story of her near-drowning in the Rhone close to the Avignon bridge is rewritten in the answering letter from her mother, who includes in her version her own reaction to the horrifying event: "j'en frissonne, et m'en suis réveillée avec des sursauts dont je ne suis pas la maîtresse" (I, L. 141, p. 176) [I shiver from it, and wake up from it with starts I cannot control]. The story is no longer of the daughter's accident, but of the mother's anguish upon learning of it. The details of the daughter's letter feed the mother's imagination, allowing her to rewrite the story and refocus the account. The daughter is at once mirrored and upstaged in the mother's text.[22]

Questions of prolixity and detail, ways of fetishizing the mother's textual body and incorporating the daughter's, signal the mode that permeates and justifies this proliferation of writing: *jouissance*. Sévigné recognizes early on that the ostensibly consolatory and compensatory act of writing to her daughter generates its own pleasure: "Je vous écris, ma bonne, avec plaisir, quoique je n'aie rien à vous mander" (I, L. 184, p. 301) [I write you, *ma bonne*, with pleasure, although I have no news to send you]. The discovery of the joys of writing, uncommitted to transmitting news, untethered by other social constraints pertaining in writing relations with others, decided Sévigné on her course of being. With her daughter, "ma bonne," as addressee, Sévigné could direct her attention to herself, could explore herself and her world through writing. As she assumes an image in her writing, we are witness to a Lacanian "flutter of jubilant activity." [23] She discovers writing as mirror, and, in writing to her daughter, the mirror least clouded by otherness. The degree of narcissistic identification of mother to daughter is such that at times she can be read to be writing herself intrasubjectively to herself rather than addressing intersubjectively an "other."

That she commonly calls her daughter "ma bonne" is telling in this regard. She uses the expression exclusively with her daughter.[24] Her other friends are always "ma chère," "ma belle," "ma très chère," etcetera. The only other figure to be evoked in remotely similar fashion is the abbé de Coulanges—"le bien bon"—and I suggest there is a reason behind this as well.

In the *Dictionnaire de l'Académie française* of 1695, the term *bonne* is not included. However, the entries from a variety of dictionaires listed below suggest an evolving nuance of definition for the term, formalized through allusion to its stabilized usage by early in the eighteenth century, a little over a decade after Sévigné's death (my emphasis is indicated by boldface type):

Dictionnaire de l'Académie française, 6th ed., tome 1 (Paris: Firmin Didot frères, 1835); under **bon**: *mon bon ami, ma bonne amie* ou simplement *ma bonne*. **Termes d'amitié** ou de bienveillance qu'on emploie surtout entre égaux ou **de supérieur à inférieur**" [Terms of friendship or benevolence used especially between equals or from superior to inferior].

Dictionnaire de la langue française, Emile Littré, ed. (Paris: Librairie Hachette, 1863); under **bonne**: "1. **femme de service; fille chargée de soigner un enfant.** étym. bon, bonne dans le sens de femme de service est **un terme d'amitié de la part des enfants ou des maîtres**" [woman in service; girl responsible for caring for a child; a term of friendship used by children or masters in a household].

Dictionnaire alphabétique et analogique de la langue française, Paul Robert, ed. (Paris: Presses Universitaires de France, 1953); under **bonne**: "nom féminin, [used in] 1708 [by] Saint-Simon: **terme d'affection donné aux domestiques par les enfants**" [term of affection given to household servants by the children of the household].

Nouveau Dictionnaire Etymologique du français. Jacqueline Picoche, ed. (Paris: Hachette-Tchou, 1971); under **bonne**: "XVIIIe siècle, substantif féminin: à l'origine **terme d'affection employé par les enfants à l'egard de la domestique qui s'occupait d'eux**" [term of affection used by children to refer to the servant who took care of them] (my emphasis).

This traced chronology of the shifting of meaning for the erstwhile adjective and its passage into nominalization suggests that, even as Sévigné used the term, it was already carrying the connotations that would crystallize in the above dictionary definitions. The combined connotation of the term's semes—affectionate mode of address for a nursemaid by the child in her charge, socially her superior if pragmatically her inferior— a relationship of patronizing dependence, suggests a way of considering the mirror relationship between mother and daughter as epitomized in the mother's mode of address.

The child, "ma bonne," is charged with the well-being of and ministers to her mother.[25] The mother-child relies on the good services of the daughter as nursemaid to guide her through her coming to self in writing. It is as if the little girl–mother stood at her mirror (her writing) rejoicing in her image, with the watchful *bonne* on the other side of the mirror, or just behind her, or next to her, wherever she is needed (and this the *bonne* is charged to know), to facilitate the coming to self of her charge. The little girl–mother, although dependent, governs the situation and enjoys the right to say whether the *bonne* is performing a good job. The *bonne* has to anticipate and internalize the little girl–mistress's every need and wish, and, above all, to be there for her. Thus while the child indulges in the necessary act of self-construction, the *bonne* stands by, attentive and responsive to her needs, doing her job. None of Sévigné's other correspondents are addressed in the same manner, nor do they ever call Sévigné "ma bonne."[26] Hence it is safe to conclude that the form of address "ma bonne" does particularize the mother-daughter relationship. It points to a specific dynamic operative in the way the mother relates to her daughter and frames the daughter's possible modes of response.[27]

Thus Sévigné's pleasure at writing to her daughter is part of "the lengthy process of learning to differentiate herself from her own daughter, her simulacrum, whose presence she is forced to confront"[28] and whose presence she must use in order to imagine herself. Sévigné's *jouissance* will hence be particularly marked in writing to her daughter:

Ce plaisir d'écrire est uniquement pour vous, car, à tout le reste du monde, on voudrait avoir écrit, et c'est parce qu'on le doit. (II, L. 417, p. 77)

This pleasure in writing is only for you, for, to everyone else one would like to have already written, and then only because one has to.

It is through this relationship of enabling specularity that Sévigné can actually pass into the realm of the symbolic, construing a shape through scriptoral representation, and delighting in the self-confirming image refracted.

The problem with this arrangement, so convenient and indeed necessary to the mother, is the total availability of the mother to this relationship since it is fundamentally a relationship to her self (a relationship of the realm of the imaginary), vital to her own self-apprehension, as opposed to the daughter's distraction now that she has entered into another relationship and assumed the role of wife. She is now under obligation to apply her training and to serve as mirror to her husband.[29] When that same woman is still engaged in serving her mother specularly (still under obligation on the filial training ground), and the mother continues to demand of her that service, tension and ambivalence necessarily characterize the wife/daughter's response to the situation, and in particular to the mother.

Discussions of leisure point to the imbalance in the relationship. Mme de Grignan's attentions are divided as she is expected to meet her obligations as daughter and as wife, doubly indentured, and the mother ruefully contemplates her displacement in the daughter's specularizing self:

Mais, hélas! ma bonne, vous n'avez pas de ces loisirs-là. J'écris tranquillement et je ne comprends pas que vous puissiez me lire de même. Je ne vois pas de moment où vous soyez à vous. Je vois un mari qui vous adore, qui ne peut se lasser d'être auprès de vous, et qui peut à peine comprendre son bonheur. (I, L. 141, p. 174)

But, alas! *ma bonne,* you do not have these sorts of leisures. I write peacefully and I do not understand how you could read me in the same way. I see that you don't have a moment to yourself. I see a husband who adores you, who cannot tire of being with you, and who can barely comprehend his own happiness.

While she seems to be congratulating herself on her own leisure and pitying her daughter because of her lack thereof—for having no time for her self/her mother (it being assumed that if the daughter did have time for her self, her thoughts would turn automatically to her mother), the pity does not appear to transfer but remains with the mother. She recognizes that the daughter has deflected her mirroring activities onto her husband and feels deprived of specular attention herself.

Sévigné needs to know that her daughter is available to serve her in her mirroring capacity, or she has difficulty in writing. She acknowledges the dubious hold she has on her daughter's attentions since the daughter is caught up in playing mirror to her husband:

Je ne veux point vous écrire davantage aujourd'hui, quoique mon loisir soit grand. Je n'ai que des riens à vous mander; c'est abuser d'une lieutenante générale qui tient les Etats, et qui n'est pas sans affaires. Cela est bon quand vous êtes dans votre palais d'Apollidon. (I, L. 207, p. 361)

I do not want to write any more to you today, although my leisure is great. I have only trifles to send you; this would be taking advantage of a lieutenant general's wife in the middle of the Estates Assembly, and who is not without concerns. It is good for when you are in your Apollidon's palace.

This reluctance to write when she feels insufficiently attended to gradually gives way to pleasure in writing as she attends to herself and as she replaces the actual daughter with the fictional one whom she invents in the process of producing her own text. Within the letter, setting up her implied daughter as nursemaid to give her the safe space needed, she established her mirror, developed and experienced her own pleasure as writer.

Sévigné quickly discovered the pleasures of writing as she sought solace in writing to her daughter. Initially, to keep herself occupied, while she waited for letters, she wrote. Although occasionally she would claim that lack of news from her daughter, a missing or delayed letter, inhibited her own inclination to write, the evidence of the *Correspondance* attests that she found in writing, and most specifically in writing to her daughter, a comforting way of coping with her solitude:

> Je suis bien assurée qu'il viendra des lettres (je ne doute point que vous m'ayez écrit), mais je les attends, et je ne les ai pas. Il faut se consoler, et s'amuser en vous écrivant. (I, L. 137, p. 163)

> I am quite assured that letters will come (I do not doubt you have written me), but I am awaiting them, and do not have them. One must console oneself, and amuse oneself in writing to you.

Thus she justifies her unsolicited writing. Initially, she was reluctant to admit to her daughter that writing afforded her pleasure. In her early letters, she usually couches her joy in one of two negative ways: either the pleasure of writing is only by way of consolation for the daughter's absence, or the pleasure of writing to the daughter is contrasted with all of the other obligatory sorts of letter writing. It is almost as if Sévigné feared her daughter's resentful jealousy of her independent satisfaction, and so had to insist that writing was always inadequate compensation for the daughter's presence. Sévigné was aware at some level that the real daughter was being supplanted in her mind by the inscribed daughter, and that there was danger for the continued correspondence in the production of tension between the fictional daughter and the daughter addressed.

That Sévigné professes to be constantly thinking of her daughter serves to justify her decision to write at will, for she is thus simply committing to paper something of that mental and affective activity that would be taking place in any case, even if she were not writing:

> C'est que je me soucie beaucoup de vous, que j'aime à vous entretenir à toute heure, et que c'est la seule consolation que je puisse avoir présentement. Je suis aujourd'hui toute seule dans ma chambre, par l'excès de ma mauvaise humeur. Je suis lasse de tout: je me suis fait un plaisir de dîner ici, et je m'en fais un de vous écrire hors de propos. (I, L. 141, p. 174)

It's just that I am very concerned about you, that I like to converse with you all the time, and it's the only consolation I can have now. I am all alone in my room today, because of the excess of my bad mood. I am tired of everything: I took pleasure in dining here, and I take pleasure in writing to you out of turn.

Breaking out of the constraining rhythm of exchange, and writing "out of turn" simply for the pleasure it affords—this signals the discovery of writing as refuge and vocation. Here we see the beginnings of Sévigné's *lettres de provision*.[30]

When Sévigné writes out of turn, out of synchrony, disregarding the balance of flow, disrupting the tacit turn-taking agreement characteristic of a correspondence situation, the nature of her epistolary project is transformed from an other-oriented endeavor into a self-oriented enterprise. It is as if, in her writing, Sévigné produced a splitting of self that transferred the mirroring relation from her daughter to her writing. The consequence is the inscription of epistolary excess, an eloquent excess, bespeaking maternal devotion, which will inveigle witnesses to the mother-daughter correspondence, and at once exclude and overwhelm the daughter.

Sévigné appears to acknowledge that there is a self-indulgent and inappropriate dimension to her writing behavior, harmful to her correspondent when she simply writes at will, rather than in turn:

J'abuse de vous, ma chère bonne. J'ai voulu aujourd'hui me permettre cette lettre d'avance; mon coeur en avait besoin. Je n'en ferai pas une coutume. (I, L. 141, p. 175)

I take advantage of you, *ma chère bonne*. I decided today to allow myself this letter in advance; my heart needed it. I won't make a habit of it.

Her vow not to make a habit of excessive writing was one she could not and did not keep.

Nor was Sévigné always able to keep her addressee paramount in her concerns as she wrote. On one occasion, she invented a clever turn to convey an image of the great crowd gathered in town for the assembly of the Estates of Brittany, but, not sure whether she had already communicated it to her daughter, she sent it again, risking the embarrassment of repeating herself: "Etait-ce à vous que je mandais l'autre jour qu'il semblait que tous les pavés fussent métamorphosés en gentilshommes?" (I, L. 190, p. 317) [Was it to you that I sent word the other day that it seemed that all the cobblestones had metamorphosed into gentlemen?]. The focus of the question is not at all the addressee, since Sévigné cannot seem to remember to whom she has sent the clever thought. The *vous* is denied importance and individuality; it is here merely one of many correspondents, one of many writing pretexts. Emphasis is placed instead on the clever metaphor itself, which is detached in the letter from any particular context. It is self-focused and self-sufficient citational wit. It is proffered as a gift; the only supposed problem is to remember to whom. Sévigné's worry is ostensibly about repeating herself, but there appears to be just as much concern that this felicity has not been circulated, or not adequately. The message is privileged here over the addressee; the unsure but equally unconcerned sender appears insensitive to the more profound message of indifference that this question might convey to the addressee. It is at moments such as these that the correspondence appears more a writing project than a communicatory one.

Eventually, Sévigné begins to assert more directly the pleasure she finds in writing. Having been absorbed in this activity as if in a trance, she returns to her epistolary senses at the closing of her letter to interrogate herself and her correspondent on the nature and meaning of the text produced:

Ma bonne, quelle espèce de lettre est-ce ici? Je pense que je suis folle. A quoi peut servir une si grande narration? Vraiment, j'ai bien satisfait le désir que j'avais de conter. (I, L. 270, p. 504)

Ma bonne, what kind of letter is this? I think I must be crazy. What can be the use of such a long narration? Truly, I have quite satisfied the desire I had to tell a story.

There is an artificial air to the opening rhetorical question and to the volunteered answer as well; the device serves to convey to the correspondent self-conscious and apologetic concern for the imposition of a long letter. It is recognized that the long text does not fit neatly into the category of letter at all, that it is admittedly hardly an exchange with the addressee. "Lettre" (the generic form) and "conter" (the narrative act) are conflated so as to appear almost synonymous, and both are subsumed under the rubric of conversation referenced by the question marks, suggesting that the text does meet, albeit univocally, the criterion of dialogical exchange central to the proper functioning of a correspondence. Inculpating in order to exculpate herself, Sévigné adds the self-deprecating questioning of her sanity. But both questions are strictly rhetorical. They are merely formal recognitions of the proper bounds of epistolary comportment. Their perlocutionary force is compromised by the provision of the answers as well, answers that confirm the positive pleasure Sévigné takes, not necessarily in corresponding, but in writing. She is both the origin of the desire to write and the agent of its satisfaction. Here her writing takes on an autonomy and sufficiency that stand in contradiction to the originally postulated epistolary motivation. No longer is writing solely other-oriented; rather, it is self-absorbed. No longer is it merely compensatory and consolatory writing; it is sheer pleasure, exceeding and flouting generic constraints.

At a later date, Sévigné further undermines the exchange rationale of the correspondence between the two women, resituating the exchange as between her world and its inscription. In this increasingly self-focused activity, Sévigné encodes her life as a letter in process. In a long epistolary communication made up of repeated visits to her desk, her stationery, and the mirror she has made of the daughter as pretext for writing, she finds respite from and reason for moments of direct social engagement with others. On the fifth page of a seven-page letter, composed of fragments of freshly gleaned news and various reflections, she reaffirms the delight she finds in writing:

Cela est plaisant avec quelle naïveté je vous écris, sans songer que la disposition de ceux qui reçoivent les lettres n'est pas toujours comme de ceux qui les écrivent. A tout moment, je vous viens dire un mot; cela me fait un amusement qui m'est toujours meilleur que toute autre chose. (II, L. 704, p. 720)

The naïveté with which I write you is amusing, without considering that the mood of those receiving letters is not always like that of those writing them. At every moment, I come to add a word for you; such an amusement always does me more good than anything else.

She claims she is writing naïvely by not focusing on the situation of reception, although she is thereby momentarily doing just that. But, through this mere nodding gesture, she effectively dismisses the importance of the addressee as structuring factor of the letter. She addresses her words to an individual *vous* but deflects the impact by shifting to *ceux*, transforming and elevating the remark from particular observation to general truth. She thus depersonalizes and legitimates her writing pleasure. This sophisticated naïveté glosses a kind of writing that takes less and less into account the addressee and focuses increasingly on its own agency, on the writer. The minimizing of the *vous*, with its necessary corollary of the maximizing of the *je*, is paralleled by greater emphasis on the context of production at the expense of that of reception. This shift in polarity is accompanied by an admission of increase in the sheer pleasure of writing and a concomitant decrease of accent on the consolatory purpose of writing. The letter becomes a more positive writing experience as the writing itself takes on importance and pretext becomes more obviously just that.

The esthetic of the letter as conversation is at once exemplified and undermined by Sévigné's occasional practice, once she has established a pattern of prolixity, of inventing not only her contribution but her addressee's response as well:

Vous me dites: "Eh, mon Dieu! pourquoi me contez-vous cela? j'en sais la plus grande partie, et je ne me soucie pas de l'autre." En vérité, ma chère bonne, je n'en sais rien; c'est que je cause. (III, L. 1201, p. 852)

You say to me: "My goodness! why are you telling me this? I know most of what it's about, and I don't care about the rest." In truth, *ma chère bonne,* I don't know why at all; it's just that I'm chatting.

The one-sided character of "conter" is presented in the guise of "causer." The invented exchange punctuates the *causerie* with a rhetorical flourish whereby Sévigné at once acknowledges and flouts the conventions of epistolary turn taking. Such short-circuiting also points up a problem: the letter is not a conversation per se; it is a written document, a circular and closed one at that, except to the extent that it succeeds in eliciting from its addressee another of its kind in turn. Both the *je* and the *vous,* while in theory referential, are textually invented in the course of producing the letter and thus pertain as much to the realm of wishful fiction as to the "real" world.

Various circumstances in the writing situation contributed, over the course of the years, to shape a self-absorbed correspondent. In time, if Sévigné no longer apologized to her daughter for her prolific and self-absorbed writing, especially since she solicited the same sort of letter from her, she did still nod to epistolary propriety and recognize her deviation from that etiquette. The theme of the inappropriateness of self as subject regularly punctuates her letters, as reminders to her addressees that she is perfectly versed in the rules. But such gestures are most often occasioned by a transgression of the rule and occur by way of acknowledgment, apology, and resolve. Of these three locutionary acts, the most forceful, since the least compromised and the most self-fulfilling, is that of acknowledgment. Sévigné wishes her addressee to see that she does know the rules even if she chooses not to abide by them, once again exercising authority informally within a supposedly intransigent codified space and building her own permission for her writing pleasure.

The *lettre de provision* marks the degree of Sévigné's commitment to writing as a self-fulfilling activity. It also emphasizes the ways in which the daughter's apprenticeship constituted the grounds for the mother's mastership. In establishing and sustaining this enabling mirror relationship, Sévigné exercised mother-right over her daughter and gave birth to herself as writer. At the same time she elaborated an articulation of that mother-right, and gave birth to herself as mother. This was entirely consonant with the wisdom of the day on the duties of a mother:

Or est-il que les mères ayant les mêmes humeurs et inclinations qu'on remarque dans les filles, connaissent parfaitement leur naturel, en se connaissant elles-mêmes; elles s'efforcent de lever toutes les tâches d'une glace qui les doit représenter . . . elles cherchent leur agrément dans leurs filles, afin qu'après elles plaisent à tout le monde.[31]

So it is that mothers, having the same moods and inclinations one notices in their daughters, know their daughters' nature perfectly, by knowing themselves; they strive to remove all the flaws from a mirror that must represent them . . . they seek their comeliness in their daughters, so that afterward they please everyone.

Maternality focused not on the eventual product of the polishing process—the daughter—but on the agent immediately responsible for conducting that process—the mother. But the mutual implication of mother and daughter in the successful outcome is signaled by the indeterminacy of the final pronoun, "elles." It is not clear whether it is the mothers or the daughters who benefit socially from the apprenticeship. This confusion of identity, invoked time and again by de Grenaille, must be understood as deliberately useful to the social order he is intent on encoding, and it is within this problematic that generational tensions between women are located. Nevertheless, the rights of the mother over her daughter are firmly stated, neatly correlated with the degree of maternal investment in her upbringing. The daughter, then, is perceived as an artifact of the mother's making, a self-portrait in process that entitles the model to particular claims on its image. The process of establishing the mirror, of polishing it, and of striving toward self-imaging, is reflected in Sévigné's epistolary relationship with her daughter. In that discursive space, she developed the maternal identity that constituted her entitlement to authority and that legitimated her writing pleasure.

FIVE

Private and Public—The Space Between

Sur ce subject de lettres, je veux dire ce mot, que c'est un ouvrage auquel mes amys tiennent que je puis quelque chose. Et eusse prins plus volontiers ceste forme à publier mes verves, si j'eusse eu à qui parler. Il me falloit, comme je l'ay eu autrefois, un certain commerce qui m'attirast, qui me soutinst et souslevast.
                          MICHEL DE MONTAIGNE [1]

On this subject of letters, I want to say this, that it is a work for which my friends insist I am gifted. And I would most willingly have taken up this form of publishing my thoughts, if I had had someone to converse with. I needed, as I once had, a certain exchange that attracted me, that sustained and inspired me.

This great lady, this robust and fertile letter-writer, who in our age would probably have been one of the great novelists, takes up presumably as much space in the consciousness of living readers as any figure of her vanished age.
                          VIRGINIA WOOLF [2]

Between writing letters, essays, and novels, there is at once a similarity and a radical difference. Michel de Montaigne in the sixteenth century claims that he would have preferred writing letters to essays had he had an appropriate correspondent.[3] And Virginia Woolf claims that, had Sévigné lived in the presumedly more liberated twentieth century, she would have written novels. Implicit in these remarks is discomfort with the generic constraints imposed by circumstance (the death of Montaigne's only intimate friend, La Boétie) and by gender (the prohibition of literary ambition for women writing in the seventeenth century). Whereas Montaigne apparently regretted the "manly" isolation in which he wrote, it is postulated that Sévigné would have flourished as author had she written from a position of greater autonomy. Both writers, then, played out in their choice of genre the restrictions imposed on them by virtue of their gender. At the same time, it must be kept in mind that at least three of Sévigné's contemporaries, Mlle de Scudéry, Mme de Villedieu, and Mme de La Fayette ventured to assume more professionally deliberate writing roles than that of family correspondent.

In respecting the generic constraints imposed on her by virtue of her gender, Sévigné chose a safe outlet for her writing ambitions, but she did not necessarily renounce hope of eventual publication and the securing of a reputation as a writer.[4] Indeed, in the seventeenth century, the distinction between the private and the public spheres was still an ambiguous one, and a private correspondence was capable of garnering as much publicity as a printed novel.[5] The following discussion explores Sévigné's negotiation of the sanctioned epistolary area of feminine authorship and her discreet cultivation of a relationship to a greater public than the immediate addressee. The eventual publication of her letters is quietly anticipated and inscribed in her text, while the immediate ostensible motivation, that of assuming and fulfilling her maternal role, operates as guarantor of her unassuming status. The construction of the mother and of the writer are conveniently elided to ease the passage of letters into literature.

While it is true that many stretches of letters between mother and daughter were of a strictly private nature, engaging only the two immediate parties to the correspondence, it is just as true, and more striking (particularly in comparison with correspondences produced today), that writing and receiving letters was a social activity in the seventeenth century, including many more participants than the simple binary schema of "writing subject–addressee" suggests. The activity of writing and receiving letters, more frequently than not, resembles that of playing an intricate codified parlor game. Woolf remarked on the active participation of various friends in the Sévigné exchange:

The flowers in this garden are a whole society of full-grown men and women from whom want and struggle have been removed; growing together in harmony, each contributing something that the other lacks. By way of proving it, the letters of Madame de Sévigné are often shared by other pens; now her son takes up the pen; the Abbé adds his paragraph; even the simple girl—la petite personne—is not afraid to pipe up on the same page.[6]

Woolf sees the epistolary situation that Sévigné invents for herself not so much as a response to a private crisis as much as a collective leisure activity, an eminently sociable affair, engaging a privileged class of people in mutually complementary behavior. The act of writing to her daughter in such a public and elite forum constitutes the necessary base for production of a particular social construction of self as mother. Sévigné's maternal role responded to one of these "lacks" Woolf refers to and was legitimated by the affirming participation of her friends. Their voices, chiming into the letter-conversations, validate Sévigné in her role as mother, thus subscribing by implication to a permanently limited view of Mme de Grignan as daughter.

Friends function in Sévigné's letters as witnesses, participants, critics, judges, and fans and play an essential role in enabling, regulating, censoring, and ensuring the playing out of the mother-daughter relationship. Woolf demonstrates, through her verbal tableau, an understanding of the social, psychological, and performatic dimensions of the Sévigné writing project ("je vivrai pour vous écrire")[7] that prepares the way to explore the nature of maternal expression in the letters. It is at once meeting the expectations of the members of a given clique and inventing them. Neither entirely structurally determined nor altogether voluntaristic, it articulates a hitherto tacit position of familial engagement and purpose that had apparently begun to weigh on this society as a whole, on this social organism caught up in a process of mutation precipitated by the crisis of its diminishment under Louis XIV, and seeking authorized outlets for its increasingly channeled energies. The maternal role, already outlined in manuals such as de Grenaille's, was ready to be played out and written in.

We have seen how, in the very first letter Sévigné wrote to her daughter upon their separation, witnesses and company were important to her as she sought to come to terms with her grief. It was not enough that she should describe how she had sought them out and how they had responded. In the early letters, her friends constituted a formidable presence, reminding Mme de Grignan that all of these eyes were upon her as well as her mother, and also invested in their relationship:

Mme de Verneuil, Mme d'Arpajon, Mmes de Villars, de Saint-Géran, M. de Guitaut, sa femme, la Comtesse, M. De La Rochefoucauld, ma tante, ma cousine, mes oncles, mes cousins, mes cousines, Mme de Vauvineux, tout cela vous baise les mains mille et mille fois. (I, L. 136, p. 163)

Mme de Verneuil, Mme d'Arpajon, Mmes de Villars, de Saint-Géran, M. de Guitaut, his wife, the Countess, M. De La Rochefoucauld, my aunt, my cousin, my uncles, my cousins, Mme de Vauvineux, they all all kiss your hands a thousand times.

Reciprocity governs the relationship between Sévigné and her friends: she performs a service for them by including their messages for her daughter; they perform one for her by entering into the epistolary pact and volunteering contributions; they literally subscribe to the arrangement. Meanwhile the ostensible purpose of such communication is to transmit compliments from the friends to the daughter. However, the emphasis on the first person possessive ("*ma* tante, *ma* cousine, *mes* oncles, *mes* cousins, *mes* cousines") highlights the centrality of the intermediary to the message. Instead

of a litany of devotion offered to the addressee, which would properly
be focused on the *vous*, it suggests an army of friends and relatives in
league with the mother, solidly backing her social role as essential filter—
as mother.

Louise Horowitz claims that the marked presence of proper names in
the letters serves as evidence that Sévigné is attempting to "extend her own
feelings to a whole social circle" because of her "self-delusion"; she attempts "to 'seduce' her daughter by rendering her a *universal* 'princesse
lointaine.' " [8] The dynamic of seduction seems appropriate as a description
of the relationship cultivated in the letters. However, I tend to read the
social dimension as much more collaborative, indeed complicitous among
Sévigné and her friends rather than simply the fruit of her individual endeavor. It served their purposes as well to codify her behavior as maternal,
to codify the maternal in terms of her behavior. Nor am I convinced that
this was an instance of "self-delusion." There can be no doubt that Sévigné
embraced her role with conviction and that her coterie subscribed to it. A
new ethos was in the making, evolving out of a set of standard practices
and attitudes, and shaping a way of being in the world for women through
writing.

In the initial letters, as the correspondence took shape, the social world
was particularly present. Horowitz, sensitive to the "haughty, command-
ing tones" in the letters, has noticed that the presence of proper names
also introduces compliments for the daughter.[9] Just as often, such presence
is accompanied by requests and demands. Sévigné asks her daughter to
write for her audience, to feed her lines for them, that she might play her
role: "Faites quelque mention de certaines gens dans vos lettres, afin que je
leur puisse dire" (I, L. 136, p. 161) [Make some mention of certain people
in your letters, so I can tell them you did]. Having assembled her league
of cohorts (see L. 136), Sévigné draws her correspondent into the game.
There is a movement from the transmission of compliments to requests for
same. In this appeal for reciprocity that will put the mother-filter in operation, the following flatteries constitute a transitional stage: "Savez-vous
que votre souvenir fait ici la fortune de ceux que vous en favorisez? Les
autres languissent après" (I, L. 140, p. 172) [Do you know that your memory makes the good fortune of those you favor with it here? The others are
languishing for it]. Then:

Je ferai vos compliments à Mme de Villars. Il y a presse à être nommé dans mes
lettres. Je vous remercie d'avoir fait mention de Brancas. (I, L. 140, p. 173)

I will convey your compliments to Mme de Villars. There is great demand to be
named in my letters. I thank you for having mentioned Brancas.

Sévigné advises the daughter on appropriate complementary behavior. She suggests in the following passage the rewards to be had for such compliant behavior:

J'ai distribué fort à propos tous vos compliments; on vous en rend au centuple. La Comtesse était ravie, et voulut voir son nom. (I, L. 146, p. 190)

I have distributed in an extremely timely manner all your compliments; they are returned to you a hundredfold. The Countess was delighted by them, and wanted to see her name.

Sévigné further reminds her daughter that she cannot invent remarks to be circulated, since her friends request proof of them; thus she emphasizes the need for their continuance and specificity.

The communicatory circuit closes up completely around Mme de Grignan when Sévigné can point to letters written by her daughter to others, assume that there must be one for her, and demand to know where it is:

Je n'ai point encore reçu une lettre que je suis persuadée que vous m'avez écrite de Lyon avant que de partir; je croirai difficilement qu'ayant pu m'écrire, et ayant écrit à M. de Coulanges, vous m'ayez oubliée. (I, L. 139, p. 168)

I have not yet received a letter which I am convinced you wrote me from Lyon before leaving; I will have difficulty in believing that, having been able to write to me, and having written to M. de Coulanges, you forgot me.

The validity of Sévigné's deductive reasoning is not at all in question here; she probably had every good reason to think that, given these other letters, her daughter must have written to her as well. What is noteworthy is the mutual visibility of the two women's behavior in the tight circle in which they moved. Sévigné was eager to define their relationship within a social context, depending thus on the daughter's willingness to participate in this circle. At the same time, it was paramount that she maintain her mediating position between her daughter and the other members of the circle. Her central role was threatened, rendered superfluous, if the daughter and these others undertook to correspond independently of her. Hence a delicate balance had to be maintained whereby the daughter was close but not too close to members of the mother's circle, and by means of which the mother's friends understood that she was pivotal in any relations they entertained with her daughter.

Just as Sévigné demonstrates concern to establish a central social role for herself as *mater* by elaborating a communicatory system in which messages between the daughter and the mother's friends would be incorporated in her text, she endeavors to control the circulation of her letters at their point of reception, to implicate the daughter's entourage in the same project. She had resented her exclusion from her daughter's exchanges with M. de Grignan ("Où est donc ce principe de cachoterie pour ce que vous aimez? Vous souvient-il avec combien de peine vous vous resolviez enfin à nous confier les dates de celles [les lettres] de M. de Grignan?" [I, L. 143, p. 181] [So where is this principle of mystery for that which you cherish? Do you recall how much difficulty you had in finally deciding to tell us the dates of the ones [the letters] from M. de Grignan?]), and was angered to learn that her daughter was not sharing the totality of her letters with her friends when they arrived:

Vous pensez m'apaiser par vos louanges, et me traiter toujours comme la *Gazette de Hollande*; je m'en vengerai. Vous cachez les tendresses que je vous mande, friponne; et moi je montre quelquefois, et à certaines gens, celles que vous m'écrivez. Je ne veux pas qu'on croie que j'ai pensé mourir, et que je pleure tous les jours, *pour qui? pour une ingrate!* Je veux qu'on voie que vous m'aimez, et que si vous avez mon coeur entier, j'ai une place dans le vôtre. (I, L. 143, p. 181)

You think you can appease me with your praise, and by always treating me like the *Gazette de Hollande*; I will get my revenge. You conceal the affections I send you, rascal; whereas I sometimes show, to certain people, those you write to me. I don't want it thought that I believed I would die, and that I weep every day, *for whom? for an ungrateful daughter!* I want it seen that you love me, and that if you have my whole heart, I have a place in yours.

Sévigné intended her letters to function neither as exclusively private professions of affection nor as mere purveyors of news from the capital. She attempted to structure, particularly in the early formative letters, appropriate reception on the part of the daughter-addressee and to ensure the collaboration of her daughter's entourage in subscribing to her preeminence and to her daughter's complementary role. Whereas Mme de Grignan was inclined to hide, Sévigné was eager to circulate evidence of her attachment to the daughter. Appeal to a witnessing public and Sévigné's insistence on its right to valuate the two women's affective behavior underscores the social nature of the role Sévigné was engaged in constructing. The two women did not merely entertain different conceptions of love;[10] they occupied very different positions in relation to each other and the world.

Sévigné insisted that third parties be privy to their private feelings ("Je ne veux pas qu'on croie que j'ai pensé mourir") in order to provide textual justification for her extravagant affective behavior, and to demonstrate that there was indeed a reciprocity of feeling between the two women ("je veux qu'on voie que vous m'aimez, et que si vous avez mon coeur entier, j'ai une place dans le vôtre."). *On*, the collective voice of social authority, is invoked as necessary witness and judge to the relationship between the two women but must have access to textual evidence in order to pronounce on their behavior.[11]

The letters themselves, as textual evidence, become central to the enterprise and anchor the performance, and the tactic of public display of affection carries implications for the structuring of the letters. The anecdotes, readily detachable and eminently readable, decorating the mother's letters, the humorous quips, messages for members of the daughter's immediate circle, intriguing quotes from other texts—all of these devices can be seen to serve as incitement for the addressee to circulate the letters in their entirety, to share not only the display texts proper but the ostensibly marginal and, in fact, central affective framing. A web of friends is thus invoked and woven around the daughter through this epistolary appeal for attention. The extent to which Mme de Grignan is mistress of her letters depends on the degree to which she resists or at least controls selectively textual appeals to and for a public.

If Sévigné makes light in her letters of the *lettre-gazette* form, which simply purports to circulate news and gossip, it is because such epistolary journalism cannot alone serve the more complicated function she assigns to her writing. For her, transmitting news was merely one of many ways of securing not only her daughter but their shared society's confirmation of her in her role as mother. Whereas Roger Duchêne claims that, for Madame de Sévigné, being herself meant being *for* her daughter,[12] I suggest that it is in being *through* her daughter, that is, vicariously, that she constructs and justifies her existence. One of the most significant strategies she employs, certainly one of the most efficacious, is the inclusion of a public in a supposedly intimate correspondence. The highly social character of the enterprise, the structuring function of concern for appearances, set the stage for the mother and recommended a supporting role for the daughter.

The degree to which letters extended beyond their specified addressees is suggested in the following passage:

Voilà une infinité de lettres que je vous conjure de distribuer. Je souhaite que les deux qui sont ouvertes vous plaisent. (I, L. 151, p. 208)

Here is an infinity of letters I beg you to distribute. I hope the two that are open will please you.

Sévigné invites her daughter to read two of the letters she is entrusting to her for distribution. She makes her daughter an extension of the courier service and thereby binds her to a certain degree of complicity. The actual addressees may never know that Mme de Grignan has read their letters, and Mme de Grignan cannot know what is in the other letters she is requested to hand out. She is at once included and excluded, forcefully reminded of the epistolary web her mother is weaving about her with daunting ("une infinité") prolixity. Mme de Grignan's assigned forwarding role is to read, appreciate, and distribute. She has no choice, unless she opts rebelliously and improbably to return the letters by post to their sender, but to lend silent, submissive attention to her mother's text, and to implicate herself tacitly in the project by then passing on the letters to their destination.

While on the one hand promulgating circulation of letters in order to bring concrete evidence to the social role she was projecting, Sévigné needed at the same time to be able to reassure her daughter of discretion in sharing her letters so as to inspire her total confidence, as was discussed in chapter 4. In that process, as well as elaborating a practice of censorship, Sévigné focused on the readability of her daughter's letters, and hence on her daughter's writing talent, which in turn justified the mother in showing those letters to others. Those same passages that can be read as evidence of Sévigné's efforts to bolster her daughter's self-confidence can be just as easily read as her establishing adequate reason to share them, to project to a greater public a hint of work in progress.

Accordingly, in Sévigné's appreciation of one of her daughter's letters, there are three audiences cited, ending with the mother alone. She identifies in the text of her daughter's letter two kinds of writing—the *narrations* and the *tendresses*—and correlates with them a distinction between public and private domain, asserting her judicious control over her daughter's disclosures:

D'Hacqueville et moi, nous étions ravis de lire certains endroits brillants; et même dans vos narrations, l'endroit qui regarde au Roi, votre colère contre Lauzun et contre l'Evèque, ce sont des traits de maître. Quelquefois j'en donne aussi une petite part à Mme de Villars, mais elle s'attache aux tendresses et les larmes lui en viennent fort bien aux yeux. Ne craignez point que je montre vos lettres à propos. Je sais parfaitement bien ceux qui en sont dignes et ce qu'il faut dire ou cacher. (I, L. 237, p. 420)

D'Hacqueville and I were delighted to read certain brilliant parts; and even in your narrations, the part about the King, your anger toward Lauzun and the Bishop, these are masterful strokes. Sometimes I give a little section to Mme de Villars to read, but she gets caught up in the affectionate parts and tears come quite easily to her eyes. Do not fear that I show your letters inappropriately. I know quite well those who are worthy of them and what should be said or concealed.

The *narrations* or *endroits brillants* function like display texts; they are apprehended as esthetic artifacts and therefore, as such, as attesting to their creator's intent that they be shared. They are construed to call for an audience and a shared appreciation by virtue of their quality, and thus to justify their circulation by the addressee. They are interpreted to constitute the obviously public domain of the letter. Mme de Villars, for her part, focuses on the supposedly marginal framing *tendresses* to which she is made privy and responds emotionally to these sentimental passages. Since they are clearly of a more private nature than the *narrations,* her access to them makes questionable the confidentiality of the writing exchange. Lest her daughter develop inhibitions and cease to communicate fully as a consequence, Sévigné reassures her of her sound judgment in distinguishing appropriate passages for public consumption as well as appropriate publics for the sharing of her daughter's letters. Self-authorized connoisseur of both texts and people, Sévigné invites her daughter to trust in her discretion and thus protects her claim to further confidences. The inclusion of other parties both potentially jeopardizes the writing relationship and stabilizes it. An excess of invasiveness must be balanced against an excess of intimacy in order to accommodate the delicate relationship between mother and daughter.

Again and again, especially in the early letters, Sévigné alludes to the sharing of letters from the daughter, often in the context of flattery, publicizing and thus further grounding the pact of reciprocal inscribed affection:

Mais je suis toujours charmée de vos lettres sans vous le dire. Mme de Coulanges l'est aussi toujours des endroits que je lui fais voir, et qu'il est impossible de lire toute seule. (I, L. 252, p. 450)

But I am always charmed by your letters without telling you so. Mme de Coulanges always is too, by the parts that I show her and that are impossible to read all alone.

As Sévigné shares her daughter's letters with others, so they in turn show her the letters they receive from Mme de Grignan, participating thus in the tightening of the communicatory and relational circle:

Je vis hier une de vos lettres à l'abbé de Pontcarré, qui est la plus divine lettre du monde; il n'y a rien qui ne pique, et qui ne soit salé. Il en a envoyé une copie à l'Eminence. (II, L. 403, p. 11)

I saw one of your letters to the abbé de Pontcarré yesterday, the most divine letter in the world; there is nothing there that doesn't pique, that isn't spicy. He sent a copy of it to his Eminence.

Style deemed brilliant constitutes reason for sharing and, once pronounced such, is cited as evidence of the writer's apparent appeal for a public extending beyond the addressee. Here this sample of the daughter's writing, once established as artful, receives its appropriate accolade in being copied and circulated. The proof of the letter's success is, tautologically, its success.

Both the meritorious quality of the daughter's writing and the mother's need to advertise her pleasure at receiving and reading these letters are regularly cited as irreproachable reasons for sharing them:

Je suis ravie, en vérité, quand je reçois de vos lettres, ma chère enfant; je ne puis me résoudre à jouir toute seule du plaisir de les lire. Ne craignez rien; je ne fais rien de ridicule là-dessus, mais j'en fais voir une petite ligne à Bayard, une autre au *chanoine* . . . et en vérité on est charmé de votre manière d'écrire. Je ne fais voir que ce qui convient, et vous croyez bien que je me rends maîtresse de la lettre, pour qu'on ne lise pas sur mon épaule ce que je ne veux pas qui soit vu. (II, L. 512, p. 298)

I am delighted, truthfully, when I receive your letters, my dear child; I cannot resolve to enjoy reading them all by myself. Do not fear a thing; I am doing nothing ridiculous about this, but I show a little line to Bayard, another to the *canon* . . . and in truth they are charmed by your writing style. I show only what is appropriate, and you can fully believe that I make myself mistress of the letter, so that what I don't want seen isn't read over my shoulder.

While the mother insists that she retains control over the material and exercises discretion, the daughter cannot help but be reminded by these frequent effusions (containing always the same combined elements of flattery, sharing, assurances of discretion) that their relationship is being constructed and played out before a greater public, that the mother controls the daughter's image in their shared society, and that she is irremediably implicated as the mother's daughter in this greater circuit of social exchange.

In those frequent instances involving several voices at the sending and receiving ends of the exchange, the communicatory circuit is a good deal more complicated than that of a simple binary movement. Sévigné comments on the punctuations that these eruptions of sociability produce in her letters as they occur; she never suggests that they are inappropriate or undesirable, save in jest when they are inscribed so as to appear to interrupt her and to compromise the illusion of unmediated contact or conversation claimed by Sévigné for the letter. Her son, Charles, frequently shares her pen to add a word for his sister; the letter then becomes a joint writing project: mother and son are writing to and for each other as well as to and for the ostensible addressee. When Sévigné says, "Je laisse la plume à cet honnête garçon" [I leave the pen to this good boy] as she closes, and then Charles opens his section of the letter with a riposte, "Que veut-on dire de *cet honnête garçon?*" (II, L. 454, p. 178) [What is meant by *this good boy?*], to whom in fact are the mother and son writing? Sévigné takes the pen again, to close the letter, and must read her son's words.

Such textual evidence of play among the characters as they write leads the latter-day reader to conjecture on conversations spilling out of the letter and into the salon and occasionally making their way back into the text again. Puzzles of dimensionality invite speculative readings and imaginative dramatization of the relationships among the participants inscribed in the *Correspondance*. These letters remind us of the at once limited and limitless nature of any text, for the letters always play along the margins of communicational aspirations. They constitute all there is and yet they are signs of what is (or was) elsewhere. As eloquent as what is fixed in them is what eludes them. The transition from one writer to another with the passage of the pen is a social act that escapes the text at the same time that it is inscribed and evidenced in it.

Such participation contributes to determine the kind of writing that will be possible in these sorts of letters. The inclusion of "third" parties has a stabilizing effect on the epistolary relationship between the mother and daughter. It ensures a censorship of emotional expression that allows for the continuance of the exchange even when the relationship is tense and strained. In a letter of 1690, there figure two writers (Sévigné and her son) and two addressees (daughter and her husband). Sévigné first addresses her daughter; then her son takes up the pen and writes to his sister; the mother closes the message to her daughter and adds a passage addressed to M. de Grignan. In a third and final passage to the daughter, Sévigné protests after the fact her son's invasion and preemption of the letter in the section preceding: "On m'enlève ma plume, on me la rend, et je n'ai quasi plus qu'à vous embrasser de tout mon coeur" (III, L. 1192, p. 829) [My pen is being taken from me, it's being returned to me, and I have practically no more to do than to embrace you with all my heart]. She continues, though, extending her closing remarks with an apparent non sequitur: "Et si je vous ai donné un moment de chagrin, vous devez me le pardonner." [And if I have given you a moment of chagrin, you must pardon me.] There is no other allusion in the letter to the misunderstanding in question. It can be safely assumed that all four epistolary participants read the letter in its entirety and are not privy solely to the sections directly pertaining to them (although perhaps her son, who has made his final contribution just above, does not read through the last lines of the letter). Thus Sévigné has at least one and possibly two witnesses for her apology and reasons of social decorum for not elaborating it. Such a strategy, if it can be considered that self-conscious, appears to be one of containment. Inclusion is a mode of incorporating and controlling images, messages, relationships. Sociability plays a prominent role in the shaping of the mother and daughter's epistolary relationship.

Throughout the *Correspondance*, there persists a flirtation with the idea of publication.[13] This might be dismissed as merely a variation on codified modes of complimenting and thus encouraging the continuance of the epistolary exchange between mother and daughter, were it not that personal letters were susceptible to this treatment during the women's lifetime. Letters written for private or limited consumption were deemed stylistically brilliant or representative of certain exchange conventions and therefore included in *manuels,* or entire correspondences were published (as was seen in chapter 1). Writing letters to her daughter so assiduously, and attuned to the trends of her time, Sévigné was hardly unaware of a possible printed destiny for their correspondence. She had actually experienced the passage of self-apprehension from private correspondent to that of writer when Bussy informed her of his gift of their letters to the king. Indeed, the notion of privacy for the intimate correspondence has already been problematized in the preceding discussion concerning the circulation and sharing of the mother's and daughter's letters among their friends. When Sévigné reports that, as she writes, her letter is being copied by a friend ("Devinez ce que fait M. de Coulanges; sans s'incommoder, il copie mot à mot toutes les nouvelles que je vous écris" [II, L. 407, p. 30] [Guess what M. de Coulanges is doing; without inconveniencing himself, he is copying word for word all the news I send you]), she must also be understanding that a certain value is being assigned to her writing, that in the very notion of a copy, particularly in the hand of and at the instance of another than herself, a future (however glorious) for her writing (however preserved) is doubly assured. Just as the delimitations of private and public spheres are not articulated as we experience them today, so publication in the seventeenth century has to be understood in its more subtle connotations.

Sévigné introduced early on, in the third month of separation, a dimension of writerly self-consciousness to the exchange she was still inaugurating with her daughter:

Mon Dieu, ma bonne, que vos lettres sont aimables. Il y a des endroits dignes de l'impression; un de ces jours vous trouverez qu'un de vos amis vous aura trahie. (I, L. 152, p. 209)

My goodness, *ma bonne*, how kind your letters are. There are parts worthy of being printed; one of these days you will find that one of your friends has betrayed you.

Clearly she considers that the greatest tribute writing can receive is its transformation into print: writer would become author. However, negotiating that passage was a delicate business: the dictates of the aristocratic ethic or esthetic of *négligence,* particularly as they codified the proper relations to be observed between "ladies" and "writing," precluded any direct expression or act of authorial ambition. The path to prominence would necessarily be more circuitous. Sévigné could not presume to publish her own writing without defying tacit prescriptions for her behavior, not to mention her writing; nor could the daughter. The only hope either genteel correspondent might entertain for eventual publication lay precisely in the possibility of admiring betrayal (such as Bussy's, discussed in chapter 2). Thus the above flattering prediction can be construed to operate as a promise rather than the threat it purports to be, and further, as an implicit directive holding out the only solution available that might see the two women's writing into print. The very fact that Mme de Grignan did conserve her mother's letters, as Sévigné conserved her daughter's, suggests that, beyond the cherishing of family documents, the two women's writerly self-consciousness assigned value to the letters as texts.

One of the significant ways in which the letters were extended beyond their immediate ostensible purposes of communication and into other ways of considering them was acknowledgment of the context in which they were written—that of leisure. The practice of corresponding satisfied a need to engage in improving, self-affirming activity without transgressing the aristocratic sanctions against more explicitly purposeful pursuits. Slack hours, morning, afternoon, and evening, find a worthy leisure occupation. The time and the freedom to invent, elaborate, and extend epistolary texts allow for a savoring of that experience. Not only writing but reading letters constitutes a way of passing time, especially in the country:

Notre solitude nous fait la tête si creuse que nous nous faisons des affaires de tout. Les lettres et les réponses font de l'occupation, mais il y a du temps de reste. Je lis et relis et relis les vôtres avec un plaisir et une tendresse que j'espère que vous puissiez imaginer, car je ne vous la saurais dire. (I, L. 205, p. 357)

Our solitude makes our minds so empty that we turn everything into an occasion. Letters and responses keep us busy, but there is still time left over. I read and reread and reread yours with a pleasure and affection I hope you can imagine, for I would not be able to express it to you.

Sévigné here depends on letters for her day's activity and for company as well. Not only is her own writing an occupation to fill the hours; reading letters received is also, literally, a pastime. While time and solitude are viewed negatively, in terms of the stark existence they impose on basically gregarious creatures, when postulated in a framework of absence, they do represent the conditions propitious to writing. The abundance of leisure and its lack of focus ("la tête creuse") is epitomized by the availability of the time evidenced in the writing out of "Je lis et relis et relis." And that act of rereading not one but a sequence of letters at a single sitting marks the passage of these letters from strictly communicational devices to pleasure texts. From there to "book" is not far.

Nor are occasions for rereading, such as the above, rare. They occur frequently enough to inform the general tenor of production and reception of the correspondence. When Sévigné cannot exalt their activity by sharing and circulating her daughter's letters, she promotes the project by stressing the virtues of writing in play. Thoughts of publicizing turn to thoughts of publishing. Four years into the writing, Sévigné reiterates her predilection for her daughter's letter; it withstands the test of time and scrutiny: "Je l'ai lu, et relu, et le relirai encore" [I read it, and reread it, and will reread it again]. By way of compliment, she explicitly elevates the letter to the status of book:

Quelle lettre, ma très bonne! Quels remerciements ne vous dois-je point d'avoir employé vos yeux, votre tête, votre main, votre temps à me composer un si agréable livre! Je l'ai lu et relu, et le relirai encore avec bien du plaisir et bien de l'attention; il n'y a nulle lecture où je puisse prendre plus d'intérêt. Vous contentez ma curiosité sur tout ce que je souhaitais, et j'admire votre soin à me faire des réponses si ponctuelles; cela fait une conversation toute réglée et très délicieuse. (II, L. 446, p. 150)

What a letter, *ma très bonne*! What thanks I owe you for having used your eyes, your head, your hand, your time to compose such an agreeable book for me! I read and reread it, and will reread it again with much pleasure and attention; there is no reading in which I can take more interest. You satisfy my curiosity about all that I wished to hear, and I admire your care in writing me such punctual responses; that makes for a well-regulated and delicious conversation.

The letter thus makes its passage from message-bearing fragment to pleasure-producing text, and this unwittingly, through the good graces of its addressee, not through any suspect effort on the part of the writer. Conversation here gives way to writing—its inscription, unlike ephemeral talk, affords endless pleasure to the interlocutor/addressee/reader.

Not only inscribed acts of reading but also stylistic appraisals signal moments of authorial self-consciousness. Frequently Sévigné will focus her praise on the daughter's writing, encouraging her thus to consider her letters not simply as informative communications but as examples of style. The corresponding couple engages regularly in exchanging volleys of compliments:

Je n'ai jamais vu de si aimables lettres que les vôtres, ma très chère Comtesse; je viens d'en lire une qui me charme. Je vous ai oui dire que j'avais une manière de tourner les moindres choses; vraiment, ma bonne, c'est bien vous qui l'avez. Il y a cinq ou six endroits dans votre dernière lettre qui sont d'un éclat et d'un agrément qui ouvrent le coeur. Je ne sais par où commencer à vous répondre. (I, L. 360, p. 658)

I have never seen letters as amiable as yours, my very dear Countess; I have just read one that charms me. I have heard you say that I had a way of phrasing the least of things; actually, *ma bonne*, it's really you who have. There are five or six places in your last letter which have a sparkle and charm which open the heart. I do not know where to begin to respond to you.

The rephrasing and returning, the reinscribing of flattery is itself the performance of a stylistic exercise that further heightens the writerly consciousness of the two correspondents. The echos and reverberations of praise advance the sealing of the mutuality of their writing pact. The praise comes to pertain, in spite of assignment, to both mother and daughter, caught up in congratulations in a relation where the very notion of self is problematic. Only to the degree that there is a clear separation between the two can there be a genuine extension and transmission of compliments. The exchange of praises between individuals as intimately related as these two suggests an intertwining of compliments and points to a profound ambiguity concerning the "real" identity of the tributee. Projection and transference are evidently in play as the two women build their writing relationship. If much of the mutual admiration expressed is frequently couched in terms of speculation on eventual publication, this is not merely flattering hyperbole deployed to sustain engagement in the exchange: it is a powerful way of reminding each other of, of keeping in view, the greater potentiality of their writing project.

The term "livre" does not always figure positively. In the following passage, it carries primarily the connotation of length, implying tediousness, an imposition on the addressee's time. Sévigné speaks here not of one but of her letters as a series or totality of texts. In generalizing about them, she is conceiving them not so much as individual missives, confided separately over a period of years to the mail, but as a whole:

Je comprends l'occupation que vous donnent mes lettres, et combien elles vous détournent de vos civilités. Vous perdez connaissance, dites-vous; je souffre deux fois la semaine que l'on m'en dise autant. Il ne faut point d'autre livre que ces abominables lettres que je vous écris; je vous défie de les lire tout de suite. Enfin, ma bonne, vous en êtes contente, c'est assez. (II, L. 417, p. 76)

I can imagine that my letters take up your time, and how they must distract you from your courtesies. You are fainting, you say; I am subjected to being told as much twice a week. You need no book other than these abominable letters I write you; I challenge you to read them all at once. But, after all, *ma bonne,* you are satisfied; that is enough.

The notion of a book of letters is at the least obliquely entertained by Sévigné in this passage. While the context is one of self-disparagement ("ces abominables lettres"), it points simultaneously to the thought of publication, imagining a collection to be read at one sitting. The shift of consideration of the letters from within the personal realm of "message" ("lettre") to the more impersonal and authorial realm of "text" ("livre") has been negotiated by the production of prolixity.[14] While this excess is encoded here as negative, it is in writing as much as she does that Sévigné develops justification for considering her writing as more than mere communication.

She goes as far as her social station and writing situation will allow her in admitting to pondering the readability of a book of her letters: "je vous défie de les lire tout de suite." Although couched in self-derogatory rhetoric, this remark gives evidence that Sévigné did think of her letters as text in something vaguely comparable to the *Correspondance* form, which she was never to see, but which has been their shape as they have made their way through copyists and editors and have been made available to generations of readers. Here was a woman writing letters, aware, at least occasionally, at least to some degree, that she might in fact be writing a book.

In 1690, Sévigné reiterates, in a veiled manner, her hopes concerning the publication of her letters, in a context of response to compliments proffered by the daughter:

Vous louez tellement mes lettres au-dessus de leur mérite que si je n'étais fort assurée que vous ne les refeuilleterez ni les relirez jamais, je craindrais tout d'un coup de me voir imprimée par la trahison d'un de mes amis. Voiture et Nicole, bon Dieu, quels noms! et qu'est-ce que vous dites, ma chère enfant? (III, L. 1196, p. 839)

You so praise my letters beyond their merit that if I weren't quite sure that you will never peruse them or read them again, I would suddenly fear finding myself in print by the betrayal of one of my friends. Voiture and Nicole, goodness gracious, what names! and what are you suggesting, my dear child?

The path to publication is circuitous, as in the earlier allusion, and here must be classed as fearful. Nothing so pedestrian as personal ambition can be admitted. The only conceivable solution to the aspiring author is, once again, friendly betrayal, and it becomes increasingly clear that there could be no more logical agent for the act than her most faithful collaborator.

While Sévigné exclaims protestingly at such illustrious names as those of Voiture and Nicole,[15] as if to emphasize modestly the distance between them and her, the very exclamation, the reinscribing in her own text, of the daughter's original complimentary comparison suggests as well a savoring of the contiguity, a pleasure at the mere thought of their comparability. That Sévigné might have been shocked or dismayed could she have foreseen the publication of the letters, as Roger Duchêne would have it, is not, despite her demurrings, substantiated in this passage.[16] The thoughts made explicit here convey, just as eloquently, an implicit premature regret for the possible ephemeral fate of her writing. She almost begs her daughter to reread her letters by the mere mention of such an activity, couched albeit in dissembling terms of confident negation.

An assurance by return mail from her correspondent to the effect that the privacy of her letters will be absolutely respected is not at all what is sought by Sévigné. Given the dynamic of the exchange of compliments well encoded by 1690 between the two corresponding women, modest denegation necessarily solicits and motivates a strong response to the contrary. Sévigné can be read to cherish contemplation of a flattering betrayal, to encourage rather than fear it. In a sense, what makes her daughter so dear to her ("ma chère enfant") is bound up in her knowledge that the daughter cherishes her letters ("Vous louez tellement mes lettres").

In the final analysis, it appears therefore that her two most devoted correspondents, Bussy and her daughter (by extension, since the granddaughter Pauline was apparently following through with her mother's wishes in an overdetermined way in disposing as she did of the carefully preserved letters) acted as traitorous friends. They provided the initial impetus and saw to it that her letters to them reached a greater public and that her status mutated for posterity from that of gifted cousin and devoted mother to that of author. In so doing, they served her well.

Sévigné's opting to privilege her maternal role as writer points up the centrality of performance to the world in which she lived: irreducible to neat categories of private and public; rather, committed to display. From a twentieth-century vantage, it seems that a mother's literary ambition spent exclusively on corresponding with her daughter would eventuate in talent lost to posterity. It was precisely under that sanctioned rubric and in mobilizing that prescribed role, however, that Sévigné established a public, projected a voice, and was easily integrated into the world of letters. She enjoyed the popularity her letters afforded her during her own lifetime and secured an enduring literary reputation as well. As the daughter's mother, she wrote herself into the canon.

Part II

•

Figures in the Mirror

SIX

Constructs of Maternity

On ne naît pas femme: on le devient. Aucun destin biologique, psychique, économique ne définit la figure que revêt au sein de la société la femelle humaine; c'est l'ensemble de la civilisation qui élabore ce produit intermédiaire entre le mâle et le castrat qu'on qualifie de féminin.   SIMONE DE BEAUVOIR [1]

One is not born, but rather becomes, a woman. No biological, psychological, or economic fate determines the figure that the human female presents in society; it is civilization as a whole that produces this creature.

Sévigné's drive to distinguish herself as a paragon of maternity paradoxically finds its roots in the misogyny to which she was bred. Only by inscribing herself as exceptional could she hope to transcend the confines of her gender. But, by seeking fulfillment in a socially authorized role rather than challenging that authority, she reinscribed and reinforced prescribed behavior and thereby reconfined herself in the very pattern she had sought to surpass. She articulated and valorized a maternal role that was to be of enduring consequence for generations of women being acculturated in their turn to the prevailing patriarchal system.[2]

While Sévigné insisted on the essential nature of her maternal identity, she also, on a few rare occasions, gave evidence of significant insight into the arbitrary character of the construct of femininity. Her discrete awareness of the ideology of womanhood as merely a facet of a particular social arrangement stands in tension with her general subscription to that order as epitomized in her epistolary celebration of motherhood.

Assessive statements concerning Sévigné's "place" in life appear more regularly in the later years of the correspondence as she adopts an increas-

Portions of this chapter previously appeared in *Stanford French and Italian Studies* 58 (Saratoga: Anma Libri, 1988); in *Competition: A Feminist Taboo?* ed. Valerie Miner and Helen Longino (New York: Feminist Press, 1987); and in *Papers on French Seventeenth-Century Literature* 13, no. 25 (1986).

ingly self-reflective tone. And they appear not so much in letters to her daughter, for in these she is generally intent on maintaining her maternal profile, but in letters to other relatives, where she can assume a position of critical distance. She comments as much on a life not lived as on the one she has lived. In contrast to the tenor of the rest of the correspondence, these moments of retrospection express dissatisfaction with the life she has known and recognize the limitations of the role in which she has been cast and which she has so assiduously cultivated. It was mainly in exchanges with her cousins Bussy and Coulanges that Sévigné voiced doubts about the gender system to which she had been raised. It was in comparing herself to these male relatives with whom, in theory, she had so much in common—ancestry, history, pedigree—that the discrepancies between their life experiences and her own stood out as that much more anomalous and gender-grounded.

To Bussy, she observed, in 1683, at the age of fifty-seven:

Je suis une petite poule mouillée, et je pense quelquefois: "Mais si j'avais été un homme, aurais-je fait cette honte à une maison où il semble que la valeur et la hardiesse soient héréditaires?" Après tout, je ne le crois pas, et je comprends par là la force de l'éducation. Comme les femmes ont permission d'être faibles, elles se servent sans scrupule de leur privilège, et comme on dit sans cesse aux hommes qu'ils ne sont estimables qu'autant qu'ils aiment la gloire, ils portent là toutes leurs pensées, et cela forme toute la bravoure française plus ou moins, selon leurs tempéraments. (III, L. 869, p. 116)

I am a little coward, and sometimes I think: "But if I had been a man, would I have brought this shame upon a family where it seems that valor and daring are hereditary?" After all, I do not believe so, and I understand by that the power of education. Since women have permission to be weak, they use their privilege unscrupulously, and as men are constantly told that they are worthy only insofar as they love glory, they focus all their ambitions there, and that more or less forms all of French bravery, according to their temperaments.

She entertains the possibility of biological determination, toying briefly with the concept of heredity. But she recognizes here that timidity and bravery are instilled in women and men respectively, so that what are commonly regarded as essential traits of femininity and masculinity are nothing more than the effects of gender-specific education. At the same time, faithful to the tenets of that same training, she describes herself belittlingly as "une petite poule mouillée" and invokes the standard norm ("Mais si j'avais été un homme"). The wistfulness of this past conditional is justified by the pathos of the present constative ("Je suis une petite poule mouillée")—manifestly untrue in its literal sense, figuratively eloquent in its self-disparaging message, but attenuated by the lucidity informing the comparison between what is and what might have been. She refuses the unfavorable comparison she has just articulated, recognizing the weight of engendering education and not accidental sex in deciding such fates. While she recognizes the norm of masculinity to be a social construct as well ("on dit sans cesse aux hommes"), she is unable to extricate herself from the system she is in the process of interrogating. She further casts aspersions on her own kind in suggesting that women exploit their social condition ("elles se servent sans scrupule de leur privilège") rather than oppositionally citing the virtues of weakness and so challenging the system that claims to privilege women while leaving them feeling like "little wet hens." Completely implicated in it, having embraced her prescribed role, she can only wonder lucidly at the irony of her insight, waffling back to "tempérament."

Bussy's glib reply both supports and dismisses her observation:

Vous êtes faible, Madame, parce qu'on vous a élevée à la faiblesse. Si vous aviez été nourrie dans la pensée que votre honneur consistait à tuer les hommes, comme vous l'avez été dans celle qu'il consiste à ne pas les aimer, je suis assuré que vous seriez aussi brave qu'une Amazone. (III, L. 870, p. 117)

You are weak, Madame, because you were raised to weakness. If you had been nurtured in the thought that your honor consisted of killing men, as you have been to think that it consists in not loving them, I am assured that you would be as brave as an Amazon.

Responding true to character, he pronounces authoritatively and reduces his concurrence to a teasing trivialization of the question. By escalating "aimer la gloire" to "tuer les hommes" he performs a reductio ad absurdum of the question. Where Sévigné had moved from "héréditaire" to "éducation," Bussy slips in the other direction, from the verb "élever" to the verb "nourrir." He substitutes a register of nutrition ("nourrie"), playing on the ambiguity of the word itself, for Sévigné's of training ("éducation"). He thereby naturalizes and defuses her more radical observation. Further, leaving aside his flirtatious banter, he concludes that if Sévigné had been brought up according to the code she has identified as masculine, she would have turned out as brave as "une Amazone." The women who had actively participated in the Fronde were known as *Amazones*. Sévigné might have been, but was not, among them. Otherwise, these warrior women exist only in texts of ancient lore. Thus, the whole question is neatly relegated to domains of history and fabulation and thereby dismissed. While paternalistically humoring her reflection, Bussy has expertly remotivated it in nature, resituated it either in the past or in fiction, deflated her statement, and effectively reinstated through linguistic manipulation the order that privileges him.

In 1690, at the age of sixty-four, another flash of retrospective insight brought home to Sévigné the realization that her life potential had been very much circumscribed by the accident of gender assignment. She wrote to her maternal cousin, Coulanges, who was visiting Rome, and who had sent her one of his songs composed in celebration of his having climbed to the cupola of Saint Peter's. She adopts a light tone of envy, but reflects seriously on her circumscribed life, now significantly behind her, with diminishing potential for new directions:

Je songeai à cette boule [la coupole de Saint Pierre] où vous étiez *grimpé avec vos jambes de vingt ans,* et à l'avantage qu'ont les hommes au-dessus des femmes, dont tous les pas sont comptés et bornés, et combien je me promènerais de jours et d'années dans le plain-pied de nos allées sans me trouver dans cette boule. (III, L. 1202, pp. 853–54)

I thought of this dome [the cupola of Saint Peter] where you had *climbed with your legs of a twenty-year-old,* and of the advantage that men have over women, whose every step is counted and marked out, and how I might walk for days and years in the straight and narrow of our garden paths without ever finding myself in this dome.

She recognizes succinctly the general condition of women to be one of submission, constraint, and routine, as opposed to men's estate of freedom, represented above by images of travel, adventure, youth. While her cousin might and did ascend to great heights, literally, she and her kind were restricted to pace the earth. As Sévigné advanced in age, she found herself in a position to take stock of her life, to reflect on her experience, and to generalize from it to a greater understanding of her condition as a woman, to speak her mind. While she bemoaned her lack of freedom, in her writing she finally exercised it, at least to a certain degree. This liberating honesty finds resonance in Carolyn Heilbrun's reversal of the traditional value set on youth in her reflections on *Writing a Woman's Life.* Instead Heilbrun sings the praises of age for women: "the coming of age portends all the freedoms men have always known and women never—mostly the freedom from fulfilling the needs of others and from being a female impersonator." [3] Sévigné had arrived at a time in her life when she could speak out of role, when there was no clear role for her.

Around her, over the years, the question of the status of women had raged: Mlle de Gournay had written her treatise on equality, Poullain de la Barre's had come out in several editions, the abbé de Pure had taken up the cause, and the *précieuses* had actually come close to realizing the social revolution of their dreams. Sévigné had been a member of the salon society that espoused liberating views concerning women and was a close friend of Mme de La Fayette as this novelist rescripted the female plot in *La Princesse de Clèves,* rejecting for her heroine the conventional closure of marriage. On the other hand, conservative voices had articulated contrary views, celebrating marriage, the family, and women's place, and, along with all subjects under Louis XIV, but even more markedly, women were reduced to ornamental and dependent signifiers of his monolithic glory.

To judge from Sévigné's practice of maternality, its implicit support of the regime, and its consistent mirror relation to at least one of the guiding voices for women,[4] she was more profoundly attuned to the conservative ideology. But Sévigné never explicitly situated herself in the debate on the woman question. Her practice and her friendships stand in contradiction with each other insofar as they represent opposed positions, but it must be remembered that Sévigné occupied an interstitial social position, neither true aristocrat nor complete bourgeoise. To the extent that seventeenth-century versions of feminism and antifeminism were propagated by these two groups respectively,[5] she can be seen to have maneuvered between the two extremes. The complexity of her status is reflected in the contradictions of her postures. Her own life experience afforded her certain lessons. But she arrived late and timidly at her conclusions and presented them to her male cousins where they were likely to produce the least of consequences, and so she at once aired and stifled her thoughts.

With her daughter, Sévigné was much more circumspect in her critique of gender roles. Here she herself was still acting in role. Intent upon inculcating in her the virtues of family life, that cornerstone of the social order, she could ill afford at the same time to raise doubts concerning the sanctity of that order. Nevertheless, in the course of these same late years, Sévigné made a few sharp observations to her. In the passage below, she evinces awareness of gender stereotyping as it informs and is transmitted by institutions. She commiserates with her daughter on the deplorable preaching to which the daughter is subjected at Grignan, pointing irreverently to a longstanding tradition of misogyny in the Church teachings:

Vraiment, cette sottise que vous nous mandez de votre prédicateur n'a jamais été imaginée, quoiqu'il y ait longtemps qu'on se mêle d'en dire: *Adam le bon papa, Eva la cruelle maman.* (III, L. 1038, p. 427)

Honestly, this nonsense of your preacher's that you send us defies imagination, although for a long time people have been chiming in to say: *Adam the good daddy, Eve the cruel mommy.*

On the verge of generalizing from particular repeated discourse to more sweeping conclusions concerning Christian doctrine, and its implied ideology of gender, Sévigné limits herself to the pointed remark above and takes the question no further. Paradoxically, Sévigné's insight regarding the misogyny of the Church is available to her through her experience of motherhood, which she finds in contradiction with the Church's teaching ("Eva la cruelle maman").

The above are the few critiques Sévigné ventures on the condition of women, all of them surfacing late in her life, but indicating personal cognizance of the inequities inherent to a social system privileging men at women's expense. Her understanding of gender stereotyping as it delimited femininity did not extend to an understanding of the institution of motherhood that she herself was in the process of elaborating through her writing behavior. Thus maternity operates at once as both her critical perspective and her blind spot.

Sévigné's route to social identity was necessarily circuitous, grounded and projected in the relational mode sanctioned as appropriate and specific to the feminine ethos. She surveyed the terrain of her allowed performance and sought models upon which to shape her persona. The following discussion focuses on the vicarious, social, and cultural dimensions of her inscribed maternal identity and hypothesizes specifically on implications for the daughter's complementary role.

The Art of Vicarious Living

> Que s'est-il passé dans la nuit de ton ventre pour que tu ne saches plus que
> j'étais? Qui était l'une, qui l'autre?   LUCE IRIGARAY [6]

> What happened in the darkness of your belly so that you no longer knew that
> I was? Who was the one, who the other?

The epistolary genre epitomizes textually the relational and connective mode of existence theorized in recent years as characterizing traditional woman's way of being culturally assimilated in the world.[7] The act of shaping and pacing epistolary discourse to the intention of the addressee reflects this social construction of a "feminine" self: typically the subject is molded in the image of the other and according to the vision of the other, in anticipatory and reactionary fashion. This accommodating mode informs profoundly the sense of self as it is articulated in Sévigné's writing: the maternal writing subject invents itself as it proceeds. It identifies a role for itself in the world and projects that image through its inscription in the letter. It cultivates and controls that image through obsessive epistolary activity and then basks in the refraction of society's complicitous recognition of that fiction. But that self-invention and self-cultivation depend quite often on others for their very substance. The writing subject assumes vicariously the experiences and concerns of all who come into contact with the *je*, incorporates, reshapes them, and then represents itself in their guise.

Two attitudes can be discerned in Sévigné's epistolary activity of self-construction: an ironic distance, betokening reflective self-knowledge, informs her projection of the subject (I/*je*) when it is engaged in relatively public affairs (accessed through her extended family network); and a lack of that self-awareness in the articulation of the subject when it is engaged in more intimate domestic affairs, specifically in moments of intense exchange with her daughter. Passages evincing traces of ironic distance of the first sort help us as readers to interpret her construction of the maternal subject in the second instance, to appreciate the process of vicarious identification that so characterizes her definition of self. It leaves us ultimately, though, with the question of whether this reading was available to her, or whether it so constituted her notion of self that the similarities between the way she represented herself in the public sphere and the way she performed herself in her most intimate relationships were invisible to her.

Sévigné's techniques of role creation and projection are aptly illustrated in a short passage from a letter addressed to her cousin Bussy. She writes in the personas of cousin and grandmother. The text shows how, through the letter, Sévigné endeavors to create and to control her world. But, in this extended relationship, the *je* assumes a stance of humorous distance that indicates awareness of the vicarious way in which she constructs her self:

J'ai été si occupée, mon cher cousin, à prendre Philisbourg qu'en vérité je n'ai pas eu un moment pour vous écrire . . . Voilà donc qui est fait, Dieu merci. Je soupire comme Monsieur de la Souche; je respire à mon aise. (III, L. 1019, p. 386)

I was so busy, my dear cousin, in taking Philisbourg that in truth I haven't had a moment to write to you . . . Here, then, it is done, thank God. I'm sighing like Monsieur de la Souche; I'm breathing easily.

Sévigné flaunts her chameleonic virtuosity here, combining four roles at once: she is, in turn, cousin, grandmother, comic figure from Molière's repertoire, and, a little less obviously but unmistakably, the endearing self-important fly from La Fontaine's "Le Coche et la Mouche."[8] All of these roles are mustered to beg pardon for a tardy reply; the ostensible intent is to charm away any annoyance her cousin Bussy might have felt at being subjected to a long wait for her letter. As is fairly typical of seventeenth-century protocol, where even the most mundane of activities are performed in exacting and frequently hyperbolic ways, Sévigné's excuses cannot be simple. She explains that she has been busy, engaged in the victorious siege of Philisbourg. Of course, she was not, in fact, there at all, except insofar as her imagination, fueled by her concerns for her grandson (who was) and news from the front, transported her there.

It is as grandmother that she worries about her grandson, who, at the age of seventeen, is embarking on his military career and is off at war. Her extraordinary capacity for identification and sympathy, complementing her vivid imagination, is such that she appropriates his experience and makes it her own. She feels herself entitled, then, because of her total emotional participation, to attribute to herself—to her involvement and anguish—the victory of Philisbourg. This passage offers further evidence to the thesis proposed earlier (see chapter 5) that, if Sévigné does live, as she claims, *for* others, she lives *through* them as well. She wills herself essential to life as it bustles indifferently around her. The writing subject dominates the world as she incorporates it and recreates it, transforming it into an epistolary drama in which she assumes, through vicarious identification, the lead role.

Sévigné recognizes, however, the comical aspect of her parasitical approach to experience. Before Bussy, exiled as he was, and removed from the center of signifying (Paris) himself, who enjoyed, however, a position of familial ascendancy and claimed authorial superiority over his cousin (see chapter 2), she humbles herself strategically and intertextually as she exalts herself textually, presenting thus a humorous self-reflective and accommodating persona. She has previously recognized a similarity between herself and La Fontaine's Dame Mouche and has frequently cited the fable before,[9] as in the following instance of an earlier letter:

Me voilà précisément comme la mouche. Je me mets *sur le nez du cocher*, je pousse la roue, je bourdonne, et *fais cent sottises pareilles*, et puis je dis: *J'ai tant fait que nos gens sont enfin dans la plaine.* (II, L. 715, p. 758)

Now I am just like the fly. I land *on the coachman's nose*, I push the wheel, I buzz, and *do one hundred such silly things*, and then I say: *I have done so much that our people are finally in the plain.*

Having incorporated that literary figure into her own epistolary persona, Sévigné alludes freely and loosely here to the importunate fly; she flatteringly assumes that her cousin will catch and appreciate the understated respiratory allusion and offers a subtle insight into her understanding of her own behavior and life role as epitomized in this minor episode from her life. She acknowledges that her claim to victory is but a delusion, just as is that of the fly, who thinks that by stinging the horses of the coach "elle fait aller la machine" [she makes the machine go]. When the coach has finally achieved the crest of the hill, Dame Mouche claims both the exhaustion and the accomplishment: "Respirons maintenant, dit la Mouche aussitôt" [Let's breathe now, says the Fly promptly].

The fly heaves a sigh of relief following its exertions, with its mistaking of sequence for cause, and so does the grandmother. The motif of breathing, introduced by the expletive expression of relief "Dieu merci," has associated and brought into intertextual play another fictional character as well: Sévigné compares herself to Molière's monomaniacal M. de la Souche in *L'Ecole des femmes*. His eloquent "ouf" translates her relief while admitting her intense concern for the grandson's well-being and her desire to control the dangerous world in which he moves.[10] Sévigné knows herself to be nonessential (unlike Dame Mouche) and ineffectual (unlike M. de la Souche) in relation to life as it bustles around her. Nonetheless, she endeavors to create an essential role for herself in the fray and to exert some control over her world through her writing.

Sévigné takes life, other people's experience of it as well as her own, and literature, indeed anything that comes her way, and she incorporates it, according to her needs, transmuting it into the substance of the *je.* All of her relationships to the world, literary and genealogical, are subsumed by the writing subject, knowingly and wittily. She perceives, in self-deprecating but insightful fashion, the appropriateness of comparing herself with such comical and pathetic figures as the busy insect and the amorous guardian. This self-conscious attitude, at once self-critical and self-indulgent, contributes regularly to the charm of her letters.

But the context of this self-caricaturing must be kept in mind: a woman in Paris is writing an apology to her cousin in the country, affirming her familial roles of cousin and grandmother. It is this familial domain, and particularly the area surrounding her daughter, that she exploits quite literally as a resource for subject matter, as an inspiration for roles, and as the center stage for her performance. In the scene just discussed she is able to affirm that she has lived the trauma of war because she has found a role by which to attach herself to the events. She has invented and elaborated it by bringing into play her family attachments, her imagination, and her literary competence. And she actualizes the role in this epistolary communication to her cousin.

Perspectives of intertextuality, maternal love, literary ambition, dramatization, and psychological motivation are factors contributing to the modulation of the voice that dominates the letters.[11] But it is precisely the invention, the projection, and the performance of this lead voice that calls for critical attention. This voice is the expression of a life role developed and played out in the letters as well as in the salons where the writing frequently takes place, and realized in the course of the epistolary project through the psychological and textual incorporation of relations into the fabric of self.[12]

Like La Fontaine's Dame Mouche, Sévigné invents and enacts her own drama in the writing process. However, Dame Mouche, in her at once delightful and troubling ignorance, is convinced that she is truly the cause of the progress of the coach to which she attaches herself. Whereas Sévigné acts advisedly: she knows she is inventing her own vehicle, her *Correspondance*, as well as propelling it along. She constructs a textual world, weaving it upon and through strands of family relations, to which she is, without question, essential.

She filters the outside world, where she knows herself to be ineffectual and nonessential, through that domestic reality. She shapes a version to which she is markedly important and of which she is significantly in control. Thus it is not merely what she says in her letters that matters but what that saying does, and to whom. She acts directly and forcefully on her family, and specifically her daughter, her privileged sphere of influence, inscribing and formalizing her central place through her epistolary activity.

Recent theorizing on mother-daughter relationships emphasizes the difficulty mothers and daughters have in separating from each other in the process of individuating.[13] Simultaneous drives on the part of both women to be at once close and autonomous in relation to each other produce a conflict of desires. The specularity of the mother-daughter tie, marked by signs of resemblance and repetition, is such that identity and role confusion characterize the relationship and structure a lack that repeats itself and is transmitted from one generation to the next through this nexus. The general result of this experience, as Marianne Hirsch puts it, is that "for women the delimited, autonomous, separated, individuated self does not exist (although much of our discourse still functions as if it did)."[14]

It is not difficult to imagine the complications that might arise when two people, conditioned to approach life vicariously, attempt to relate to one another. The mother-daughter relationship, as inscribed in Sévigné's letters to her daughter, offers a striking example of the tensions inherent to the dilemma of two people equally dependent one on the other for self-definition and therefore, in relation to each other, equally frustrated.

In a contemporary account, Luce Irigaray writes in a daughter's voice of her relationship with her mother and points to the seemingly inevitable alternating of well-being and frustration inscribed in the experience of the traditional mother-daughter dynamic:

Et l'une ne bouge pas sans l'autre. Mais ce n'est ensemble que nous nous mouvons. Quand l'une vient au monde, l'autre retombe sur la terre. Quand l'une porte la vie, l'autre meurt. Et ce que j'attendais de toi, c'est que, me laissant naître, tu demeures aussi vivante.[15]

And the one does not budge without the other. But it is not together that we stir. When the one is coming into the world, the other is falling back to the ground.

When the one is bearing life, the other is dying. And what I expected of you is that, letting me be born, you remain alive as well.

This difficulty in self-delimitation from a maternal perspective is eloquently expressed in Sévigné's letters to her daughter. However, those passages that exhibit signs of identity confusion might also be interpreted simply as appropriations by her from a traditional masculine-generated amorous rhetoric expressing the lover's desirous impression of merging with the beloved. Thisbé's avowal to her lover Pyramus, from Théophile de Viau's tragedy of 1617, offers an example of this sort of discourse so prevalent in Sévigné's time, and, importantly, the only kind available to her (other than that of religious mysticism) as she formulated in her writing a social role that, although already prescribed by patriarchal ideology (as witness François de Grenaille's treatise *L'Honneste fille*), had not yet been culturally assimilated and encoded:

> Hors de l'empêchement qui nous sépare ici,
> Tu sauras que *tes voeux* sont *mes désirs* aussi,
> Que ton mal est celui dont je me sens pressée.[16]

> Beyond the obstacle that separates us here,
> You will know that *your wishes* are also *my desires*,
> That your sorrow is the one by which I feel beset.

The fictional female beloved is generally poeticized, when given voice by the male writer (in those fleeting moments of felicitous harmony) as a figure of total identification and compliance, distinguished from her male counterpart only by the fissure of circumstance—the other onto whom he projects his narcissistic desire. The formative relationship between mothers and daughters as psychically organized within the patriarchal system offers an apprenticeship to the daughter for her eventual subsumption and consumption by her mate. For this reason, perhaps, little attention has been accorded by male theorists to the trauma and conflict that frequently characterize mother-daughter relationships. In that nexus is engendered a pattern of behavior that serves the prevailing system well. Hence, Sévigné's borrowings from traditional amorous discourse both accurately reflect and effectively reinforce systems of already profoundly complicitous relations.

Sévigné both attests to her radical dependency on her daughter and suggests a privileged position (comparable to the structuring Pyramus's) for herself in the relationship in the following statement:

Je ne pense qu'à vous; si, par un miracle que je n'espère ni ne veux, vous étiez hors de ma pensée, il me semble que je serais vide de tout, comme une figure de Benoît. (I, L. 152, p. 213)

I think only of you; if, by a miracle I neither hope for nor want, you were outside of my thought, it seems to me I would be empty of everything, like a Benoît statue.

Sévigné offers the painter Antoine Benoît's model in wax as an illustration of the existential void she imagines and fears without her daughter as content for her. She posits a split in herself of her self: alone, she would reduce simply to incomplete *form*; thoughts of her daughter constitute her *substance*.[17] Without her daughter as content, Sévigné imagines herself to be incomplete but, it is suggested, privileged, as pure active form is classically over pure passive matter. She thus voices her extreme dependence on her daughter and claims her as an integral and necessary element to flesh out her own structuring self.

Insatiable neediness translates into insistent pleas for the daughter's cooperation in assuring the continuance of the mother's life, inconceivable otherwise:

Ma fille, aimez-moi donc toujours. C'est ma vie, c'est mon âme que votre amitié; je vous le disais l'autre jour, elle fait toute ma joie et toutes mes douleurs. (I, L. 170, p. 263)

My daughter, love me, then, always. Your friendship is my life, my soul; I was telling you this the other day, it makes for all my joy and all my sorrows.

As surely as her celebration of identity (con)fusion denotes recourse to a familiar Platonic courting rhetoric, it reads as symptom. It points to a specific condition of "flexible and permeable ego boundaries," particularly fraught with potential problems, developed as it is, in the context of the specular mother-daughter relationship.[18] Sévigné begs her daughter for "content," for information that will feed her continuance through the vicarious relationship:

Parlez-moi de vos balcons et de votre terrasse, du meuble de ma chambre, et enfin toujours de vous: ce *vous* m'est plus cher que mon *moi*, et cela revient toujours à la même chose. (II, L. 519, p. 318)

Tell me about your balconies and your terrace, about the furniture in my room, and finally always about you: this *you* is dearer to me than my *me*, and always comes back to the same thing.

If a rhetoric of persuasion is engaged to incorporate the daughter in the maternal project, it is at the service of the mother's neediness and functions just as readily as a rhetoric of dissuasion, discouraging the daughter from considering her self and her needs other than in relation to her mother's. Constant requests of the sort illustrated above attest to Sévigné's inability to recognize and relate to her daughter as a person in her own right, and they demonstrate the narcissistic nature of the attachment.

Sévigné and her daughter are caught up in a contest of neediness that escalates emotionally in a circle of claims and demands:

Adieu, ma très chère bonne. Ne vous faites aucun *dragon*, si vous ne voulez m'en faire mille. N'est-ce pas déjà trop de m'avoir dit que *vous ne valiez rien pour moi?* quel discours! ah! qu'est-ce qui m'est donc bon? et à quoi puis-je être bonne sans vous? (II, L. 598, p. 523)

Goodbye, *ma très chère bonne*. Make no dark clouds for yourself if you do not want to make a thousand for me. Is it not already too much to have told me that *you are worth nothing to me?* what a speech! ah! so what worth is anything to me then? and what can I be worth without you?

The mother, always professing to suffer and to love more than the daughter, is fed self-disparaging remarks by the cooperative daughter, who seeks thereby to elicit from the mother the nurturance she craves. Instead, she is simply subjected to hearing more about the mother's always greater needs.

Except in the instances where the fusion drive is overtly frustrated and refused by the daughter, Sévigné probably finds satisfaction in the mere expression of her desire. The articulation of desire constitutes part of the inscriptional construction of the writing subject, while anchoring a maternal social role; so simple expression can satisfy this desire in that it performs the act. This would explain the repetition throughout the letters of her equation of living and loving, variations on the following:

Je ne sais pas trop bien si cela se peut dire, mais je sens parfaitement que de vivre et de vous aimer, c'est la même chose pour moi. (II, L. 723, p. 784)

I don't much know if this can be said, but I feel completely that to live and to love you is the same thing for me.

The most direct way Sévigné finds to express the existential oneness she feels with her daughter is to play with grammatical terms:

Si vous me demandez de quoi je me mêle de vous gronder ainsi, je vous répondrai que je me mêle de mes affaires, et que, prenant à votre personne et à vos intérêts une part aussi intime que celle que j'y prends, je trouve que tous ces arrangements et dérangements ruineux sont les miens. (II, L. 822, p. 57)

If you ask me by what right I am interfering by scolding you like this, I will respond that I am interfering in my own business, and that, taking as close an interest in your person and your affairs as I do, I find that all of these ruinous arrangements and disarrangements are my own.

Intimate concern breeds and justifies a conflation of possessive pronouns whereby the daughter's business becomes the mother's. The adult daughter, aged thirty-four at the time of this letter and mother herself, must perforce have difficulty in realizing her own person and in cultivating relationships with others when the mother insists on retaining her in an infantile state so as to satisfy, paradoxically, her own need for nurturance. The ever recurrent hope for assuaging empathy, so desired by the two women from each other, feeds and perpetuates the tension as well as the correspondence.

The success of Sévigné's epistolary role invention is ultimately not only hers but her audience's to judge as well.[19] As essential to the letters as the rhetorical strategies represented therein is their reception. The social circle regularly inscribed in the letters, bearing witness to and participating in the constitution of the subject—the daughter, the cousin, and all those friendly souls, named here and there, peering over shoulders and adding messages, spilling into referentiality—reminds the reader of the social and pragmatic goal of the letters, that of establishing visible identity and purpose for the *je* through incorporation of these voices into her own inscribed self.[20]

These presences attest to the dependence on relationships for self-knowledge which is a general fact of the human condition.[21] Sévigné appears, however, to evince the acquisition of ineffectual self-knowledge. That is, her acknowledgment of lack of control in her world, conveyed by tones of ironic distance and levity in certain instances, does not prevent her from trying to exert control at other moments, particularly with regard to her daughter. Observation of a systematic difference between the events and people she mocks herself for trying to control and those she actually does try to control in her correspondence suggests that her self-knowledge is not so much ineffectual as blinded when focused on her intimate relationship with her daughter.

Sévigné's contradictory attempt to transmit a specific image of her persona while being dependent on other people and other texts for the fabrication of this self is epitomized and explained in the tension she experiences between living through the daughter and constructing her inscribed self out of the material of the daughter. The interplay of vicarious and incorporative acts evident in the articulation of Sévigné's *je* offers a telling example of the traditional structure of maternity. Its epistolary encoding represents one of the earliest instances of the formalizing of the mother-daughter relationship and illuminates, without necessarily clarifying, the murky area between essentialism and constructionism currently being explored for traces of the maternal.[22]

Measuring Maternity

Ambition inconcevable que cette aspiration à la singularité, non naturelle, en ce sens inhumaine, et que la rage éprise d'Unicité ("Il n'y a qu'Une femme") ne peut que récuser en la condamnant "masculine"   JULIA KRISTEVA [23]

An inconceivable ambition, this aspiration to singularity—not natural, in this sense inhuman—and which the passion for uniqueness ("There is but One woman") can challenge only by condemning it as "masculine."

The theme of competition traverses and informs, in both subtle and blatant modulations of emulation and rivalry, Sévigné's expression of maternal feelings. The epistolary site of reciprocity and mutuality is just as importantly the privileged space of self-assertion implicating the other in a dialectic of necessary denial. Feminist thinking has recently been sensitive to the important place that competition occupies in what Helen Longino calls "culturally formative thinking about issues in modern western social thought," and in the extent to which relations among women are structured within and according to the dominant ideology. As she points out, competition has been posited by such social theorists as Hobbes, Malthus, and Darwin as fundamental to social behavior. It is summed up in such formulas as "survival of the fittest" and justified by such models as the economic one of limited resources.[24] So pervasive is the concept that it appears to govern even those areas of human concern that do not determine survival and that constitute in themselves their own resources. Sévigné's tendency to compare herself, her daughter, their relationship, with her contemporaries and theirs suggests perhaps a search for behavior models and guidance in a recently identified and relatively uncharted domain of competence, but her drive to excel in her performance of motherhood and to surpass even her own daughter in professing affection suggests a need to valorize herself publicly in that role.[25] Why need a mother compete for a reputation of affective excellence with other mothers, and why need a mother and her daughter compete with each other affectively? Such striving indicates a will to lay claim to a limited resource: the only resource evident in such circumstances being that of public acclaim, the acclaim of the Father, of the patriarchy.

Social recognition and approbation as meted out within the confines of patriarchal society appear to answer a paramount need in Sévigné's inscribed experience of motherhood. She regularly alludes in her letters to the maternal behavior of her contemporaries and to other mother-daughter ties, returning in each case to a consideration of her own. This penchant for comparing other mother-daughter relationships with their own indicates Sévigné's drive to compete, to excel in her role of "mother," and to encourage complementary rivalrous behavior in her daughter. There appears to be a deliberate attempt to pass from the private sphere of domestic relations into the public domain of social performance, the success of which will be crowned finally by the publication of this personal correspondence.[26]

Sévigné inscribes her drive to distinction within a politically conservative framework; she affirms "her friends, her daughter and herself as exceptional women, since their coding as exceptions does not undermine the prevailing system of sex roles."[27] Sévigné does not content herself, however, with functioning as merely another member of an exceptional female community; she seeks, through her relationship with her daughter, to distinguish herself even within that group:

Il n'y a que vous, ma bonne, et moi, si je l'ose dire, qui la [une si chère et précieuse amitié] mettons au premier rang, et qui en soyons plus touchées que de toutes les autres choses de ce monde. Ces sentiments sont rares; on voit tous les jours des arrangements bien contraires, mais jouissons du plaisir de n'être point comme les autres. (III, L. 1203, pp. 854–55)

Only you, *ma bonne,* and myself, I dare say, rank such a dear and precious friendship foremost, and are more moved by it than by all the other things in this world. These feelings are rare; every day we see arrangements quite the contrary, but let us rejoice in the pleasure of not being at all like the others.

Sévigné revels in her achievement in the maternal sphere, not necessarily because of any specific gratification to be had there, but, at least as she expresses it in the passage cited above, because it represents for her a mark of difference, and, therefore, of superiority over others. She derives pleasure from the self-favoring act of comparison and includes her daughter as she exults in a spirit of self-congratulation.

It does not suffice that Sévigné should enjoy an intense and intimate relationship with her daughter; she seeks, through her epistolary performance of maternity, visibility and acclaim in the social arena. Maternal affection, commonly viewed as pertaining to the sacred realm of the unconditional, the instinctual, regulated only by its own private momentum, appears paradoxically measurable here as it enters the world of display. In transforming maternity through her writing into a public role, Sévigné shapes her experience according to values borrowed from the patriarchal social sphere in which she seeks distinction. She invents and savors a dynamic of competition in her newly established domain of affective competence and can be seen thereby to "masculinize" maternity.

Sévigné's incitements to epistolary reciprocity appear to function most effectively in those relational situations where the power structure already favors the amenability of the addressee—within the family and particularly addressed to the daughter. Mme de La Fayette, Sévigné's closest woman friend, refused to be coerced into a regular writing relationship with her:

Et si j'avais un amant qui voulut de mes lettres tous les matins, je romprais avec lui. Ne mesurez donc point notre amitié sur l'écriture; je vous aimerai autant, en ne vous écrivant une page en un mois, que vous en m'écrivant dix dans huit jours. (I, L. 319, p. 583)

And if I had a lover who wanted letters from me every morning, I would break off with him. So don't measure our friendship by writing; I will love you as much, in writing you not one page in a month, as you in writing me ten in a week.

La Fayette condemns the economy that equates loving and writing and that insists on ceaseless demonstration, on measuring. In that sense, she protects their friendship from the insidious implications of quantifying. Only with her daughter, in a position of filial obligation, could Sévigné elaborate a relational identity in writing. Her maternal role, because the most powerful posture she enjoyed, was the most effective position from which to write.

The projection of the maternal persona depends crucially on the cooperation of her daughter, cast in a supporting role. As Sévigné measures maternity by scrutinizing other mother-daughter relationships, she seeks to shape supportive behavior in her daughter, Françoise-Marguerite. To that end, she dwells particularly on the behavior of the other daughters. In an early letter to her daughter in Provence, Sévigné introduces the first filial comparison, and she does not at all assure Françoise-Marguerite of her primacy as model daughter. She confronts her with the example of another daughter, Mme de Soubise, who writes superb letters because she is inspired by the subject matter, her own mother Mme de Rohan, and who inscribes herself socially and textually in her mother's domain via the letter:

Ma bonne, vous n'êtes pas seule qui aimez votre mère. Mme de Soubise écrit ici des lettres qui surpassent sa capacité ordinaire . . . Mme de Rohan m'a bien fait souvenir d'une partie de mes douleurs dans la séparation de sa fille. (I, L. 162, p. 246)

Ma bonne, you are not the only one who loves her mother. Here, Mme de Soubise writes letters to hers that surpass her usual abilities . . . Mme de Rohan reminded me of a measure of my own sufferings in her separation from her daughter.

Sévigné devotes more admiring attention to the filial devotion exemplified in Mme de Soubise's letters than to the maternal model afforded in Mme de Rohan. This mother's grief is equal to only part of her own, whereas Mme de Soubise, the daughter, outdoes not only herself but, by implication, Françoise-Marguerite as well. The subliminal message proposes a relationship of rivalry; it instructs the daughter to do the same and to surpass Mme de Soubise, just as Sévigné surpasses the mother, Mme de Rohan, in the plenitude of her suffering.

Such comparisons suggest an invitation to compete for mother-daughter epistolary excellence and renown. Françoise-Marguerite resisted her mother's urgings and preferred to protect the privacy of their exchange, as evidenced by her mother's reproaches:

Vous cachez les tendresses que je vous mande, friponne; et moi je montre quelquefois, et à certaines gens, celles que vous m'écrivez . . . je veux qu'on voie que vous m'aimez. (I, L. 143, p. 182)

You hide the tender thoughts I send you, rascal; whereas I show sometimes, and to certain people, those that you write to me . . . I want people to see that you love me.

The daughter's reluctance, in the interest of forging a less dependent identity for herself, to circulate her mother's outpourings in her salon was a source of continued frustration to Sévigné. Nevertheless, by keeping up her end of the exchange, the daughter participated, in passive-aggressive fashion, in enabling and sustaining her mother's project.

Sévigné actually expresses territoriality regarding the domain of maternity as she scans the horizon for other mother-daughter pairs. She needs such other figures in order for there to exist such a domain within which to establish the grounds of her own excellence. She has staked out her claim as maternal paragon, and all pretenders to the title are subject to her scrutiny. Again, she focuses on a daughter's active part in the relationship rather than on the mother's, in a subtle gesture of coercion:

Il y a ici une petite fille qui se veut mêler d'aimer sa maman, mais elle est cent pas derrière vous, quoiqu'elle fasse et dise fort joliment; c'est Mme de Nangis. (III, L. 981, p. 322)

There is a young girl here who wants to get involved in loving her mother, but she is a hundred steps behind you, although she speaks and acts quite nicely; it's Mme de Nangis.

Here Françoise-Marguerite receives an actual compliment, but she receives with it forceful reminders that she is engaged in a competition of filial devotion, even though it be of her mother's devising rather than of her own choosing. The daughter's performance is measured, weighed, and compared; it could conceivably some day be found lacking. Such comparative vignettes function parabolically in the Sévigné rhetoric of maternity. They are not subtle; the immediate references—Sévigné and her daughter— always dominate in those related, and the lessons more often than not seem to be designed for the specific edification of the daughter.

Sévigné privileges the Rohan-Soubise mother-daughter couple as a convenient standard. In the passage below, she locates herself as judge of the compared daughters' epistolary prowess and thus devises and occupies a position of authority on proper filial address. In her evaluation, she distinguishes between content and form, and Françoise-Marguerite receives a compliment, via the comparison, on her writing:

J'en ai vu une [lettre miraculeuse] d'une fille à une mère. Cette fille n'écrit pas comme vous, elle n'a pas de l'esprit comme vous, mais elle a de la tendresse et de l'amitié comme vous; c'est [Mme] de Soubise à Mme de Rohan. Je fus surprise hier de voir le fond de son coeur pour Mme de Rohan, et aussi quelle tendresse naturelle Mme de Rohan sent pour elle. (I, L. 197, p. 336)

I saw a marvelous letter from a daughter to her mother. This daughter does not write as you do, she does not have your wit, but she does have affection and tenderness like you; it's [Mme] de Soubise writing to Mme de Rohan. I was surprised yesterday to see the depth of her feeling for Mme de Rohan, and also what natural tenderness Mme de Rohan feels for her.

This comparison is distinguished from the preceding citation concerned with filial devotion by Sévigné's attention to the reciprocity of affection between the mother and daughter. One wonders what kind of "tenderness" other than "natural" Sévigné might have in mind that requires her to use the qualifier, or is it simply her urge to prolixity—ever obedient to the phatic function of the letter, as she satisfies her need to write—that insists on such expansion?

On another occasion, Sévigné generously admires a daughter's self-sacrificial attentions to her ill mother, Mme de Montlouet, and comprehends the mother's consequent concern for the daughter's health:

Mme de Montlouet a la petite vérole. Les regrets de sa fille sont infinis; la mère est au désespoir aussi de ce que sa fille ne veut pas la quitter pour aller prendre l'air comme on lui ordonne. Pour de l'esprit, je pense qu'elles n'en ont pas du plus fin, mais pour des sentiments, ma belle, c'est tout comme chez nous, et aussi tendres et aussi naturels. (II, L. 404, p. 19)

Mme de Montlouet has smallpox. Her daughter's worries are infinite; the mother is in despair as well since her daughter refuses to leave her side to take some fresh air as she has been told to do. As for wit, I do not think they have the sharpest, but for feelings, my dear, it is just as with us, just as tender and just as natural.

In discussing what appears to be a private sickroom drama, Sévigné indicates the potentially public dimension of all situations in her society and the performative aspect of all relational activity. The world at large is privy to the mother-daughter dynamic as it is played out around the sick bed, and it sits in constant judgment; the "natural" consistently has a concern for effect and must be understood as a contradiction in terms within the Sévigné discourse.

Sévigné reads a visual and behavioral text in her observation of the sickroom drama here. As she evaluates the relational manifestation, she reiterates the textual distinction of form and content and amplifies it once again as she opposes "esprit" and "sentiment." The intellectualizing of experience corresponds with "wit" and aligns thus with form, and the emotional apprehension of life underlies the equation of "feeling" and content. It is not surprising that in her repeated dichotomizing, Sévigné should be prepared to concede comparability with this other couple in those affective areas (feeling and content, in the sense of material experience) traditionally allotted to women, while she expresses more competitive concern for excellence in the traditionally male domains of writing, of expression, wit, and form. It is telling that Sévigné's privileging of the rational eventually backfired. The daughter-disciple carried it to the extreme and became a fervent practitioner of Cartesianism, leaving the mother-model behind in a muddle of puzzled emotional bewilderment and resentment toward her daughter's passion for reason.[28]

Occasionally Sévigné congratulates herself and her daughter on their epistolary fidelity; not only the relationship, but the exchange of letters itself, seems to have stabilized into an unusual routine:

Je ne crois pas qu'il se soit jamais vu un commerce comme le nôtre; il n'est pas fort étrange que j'en fasse mon plaisir. Aussi c'est ce qui ne se voit guère, et c'est ce que je sens délicieusement. (I, L. 359, p. 657)

I do not think there has ever been seen an exchange such as ours; it is not strange that I should take pleasure in that. And it is something that is hardly ever seen, and that is what I savor thoroughly.

What seems to please Sévigné particularly about the correspondence, just as with the relationship, is not the exchange itself but the fact that it is unparalleled, that it defies comparison. As exceptional, it has succeeded in transcending the vicious circle of comparability and has established itself as unique, that is, so excellent as to surpass all similar others. She reiterates the same pleasure at its singularity in the following passage, written a few weeks later:

C'est une grande consolation pour moi que la vivacité de notre commerce; je ne crois pas qu'il y ait d'exemple d'un pareil. (I, L. 364, p. 677)

The liveliness of our exchange is a great consolation for me; I do not believe there exists an example of a similar one.

While the concern to conform to prescribed etiquettes characterized the general tenor of social exchange under Louis XIV, the corollary to that movement of submission was the drive for distinction, the need to establish an independent identity and stand out from the crowd—ultimately, to attract the monarch's attention and favor. Such a competitive environment influenced even the most discreet of activities. Not only does Sévigné find pleasure and consolation in writing to her daughter; she also takes obvious pride in the novelty of her maternal and epistolary enterprise. While pleasure and consolation are feelings that might result from the most private of exchanges, the feeling of pride can derive only from a scanning of the social horizon, from finding and classing as inferior other similar arrangements, thus establishing as outstanding, and therefore meritorious, her own.

Such competitiveness characterizes Sévigné's attitude toward other mother-daughter pairs. It motivates her to invent incentives for securing demonstrations of filial devotion from her daughter. These appear, in the course of the correspondence, to be ever greater, and never sufficient. This drive reaches even into the relationship between the two women, where it stimulates comparison, protest, and controversy. When the two women exchange compliments on style, they vie at insisting on the greater talent of the other. This is in keeping with the greater value assigned, as seen earlier, to form and wit. But each insists on claiming for herself the greater love for the other. Sévigné fuels the contest of the greater affection by insisting on the naturalness of maternal love, maternal instinct, as opposed to a lack of tradition of filial devotion. This insistence on the primacy of maternal instinct functions as a pretext for self-absorption in the letters of the mother and generates appropriate cooperative protest on the part of the daughter.

Sévigné generalizes about maternal and filial capacities for affection. Having established that her caring is merely in keeping with the nature of the maternal, while her daughter's is not at all typical of the filial response and is therefore the more extraordinary of the two, she then claims to surpass her daughter's remarkable affection by virtue of that same unique and so inspiring daughter:

Je suis persuadée que personne ne sait aimer comme vous, je dirais, si ce n'est moi, mais la tendresse de la maternité est si naturelle, et celle des enfants si extraordinaire, que quand je fais ce que je dois, vous êtes un prodige. Je crois pourtant qu'il y a une dose de tendresse dans mon coeur qui tient à votre personne et dont les autres mères ne tâtent pas, ce qui me faisait dire, il y a quelque temps, que je vous aimais d'une amitié faite exprès pour vous. (III, L. 1196, p. 837)

I am convinced that no one else is capable of loving as you do, that is, if not me, but maternal affection is so natural, and that of children so extraordinary, that whereas I do simply as I must, you are a prodigy. I believe, however, that there is a measure of affection in my heart that is inspired by you personally and that other mothers do not experience, which is what made me say, a while ago, that I loved you with an affection tailored specifically for you.

Such a position at once denies to Françoise-Marguerite (mother of three) perspective as mother herself and subordinates her as daughter, locating her value in the appreciation the mother assigns, encoding her fixedly as instrument of her mother's agency. Sévigné's insistence on the natural character of maternal love stands in contradiction to views more recently posited by women writers and thinkers, many of them mothers themselves. The social historian Elisabeth Badinter, on the basis of research done on maternal behavior in France from the seventeenth century to the present, finds grounds to refute the notion of any primordial maternal instinct:

L'amour maternel n'est qu'un sentiment humain. Et comme tout sentiment, il est incertain, fragile et imparfait. Contrairement aux idées reçues, il n'est peut-être pas inscrit profondément dans la nature féminine.[29]

Maternal love is a human feeling. And like any feeling, it is uncertain, fragile, and imperfect. Contrary to popular belief, it is perhaps not deeply inscribed in women's nature.

The assumption of maternal instinct, traditionally expressed in mythological, religious, literary, and folkloric modes, reflects perhaps not so much a truth as a profound human desire shaped by the history of social organization. It provides, in Sévigné's rhetoric, the context essential to her aspiration to exceptionality, while the emphasis on the superiority of her daughter as love object offers even further justification.

In order to sustain the epistolary and affective dialogue that constitutes her exceptionality, Sévigné has been obliged to share some of the glory with her correspondent daughter. She weaves a discourse of seductive flattery regularly into later letters, as she acknowledges expressions of affection received from her daughter and sustains the epistolary exchange: "La tendresse des mères n'est pas ordinairement la règle de celle des filles, mais vous n'êtes point aussi comme les autres" (III, L. 1206, p. 868) [The affection of mothers does not usually set the rule for that of daughters, but then you are not at all like the others]. The pact of mutual admiration, instigated by the mother, implicating and isolating the daughter, has served to posit the mother in the authoritative "ruling" role within the couple and has ensured her incontestable title to her self-designed but publicly recognized maternal crown. Her affection, her daughter, their relationship, their correspondence—these are different from and superior to all other comparable arrangements, so she claims. Paradoxically, this epistolary celebration of maternal love suggests a will to social alienation just as persuasively as it points to an example of intimate harmony. At the heart of the project is self-apprehension, which appears to require constant sustenance from the testimony of the other: of the daughter, of society, and—ultimately—of the father. That testimony is predicated upon an activity of establishing a common ground, seeking and emphasizing difference, measuring it and coming out ahead—of inventing and surpassing the necessary other.

The theme of comparison, as traced through the examples above, points to currents of competition and rivalry, to instances of performatic behavior, and to ambitions for excellence. Such traits lead me to construe the process of measuring maternity as endemic to its introduction into the public domain and to the elaboration of maternality as a social role at least in the more elite circles of seventeenth-century French society.

Patterns of Excellence: The Classical Maternal Tradition

On peut concevoir des mythes très anciens, il n'y en a pas d'éternels; car c'est l'histoire humaine qui fait passer le réel à l'état de parole, c'est elle et elle seule qui règle la vie et la mort du langage mythique. Lointaine ou non, la mythologie ne peut avoir qu'un fondement historique, car le mythe est une parole choisie par l'histoire: il ne saurait surgir de la "nature" des choses.
ROLAND BARTHES[30]

One can conceive of very ancient myths, there are no eternal ones; for it is human history that makes the real pass into words, it is history alone that regulates the life and death of mythic language. Distant or not, mythology can only have a historical base, for myth is a word chosen by history: it could not arise from the "nature" of things.

Few expressions of the classical world permeate the fabric of the seventeenth century so thoroughly as the mythological. Under the absolutist sway of Louis XIV, cultural expression sought firm grounding through affiliation with a golden past of supposed perfection. Mythology, then, is frequently cited, not merely for its ornamental value, but with a view to legitimizing contemporary conventions through appeal to its enduring authority. The king's personal penchant for identifying with that other *roi-soleil*, Apollo, epitomizes the official attitude of the period.[31]

Sévigné's cultural construction of maternity offers a more subtle example of myth matching and self-mythicization. A similar legitimizing practice is indicated in the elaboration of her social role as it is both projected and received through reference to a shared tradition. Three mythological figures, all sharing the seme of "mother"—Niobe, Ceres, and Latona—are privileged in relation to her. An examination of the context of occurrence for these allusions in the *Correspondance*, and of the purposes that they can be construed to serve, illuminates Sévigné's performance of the maternal. It highlights the socially concerted configuring of her maternal persona. At the same time, it illustrates the dynamic of legitimation and conservative perpetuation that characterizes instances of allusion to the mythological through the appeal to the authority of origins.

Throughout the *Correspondance*, Sévigné expresses concern for the image she projects as mother, indicating a preoccupation as marked for the reception of her role as for its performance. Although she views her relationship with her daughter as unique, she does seek confirmation of the distinction of such an affective attachment through its precedence in classical tradition. Familiar with translations and versions of Ovid's *Metamorphoses* by her contemporaries Du Ryer, Thomas Corneille, and Benserade, she finds therein adequate parallels and models for her performance.

Sévigné alludes to the maternal figure of Niobe in the second month of separation from her daughter, as she fashions by pen her own sense of maternity and seeks to shape their burgeoning epistolary exchange. Here she actively seeks, in mythology, a measure of comparison for her own exceptionality. Her reference to Niobe punctuates a mildly Oresteian outburst of frustration at her distant daughter's failure to cooperate in the elaboration of the maternal project, the dimensions of which exceed mere correspondence between the two women. As was seen in chapter 5, Sévigné takes umbrage at the fact that Françoise-Marguerite circulates only excerpts from her mother that are of obvious general interest, and that she keeps to herself those more intimate parts of the letters that are ostensibly addressed to her alone, and she underscores this accusation with the contrast of her own practice (I, L. 143, p. 182).

Sévigné's performance of maternity carries social implications for her. Since her tears are publicly displayed and apprehended, they must be perceived as inspired by a worthy cause. The onus is on the daughter to prove that. Sévigné requests that her daughter provide in her next letter not a text for her own consumption, but a pretext for the mother's public display of an attachment of mythic proportions: "Par exemple, nommez-moi un peu M. d'Ormesson et les Mesmes" (I, L. 143, p. 182) [For example, name to me a bit M. d'Ormesson and the Mesmes]. As bearer of greetings to her friends from her daughter, Sévigné will situate herself within her social circle as *mater*.

After requesting cooperation in this tactical maneuver, Sévigné tempers the accusatory and demanding tone of her letter with a compliment: "Vous êtes aimable, et rien n'est comme vous" (I, L. 143, p. 182) [You are kind, and there is nothing like you]. She authorizes her daughter to censor this particular instance of admiring affection, invoking the dangers of maternal hubris and positing a parallel between herself and Niobe: "Voilà du moins ce que vous chacherez, car, depuis Niobé, une mère n'a point parlé ainsi" (I, L. 143, p. 182) [This at least you will hide, for, since Niobe, a mother has not spoken like this]. She legitimizes her demanding behavior by comparing her love for Françoise-Marguerite with that of Niobe for her children.

The hyperbolic equation mitigates the preceding fit of maternal anger and absolves the daughter of her habitual failure to publicize the mother's love for her. In keeping with the lesson from the myth of Niobe, to do so would be tantamount to endangering the mother's life. As Niobe's maternal boastings brought down upon her the ire of Latona, so also could Sévigné's if they were to be broadcast by her daughter.

The allusion to the myth of Niobe serves two purposes in the mother's letter: it veils the reciprocal victimizing in the mother-daughter dynamic spelled out just above—the mother's demanding demonstrativeness and the daughter's frustrating reticence—and it legitimizes this status quo. The irresolution of the antagonism is minimized and authorized at once. Since Sévigné can identify her match in an accepted mythological archetype, she can encode her behavior as equally exceptional, but plausible and valid. Sévigné invokes a sense of temporality as she situates her discourse in relation, "depuis," to Niobe's. She elevates her own status to that of the eternal myth as she inscribes herself in immortal time, while reducing Niobe to mere historicity by framing her in mortal time. The positing of similarity at once deflates the myth as it inflates the myth matcher. Sévigné's myth matching lends an aura of sanction and exaltation to the maternal role she is cultivating. It transposes her performed role from the realm of the banal experiential to that of the sublime symbolic.

On a later occasion, Sévigné expresses particular pleasure as she reports to her daughter that her friends have compared them to Ceres and Persephone. The premiere of Quinault and Lulli's opera *Proserpine* in 1680, nine years after Françoise-Marguerite's initial departure for Provence to follow her husband, occasions the circulation of this apt analogy. Sévigné expresses pleasure at this specular confirmation of her projected self-image: she has succeeded, through such myth matching, in establishing a formal identity for herself in her world:

Je veux parler de l'opéra. Je ne l'ai point vu (je ne suis point curieuse de me divertir), mais on dit qu'il est parfaitement beau. Bien des gens ont pensé à vous et à moi. Je ne vous l'ai point dit, parce qu'on me faisait *Cérès*, et vous *Proserpine;* tout aussitôt voilà M. de Grignan *Pluton*, et j'ai eu peur qu'il ne me fît répondre vingt mille fois par son choeur de musique:
Une mère
Vaut-elle un époux?
C'est cela que j'ai voulu éviter, car pour le vers qui est devant celui-là:
Pluton aime mieux que Cérès,
je n'en eusse point été embarrassée. (II, L. 740, p. 857)

I want to speak of the opera. I have not seen it (I am not at all interested in being amused), but they say it is perfectly beautiful. Many people have thought of you and of me. I did not tell you, because they saw me as Ceres and you as Persephone; that automatically cast M. de Grignan as Pluto, and I was afraid that he would have his choir repeat to me twenty thousand times:

Is a mother
Worth a husband?
That's what I wanted to avoid, since as for the verse which comes before that one:
Pluto loves better than Ceres.
I wouldn't have been at all troubled.

Sévigné betrays or decenters the major issue of the Ceres myth in the company of the interpreting community (Quinault and those operagoers) to which she belongs. For the focus of the *Proserpine* libretto, as evidenced by the verses cited, is not solely the celebrated mother-daughter paradigm but the celebration of love in its various guises, expressed here through competitive comparisons of Ceres' and Pluto's amorous competence. Sévigné, as well as her contemporaries, opts to dwell on that interpretation of the myth which focuses on and privileges the disruptive male figure.[32] She jests about her hesitation in communicating the comparison to the Grignan couple, attributing her reluctance to delicate concern for the implications in the configuration for M. de Grignan. He would be cast, by extension of the myth logic, as her antagonist.

The drift of Sévigné's humor here is clearly designed to be shared with the son-in-law, although it is inscribed in her letter to the daughter. Sévigné peers beyond her immediate addressee and seeks to engage in flirtatious banter with the more important male in the background. She cites light-heartedly the mother-husband dynamic of rivalry that is generated around the figure of the daughter-wife. She seems to be oblivious that such treatment of Françoise-Marguerite recognizes no autonomous identity for her but figures her strictly as a relational creature, serving the needs of mother or of husband according to the season, a mere object of exchange in the familial economy.

Sévigné reshifts her attention as she concludes her interpretive play and then returns to the ostensible subject: "Tant y a, ma fille, je suis fort persuadée que nous nous retrouverons, et je ne vis que pour cela" (II, L. 740, p. 857) [So much so, my daughter, that I am quite convinced that we will be reunited again, and I live only for that]. The expressed intensity of Sévigné's desire for reunion with her daughter, "je ne vis que pour cela," justifies her earlier textual attention to the husband-obstacle and resituates her daughter as the object of her desire. Nevertheless, her maternal attachment, as she has expressed it through her interpretation of the Ceres myth, seems to function as an oppressive exercise of mother-right, competitively shared and played out with the other master, M. de Grignan.

This impression is confirmed by the most obvious and rarest of sources. On one of the few occasions where the textually speechless daughter's voice is still extant, where an actual letter of hers, addressed to her husband, has survived, she articulates her own position regarding this double-edged tyranny:

Eh, mon Dieu! Ne viendra-t-il pas une année où je puisse voir mon mari sans quitter ma mère? En vérité, je le souhaiterais fort, mais quand il faut choisir, je ne balance pas à suivre mon cher Comte. (II, p. 1392)

Oh, my goodness! Will there not come a year when I can see my husband without leaving my mother? In truth, I would truly hope so, but when I have to choose, I do not hesitate to follow my dear Count.

It seems merely politic that, in the context of a letter to her husband, Françoise-Marguerite should profess to prefer him to her mother. But the fact that the daughter-Persephone is torn and must choose points to a perceived equivalence for her of love-objects, mother and husband, and suggests the effective preparatory function of the formative mother-daughter relation that eventuates in her choice of husband over mother, thus ensuring her integration in the social order and, reciprocally, that social order's continuance. Ironically here, the mother's claims on her daughter only serve the order that disserves her, and they can be understood as already contained within and necessary to that order.[33]

Later, that spring, Sévigné extends the Ceres analogy, finding that figure increasingly appropriate to categorize her own familial self. To her daughter, she writes:

Vous faites un merveilleux usage de vos *Métamorphoses*; je les relirai à votre intention. Si j'avais de la mémoire, j'aurais appliqué bien naturellement le ravage d'Erisichton, dans les bois consacrés à Cérès, au ravage que mon fils a fait au Buron, qui est à moi. (II, L. 774, p. 978)

You put your *Metamorphoses* to marvelous use; I will reread them especially for you. If I had a good memory, I would have quite naturally applied the destruction by Erisichton, in the wood consacrated to Ceres, to the destruction my son wreaked on Buron, which is mine.

In the myth of Ceres, Sévigné finds not merely figurative ornamentation for her discourse but comforting structural parallels that at once echo her experiences and inform them in such a way as to render them coherent and meaningful. As a latter-day Ceres, she can interpret, again and again, the mundane concerns of her life deriving from her maternal relationship to both her daughter and her son as imbued with transcendent significance, while she celebrates the importance to which her role as mother entitles her (e.g., III, L. 1229, p. 934).

Sévigné moved in a world that recovered its meaning regularly through appeal to classical tradition. Her own image was invented and understood by a filtering through that semantic grid. Mention of the third model, Latona, figures actually as an analogous perception of Sévigné and comes from without the text of the *Correspondance*. We are indebted to Roger Duchêne for including the allusion in a footnote to his edition of the letters. He was evidently struck by the pertinence of a vision inscribed by the abbé Arnauld in his *Mémoires*:

"Il me semble que je la vois encore," dit-il de Mme de Sévigné, "telle qu'elle me parut la première fois que j'eus l'honneur de la voir, arrivant dans le fond de son carrosse tout ouvert, au milieu de monsieur son fils et de mademoiselle sa fille, tous trois tels que les poètes représentent Latone au milieu du jeune Apollon et de la petite Diane, tant il éclatait d'agréments et de beauté dans la mère et dans ses enfants." (I, L. 362, n. 4, p. 1386)

"It seems to me that I see her again," he says of Mme de Sévigné, "just as she appeared to me the first time I had the honor of seeing her, arriving in the back of her open carriage, between her son and her daughter, the three of them just as the poets represent Latona between the young Apollo and the little Diana, so much did the mother and her children sparkle with charm and beauty."

This interpretive recollection is dated approximately 1657: the radiant widow Sévigné would have been thirty-one, her magnificent offspring nine and eleven years old respectively. Here is an early instance of a vision and deification of Sévigné in her maternal role. The abbé's interpretation of this scene may be strictly retrospective, reading a later projection of Sévigné into his past perceptions. And, for her part, Sévigné may never have been aware that he viewed her, at that time or later, as a latter-day Latona. Nevertheless, that such a rapprochement of Sévigné and Latona is made at all points to the common cultural context within which both Arnauld and Sévigné seek meaning and assign significance to their experience.

Whether such an image projects consciously or unconsciously on the part of Sévigné, it attaches to a familiar paradigm in Arnauld's memorative repertoire and is thereby at once contextualized and exalted.[34] An important aspect of the function of myth as it relates to Sévigné is thus introduced. As model for a life-role, the mythological figure is imposed from without. Maternity as annotated here is celebrated by Arnauld rather than necessarily experienced by Sévigné. The abbé's classical orientation informs his view of his world and suggests a deified maternal model that Sévigné, in his mind's eye, meets. The complimentary correlation is the consequence of his cultural heritage. To the extent that Sévigné is attuned to reverberations of that same heritage in her own milieu, it could be argued that her self-mythicizing in the maternal mode, her cultivation of existential fact as a social role, derives, at least in part, from a patriarchal suggestive perception. She models herself according to a male assignment of appropriate significance for her, in keeping with his inherited vision of social order, contained in the mythological allusion.

Beyond her identification, projected and imposed, with such figures as Niobe, Ceres, and Latona, Sévigné advances her self-mythicizing in the maternal mode through the deployment of scriptoral and thematic strategies. The direction of such an activity is indicated by Barthes in his broader consideration on the "principle of the myth": "il transforme l'histoire en nature" [it transforms history into nature].[35] An active illustration of an attempt at this process is offered in the following passage addressed by Sévigné to her daughter:

Il faut qu'il y ait une Mme de Sévigné qui aime sa fille plus que toutes les autres mères, qu'elle en soit souvent très éloignée et que les souffrances les plus sensibles qu'elle ait dans cette vie lui soient causées par cette chère fille. J'espère aussi que cette Providence disposera les choses d'une autre manière, et que nous nous retrouverons comme nous avons déjà fait. (II, L. 760, p. 916)

There must be a Mme de Sévigné who loves her daughter more than all the other mothers, she must often be very far from her and the most painful suffering she has in this life must be caused by this dear daughter. I also hope that this Providence will arrange things in another way, and that we will be reunited as we have been in the past.

In the process of self-mythicization, Sévigné projects a grammatically indefinite persona committed by grammatically imperative fate to her role.[36] By attributing her maternal vocation to the will of "cette Providence," she situates herself in mythic eternity, as elect victim of a preordained destiny. She inscribes herself in the third person singular, as already the subject of recognized discourse, removed from the contingency of the subjective *je* mode, with an already familiar story. And she justifies her self-exaltation by postulating her comparative maternal superiority. If abstraction, fate, factuality, and exceptionality do not suffice in themselves to entitle her to the recognition she seeks, she points as well to a significant dose of evidential suffering. As Barthes states it: "le mythe est une parole *excessivement* justifiée" [myth is an *excessively* justified word].[37]

Sévigné's dependence on classical maternal figures as glorious precedents and convenient models illustrates a mythological paradigm in the historical process of elaborating and perpetuating itself, an archetype in the making. It is against and through this conservative tradition of the exaltation of the maternal that Julia Kristeva writes, tracing the effects of *his*-stories of mothering in shaping patriarchal cultural formulations of maternity.[38] She points beyond the need for radical revision of the conscious performance of motherhood, to the more revolutionary need to restructure the subconscious that harbors the motivating desire:

If the archetype of the belief in a good and pure substance, that of utopias, is the belief in the omnipotence of an archaic, full, total, englobing mother with no frustration, no separation, no break-producing symbolism (with no castration, in other words), then it becomes evident that we will never be able to defuse the violences mobilized through the counter-investment necessary to carrying out this phantasm, unless one challenges precisely this myth of the archaic mother.[39]

In Sévigné's epistolary adventure of self-expression, self-discovery, and self-invention, the cult of the mythic maternal legitimizes and glorifies a relation that today is more ambivalently considered: on the one hand, it is clinically diagnosed and labeled separation anxiety, neurotic neediness, drive to control, and identity confusion; and, at the same time, it is poeticized and valorized as a seminal model of interdependence and subjectivity. By inscribing herself in the mythic mother mode, Sévigné justifies her obsessive behavior, embraces and legitimates her "symptoms," and exalts her performed self into the visible and signifying realm of circulating metaphors.

Sévigné's self-inscription in the mythology of maternal archetypes can only be validated, in the end, through the recognition and tribute of others. By this logic, she is "mother" to the extent that she appears to be and is perceived as "mother." Her sense of self depends upon a relational world construct, a network of affective ties, to which she can assign, and from which she can derive, meaning in her maternal capacity. Hence such exhortations to the implicated daughter as: "Je veux qu'on voie que vous m'aimez" (I, L. 143, p. 182), along with her recourse to familiar and authorizing mythological paradigms.

That Sévigné was successful in projecting her maternal identity not only within her family but for the consumption of a greater public is attested by its susceptibility to parody. She revels in her friend M. de Chaulnes's humorous confirmation and endorsement of her relationship with her daughter:

Il [M. de Chaulnes] assure que vous êtes son bon génie, qu'il vous parle toujours, et vous entend. L'autre jour il me dit: "Pourquoi touchez-vous à votre tête, ma mère? Vous y avez mal?" Je l'entends, et je lui réponds: "Non, ma fille point du tout." Cela nous fait un jeu, et un souvenir continuel de l'amitié que vous avez pour moi. (III, L. 1134, p. 658)

He [M. de Chaulnes] insists that you are his good spirit, that he is always in communication with you, and understands you. The other day he said to me: "Why are you touching your head, mother? Does it hurt?" I understood him, and replied: "No, daughter, not at all." This is a game for us, and a constant reminder of the affection you have for me.

She looks not only to her daughter, but to society also, as a mirror for self-affirmation, and she is dependent on that reflection for a sense of her own being. She revels in her daughter-in-law's accolade: "Ma belle-fille a dit fort joliment: 'Ah! voilà la vraie mère!' Je suis donc la vraie mère!" (III, L. 1113, pp. 604–5) [My daughter-in-law said quite prettily: "Ah! Here is the real mother!" So I am the real mother!] Such a statement reads as an amusing and amused relational and gendered variation on Descartes's autonomous and presumably universalizing *cogito, ergo sum*. Sévigné says rather: *elle dit, donc je suis*.[10] She is, then, to the extent that she is perceived to be, and projection and perception of herself depend on her society's collective subscription to the maternal archetype.

As Sévigné has looked to mythology, to that collective memory, for valuation and validation, finding there both contexts and models for her privileging of the maternal, so there does society find and elaborate an operative perspective on her as well. Arnauld's interpretive recollection of Sévigné as Latona, her friends' comparison of her with Ceres, her own allusion to Niobe—these instances point to the structuring nature of their common cultural heritage. Sévigné and her society collaborate, then, in sustaining and furthering a traditional exaltation of the maternal, drawing on their shared classical frame of reference as authoritative alibi and enduring measure of excellence.

Vicariously, socially, culturally, Sévigné maps out and lays claim to the domain of maternity. But she respects the borders already drawn for her and elaborates her role only within those permissible bounds as they are suggested to her by the prevailing ideology in all its manifestations. Recognizing implicitly her greater power as mother of a daughter than of a son within this system, she cultivates that relation and moves selectively through the repertoire of available models from which to fashion her persona. Thus, at once conservative and radical, she toys briefly with the figure of the Virgin Mary in a letter written to her daughter on the feast of the Annunciation in 1689:

Cette fête est grande et me paraît le fondement de celle de Pâques et, en un mot, la fête du christianisme et le jour de l'incarnation de Notre Seigneur; la sainte Vierge y fait un rôle, mais ce n'est pas le premier. (III, L. 1090, p. 556)

This feast is important and seems to me to be the foundation of that of Easter, and in a word, the feast of Christianity and the day of the incarnation of our Lord; the holy Virgin plays a role in it, but not the most important one.

The Virgin operates as the dominant model for Christian womanhood and would have been the most obvious choice for emulation, but Sévigné borrowed from her only her posture of *mater dolorosa* and reoriented her sorrow toward her distant mirror image, her daughter. The Virgin, as self-effacing medium of the birth of the father's son, is inscribed to be eternally upstaged by that paternal relation and eclipsed by her son. For that reason, and because her example, while sacred, is emphatically unique, does not bear repeating, Sévigné dismissed it with these few remarks. She clung to models she had found in a more distant but still authorized past, figures that were more congruent with her assigned place and allotted role, images that were more propitious to her project.

SEVEN

Complementary Constructions

The construction of Sévigné's maternal persona intersects with, touches on, and activates other constructions as well. The correspondence, and thereby the textual mother-daughter relationship, takes shape upon Françoise-Marguerite's departure from Paris to join her husband. Hence, it must be remembered that Sévigné was relating to a married daughter, and that a third and important figure, the husband, inflects the inscribed relationship between the two women. The socioeconomic structuring of the marriage itself bears implications for the way Sévigné relates to her son-in-law as well as for the way Sévigné and her married daughter interact.

The tensions generated in the daughter by her position in the triangulated family configuration are refracted and encoded by the writing mother in metaphors that eloquently bespeak both Françoise-Marguerite's inability to thrive as daughter and her attempts, in positioning herself oppositionally, to relocate her self symbolically, primarily in her role as wife. Those tensions are played out in the daughter's self-defeating retreat to invalid status, as she attempts to deviate and extricate herself from the imaginary dyadic relationship to which her mother accessorily binds her in her own project of passage into the symbolic. Françoise-Marguerite's regular alibi of illness is endorsed by the writing mother as justification for continual concern, thus recuperating her own perceived excessive maternal discourse, and, at the same time, it is ignored in maternal adjurations to her daughter to put aside her complaints, and to write, to visit, to maintain her filial posture.

Sévigné completes the figuration of her maternal persona in the identification and cultivation of another, more satisfying relationship. She projects onto the world of nature a more pliant child than her own, and through the inscribing of her relation to it, constructs herself as "Mother Nature," thereby meeting fully the conventions of her cultural encodement as *mater*.

Mediating Maternity

Un beau-père aime son gendre, aime sa bru. Une belle-mère aime son gendre,
n'aime point sa bru. Tout est réciproque.   LA BRUYÈRE[1]

A father-in-law loves his son-in-law, loves his daughter-in-law. A mother-in-
law loves her son-in-law, does not love her daughter-in-law. All of this is
mutual.

The separation of mother and daughter does not provide the initial impetus for Sévigné's epistolary attention to Provence. The inaugural gesture
of maternal letters is directed rather toward the daughter's husband. The
first letters addressed by Sévigné to her daughter's future home, Grignan,
are those she writes to the count, her newly acquired son-in-law, while
her daughter is still with her. The count departed from Paris in April 1670
to assume his responsibilities as the king's lieutenant general in Provence.
For reasons of health (and at Sévigné's insistence in particular), his pregnant wife remained behind, in her mother's care, with the understanding
that she would join him following the birth of their child. From June 1670
until her daughter's departure in February 1671, Sévigné wrote regularly
to her son-in-law, establishing for herself a position in the relation she had
contracted between him and her daughter.[2] At times, she and her daughter
wrote together in one letter, at others they wrote separately but at the same
time, and when her daughter was physically unable (just after giving birth),
Sévigné wrote in her place. Once Françoise-Marguerite was reunited with
her husband, there was no further attempt on Sévigné's part to sustain an
independent exchange with Grignan, but he is continually addressed in letters to the daughter: some missives are written to both of them explicitly;
others, sent to the daughter, bear messages for him, or include passages
written specifically to him. Grignan figures as a constant third term to be
reckoned with in the mother-daughter relationship.

Even before the role of mother is encoded, that of mother-in-law (a
role with a long history and tradition in French folklore; see Perrault's
Contes) is in play. In one of Sévigné's first letters to her departed son-in-
law, she grounds her relationship to him in the bargain they have already
contracted by law:

Est-ce qu'en vérité je ne vous ai pas donné la plus jolie femme du monde? Peut-on
être plus honnête, plus régulière? Peut-on vous aimer plus tendrement? (I, L. 112,
p. 129)

Have I not in truth given you the prettiest wife in the world? Is it possible to be
more virtuous, more right? Can anyone love you more tenderly?

Their bond is premised on the "gift" exchanged: to the extent that Sévigné represents her daughter as a prized object at her disposal and encodes her marriage to Grignan as a gift to him, she invokes an etiquette of gratitude and a social economy of indebtedness and reminds her son-in-law of her entitlement to his devotion.

While Sévigné plays on the superfluity of her role in the marital configuration as represented in the double communication line to Provence ("Je vois un commerce si vif entre vous et une certaine dame qu'il serait ridicule de prétendre vous rien mander" [I, L. 113, p. 131] [I see an exchange so lively between you and a certain lady that it would be ridiculous to claim to send you any news]) and claims to respect it ("Je ne vous dis aucune nouvelle, ce serait aller sur les droits de ma fille" [I, L. 112, p. 130] [I tell you no news; this would be to infringe on my daughter's rights]), she manifestly uses her daughter as pretext for entrée into Grignan's affections and attempts to factor her supposed redundancy into the relational equation:

S'il y a une petite place de reste dans votre coeur, vous me ferez un plaisir extrême de me la donner, car vous en avez une très grande dans le mien. Je ne vous dis point si j'ai soin de votre chère moitié. (I, L. 113, p. 131)

If there is a little place left over in your heart, you will do me an extreme pleasure by giving it to me, for you have a very great one in mine. I don't have to tell you that I'm looking after your dear half.

On the grounds that she has his interests (that is, his wife) at heart and entrusted to her keeping, she requests whatever portion of affection remains once he acquits himself affectively of his conjugal relation. The introduction of the notion of apportionment ("une place de reste dans votre coeur") implies a quantifying of affection that prepares the way for calculations of doses to be distributed by the son-in-law according to his various obligations.

The framing of the relation in economic terms enables the mother to claim a position for herself in the new household. By strategically identifying and claiming an affective place for herself, Sévigné secures her inclusion in the couple's life. This is, however, at the daughter's expense: the act of quantifying also invokes and ratifies the limits of the husband's conjugal affections. The flirtatious insistence that he distribute his devotion between wife and mother-in-law is grounded in the understanding that the marriage is a contractual agreement premised on the circulation of goods, that the daughter, given and taken, constitutes the signifier of the transaction, but that the contract itself has been struck between the representatives of the two households, the mother and the count. The daughter would attempt to counter her mother's claims on Grignan by asserting her own. She responded playfully but tellingly to her mother's words once she had joined the count; her mother in turn echoed them back to her:

Vous ne pouviez pas me donner une plus petite idée de la place que j'ai dans le coeur de M. de Grignan qu'en me disant que c'est le reste de ce que vous n'y occupez pas. (I, L. 202, p. 350)

You could not give me a more minuscule idea of the place I have in M. de Grignan's heart than by telling me that it is the remainder that you don't occupy.

The superfluity is ceaselessly circulated among the three figures, each refusing that position and claiming primacy in the relationship. The arrangement is triangular, and the daughter most often, in her mother's letters, represents the position of negotiation between the other two.

Normally, in the seventeenth century, responsibility for contractual agreements would devolve on male heads of household and bring them together in an alliance of interests. As widow, Sévigné assumed the paternal role in administering her family, nor was this unusual. As Badinter points out:

Au XVIIe siècle encore elle [la mère] suit résolument l'ordre social qui impose le pouvoir paternel. Elle épouse si bien les valeurs paternelles, valeurs dominantes de la société, qu'en cas de disparition du père, devenue veuve, elle sait s'identifier et se substituer à lui.[3]

Still in the seventeenth century she [the mother] resolutely follows the social order that imposes paternal power. She adopts paternal values, the dominant values of society, so well that, in the case of the father's disappearance, having become a widow, she can identify with and substitute herself for him.

Thus, in cultivating her relationship with Grignan, Sévigné was simply playing out the complex social position she occupied and performing her assigned duty. But she did so with such enthusiasm as to confound and expand the bounds of her role. Circumstance combines with personality in Sévigné to produce the profile of the phallic mother.[4] This construction, both imposed on and embraced by her, shapes decisively the maternal discourse of the correspondence.

The appeal to an economy of affective indebtedness with the son-in-law is reproduced in Sévigné's attempts at setting up an economy of epistolary indebtedness and marks a materialization of the sentimental, an attempt to concretize relations: "Si je vous écris souvent, vous n'avez pas oublié que c'est à condition que vous ne me ferez pas de réponse" (I, L. 113, p. 130) [If I write to you often, you have not forgotten that it is on the condition that you will not respond to me]. Her refusal to accept repayment in kind, while ostensibly testifying to her generosity, poses just as pertinently the question of what kind of recompense it is that she does seek. The reiteration of her proposed (and their apparently sealed) bargain articulates a will to solidify and perpetuate the initial contract and her powerful position as "donor" over Grignan. It also contingently protects her from wounded feelings in the event he doesn't respond, thereby effectively canceling the possibility of rejection, and so it disempowers him in this relation of her apparent devising.

The rhetoric of seduction Sévigné addresses to her son-in-law as she seeks to ingratiate herself with him and to insinuate for herself a place in the economy of household affections sets her in competition with her daughter. Double but not identical strands of discourse operate between Paris and Provence, since Françoise-Marguerite is in correspondence with her husband during their separation as well. Accordingly, Sévigné tacitly acknowledges the superfluity of her letters to him in repeatedly denying the desire of any "commerce" with him:

Ce n'est point pour entretenir un commerce avec vous; j'en ferais scrupule, sachant de quelle sorte vous êtes accablé de celui de Mme de Grignan. Je vous plains d'avoir à lire de si grandes lettres. (I, L. 114, p. 131)

It isn't that I want to maintain an exchange with you; I would have scruples about it, knowing how you are overwhelmed by Mme de Grignan's. I pity you for having to read such long letters.

That this is the mother's third letter in a series of eight addressed in rapid succession to Grignan somewhat belies her denial of desire for "commerce." The allusion to exchange operates further as a reminder of the fundamental relation in place and puts in question the locus of the superfluity. It is she and Grignan who drew up and agreed on the marriage contract. The daughter is merely the object of their exchange in the uniting of the two households, and that original exchange is to be mutually beneficial to the two consenting parties, herself and Grignan.

It is in fact the daughter who is encoded above as superfluous to the arrangement, whose participation, in her attempts at maintaining marital intimacy and codifying the conjugal bond in long letters is interpreted by the mother as an imposition on the husband. By expressing, even facetiously, pity for Grignan, Sévigné devalorizes the daughter's writing and posits her own as the more deserving of his appreciation because respectful of demands on his time, demonstrated by limiting the volume and number of her letters to him. Commiserating with the husband may also effectively channel her resentment that she no longer holds her daughter's attention exclusively; she must now share it with the new husband and, in order to reclaim it, needs to assert herself as the focus of their shared world.

Sévigné's insertion of herself into the husband-wife relation, her insistence on keeping in view and operative the originating pact between herself and Grignan, has repercussions that only affirm the consolidating of the triangular shape of the marriage. In the same letter, Sévigné inscribes her binary relation to Grignan (*je-vous-nous*), confirmed by the fact of the letter she has had from him, and isolates her daughter, effectively objectivizing and excluding her (*la, elle*):

Elle a été au désespoir que vous m'ayez écrit; je n'ai jamais vu une femme si jalouse ni si envieuse. Elle a beau faire, je la défie d'empêcher notre amitié. (I, L. 114, p. 132)

She has been in despair that you have written to me; I have never seen a woman so jealous or so envious. No matter what she does, I challenge her to prevent our friendship.

Sévigné offers up her daughter's jealousy and envy to Grignan as the price she willingly pays for his friendship. Where the daughter had perhaps sought escape from the mother in this marriage and entertained hopes for a more independent existence, she is confronted instead with the threat of conspiracy between the two rational writing partners and (to the extent that she actually is jealous and envious) reduced to emotional turmoil. Paradoxically, while undermining the couple's relationship through her intrusiveness, Sévigné was in fact accomplishing the solidarity of the marriage. By setting in play a dynamic of competition that continually privileged symmetry, and by continually threatening to eclipse Françoise-Marguerite in Grignan's affections, Sévigné incited her daughter to claim her place in her husband's heart. But this ensuring of marital unity would be at the cost of mother-daughter harmony.

Sévigné would evoke the superfluity of her letters to Grignan regularly ("Vous avez une lettre de votre chère femme; n'est-ce pas une folie de se mêler de vous écrire?" [I, L. 116, p. 134] [You have a letter from your dear wife; is it not a folly to join in writing to you?]) and then point to the superfluity of her daughter, reinforcing the either/or dynamic endemic to the triangulated affective system. In November, shortly after Françoise-Marguerite had given birth (fulfilling imperfectly her assigned role in the marriage agreement, having produced only a daughter instead of the desired male heir), Sévigné wrote directly to her son-in-law, dismissing peremptorily the pretext that bound them:

Ne parlons plus de cette femme; nous l'aimons au-delà de toute raison. Elle se porte très bien, et je vous écris en mon propre et privé nom.

Let us speak of that woman no longer; we love her beyond all reason. She is feeling very well, and I write to you in my proper and private name.

and addressed more pressing and substantive issues:

Je veux vous parler de Monsieur de Marseille et vous conjurer, par toute la confiance que vous pouvez avoir en moi, de suivre mes conseils sur votre conduite avec lui. Je connais les manières des provinces. (I, L. 117, p. 135).

I want to speak to you of Monsieur de Marseille and beg you, by all the confidence you can have in me, to follow my advice on your conduct with him. I know the ways of the provinces.

The daughter relegated to responsibilities of reproduction and acquitted momentarily of these, Sévigné turned to the more important politics of the now combined households. Extending her less distinguished family interests and embracing the more prominent and crucial ones of the Grignan household, she paternally offered advice and placed her experience and wisdom at her son-in-law's disposal. Grignan might operate as the vehicle for her participation in the political discourse of their time. She could advise from behind the scenes and influence the world indirectly by guiding his behavior. She might vicariously wield power.

As the time for the daughter's departure approached, Sévigné reconfirmed and more explicitly claimed her place in the relationship. Once the daughter was reunited with her husband, Sévigné risked becoming definitively superfluous to the marriage. She delighted in the report of Grignan's professed devotion to her and repeated it back to him as if to lend it even greater substance through its reinscription:

Vous pouvez juger à quel point mon coeur est content d'apprendre que vous répondez à cette inclination que j'ai pour vous depuis si longtemps. (I, L. 119, p. 127)

You can judge to what extent my heart is content to learn that you respond to this inclination I have had for you for such a long time.

She reiterated her proposal of an epistolary relation of indebtedness between herself and Grignan. And she reinforced the premises of that arrangement by approving epistolary reciprocity between her son-in-law and her daughter. Her gesture of self-effacement at once veils and enacts a strategic power positioning:

Je vous défends de m'écrire. Ecrivez à ma fille, et laissez-moi la liberté de vous écrire ... Aimez-moi toujours mon cher Comte; je vous quitte d'honorer ma grand-maternité, mais il faut m'aimer, et vous assurer que vous n'êtes aimé en nul lieu du monde si chèrement qu'ici. (I, L. 119, p. 138)

I forbid you to write to me. Write to my daughter, and leave me the freedom to write to you . . . Love me always, my dear Count; I absolve you of honoring my grandmotherhood, but you must love me, and be assured that you are loved nowhere in the world as dearly as here.

The triangular configuration proprietarily features the count ("*mon* cher Comte") and the daughter ("*ma* fille") as subordinated to the organizing *je*. This *je* is emphatically to be understood by the addressee son-in-law not as grandmother, nor even, implicitly, as mother. Sévigné seeks an affective relation with Grignan independent of those prescribed and thereby emptied of meaning by ritualistic family obligation. As long as her daughter is still with her, their affections for the count are completely localized between them, "ici," and indistinguishable one from the other. Under cover of this competitive confusion, Sévigné lays seductive claims of her own to his affections.[5] In this way, the groundwork for rivalry between mother and daughter, mother-in-law and wife, around the central male figure is laid.

Despite attempts to suppress or disguise the unpleasant truth from themselves, each other, and the world at large, antagonistic eruptions occurred between the two women that could not be ignored and made their way eventually into the letters. Three full months of the initial separation elapse before the first epistolary allusion to the tensions experienced between the two women when they had been together. In May 1671, Françoise-Marguerite and her husband had been reunited for three months. For the first time in the mother's stream of letters to Provence, reverberations surface that point tellingly to the fact that their relations while together in Paris had been strained, that their separation had eased the tensions, at least for the daughter. Sévigné refuses the daughter's observation, seconded by her husband, that the two women get along better when apart:

Je vous prie, ma bonne, ne donnons point désormais à l'absence le mérite d'avoir remis entre nous une parfaite intelligence et, de mon côté, la persuasion de votre tendresse pour moi . . . N'allons point faire une séparation de votre aimable vue et de votre amitié, il y aurait trop de cruauté à séparer ces deux choses.

I beg you, *ma bonne,* let us henceforth not credit absence with reestablishing perfect understanding between us and, for me, the persuasion of your tenderness for me . . . Let us not make a distinction between your wonderful presence and your affection; there would be too much cruelty in separating these two things.

Sévigné now appears to occupy the position of outsider; apparently Françoise-Marguerite has told her husband of the unhappiness she experienced while with her mother, and he subscribes with his wife to the separation of mother and daughter as the solution:

Et quoi que M. de Grignan dise, je veux plutôt croire que le temps est venu que ces deux choses marcheront ensemble, que j'aurai le plaisir de vous voir sans mélange d'aucun nuage, et que je réparerai toutes les injustices passées, puisque vous voulez les nommer ainsi. (I, L. 162, p. 243)

And whatever M. de Grignan says, I prefer to believe that the time has come when these two things will work together, that I will have the pleasure of seeing you without the hint of any clouds, and that I will redress all the past injustices, since that is what you choose to call them.

Sévigné must now counter the opinion of a couple without acknowledging the veracity of their shared perception. This can only be done by splitting that couple ("Et quoi que M. de Grignan dise"), challenging the husband's authority, and denying the truth of the daughter's charges without alienating either one. Sévigné negotiates a delicate maneuver: she refuses to accept that there have been past injustices and effectively returns them to her daughter as her own misperceptions ("puisque vous voulez les nommer ainsi"), but at the same time she promises to right them. She suggests that the solution to the mother-daughter tensions is merely a matter of mutual resolve ("N'allons point faire . . ."), and she attempts to impose her will ("je veux plutôt croire") to reconstruct a scenario for more satisfactory reunions. She thus simultaneously addresses and evades the issue of the problematic relationship, inscribing it as a monolithic project of their concerted will, and attempts to assure her place in the affections of the couple.

As the span of the letters over the years attests, Grignan was not amenable to the subordinate, emotionally indebted, and instrumental role Sévigné had suggested to him at the outset of her epistolary relation to him. He appears to have left it to his wife to relate as best she could to her mother. There remains no evidence of any sort of actual rejection on his part; in fact, his warm letter of tribute to Sévigné, written to their mutual friend Moulceau shortly after her death (III, p. 1689), indicates that he was indeed attached to her. One assumes he prudently distanced himself from the mother-daughter drama, and that his own life was only minimally disturbed by the tensions that raged around him. For her part, Sévigné continued to cultivate her relationship to him and to the Grignan household generally, but diplomatically, through the sanctioned mediation of her daughter rather than independently. Thus it is, for the most part, in letters to Françoise-Marguerite that she addresses her son-in-law more circumspectly.

Apart from Sévigné's constant dedication to helping secure advancement and prestige for Grignan and the members of his family, her remarks to or concerning him were significantly informed by two themes: the daughter's childbearing troubles and the family's precarious finances. Both of these issues could be considered to be legitimately her business as a consequence of the determining role she had played in negotiating the original marriage contract and the implied if not explicitly articulated purposes of that contract.

Sévigné held her son-in-law as directly implicated and personally accountable to her for these domestic problems. She claimed authority for herself over these issues in his household and effectively distributed the tension of the rivalry so that it was not exclusively between herself and her daughter for Grignan's attention and affection, but between herself and her son-in-law for prime sway over the daughter as well. The same rivalrous energy continued to course through the family but was strategically rerouted in the letters as the need arose, to serve Sévigné's needs.

Sévigné's daughter's constant, difficult, and debilitating pregnancies are regular and serious cause for the mother's concern, and she holds Grignan responsible. He had already been through two wives, both of whom had died shortly after giving birth,[6] and she recognized that her daughter, her investment in social advancement, was literally her lifeline to the family. Her cousin Bussy had facetiously voiced the fears that she must genuinely have felt for her daughter in this alliance:

Il n'y a qu'une chose qui me fait peur pour la plus jolie fille de France: c'est que Grignan, qui n'est pas vieux, est déjà à sa troisième femme; il en use presqu'autant que d'habits, ou du moins que de carosses. (I, L. 90, p. 106–7)

There is only one thing that frightens me for the prettiest girl in France; that Grignan, who is not old, is already on his third wife; he wears them out almost as quickly as clothing, or at least carriages.

Sévigné was more understanding of this taxing of her daughter's strength prior to the birth of a male heir since the continuance of the family line was a tacit premise of the marriage contract she had negotiated with Grignan. But, from the first, each newborn was anticipated as the male child that would put an end to the reproductive demands on Françoise-Marguerite's frail constitution. A month before the much desired birth of a male son (after two and a half years of marriage, during which time Mme de Grignan had already had one miscarriage and had produced a daughter, Marie-Blanche), Sévigné was already referring optimistically to the unborn child as a "garçon," as she remonstrated with Grignan in a letter to her daughter:

Ecoutez, M. de Grignan . . . Il paraît bien que vous ne savez ce que c'est que d'accoucher . . . Si après ce garçon-ci vous ne lui donnez quelque repos, je croirai que vous ne l'aimez point, que vous ne m'aimez point aussi, et je n'irai point en Provence . . . Et de plus j'oubliais ceci, c'est que je vous ôterai votre femme. Pensez-vous que je vous l'aie donnée pour la tuer, pour détruire sa santé, sa beauté, sa jeunesse? (I, L. 210, p. 365)

Listen, M. de Grignan . . . It really seems that you do not know what it means to give birth . . . If after this boy you don't give her some rest, I will believe you do not love her, that you do not love me as well, and I will not go to Provence . . . And

I was also forgetting this, that I will take your wife from you. Do you think I gave her to you in order to kill her, to destroy her health, her beauty, her youth?

She continues to claim sovereign power over her married daughter and feels authorized to exercise it if she decides the relationship constitutes a threat to her daughter's life. While these remarks are made lightly, they also serve as reminders of the terms of the marriage contract and her role in negotiating it. On the one hand, such concern and protectiveness must have been comforting and reassuring to the daughter; she must have appreciated her mother's devotedness. On the other hand, the competing claims of mother and husband on her very body ("Pensez-vous que je vous l'aie donnée pour la tuer?") was a reminder to her of her status as object of exchange in a bargain not of her making.

That bargain was founded on the alliance of fortune and prestige. Sévigné herself was of a complicated lineage that positioned her in the interstices of an at once rigidly hierarchized and somewhat fluid society. Maternally a Coulanges and paternally a Rabutin, she was the product of a minor *mésalliance* that had wed fortune to prestige. In turn, by her own marriage into the Sévigné line, if she had not surpassed the social standing of the Rabutin household, the marriage was considered quite acceptable to the less distinguished Coulanges. As Roger Duchêne summarizes: "Marie épousa un provincial aux terres médiocres et à l'avenir incertain" [Marie married a provincial of mediocre land and uncertain future].[7]

That Sévigné was intent on social advancement for her family through her daughter is indicated by the reassessment of the Sévigné lineage (and its purported revalorization) she reports to Bussy in the same letter announcing the marriage of her daughter to M. de Grignan (I, L. 89, p. 106), as if attempting to justify the match and to counter any possible hint of *mésalliance*. While Sévigné apparently aspired to greater social prominence for her daughter (and any redounding prestige for herself) through marriage, she herself brought to the union a solid bourgeois set of values and concerns that conflicted regularly with what she perceived to be the profligacy of her aristocratic son-in-law.

Sévigné married her daughter into a family of greater distinction than her own composite one, providing a dowry that, it was hoped, would enable the indebted, impoverished noble Grignan to restore and maintain the appearances required of his social standing.[8] The marriage of title and wealth was a standard and mutually beneficial practice in seventeenth-century polite society. It was one of the few solutions available to the aristocracy to increase revenue while meeting obligations of display; and it afforded social mobility to well-placed and more financially secure members of the lesser nobility or the more recently enriched bourgeoisie.[9] It was particularly seconded by the ethos of *préciosité*, intent on grounding a social system in merit rather than birth, and in thereby establishing a more clement environment for women's claims of equality.[10] Sévigné appears to have occupied an ambivalent position with regard to her daughter's marriage: on the one hand, she subscribed to the practice of *mésalliance,* as witness her daughter's marriage; on the other hand, the financial burden caused by that marriage, which devolved on her as the familial agent responsible for having negotiated the match, was a heavy one. Thoroughly imbued with bourgeois values (inculcated in her by the maternal side of her family, by "le bien bon" abbé Coulanges especially) that were premised on the subordination of expenditure to income, she was uncomprehending of the financial affairs of Grignan. She could neither understand nor countenance the constant drain on the family income that, as far as she could tell, was merely the consequence of self-indulgent ostentation on the part of her son-in-law.

Sévigné and her uncle had taken pains to try to instill in Françoise-Marguerite, while she was still with them in Paris, a sense for finances and a conservative attitude toward expenditure. And, before her departure, the abbé Coulanges had undertaken to write to his counterpart, the accountant for the Château de Grignan, in the hopes of setting a conservative budget that would avoid the threatening ruination of the Grignan household (I, n.1 to L. 127, p. 147, on p. 977). Apparently the maternal lessons did not take, and Françoise-Marguerite espoused her husband's ethos.

Sévigné was infuriated by the constant precariousness of the Grignan finances. She held her son-in-law responsible for the ever disastrous state of the household and pitied her daughter's inescapable involvement in such an anxiety-producing situation; at the same time it was to the daughter that she addressed her frustration:

La rage de M. de Grignan pour emprunter, et pour des tableaux et des meubles, c'est une chose qui serait entièrement incroyable si on ne la voyait. Comment cela se peut-il accorder avec sa naissance, sa gloire, et l'amitié qu'il vous doit? Croit-il ne point abuser de votre patience, et qu'elle soit intarissable? N'a-t-il point pitié de vous? Qu'avez-vous fait pour être misérable et abîmée? Et il croit que nous croirons qu'il vous aime! Ah, la plaisante amitié! Comptez sur la mienne, ma chère enfant, qui assurément ne vous manquera jamais. (II, L. 404, p. 20)

M. de Grignan's passion for borrowing, and for paintings and furniture, is something that would be entirely unbelievable if one didn't see it. How can this be in keeping with his birth, his glory, and the affection he owes you? Does he believe he isn't taking advantage of your patience, and that it is unfailing? Has he no pity for you? What have you done to be miserable and injured? And he would have us believe that he loves you! Ah, a strange affection. Count on mine, my dear child, which assuredly will never fail you.

Evidently the seigneurial code of prodigality was unavailable to Sévigné to help her understand the pressures brought to bear on her daughter's household; what was altogether too evident to her was her responsibility to help out that household as she could, to meet indefinitely her part of the marital bargain. She operated as a creditor to the family, as an advisor, and as a model of moderate ways, and she frequently sacrificed her own comfort to ensure theirs. But none of these roles had the slightest effect on the Grignan account books. If they produced indebtedness, it was on another register and was perhaps repaid in the daughter's epistolary fidelity to her mother. It generated a constant and legitimate pretext for maternal intrusiveness that threatened to animate conjugal discord but appears to have only further alienated the daughter from her mother.

Mésalliance was most commonly practiced by marrying daughters of financially sound families to sons of distinguished families rather than the reverse.[11] So the entire system, premised on the desirability of familial prestige already in place but no longer able to afford itself (particularly as exemplified in Françoise-Marguerite's marriage), appears calculated to benefit and sustain a patriarchically organized social configuration. It is not surprising that subscription, however unwitting, to that economy should have been detrimental to relations between the women involved.

The wedding of Sévigné dowry to Grignan title generated a dynamic of indebtedness that was useful to the mother-in-law in maintaining a position of influence in her daughter's household, but, at the same time, it caused her frustration in her incomprehension of the aristocratic ethos of prodigality that was continually draining the Grignan coffers and her own. Sévigné's reaction was constantly to reclaim her daughter, to insist on her continued rights over her as long as she was so deeply implicated in the finances of the Grignan household. While the position was consistently sentimentalized and cast in a rhetoric of affection, the subtext points to the mother's calculations of her dues. She exacted those dues in claims on her daughter that she measured against those of the contracting partner, M. de Grignan. Hence a repetition throughout the *Correspondance* of the Ceres-Persephone-Pluto paradigm of mother-husband turn taking, in various mutations, for example:

Plus j'y pense, ma bonne, et plus je trouve que je ne veux point vous voir pour quinze jours. Si vous venez à Vichy ou à Bourbon, il faut que ce soit pour venir ici [à Paris] avec moi. Nous y passerons le reste de l'été et l'automne . . . et M. de Grignan vous viendra voir cet hiver et fera de vous à son tour ce qu'il trouvera à propos. (II, L. 496, p. 265–66)

The more I think of it, *ma bonne,* the more I find that I do not want to see you for only two weeks. If you come to Vichy or Bourbon, it must be to continue on here [to Paris] with me. We will spend the rest of the summer and fall here . . . and

M. de Grignan will come to see you this winter and will do with you in turn what he finds suitable.

The significant difference between the Sévigné model and the Ceres myth is located in the resistance of the daughter to her mother's desire and the humiliating need Sévigné regularly confronted to persuade her daughter of her greater attachment and to motivate their relation to her advantage.

Sévigné directly adjured not only her daughter but her son-in-law as well to keep in mind the triangular nature of their arrangement, pitting herself fitfully as rival to Grignan for her daughter's affections. She addressed messages to him in letters to her daughter, such as the following:

Vous faites ma fille jalouse; ne craignez-vous point ses emportements, et que, pressée par vos mauvais traitements, elle ne vienne me trouver, moi qui ne lui ai jamais donné aucune jalousie? (II, L. 742, p. 864)

You are making my daughter jealous; do you not fear her anger, and that, incited by your bad treatment, she might come seek me out, I who have never caused her any jealousy?

Under cover of such light and facetious remarks, Sévigné identified her daughter as the emotional target and barometer of strategies played out around and through her by the two contenders in the relation, herself and Grignan.

Increasingly, as the Grignan household persisted in squandering (as far as Sévigné could understand) its fortune and her own, and as her daughter's health deteriorated, Sévigné found M. de Grignan unworthy of her daughter. She did not hesitate to object to his cavalier ways with his wife, and to voice her disapproval to her daughter, sowing the seeds of conjugal dissension:

Je vous demande, ma fille, comme vous vous portez de votre voyage de Marseille. Je gronde M. de Grignan de vous avoir menée; je ne saurais approuver cette trotterie inutile. (II, L. 745, p. 875)

I ask you, my daughter, how you feel after your Marseille trip. I scold M. de Grignan for having taken you there; I hardly approve of this useless scampering.

Sévigné gradually accepted Grignan's lack of interest in financial matters. She continually aired her worries to her daughter and placed on her, as the member of the family over whom she had the greater influence, the burden of responsibility for the untenable Grignan situation. Ironically, as she accepted her son-in-law's seeming insouciance, she held her daughter as that much more accountable:

Je ne comprends pas que mes lettres puissent divertir ce Grignan, où il trouve si souvent des chapitres d'affaires, de réflexions tristes, des réflexions sur la dépense.

Que fait-il de tout cela? Il faut qu'il saute par-dessus pour trouver un endroit qui lui plaise. Cela s'appelle des landes en ce pays-ci; il y en a beaucoup dans mes lettres avant que de trouver la prairie. (II, L. 785, p. 1008)

I do not understand how my letters could amuse this Grignan, where he so often finds chapters of business, of sad reflections, of thoughts on spending. What does he make of all this? He must have to skip over them to find a part that pleases him. These are called moors in this country; there are many of them in my letters before arriving at the meadow.

Sévigné recognized the lack of appeal in her letters when she had to address the hard and unpleasant facts of finance, and Grignan's particular distaste for such topics. While she decried his lack of interest and irresponsibility, at the same time she catered to him in offering news and stories more calculated to amuse him. She deferred to his status and visited her worries primarily on her daughter.

A consequence of this arrangement was to cast Françoise-Marguerite in two conflicting roles at once. On the one hand, when Sévigné addressed her daughter directly in the discussion of finances, she projected a responsible, mature adult, accountable for her household. On the other, when she addressed her son-in-law, she projected a very different profile of Françoise-Marguerite—an amenable child without will or direction of her own, who was the good wife or the good daughter depending on the husband's or the mother's need. In this tone she appealed repeatedly to Grignan for her share:

Rien ne se préfère à vous, en quelque état que l'on puisse être, mais soyez généreux, et quand on aura fait encore quelque temps la bonne femme, amenez-la vous même par la main faire la bonne fille. (III, L. 503, p. 279)

Nothing is preferable to you, no matter what state one is in, but be generous, and when she has played the good wife for a while, bring her here yourself by the hand to play the good daughter.

Françoise-Marguerite was framed in a position where ceding to her mother's will automatically implied refusing her husband's, and vice-versa. Demands on her were such as to construct a self that was composed of fragmented and conflicting obligations, riddled with unlocalizable and passive resentments, with no sense of autonomy and only a fragile surface identity.

The following passage bespeaks eloquently the daughter's dilemma, illustrating the tensions grounded in and ratified by the marriage contract and played out through the course of her life in the mother-husband rivalrous claims on her. In 1685, when it was penned, Sévigné was fifty-nine years old, her son-in-law was fifty-three, her daughter, thirty-nine. M. de Grignan and Françoise-Marguerite had been married for sixteen years and had three living children. If precariously funded, their household was well established and reproducing itself. Nevertheless, Sévigné persisted in attempts at inculcating in her daughter her own virtues of fiscal conservatism, resolutely opposing the extravagance of her son-in-law:

Pour votre chambre, ma bonne, je comprends qu'elle est fort bien avec tout ce que vous me mandez. Si la sagesse ne faisait point fermer les yeux sur tout ce qui convient à la magnificence des autres et à la qualité, on ne se laisserait pas tomber en pauvreté. Je sais le plaisir d'orner une chambre; j'y aurais succombé, sans le *scrupule* que j'ai toujours fait d'avoir des choses qui ne sont pas nécessaires quand on n'a pas les nécessaires. J'ai préféré de payer des dettes, et je crois que la conscience oblige, non seulement à cette préférence, mais à la justice de n'en pas faire de nouvelles. Ainsi, je blame maternellement et en bonne amitié, l'envie qu'a M. de Grignan de vous donner un autre miroir. Contentez-vous, ma chère bonne, de celui que vous avez. Il convient à votre chambre, qui est encore bien imparfaite. Il est à vous par bien des titres, et tout mon regret c'est de ne vous en avoir donné que la glace. J'aurais été bien aise, il y a longtemps, de le faire ajuster comme vous avez fait. Jouissez donc, ma bonne, de votre dépense sans en faire une plus grande qui serait superflue et contre les bonnes moeurs dont nous faisons profession. (III, L. 912, p. 201)

As for your room, *ma bonne*, I understand that it is quite nice from all you tell me. If wisdom didn't make one close one's eyes to all that is in keeping with other people's magnificence and to quality, one would not allow oneself to become poor. I know the pleasure of decorating a room; I would have succumbed to it, without the *scruples* I have always had concerning having things that aren't necessary when one doesn't have those that are. I have preferred to pay debts, and I believe that conscience obliges not only this preference, but the rightness of not incurring new ones. Thus, I reproach maternally and with affection the desire M. de Grignan has to give you a new mirror. Be happy, *ma bonne*, with the one you have. It suits your room, which is still quite imperfect. It is yours by many rights, and all my regret lies in having given you only the glass part. I would have been quite pleased, a long time ago, to have it set as you have done. Enjoy then, *ma bonne*, your expense without making it greater, which would be superfluous and against the morality that we profess.

The issue of contention is ostensibly a mirror for the daughter, and if this passage appears particularly charged, it is because of the metaphorical connotations of the mother's message, centered on this object of specularity, resonating with energy deriving from the investment in the term "mirror" of cultural meaning that exceeds the economy of the mother's words. The "mirror" has already been seen as encoded to signify the mother's socially endorsed position of influence over her daughter, in de Grenaille's *L'Honneste fille*, for example (see chapter 4):

L'honnête femme étant le miroir de sa fille . . . celle-ci ne peut recevoir de plus utiles leçons que de celle qui la précède, et qui joint l'exercice aux enseignements.[12]

The honest woman being the mirror of her daughter . . . the latter cannot receive more useful lessons than from her who precedes her, and who joins practice to teaching.

In countering the husband's desire, Sévigné is defending one of the few spaces of authority to which she holds title as mother, the space of mirror for her daughter's edification and emulation. Grignan proposes to replace his wife's mirror, a gift from her mother, with a new one, from him. He also has claims on Françoise-Marguerite: wisdom of their day decrees that the wife is to serve as mirror to her husband.[13] The husband's and the mother's claims on the mirror wife/daughter are equally weighted and are represented in their competition each to be the one to give her a mirror of her own. Sévigné objects that Grignan cannot afford to offer such a gift; she refuses his pleasure, his "envie." She begs her daughter to keep the original rather than incur further debt with her husband, rather than further implicate herself in that other relationship. That other relationship, with the husband, constantly threatens to replace the one with the mother, so vital to the mother's self-image.

Psycho-economics are in play as Sévigné holds herself up as paragon of bourgeois virtue, with her *scruples,* and invites her daughter to look to that mirror—the maternal one—and to forgo the husband's extravagant and superfluous one. The mother is in a position to give, and he is not; the daughter is enjoined to recognize that, and to prefer the mother's more reliable gift, already hers. Both the husband's desire and the mother's wish cover invitations for Françoise-Marguerite to specular relations with each, respectively and exclusively. The two options are identical in the totally relational and dependent identity they propose to her, with the difference that the mirror of the mother is already in place and operative, attempting to elicit its image in a daughter who would mirror back to her her *scruples.*

On the epistolary, affective, and economic registers, superfluity is constantly an issue in this triangular familial configuration. The relation of reciprocity implicit in letter exchanges is complicated by the potential participation of three correspondents. The coupling paradigm fundamental to the marriage convention is always already disturbed by its negotiated inception featuring three parties to the contract. And the desired balance of income and expenditure is forever eluded by the demands of prodigality and display on the aristocratic household. Superfluity is a consequence of the privileging of a binary organization as the governing principle of these relations. This results in constant attempts at forcing a more complicated reality into tidy symmetry, and identifying all that cannot be contained in that neat arrangement as excessive. Excess in the familial discourse is thus regularly produced and ceaselessly displaced, now assumed by the mother, then visited on the daughter, occasionally levied on the husband. The restless energy generated by discomfort with contractual, institutional molds shaped by a patriarchal ideology of relations grounded in the binary, aggravated by shifts and contradictions in those as they reflect and adjust to changing economies, engenders excess that is ultimately localized and contained in the figure of the mother and is reproduced in her own discourse. That excess is epitomized and fixed in the figure of the mother conventionalized, caricatured, and vilified as mother-in-law. She is always *de trop* in the governing economy.[14]

Negotiating Maternity

> This cathexis between mother and daughter—essential, distorted, misused— is the great unwritten story. Probably there is nothing in human nature more resonant with charges than the flow of energy between two biologically alike bodies, one of which has lain in amniotic bliss inside the other, one of which has labored to give birth to the other. The materials are here for the deepest mutuality and the most painful estrangement.   ADRIENNE RICH [15]

Françoise-Marguerite's marriage figured a new orientation for her. She turned to her husband, and away from her mother, for direction, affection, and social identity. This shift was all the more radical and destabilizing for the two women in that it had not been prepared over the years by the participation of a father in the familial affective economy. While paternal figures from Sévigné's family and circle of friends had been formally available to perform societal rituals as required, none was incorporated intimately in the familial nexus.[16] This much is clear from the intense and exclusive way in which the two women proceed to relate to each other by letter. Even the son-brother, Charles, is relegated to an ancillary role in their exchange. The new husband, M. de Grignan, comes to claim the symbolic role and to occupy the affective void that was the father's, a void that the widow-mother had tacitly filled over the years. The introduction of this new element to the familial configuration prompts both mother and daughter to confront and contend with that figure, the embodied paternal one, and to accommodate it through adjustments in their relations to each other.

Little is known of the relationship between the two women prior to Françoise-Marguerite's marriage, their separation, and the subsequent epistolary tracing of those years. The formative period of Sévigné's motherhood and Françoise-Marguerite's daughterhood constitutes an inaccessible prehistory. However, upon their separation, a relationship is figured that resonates with meanings that have been codified in recent descriptions of relations between mothers and daughters within the psychological economy of the patriarchal family.[17]

This relationship is reformulated and rearticulated repeatedly, for separations recur throughout the correspondence, and it is at these textual junctures, as the trauma of the initial separation is remembered and re-enacted, that feelings surface, that the women give voice to the nature of their attachment to each other. Correlatively, when the women are reunited, there is only a textual void, the inscription of the relationship is (with only one notable exception) interrupted.

Sévigné and her daughter were significantly separated nine times over a period of twenty-five years, between the daughter's first departure from Paris in 1671 and the mother's death at Grignan in 1696. However, they spent only a total of approximately seven years apart from each other, and the longest separation (the first one, from 4 February 1671 until 13 July 1672) lasted merely eighteen months.[18] That they were actually together for roughly eighteen of Mme de Grignan's married years is not at all evident at an initial reading of the voluminous letters, penned almost entirely during periods of separation.

A reading of the *Correspondance* as a continuous text (both written and unwritten, some preserved and some destroyed) spelling a narrative available through attention to the eloquent chronological gaps afforded by the two women's presence to each other as well as the letters themselves, orders a coherent if speculative view of the dynamic of the mother-daughter relation in play. Particularly valuable are the punctuations of the repeated separations for tracing the history of that relationship as it develops over time. The discussion pauses at these moments and lingers over these texts in efforts to catch glimpses, in the mother's discourse, of the daughter's. It represents an attempt to reconstruct their relative positions, both to understand the energy mobilizing this maternal inscription and to locate the fleeting daughter's.

This focused overview of the letters yields a clear pattern of alternation: reunion of the two women spells crisis for the daughter and euphoria for the mother, and their separation offers relief to the daughter and plunges the mother in mourning. The pattern of extreme tension relaxes and promises serenity as it spans the later years of the correspondence and moves toward the final reunion of the two women.

It is rarely Sévigné who initiates epistolary discussion of the dissension that has marred periods of reunion. Her first letters to her daughter upon each separation typically express only her great sorrow; she contemplates a bleak present and grimly wills herself to survive until their next reunion (see chapter 3). Allusions to discord experienced during visits surface only in letters of reply to the daughter, most often upon reception of the departed daughter's first letters. This trend is consistent enough to suggest that the visits were more painful for the daughter than for the mother, that Sévigné at the least feigned to be oblivious of the negative effects of their reunions for the daughter, and that, for her part, Françoise-Marguerite found release from her inhibitions and gave voice to her unhappiness only upon leaving her mother.

Françoise-Marguerite left her mother for the first time on 4 February 1671. By 11 February, a week later, Sévigné was already responding to letters received and reacting to the first in what would be a steady series of critiques of their relationship:

Mais je ne veux point que vous disiez que j'étais un rideau qui vous cachait. Tant pis si je vous cachais; vous êtes encore plus aimable quand on a tiré le rideau. Il faut que vous soyez à découvert pour être dans votre perfection; nous l'avons dit mille fois. Pour moi, il me semble que je suis toute nue, qu'on m'a dépouillée de tout ce qui me rendait aimable. (I, L. 133, p. 155)

But I certainly do not want you to say that I was a curtain that hid you. Too bad if I concealed you; you are even more endearing when the curtain is opened. You must be exposed to be in your perfection; we have said it a thousand times. As for me, it seems to me that I am completely naked, that all that made me loveable has been stripped from me.

The symbiotic relationship of the two women is both illustrated and refuted in the daughter's attempted metaphorizing. According to her reported rendering of the image, when the two women were together, the mother eclipsed the daughter, kept her from appearing as she "was," in some sort of imaginary unmediated truth. But the "curtain" figure lends itself to a more complicated reading than the daughter's. A curtain is only a curtain by virtue of that which it conceals, shuts off, covers. It derives its own meaning from what is, or is imagined to be, behind it; it is dependent by definition on that which it obscures. Conversely, that which is veiled, the object behind the curtain, is but a suggestive figment of the imagination, empowered and magnified by virtue of its very mystification and concealment. That either the curtain or the object behind it might be better off without the other is unsure: they function in symbiotic relation to each other.

The daughter rejected the curtain; she claimed to be better off parted from her mother. But the notion of a maternal veil and of a daughter concealed implies a third perspective, that of the projected viewer whose gaze on the daughter is obstructed by the mother's presence. Who is that viewer who is structuring the daughter's understanding of her relation with her mother, whose desire to see is to be gratified in the daughter's flight from behind the curtain? Most immediately and concretely, that gaze can be assigned to the husband, who by marriage has rights to what is behind the curtain. More generally, and as suggested by the text itself, that gaze belongs to *on*, to that anonymous but gendered collectivity, patriarchal society. As the daughter attempts to assume her place in society, passing into her new role of wife, she attempts to leave the place she has hitherto occupied, behind her mother. Those two locations cannot be simultaneously occupied by her.

Sévigné objects willfully ("je ne veux point") to this scenario and instructs her daughter to cease circulating ("que vous disiez") the offensive image; then, since she cannot reason against a metaphor, she simply reverses the comparison to her supposed advantage. However, implicit in both the daughter's and the mother's manipulations of the image is that fixed gaze, the desire of the other, in view of which they position themselves in relation to each other. Sévigné prefers to modify the image, to feature herself as a curtain drawn back, framing her daughter to their mutual advantage. "A découvert" implies both concealment and revelation, possible only through the mediation of the curtain. In this version she inscribes herself as essential to her daughter's charm.

Then a curious reversal is operated by the writing mother whereby she casts herself in the concealed role and appropriates her daughter's metaphorized desire for autonomy only to reinterpret it as lack: suddenly it is she who is "nue" and "dépouillée." She has rewoven her daughter's words in her reinscription of them and has fabricated the daughter as curtain to her own self. She effectively supplants the daughter at centerstage in her response. While the maternal veil hid Françoise-Marguerite and, she claims, prevented her from being appreciated on her own merits, the daughter-curtain protected Sévigné and enabled her to construct her maternal persona. What produced inhibition for the one provided security for the other. Now it is Sévigné who finds herself exposed and vulnerable to the world as a consequence of the rift in the protective veil caused by the daughter's departure. Nor does a happy compromise appear possible; one or the other of the pair must be victim as long as either of their scenarios is operative. When they are together, that will be the daughter; when apart, the mother. But, in whatever social configuration they find themselves and each other (in Paris, in Provence, among family, among friends), they perform their roles with ever an eye to the presumed gaze. Their symbiotic relationship is constructed within that line of vision and according to its perspective, the assumed desire of the other.

In their respective circles, each woman occupied center stage. Sévigné acknowledged her daughter's claim that she appeared to greater advantage now that she was in Provence without her mother:

Vous faites des merveilles. Vous êtes aimée de tout le monde. Il me semble que je vous vois valoir mieux; écu, vous ne valiez maille derrière moi, comme dit M. de La Rochefoucauld. (I, L. 171, p. 267)

You perform miracles; you are loved by all. It seems to me that I see you increase in value; a crown now, you weren't worth a penny behind me, as M. de La Rochefoucauld says.

Sévigné bestows a compliment that in no way detracts from her own value and concedes nothing to the daughter. Rather, it firmly backs the standard of the mother's currency. Her mere presence, according to her simile, diminishes the daughter, always figured behind her, after her, consequently less than her. As the crown reduces in value to a paltry penny, so the daughter, when contiguous to the mother, suffers a comparable devaluation. But, as in the earlier metaphorizing, here again a third and unexplicitated term is crucial to the operation of the comparison. It is the market that assigns, deflates, or inflates value. It is not so much in direct relation to each other but through the mediation of the social marketplace and along its continuum of valuation (here epitomized in the reductive maximal authority of M. de La Rochefoucauld) that Sévigné and Françoise-Marguerite are assigned and apprehend their relative worth. In an ultimately self-defeating but accommodating and preservative gesture, Sévigné here acknowledges her daughter's greater value when they are apart. Little wonder that the daughter will continually strive to keep her distance.

In the early letters of separation, the two women struggle to come to terms with the nature of their relationship, no longer self-evident, since they are now apart. Sévigné counters her daughter's attempts at separation by invoking another vision of their relationship, reminding her of their shared identity. From Les Rochers, her world, during the celebrations at the Assembly of the Estates of Brittany, she magnanimously writes that they, together, are the toast of the town:

Au reste, ne croyez pas que votre santé ne soit point bue ici, cette obligation n'est pas grande, mais telle qu'elle est, vous l'avez tous les jours à toute la Bretagne. On commence par moi, et puis Mme de Grignan vient tout naturellement. (I, L. 191, p. 319–20)

Moreover, don't think that your health is not toasted here; this obligation is not great, but such as it is, you have it every day from all of Brittany. They begin with me, then Mme de Grignan comes quite naturally.

In her world, as opposed to the daughter's Provence, it is Sévigné who occupies center stage, and the relational order she favors (so favorable to her) is naturalized in its ready endorsement by her toasting entourage, "on," that ubiquitous third term. Her vision of a naturally hierarchical order, confirming her precedence as mother, is operative in her world if not in her daughter's. Mother and daughter respectively enjoy preeminence, but only at the cost of the other, and in their separate worlds.

Again and again, those two worlds collided when the two women were reunited. Following unhappy visits to her mother in Paris, the daughter was reduced to apologies upon her departure, thereby effectively submitting to the order of the world she had found there, her mother's. In May 1675, Sévigné responds to her departed daughter's first letter in a tone of gracious denial, preferring, it would seem, to efface through silence any discordances experienced rather than lend them weight with words: "Je vous conjure donc, ma bonne, de n'être point persuadée que vous ayez manqué à rien" (I, L. 387, p. 717) [I beg you then, *ma bonne,* not to believe that you were remiss in any way]. Again in June 1677, she repeats forgiving assurances in response to what appears to be an apology for a precipitate departure, denying the daughter's need to make an act of contrition, but stipulating all the while the appropriate act of repentance, a return visit:

Songez à vous, ma chère enfant, ne vous faites point de *dragons;* songez à me venir achever votre visite, puisque, comme vous dites, la destinée, c'est-à-dire la Providence, a coupé si court, contre toutes sortes de raisons, celle que vous avez voulu me faire. (II, L. 578, pp. 461–62)

Take care of yourself, my dear child, make no dark moods for yourself; think of coming to complete your visit to me, since, as you say, destiny, that is, Providence, cut so short, against all sorts of reasons, the one you wanted to pay me.

And again, in September 1679, Sévigné acknowledges her daughter's apology sent immediately following their separation. Here, Sévigné admits at least that there has been tension during the visit by indicating how the daughter's letter eases the residual effects:

Ah! ma très chère, que voulez-vous dire de pénitence et de pardon? Je ne vois plus rien que tout ce que vous avez d'aimable, et mon coeur est fait d'une manière pour vous qu'encore que je sois sensible jusqu'à l'excès à tout ce qui vient de vous, un mot, une douceur, un retour, une caresse, une tendresse me désarme et me guérit en un moment. (II, L. 689, p. 677)

Ah! my very dear one, what do you mean, talking of penitence and pardon? I no longer see anything but what is loveable about you, and my heart is made for you in a way that, while I am sensitive to the point of excess to all that comes from you, one word, one sweetness, one return, one caress, one endearment disarms me and cures me in a moment.

By September 1684, an equilibrium seems to govern the relationship. Although Mme de Grignan continues to suffer from and to voice feelings of inadequacy aroused while in her mother's world, the separation, at least as evidenced by the mother's easy dismissal of the daughter's words, does not appear as traumatizing as earlier ones:

Ah! ma bonne, que mon coeur est pénétré de votre amitié! . . . et que vous me fâchez quand, même en badinant, vous dites que je devrais avoir une fille comme Mlle d'Alérac et que vous êtes imparfaite. (III, L. 887, p. 139)

Ah! *ma bonne,* how full my heart is of your friendship! . . . and how you anger me when, even in bantering, you say I should have a daughter like Mlle d'Alérac and that you are imperfect.

By 1688, Mme de Grignan was firmly integrated socially as mother herself, and the Grignan household was subsuming her mother's. When the countess left Paris this time, she did not leave her mother alone; she left behind her brother-in-law and guardian of her son: the chevalier de Grignan. His company was obviously a greater consolation to Sévigné than had been her two-and-a-half-month-old granddaughter when the daughter had first left in 1671. No allusion to dissension figures in the mother's letters to her departed daughter: "Il nous faut notre chère Comtesse, que nous ne trouvons plus, et sur cela, les yeux rougissent, tout est perdu" (III, L. 1006, p. 362) [We need our dear Countess, whom we no longer find, and upon that note, all eyes redden, all is lost]. Sévigné inscribes herself here, from a collective position of social security, anchored in her daughter's family, as merely one of her daughter's many admirers, and thus can afford to accord a more prominent place to her in her world than previously. Their worlds have in fact melded through the proliferation of grandchildren and recognition of the need for concerted effort to assure their place in society through increased Grignan presence in Paris, a project in which Sévigné participates enthusiastically.

The last separation, in March 1694, is relaxed and confident. It is as much animated by anticipation of the final and enduring reunion to take place only a few months hence, in May, for which preparations are already underway, as it is by regret at the daughter's departure. Sévigné responds brightly to her daughter's first letter:

Je suivrai votre conseil, ma chère bonne; je suivrai ce que j'aime, et je ne suis plus occupée que de me ranger pour partir au commencement de mai. (III, L. 1295, p. 1026–27)

I will follow your advice, *ma chère bonne,* I will follow the one I love, and I am no longer concerned with anything but getting organized to leave at the beginning of May.

A role reversal has taken place: now it is the mother who is following the daughter's advice and who will join her in her world. She will repair to Grignan, where the daughter reigns as mother and countess, leaving behind the world that was organized around her. Integrated as grandmother into that society, she no longer eclipses but contributes to the aggrandizement of the daughter as mother herself.

Having traced the span of the relationship as registered over time at the junctures of separation, I return here and pause over the letters that are produced at the height of the crisis in the relationship between mother and daughter. These letters are written around Mme de Grignan's second and third visits to her mother in Paris (December 1676–June 1677 and November 1677–September 1679). It is before, after, and even during these visits that the tension is most explicitly addressed by Sévigné in writing, that the problems between mother and daughter are aired and spelled out from the mother's perspective.

The first of these visits threatened to be disastrous four months before it actually began. In September 1676, Sévigné was imperiously shaping her daughter's future ("vous partirez" [you will leave]), requesting that her daughter change her plans, that she leave her husband to his assembly and come in October so that they might have some time alone together, rather than accompany Grignan in December as planned. The firmness of Sévigné's tone contrasts eloquently with the indecisiveness ("l'irrésolution") of which she accuses her daughter (II, L. 549, p. 404). Evidently, Françoise-Marguerite's strategy for parrying the demands of her mother was to vacillate and to passively resist her will (while contending at the same time with the demands that were being placed on her by her husband). Her indecision would be regularly invoked and rekindled by its very cause. But while she was able to change her mind, to defer decisions and visits, she could not postpone them indefinitely. She arrived in December.

In June 1677, six months later, the daughter left Paris precipitately (II, L. 578, pp. 461–62). Although her mother had initially accepted the lame explanations of "Providence" with which the daughter had eased herself away, she finally had to confront the failure their reunion had been. She could not ignore or dismiss the message of her daughter's "dragons" [dark moods]. Mme de Grignan's passive resistance to her mother, prefigured in the negotiations of the date of her arrival, had taken the form of illness while with her and had ultimately justified her departure. The daughter's poor health provides an excuse for leaving and functions as well as an accusation of the mother, ostensibly devoted to her well-being. It constitutes sufficient proof to society that the two are better off apart. The mother cannot object to the daughter's leaving Paris for reasons of health without being in self-contradiction. She is reduced to submit to the incontrovertible evidence, witnessed by others, of the daughter's health. Françoise-Marguerite is better off away from her:

Enfin, ma fille, il est donc vrai que vous vous portez mieux, et que le repos, le silence et la complaisance que vous avez pour ceux qui vous gouvernent vous donnent un calme que vous n'aviez point ici. (II, L. 579, p. 463)

Well, my daughter, it is true, then, that you feel better, and that rest, quiet, and the affection you have for those who are looking after you give you a calmness you didn't have here.

A liability in the daughter's exploitation of the alibi of health (witting or unwitting) is that it commits her to a lifetime of various ailments and complaints, beyond those already significant ones related to her childbearing. She seems, in her determined striving toward an ever elusive autonomy, to be constantly fighting depression, those "dragons," unable to locate and confront their provenance. Illness is her way of deviating from an expected role, that of the dutiful daughter; but ironically, the only cure is submission to authority—the doctor, the husband, the mother. Her escape into ill health only further entitles the mother to flood her with advice, to exercise authority from a position of maternal strength. And so her deviance is recuperated and incorporated in the mother's discourse.

Social consensus, ever crucial to the mother's and daughter's apprehension of themselves and their relationship, played a prominent role in determining the separation. The conflict between them had been played out before their friends in Paris, and, to Sévigné's mortification, these witnesses approved and even encouraged the daughter's flight from her mother. She exclaims at their verdict to her departed daughter: "Je saute aux nues quand on vient me dire: 'Vous vous faites mourir toutes les deux, il faut vous séparer'" (II, L. 579, p. 464) [I am outraged when someone comes to tell me: "You two are killing each other; you must be separated"]. In another letter, two days later, she returns to that verdict, now confirmed by reports of her daughter's improved health since their separation, and expands her reflections:

Et quand on me vient dire présentement: Vous voyez comme elle se porte, et vous même, vous êtes en repos; vous voilà fort bien toutes deux. "Oui, fort bien, voilà un régime admirable! Tellement que pour nous bien porter, il faut être à deux cent mille lieues l'une de l'autre!" Et l'on me dit cela avec un air tranquille! Voilà justement ce qui m'échauffe le sang et qui me fait sauter aux nues. Ma chère bonne, au nom de Dieu, rétablissons notre réputation par un autre voyage, où nous soyons plus raisonnables, c'est-à-dire vous, et où l'on ne nous dise plus: "Vous vous tuez l'une l'autre." Je suis si rabattue de ces discours que je n'en puis plus; il y a d'autres manières de me tuer qui seraient bien meilleures. (II, L. 580, p. 466–67)

And when someone comes along these days to tell me: You see how well she feels, and yourself, you are relaxed, you are both quite well. "Yes, quite well, this is an admirable state! So much so that in order for us to feel well, we have to be two hundred thousand leagues away from each other!" And they tell me this in a casual way! This is exactly what makes my blood boil and makes me furious. *Ma chère bonne*, in the name of God, let us reestablish our reputation with another reunion, where we are more reasonable, that is, you are, and where we are no longer told: "You are killing each other." I am so dejected by these comments that I can't take it anymore; there are other ways of killing me that would be quite preferable.

It is precisely its reputation as much as the jeopardized relationship itself that concerns Sévigné. She has a quarrel with her public as well as with her daughter but can only resolve that through negotiations with the daughter. That same "on" that Sévigné would impress as maternal paragon has turned instead to favor mother-daughter separation. She blames the daughter directly for this state of affairs ("soyons plus raisonnables, c'est-à-dire vous"), and acknowledges no behavior of her own that might have contributed to bring upon her this humiliation, or modifications in her own demeanor that might improve future visits. She does not appear to realize that she has caused her daughter as much anguish as the daughter has caused her. The reciprocal nature of the unhappy relation discerned and deplored by the public ("vous vous tuez l'une l'autre") is understood by her to be strictly unilateral and directed by society and the daughter directly against her ("il y a d'autres manières de me tuer").

Sévigné returns obsessively to the public's verdict in her next few letters. Shocked and mortified to find herself the center of negative attention from members of her circle, their words ring in her ears, burn on her tongue. She inscribes them again and again, framing them with pleas to her daughter:

N'ôterons-nous point les épines, et n'empêcherons-nous point qu'on ne nous dise tous les jours, avec une barbarie où je ne me puis accoutumer: "Ah! que vous voilà bien à cinq cents lieues l'une de l'autre! voyez comme Mme de Grignan se porte. Elle serait morte ici. Vous vous tuez l'une l'autre." Je ne sais pas comme vous vous trouvez de ces discours; pour moi, ils m'assomment, et si c'est comme cela qu'on me veut consoler, j'en suis fort satisfaite! Faisons donc mieux, ma bonne, une autre fois. N'apportez point ou ne faites point de dragons. Aimez votre santé, et jouissez de la mienne. Remettons-nous en bonne réputation; faisons voir que nous sommes assez raisonnables pour vivre ensemble quand la Providence le veut bien. (II, L. 584, pp. 476–77)

Will we not remove the thorns, and prevent people from telling us every day, with a barbarity I cannot get used to: "Ah! how well off you are five hundred leagues away from each other! see how well Mme de Grignan feels. She would die here. You kill each other." I do not know how you find these comments; as for me, they are killing me, and if this is how one wants to console me, I have had quite enough of it! Let's do better, then, *ma bonne,* another time. Do not bring with you or make any dark moods. Cherish your health, and take pleasure in mine. Let us restore our reputation; let's show that we are reasonable enough to live together when Providence so wants it.

These words, celebrating the daugher's near escape, are killing her, she says ("ces discours . . . m'assomment"), as she fixates on them repeatedly. In this manner she restages and reenacts her own death before her daughter; she positions herself as victim of generalized discourse and casts her daughter as traitorous accessory to the crime, guilty by implication of matricide. She inscribes her horror at the ritual murder of the mother. Sévigné begs for a reconciliation that will reintegrate her socially. Her distress indicates to what extent she has constructed a social persona premised on her relationship with her daughter. Her very identity is threatened with annihilation by the exposed and socially apprehended pathology of that bond. She requires a display of solidarity if her center is to hold. Sévigné insists, in a consistent mode of denial, on the fictional and willful nature of her daughter's depressed moods, her "dragons," and bans them from Paris without pausing to consider their cause. The only remedy to this failed visit is another, to rehabilitate their reputation if not their relationship.

Apparently, not only the daughter but the world at large was resistant to her proposed solution. When she failed to comprehend more generalized comments ("vous vous tuez l'une l'autre," "Elle [Mme de Grignan] serait morte ici"), and when her own victimization was not endorsed, she had to face a verdict that was specifically leveled against her:

On ne me parle que d'absence; c'est moi qui vous tue, c'est moi qui suis cause de tous vos maux. Quand je songe à tout ce que je cachais de mes craintes, et que le peu qui m'en échappait faisait de si terribles effets, je conclus qu'il ne m'est pas permis de vous aimer, et je dis qu'on veut de moi des choses si monstrueuses et si opposées que, n'espérant pas d'y pouvoir parvenir, je n'ai que la ressource de votre bonne santé pour me tirer de cet embarras. (II, L. 590, p. 494)

People are speaking to me only of absence; it is I who kill you, it is I who am the cause of all your woes. When I think of all I hid of my fears, and that the little that escaped me had such terrible effects, I conclude that it is not permitted for me to love you, and I say that one wants things from me so monstrous and so contrary that, not hoping to be able to achieve them, I have only the resource of your good health to get me out of this difficulty.

Sévigné is forced to acknowledge an affective economy in which she is excessive, a societal structure to which she is superfluous: society holds her responsible for her daughter's state and favors the daughter's cause over her own. Only the daughter's good health can signal room for her, and that can only be assured by a diminution in her expression of concern, by her own emotional discretion. Françoise-Marguerite has identified an instrument of power over her mother, her own health, but can wield it only at risk to herself. The daughter's health functions throughout the correspondence as a barometer of the women's relationship, and if Sévigné is constantly solicitous of Françoise-Marguerite's state, it is with the understanding, at some level, that her own depends on it. Both women have an eye ever to the judgmental public, that *doxa* not so *vaga*, that mediates, regulates, and pronounces on their allowed performance.

In November 1677, only six months after her precipitate departure, trailed by her mother's remonstrations, Françoise-Marguerite returned to Paris to accomplish the visit that was to reinstate the two women socially as reasonable and loving mother and daughter, and particularly to redeem the mother's reputation. Sévigné had just moved into the exquisite and spacious Hôtel de Carnavalet that would be her permanent residence in the city and had designated certain apartments for her daughter's exclusive use. She was making room for her. Françoise-Marguerite stayed for almost two years, until September of 1679. But those years were fraught with tensions that were only just contained through respites of separations and writing. The mother repaired for short periods to Livry during the summer months, and from there renewed her assault on her daughter's affections, begging her to join her there. Françoise-Marguerite resisted her mother's invitations; these separations provided the intermittent relief that allowed her visit north to last as long as it did.

From her arrival, Françoise-Marguerite's health was poor (II, L. 628, p. 588). By May 1678, six months later, she was ill and threatening to leave. Fearful of her moodiness, Sévigné resorted to writing in attempts to persuade her to stay (II, L. 642, p. 607). Further, she proceeded to reason with her son-in-law, to enlist his support, seconded by her daughter's doctor, M. Fagon, to prevail on his wife, since she could not, to stay. By the spring of 1679, Mme de Grignan was anxious to leave, and reasons of health were invoked both to delay her departure and to impel it. It was resolved that she would not leave until that fall (II, L. 673, p. 655), but the final months of their reunion were strained to the point that Sévigné preferred to write to her daughter rather than addressing her directly. However, in that writing, she recriminates her daughter in a rare display of angry and forceful righteousness: "J'ai mal dormi. Vous m'accablâtes hier au soir; je n'ai pu supporter votre injustice" (II, L. 681, p. 665) [I slept badly. You crushed me yesterday evening; I couldn't bear your unfairness]. The gravity of the offense is rendered and permanently affixed by the use of the historicizing past historic tense, as well as signaled by the reported disruption of Sévigné's sleep. As if pushed finally to her limits, the mother lashed back and unleashed fury that had been repressed over time in efforts to mend relations with Françoise-Marguerite. No longer containable in silence, seizing on the pretext of this particular offense, it erupted in language, but language contained by its inscription rather than gambled and perhaps exploded in direct confrontation with its addressee. Sévigné has learned the advantages of writing as opposed to speaking with an uncooperative and unpredictable interlocutor.

At the heart of their quarrel is the collision of their worlds. Symptomatic of the irreconcilability of their differences and yet also indicative of their attempts to develop respective modi vivendi is their cultivation of separate social spheres, recourse to their own worlds, which operate to the exclusion of each other. Françoise-Marguerite purportedly resents Sévigné's circle, where the mother is the central organizing figure and in which she figures merely as a topic of conversation: "Vous m'accusez aussi de parler à des personnes à qui je ne dis jamais rien de ce qu'il ne faut point dire" (II, L. 681, p. 665) [You also accuse me of talking to people to whom I never tell anything that is not to be told]. The daughter is particularly annoyed that her mother confides in members of her own new family, in this instance the chevalier de Grignan, whose loyalty and affection should be, she feels, exclusively hers. Sévigné's broadcasting of their relationship, and her ceaseless cultivation of her role through it, entraps the daughter in a maternal discourse that inevitably objectivizes her, while enhancing her own constructed subjectivity.

Sévigné in turn mourns her exclusion from the protective intimate circle the daughter has structured around herself:

Il est vrai que je suis quelque fois blessée de l'entière ignorance où je suis de vos sentiments, du peu de part que j'ai à votre confiance, . . . Je sais que vos amis sont traités autrement. (II, L. 682, p. 668)

It is true that I am sometimes hurt by your keeping me in complete ignorance of your feelings, by your taking me into your confidence so seldom . . . I know your friends are treated differently.

Just as the daughter suspects and resents her mother's objectification of her, so Sévigné imagines a similar fate in conversation centering on her daughter. The two women have encircled themselves socially to the exclusion of the other, and each resents the separation the other has fortified in order to render the relationship tolerable. In so doing, they double each other's behavior: it is not so much the other's actual behavior as its uncanny mirror reflection of her own defense that disturbs each of the two women. It calls ceaselessly into question their independent identities and proffers frightening models of intrasubjectivity against which they struggle by enacting defenses of objectification, by insisting on the other's "otherness."

They appear to be locked into patterns of repetition and reproduction; neither can satisfy herself or the other, and yet they persist in looking to each other for what neither can provide. Neither can remove herself from psychic bondage to the other. They appear committed in tandem to mutual frustration in spite of the buffer zones of separate circles they have attempted to construct. That social world which was univocally "on," an unaligned group to which they both played, now together, now separately, has been divided into two camps but, even so, does not adequately protect the mother and daughter as they continually seek each other out only to rediscover and reinvent their unhappiness.

Upon Mme de Grignan's departure in 1679, the correspondence is re-inaugurated by the mother under the familiar aegis of hope, all dissension relegated to oblivion. But shortly, with the daughter's first letter, the familiar refrain of filial repentance and apology is replayed (II, L. 689, p. 677), and maternal magnanimity is once again reenacted. The internalized mother travels with the daughter and is much more powerful than the mother herself. The daughter's flight is futile.

Still, a year later, in November 1680, Sévigné was intent upon coaxing her daughter into another trip to Paris, and pressing her to hasten her arrival: "Je vous conseille toujours, ma fille, de partir le plus tôt que vous pourrez" (III, L. 821, p. 53) [I still advise you, my daughter, to leave as soon as you can]. She blamed her daughter's ill health on the worries and obligations of keeping up appearances with M. de Grignan in Provence and presented the prospect of Paris as a means both of escaping those pressures and of economizing.

As if to underscore how easy she now was to live with and to enhance the appeal of a visit, Sévigné went to great lengths to describe the amicable relationship between herself and the difficult Mlle de Méri, who was at that time staying with her. Although this is initially and ostensibly the subject of her discourse, she takes an unusual and seemingly gratuitous detour to describe just how unpleasant their relations have been in the past. Her sweeping impersonal observations make her message universally applicable, but the one eruption of an addressed subject, "vous," redirects the description, transforms it into a message, and addresses it obliquely to her daughter:

Mais quand *on* ne peut jamais rien dire qui ne soit repoussé durement; quand *on* croit avoir pris les tours les plus gracieux et que, toujours, ce n'est pas cela, c'est tout le contraire; qu'*on* trouve toutes les portes fermées sur tous les chapitres qu'*on* pourrait traiter; que les choses les plus répandues se tournent en mystère; qu'une chose avérée est une médisance et une injustice; que la défiance, l'aigreur, l'aversion sont visibles et sont mêlées dans toutes les paroles: en vérité, cela serre le coeur, et franchement cela déplaît un peu. *On* n'est point accoutumé à ces chemins raboteux, et quand ce ne serait que pour *vous* avoir enfantée, *on* devrait espérer un traitement plus doux. (III, L. 821, p. 54; my emphasis)

But when *one* can never say anything that is not harshly rejected; when *one* believes one has been most gracious, and when, always, it isn't the case, it's just the opposite, when *one* finds all the doors closed on all the subjects one could discuss; when the most widely known things turn into mystery; when a confirmed fact is a scandal and an injustice; when distrust, bitterness, and aversion are visible and mixed in with all the words; in truth, this saddens the heart, and frankly it's a bit displeasing. *One* is not accustomed to these rough roads, and be it only for having given birth to *you, one* would hope for kinder treatment.

Without specifying, and thereby alienating her daughter-correspondent as the addressee of the message, jeopardizing the promise of her arrival, Sévigné guides the unwitting daughter through the reading of the passage with the understanding that it at once concerns someone else, Mlle de Méri, and everyone, "on." At the conclusion of the diatribe, she shifts direction and abruptly targets the reading daughter, "*vous.*" Artfully or artlessly, she effectively vents her resentment against Mme de Grignan's constant opposition and resistance to her and issues a stern warning against further such behavior, demonstrating her ability to vocalize, if necessary, her case. She invokes the authority of maternal relation to her daughter as entitling her to better treatment, if from others, certainly even more fundamentally from that same daughter. Maternity, then, is authority. She appeals to a spirit of obligation where she suspects that one of affection might not suffice.

Immediately following, she both emphasizes the reconciliation that has been effected between herself and Mlle de Méri and explains how it has come about, as if to suggest a comparable solution for herself and her daughter:

Cependant, ma fille, j'ai souvent éprouvé ces manières si peu honnêtes. Ce qui fait que je vous en parle, c'est que cela est changé, et que j'en sens la douceur. Si ce retour pouvait durer, je vous jure que j'en aurais une joie sensible, mais je vous dis sensible. Il faut me croire quand je parle; je ne parle pas toujours. Ce n'a point été un raccommodement, c'est un radoucissement de sang, entretenu par des conversations douces et assez sincères. (III, L. 821, p. 54)

Nevertheless, my daughter, I have often experienced such poor manners. The reason why I am speaking of it to you is that this has changed, and I feel the sweetness of it. If this change could last, I swear to you that it would give me considerable joy, considerable, I tell you. You must believe me when I speak; I do not always speak. This has not been a reconciliation; it's a sweetening of blood, kept up by conversations that are sweet and sincere enough.

She claims that her relationship with Mlle de Méri has improved as a consequence of their conversations together. But this claim merely follows rather than erasing the immediately preceding outburst. She remembers and forcefully inscribes, in strong and bitter tones, Mlle de Méri's earlier impossible ways and only tentatively, conditionally—even dubiously— records their improvement ("si ce retour pouvait durer"). She signals the rarity of her giving voice to such strong feelings as if to illuminate their importance to her daughter, their receiver. The juxtaposition implicit in the mother's discourse, her fierce anger and her hopeful joy, her show of force and her conciliatory gesture, offers the addressee-daughter a choice. It reminds her that the mother is capable of lashing out at or, worse yet perhaps, about her, as she has just ostensibly dealt with Mlle de Méri, but that she is equally capable of being appeased and gratified by a co-operative daughter. As for her own contributions to either her problematic relationship with Mlle de Méri or with her daughter, Sévigné will never admit to fault. Her position will always be one of loving denial. Never will she evince the slightest comprehension of the oppressive effect of her maternal devotion on the object of that affection, her daughter.[19]

The curve of the relationship's history, marked by the mother's reactive letters following periods of reunion with the daughter, as traced above, can be seen to describe a pattern of pain for Mme de Grignan when the two are together, and for Sévigné when they are apart. The crisis of the mid-years 1677–80 I have just focused on, the moment of forced recognition and confrontation, marks a turning point in the strained relations. The tension eases in later years with the diffusion of attention and common concern for the grandchildren, further integrating Sévigné, no longer dependent exclusively for social definition on her roles as mother and mother-in-law, in the Grignan household. It abates as Sévigné increasingly relaxes her maternal authority and comes to look to her daughter for guidance, and as she invests her energies in her familial role as grandmother. The two women do not so much invent new ways of relating to each other as simply change places before that same unstable and disputed mirror, embracing roles and patterns of behavior already prescribed and mapped out for them in the preordained social order.

If Sévigné gradually renounces her maternal authority over her daughter and distributes her attention throughout her daughter's family, her fixation on Françoise-Marguerite, the conduit both to that household and to her own subjectivity, continues to be played out on the register of writing, in the shape of letters—long letters, demanding of her the time required to read them, pleading letters, insisting on replies, display letters, calling for collective attention and sharing. She persisted in calculably imposing herself in her daughter's world, and on her daughter specifically, by writing. This was justified and accomplished in her unwitting encodement of the daughter as invalid and the daughter's complementary (if otherwise motivated) subscription to her mother's vision of her.

While Sévigné continually challenged any interpretation of her maternal devotion for her daughter as excess in the patrocentric familial economy of affections, she displaced the question and addressed it in terms of writing. She alluded regularly and apologetically to her epistolary habit as excessive and acknowledged its burdensome demands on her daughter, obligated to play her supportive role in sustaining the correspondence. Whereas she could not bring herself to see that their reunions were painful for the daughter, she was only too ready to volunteer that her writing was. As early as April 1671, she cheerfully and melodramatically signed off: "Adieu, ma très chère, je fais de la prose avec une facilité qui vous tue" (I, L. 158, p. 232) [Farewell, my very dear one, I am composing prose with an ease that kills you]; this is followed five days later by "Je suis bien folle de vous écrire de telles bagatelles; c'est le loisir de Livry qui vous tue" (I, L. 160, p. 240) [I am quite mad to write you such trifles; it is the leisure of Livry that is killing you]. In that same vein, she exhorted her daughter to write less, even not at all, understanding the demands of their correspondence to be in addition to the married daughter's other obligations and a threat to her health:

Cependant, ma bonne, quelque joie que me donnent vos lettres, je voudrais que vous n'écrivissiez point, tant je crains que cela ne vous fatigue, et votre santé m'est plus chère que tout le plaisir qu'elles me donnent. (I, L. 171, p. 267)

Nevertheless, *ma bonne,* no matter what joy your letters give me, I would prefer that you not write, so much do I fear it tires you, and your health is dearer to me than all the pleasure they give me.

This gesture of understanding contrasts of course with Sévigné's even more frequent plaintive panics when she has not heard from her daughter, but at least it suggests that she was more cognizant of, and prepared to acknowledge, the demands of the correspondence on her daughter than of the exacted visits.

Most often she blamed the exertions of Mme de Grignan's conjugal and social obligations (i.e., her husband, the other) for her poor health:

Ma fille, vous ne vous reposez jamais, vous êtes toujours dans le mouvement, et je tremble quand je pense à votre état et à votre courage, qui assurément passe de beaucoup vos forces. Je conclus comme vous que quand vous voudrez vous reposer, il ne sera plus temps, et qu'il n'y aura aucune ressource à vos fatigues passées. (I, L. 206, p. 359)

My daughter, you never rest, you are always on the move, and I tremble when I think of your state and your courage, which assuredly is greater than your strength. I conclude as you do that when you want to rest, it will be too late, and there will be no cure for your past exhaustions.

She seized on her daughter's complaints and dwelled compassionately on the demands her new life made on her. In repeatedly echoing her daughter's laments, in faithfully corroborating her frailty, she contributed to the daughter's construction of her identity as invalid. By 1672, Mme de Grignan's *dragons,* her dark moods, were encoded by Sévigné, fixed in place, inscribed in the epistolary persona of the daughter, to be repeatedly invoked as a shorthand for all that persistently troubled the daughter, to be reinvested as "Pascalian" headaches and other figures, and that fiction fixed the daughter in a definition of debility while empowering the writing mother (I, L. 269, p. 499).

In 1679, when Mme de Grignan had fled Paris after that second unhappy visit, she was seriously ill upon her return to Provence. Sévigné insisted that she not further tax her strength in writing, but that her attendant and friend Montgobert write in her place. She implored her daughter to leave her desk, a gift from her, reminding her that, even when she had given it to her, she had recognized in it a potentially lethal weapon:

Laissez, laissez un peu la vôtre [écritoire], toute jolie qu'elle est; ne vous disais-je pas bien que c'était un poignard que je vous donnais? (II, L. 721, p. 778)

Leave, leave yours [your desk] a bit, pretty as it is; did I not tell you that it was a dagger I was giving you?

To preserve her daughter's strength, she proposes an epistolary relation-ship reminiscent of that which she had earlier attempted to establish with her son-in-law:

Ne m'écrivez qu'une page, ma chère bonne. Laissez-moi vous conter tout ce qui me vient . . . je dois écrire des volumes, et vous trois mots. (II, L. 731, p. 824)

Write me only one page, *ma chère bonne.* Let me tell you everything that comes to me . . . I must write volumes, and you three words.

Whereas she had suggested to Grignan that she write and he merely re-ceive, putting him in her debt, here to her daughter she proposes a dispro-portioned writing relationship. Her more active, energetic participation in the exchange will be measured in volumes, her daughter's in words. The daughter is thus encouraged to assume a more passive role in the correspondence and to allow the mother to dominate it with her pro-lixity. Repeated emphasis on her daughter's invalid status and moderated expectations of her together suggest unconscious maternal strategies for shaping filial complacency, diminishing the space of the daughter, and thereby making space for herself. The constant intertwining of the themes of her daughter's health and her own voluminous writing suggests that the mother sought to incorporate her symbolic excess into the patrocentric economy and to legitimize it by locating justification for the excess of her writing in her daughter's poor health.

Sévigné spoke from a position of special knowledge, maternal knowl-edge, and her authority over her daughter entitled her to make observa-tions about the daughter to the daughter that were more founded than any the daughter might venture about herself. She congratulated Françoise-Marguerite upon coming around to an opinion that Sévigné held and that she had known, even while her daughter did not, that the daughter shared:

Je vous assure que, quoique vous m'ayez souvent repoussée politiquement sur ce sujet, je n'ai jamais cru que vous fussiez d'un autre sentiment que moi, et j'étais quelquefois un peu mortifiée qu'il me fut comme défendu de causer avec vous sur une matière que j'aime, sachant bien qu'au fond de votre âme, vous étiez dans les bonnes et droites opinions. (III, L. 813, pp. 32–33)

I assure you that, although you often rejected me politically on this subject, I never believed you were of an opinion other than mine, and I was sometimes a bit mor-tified that I was as if forbidden to chat with you about a subject I love, knowing well that in the depths of your soul, you had the good and the right opinions.

In attempts to differentiate herself from her mother, to construct her own identity, Françoise-Marguerite had evidently resorted to differences of opinion. Sévigné, in her greater wisdom, always knew they were of the same mind ("je n'ai jamais cru"), claiming to know the depths of her daughter's soul ("[le] fond de votre âme"), to know the daughter better than the daughter knows herself. Paradoxically, and disturbingly, her claim takes on a less specious quality if it is recognized that there does exist genuine identity confusion between the two women, that the mother is imprinted inescapably in the daughter. The mother can speak authorita-tively both to the daughter and within the daughter. In addressing the "corresponding" daughter, she engages the internalized mother and, in a sense, converses with a projected fiction of herself. The suggestibility of the daughter to her mother's vision for her is concretized in her easy acquiescence to the role of invalid.

Sévigné repeatedly insisted on the threats to her daughter's health that writing represented, and she recommended that she dictate her letters:

Faites-moi écrire par M. du Plessis; mettez une ligne en haut et une en bas, car il faut voir de votre écriture, et je serai ravie de penser que, toute couchée et toute à votre aise, vous causerez avec moi, et que vous ne serez pas contrainte, deux heures durant, dans une posture qui tue la poitrine. (III, L. 893, p. 152)

Have M. du Plessis write; write one line at the top and one at the bottom, for I must see some of your writing, and I will be delighted to think that, lying down and comfortable, you will chat with me, and you will not be constrained, for two hours at a stretch, in a posture which exhausts the chest.

Contrasted with this frequent advice is the fact that Sévigné never admitted to the slightest discomfort when it was she writing. Nor did she find the solution of dictating letters at all to her own liking. Only in 1676, when she suffered from rheumatism, was she unable to wield her own pen and obliged to allow others to write down her words. This interval was treated lightly and bravely, the problem collectively and gaily surmounted, so that it hardly interfered with her compulsion to be in communication with Grignan. But she was not happy with the writing it produced. "La petite personne" was serving as her secretary as she convalesced at Les Rochers (II, L. 486, p. 247), and her friend Corbinelli commented on the effect this had on her style:

Corbinelli dit que je n'ai point d'esprit quand je dicte, et sur cela il ne m'écrit plus. Je crois qu'il a raison; je trouve mon style lâche. (II, L. 492, p. 257)

Corbinelli says I have no wit when I dictate, and, on that note, he is no longer writing to me. I think he is right; I find my style lax.

The solution Sévigné constantly proffered to her daughter, a secretary, was not one she embraced for herself. The inhibition she experienced when dictating was precisely what she prescribed for her writing daughter. She minimized her own health problems, magnified her daughter's, and pronounced from a position of health and strength on her invalid daughter, as a doctor on a patient. And she prescribed for her regimes and cures that were unacceptable to herself.

While Sévigné recognized that holding her daughter to their correspondence was further debilitating to her already poor health, she persisted in the contradictory message that her own very life depended on hearing from her. So well was this lesson internalized in the daughter that, when Sévigné echoes Françoise-Marguerite below, she is only reproducing and reconfirming her own words, discoursing with her fictional foil:

Enfin, voilà l'heure qui presse, *tout est perdu si je n'écris point à ma mère*, et vous avez raison, mon enfant, il faut nécessairement que j'en reçoive peu ou prou, comme on dit; il faut que je voie pied ou aile de ma chère fille, et nul ordinaire ne se peut passer sans qu'elle me donne cette consolation. C'est ma vie, c'est manger, c'est respirer. (III, L. 896, p. 162)

Finally, the hour has come, *all is lost if I do not write to my mother,* and you are right, my child: I must absolutely receive something, be it more or less, as they say; I must see foot or wing of my dear daughter, and no mail delivery can come without her giving me this consolation. It is my life, it is to eat, to breathe.

Underscored in this message is the vital necessity that Sévigné receive signs of life from her daughter. The repetition of "il faut," the intransigence of tone conveyed by the "all or nothing" rhetoric ("tout," "nul"), and the allusion to basic survival needs ("manger," "respirer") all contribute to the urgency of her message. Not only does she need letters; she needs them each time the mail is delivered: "nul ordinaire ne se peut passer." In the passage preceding, Sévigné has paid lip service to her daughter's busy schedule and to the imposition that her requirement of regular letters must represent. She proceeds to insist nonetheless.

In 1689, she continues to pity the state to which writing reduces the daughter, evoking in detail the physical effects, and experiencing her daughter's if not her own pain:

Je ne laisse pas d'être en peine de la quantité de lettres que vous écrivez et de cette longue résidence que vous écrivez dans ce petit cabinet, dont il faut que vous sortiez avec un grand mal au dos, un grand mal à la tête, un grand épuisement. Ainsi le plaisir que je reçois en lisant vos lettres est toujours mêlé de peine, comme les autres choses de cette vie. (III, L. 1067, p. 498–99)

I do not cease to be pained by the number of letters you write and this long stay during which you write in this little office, from which you must come out with a bad backache, a bad headache, great exhaustion. So the pleasure I get in reading your letters is always mixed with pain, like the other things in this life.

Sévigné has no trouble imagining the ill effects of writing but assigns them to her daughter. Nowhere in the forty-eight years spanned by the *Correspondance*[20] does Sévigné herself ever admit to any discomfort brought on by writing. At the same time, she dwells frequently on her daughter's ailments. Although this might be interpreted as a polite dynamic of self-effacement and expression of concern for the other, it also functions as a reinforcement of the power relationship obtaining between the two women. Sévigné cultivates an active, healthy role and assigns her daughter, who compliantly obliges, a passive and sickly one. She thereby makes room for herself at the cost of her daughter. Her double messages to her daughter (write—my life depends on it; don't write—your life depends on it) signal the ambivalence of her maternal feeling. Both dependent on her daughter and superfluous because of her daughter, she inscribes her excess and visits it on her daughter, at the daughter's expense.

Filling in the Fiction/Writing out the Role: Mother Nature

L'historien de la Nature se plaint avec quelque sorte de raison, de ce que la Terre, qui est la commune mère des vivants, nous faisant une infinité de biens, nous lui faisons une infinité de maux.   FRANÇOIS DE GRENAILLE[21]

The historian of Nature complains, with some reason, that whereas the Earth, who is the common mother of the living, does us an infinity of good, we do her an infinity of evil.

In the cultural encodement of "woman" as exemplified in the myth of Ceres, if she enjoys a privileged relationship, it is not only as mother to her daughter, but it is just as categorically to nature. Figured as the dramatic reason behind the seasons, willfully fertile and deliberately barren, generous and stinting, predictable and wild, both nurturing and cruel, cause of life and death, nature is personified as woman in the humanist tradition of anthropomorphism.[22] In this elision of woman and nature is represented all that escapes man's understanding and dominion. Under the rubric of "Mother Nature" is subsumed all that man holds in veneration and in terror.

The extent to which Sévigné embraced and internalized this commonplace as constitutive of her own appropriate place and suggestive of her assigned role in the world cannot be ascertained. What can be said, what is manifestly evident from her letters, is that Sévigné derived deep pleasure from her relation to nature; and, as she had demonstrated particular verve for other conventionally sanctioned behaviors, this one also may be indicative of her ready acceptance of and drive to excellence in designated arenas of "feminine" competence. Sévigné savored her sojourns in the country, at Livry and at Les Rochers in particular. Her visits were most often immediately motivated by the need to economize, to reduce expenditures by regularly removing herself from the enforced ostentation of Paris, and to oversee the administration of her lands, upon which she depended for income. But rather than consider these stays in the country as forced retreats imposed on her by difficult circumstances, she relished them and delighted in her time there. She inscribed in her letters the cultivation of her relationship to nature and her pleasure in that world of both passing seasons and cyclical permanence.

She delights in observing patiently and exactly the minute manifestations of the changes in seasons, the patterns of life of birds and other small creatures. She appreciates the spectacles of moonlight, of dark overgrown woods, of the fall foliage, of summer haze. All of these scenes afford her entertainment, enhance and intensify her moods, and, in their epistolary inscription, convey her state of mind. She feels protective of the forests, especially as they are regularly threatened and occasionally mutilated by the woodcutters' axes at the service of her son Charles's perpetual need for ready cash.[23] She takes satisfaction in full harvests, participating in both the preparations and then the celebrations; she takes pride in planting her park with trees, in arranging them so as to ensure shade for her paths, and in watching them grow. She has a special fondness for her gardener Pilois who shares her enthusiasm and anticipates her every will; she consults regularly with him on the various concerns of her property. She appears to have a strong respect for the ecology of the land and to feel responsible to protect it as well as to profit from it.

Her relationship with nature seems generally more serene than the one that she cultivates with her daughter. With nature, she is concerned to plant, to organize and arrange, to prune, to tend, to clear, but she can also be content merely to observe and appreciate, to practice benign neglect, and to marvel. There is no conflictual dimension to Sévigné's relation to nature; rather, the flourishing of nature is essential to her own prosperity, and vice versa. There is no alternation whereby what benefits the one threatens the other; rather, there is a clear relation of complementary and mutual interest. Gardening offers much more pliant material to work with than does mothering. Sévigné takes on more completely the role of artist in shaping her world at Les Rochers than she can in shaping her absent and resistant daughter. Her loving artistry is realized in her inscription of that world through letters to her daughter.

But, just as she imprints herself on her daughter, so she imprints herself on nature. In the parks and along the wooded paths that Sévigné frequented, where she repaired for her daily constitutionals, and where she found quiet nooks to read and write, Sévigné humanized her trees. In a curious but not uncommon practice, she attached mottos and slogans to the trunks of the trees, orchestrating verbal contradictions by juxtaposing the signs to one another, for the benefit of herself and her entourage:

Voici un mot que j'ai écrit sur un arbre pour mon fils qui est revenu de Candie: *vago di fama;* n'est-il point joli pour n'être qu'un mot? Je fis écrire hier encore, en l'honneur des paresseux: *bella cosa far niente.* (I, L. 170, p. 263)

Here is a word I wrote on a tree for my son, who has returned from Candie: *vago di fama;* is this not pretty for being only a dictum? Further, I had written yesterday, in honor of the lazy: *bella cosa far niente.*

The trees function as monumental and perfectly obedient extensions of herself, "ideal children." She projects herself effectively through their embodiment, splitting and assigning her fragmented feelings, lending each of them voice. She imposes her inner conflicts on them textually and makes of them mouthpieces for her own various derivative thoughts, to be apprehended by her son and other companions, and reflected back to her as well for her further meditation. The trees, in their silent acquiescence to her authority, constitute more compliant children than her own. They say and represent her will and send back to her self-confirming messages:

Je lis, je travaille, je me promène, je ne fais rien. *Bella cosa far niente,* dit un de mes arbres; l'autre lui répond: *amor odit inertes.* On ne sait auquel entendre. (II, L. 435, p. 121)

I read, I work, I stroll, I do nothing. *Bella cosa far niente,* says one of my trees; the other answers: *amor odit inertes.* One knows not which to heed.

In the borrowed languages of humanism, Italian and Latin, she finds truths to reflect and validate her various moods, and in assigning them to her trees, she invents a way to revel in the diversity of her feelings. She produces meaning by imposing her multiple well-read voice on nature, thus subscribing to and furthering the humanistic tradition of anthropomorphism.

However, in writing about nature to her daughter, Sévigné presents herself not simply as an enthusiastic amateur or a learned ventriloquist; she posits herself as a knowledgeable authority as well and challenges her daughter's competence:

Mais où prenez-vous, ma bonne, qu'on entende des rossignols le 13e de juin? Hélas! ils sont tous occupés du soin de leur petit ménage. Il n'est plus question ni de chanter ni de faire l'amour; ils ont des pensées plus solides. Je n'en ai pas entendu un seul ici. Ils sont en bas vers ces étangs, vers cette petite rivière, mais je n'ai pas tant battu de pays. (III, L. 913, p. 204)

But where do you get the idea, *ma bonne,* that one hears nightingales on 13 June? Alas! they are all busy caring for their little household. It is no longer a question of singing or making love; they have more solid concerns. I haven't heard even one of them here. They are below toward those ponds, toward that little river, but I haven't searched for them that far.

She knows nature better than her daughter. She has an intimate acquaintance with the ways of nightingales, their schedules and habits, and contests her daughter's claim to have heard their song in mid-June. Apparently her daughter cannot distinguish between one bird and another. Sévigné's knowledge of nature, her expertise, here operates as yet another manifestation of her authority over her daughter's. Just as she lays claim to and exercises her maternal authority as constitutive of her social identity, so she lays claim to and defends her privileged relation to nature against her daughter's through demonstrations of her superior understanding of its workings.

She instates herself as "Mother Nature" particularly in relation to her trees, reporting on the progress of these her "children," which she planted and encouraged to grow over the years. Returning to Les Rochers with her son and daughter-in-law after an extended absence, Sévigné rejoices in the refreshing calm of her woods:

Mon Dieu, quel repos, quel silence, quelle fraîcheur, quelle *sainte horreur*! Car tous ces petits enfants que j'ai plantés sont devenus si grands que je ne comprends pas que nous puissions encore vivre ensemble. Cependant leur beauté n'empêche pas la mienne. Vous la connaissez, ma beauté. Tout le monde m'admire en ce pays; on m'assure que je ne suis point changée. Je le crois tout autant que je le puis. (III, L. 1113, p. 604)

My God, what calm, what silence, what coolness, what a *holy horror*! For all these small children I planted have grown so tall that I do not understand how we can be alive at the same time. Nevertheless their beauty does not prevent my own. You know it, my beauty. Everyone admires me here in the country; they assure me I have not changed at all. I believe it as much as I can.

The only jarring note in her soliloquy is a dissonant if eloquent citation (the italicized phrase) from Saint-Amant's "La Solitude," suggesting to what extent her relation to nature has already been culturally encoded and is filtered through her literary repertoire. She takes parental pride in the growth of her trees, "ces petits enfants," and considers their relations as they grow together and encroach on her paths:

Ces allées sont plus tristes et plus sombres . . . elles paraissent moins grandes par les empêchements qu'elles se font à elles-mêmes. Enfin, c'est une sorte de beauté plus sérieuse. (III, L. 1113, p. 604)

These paths are sadder and darker . . . they seem smaller because of the obstacles they make for themselves. After all, it's a more serious kind of beauty.

And it is in this context, in the contemplation of Sévigné surveying her property with affectionate detachment, that the daughter-in-law produces, for the benefit of the accompanying "dames de Rennes"—those ever necessary witnesses to the maternal performance, the accolade (cited earlier) [24] that the mother reproduces for her daughter with such evident pleasure: "Ma belle-fille a dit fort joliment: "Ah, voilà la vraie mère!" Je suis donc la vraie mère!" (III, L. 1113, p. 605) [My daughter-in-law said quite prettily: "Oh, here is the true mother!" I am then the true mother!]. As significantly as in her relation to her daughter, in her relation to nature, Sévigné constructs and projects her maternal persona.

Sévigné has carefully planted and nurtured these trees but now is able to delight in what they have become of themselves in a demonstration of detached affection and wonderment. But even this experience of parental attachment triggers a reflex of comparison. She is pleased to note that their adult beauty does not eclipse her own. The fact that the trees have matured reminds her that she also has aged, but she is reassured by her warm reception at Les Rochers and reports that she willingly embraces her friends' flattery. That this return to find her trees so grown should prompt comparative thoughts in Sévigné indicates to what extent Sévigné's world, even this completely pliant world of nature, is viewed by her as an arena of performance and competition.

She asserted herself over this world, as over her daughter's, as mother. In 1690, she triumphantly figured herself as "Mother Nature" and inscribed her personal accomplishment of the seasonal passage to spring in a letter to her daughter:

Il fait un temps tout merveilleux, Dieu merci. J'ai si bien fait que le printemps est achevé. Tout est vert. Je n'ai pas eu peu de peine à faire pousser tous ces boutons, à faire changer le rouge en vert. Quand j'ai eu fini tous ces charmes, il a fallu aller aux hêtres, puis aux chênes; c'est ce qui m'a donné le plus de peine, et j'ai besoin encore de huit jours pour n'avoir plus rien à me reprocher. Je commence à jouir de toutes mes fatigues, et je crois tout de bon que non seulement *je n'ai pas nui* à toutes ces beautés, mais qu'en cas de besoin je saurais fort bien faire un printemps, tant je me suis appliquée à regarder, à observer, à épiloguer celui-ci, ce que je n'avais jamais fait avec tant d'exactitude. Je dois cette capacité à mon grand loisir et, en vérité, ma chère bonne, c'est la plus jolie occupation du monde. C'est dommage qu'en me mettant si fort dans cette belle jeunesse, il ne m'en soit demeuré quelque chose:
       Mais, hélas! quand l'âge nous glace
       Nos beaux jours ne reviennent jamais!   (III, L. 1207, p. 875)

The weather is marvelous, thank God. I have done so well that spring is complete. All is green. I had not a little trouble in making all the buds grow, in making the red change to green. When I had finished all these charms, I had to go the beeches, then to the oaks; this is what gave me the most trouble, and I still need another eight days in order to have nothing else to reproach myself. I am beginning to receive pleasure in return for all my troubles, and I believe that not only *have I not harmed* all these beauties, but that if need be I could make a spring quite well, so much have I applied myself to watch, to observe, to epilogue this one, something I had never done with so much exactness. I owe this capacity to my great leisure and, in truth, *ma chère bonne*, it is the most delightful pastime in the world. It is too bad that in putting myself so much into this beautiful youth, nothing of it was left over for me:

But, alas! when age chills us
Our beautiful days never return!

This passage actually continues a letter from ten days before (19 April 1690), in which Sévigné had begun her careful notation of the blossoming of spring. She prides herself in her powers of observation and corrects banal assumptions on the rites of spring:

Que pensez-vous donc que ce soit que la couleur des arbres depuis huit jours? Répondez. Vous allez dire: "Du vert." Point du tout, c'est du rouge. Ce sont de petits boutons, tout prêts à partir, qui font un vrai rouge, et puis ils poussent tous une petite feuille, et comme c'est inégalement, cela fait un mélange trop joli de vert et de rouge. Nous couvons tout cela des yeux. (III, L. 1205, p. 867)

So what color do you think the trees have been for a week? Answer. You are going to say: "Green." Not at all, they're red. They are little buds, all ready to burst, that make a real red, and then they each grow a little leaf, and this unevenly, so that it makes a very pretty mix of green and red. We feast our eyes on this.

As she notes the transformation of nature, her perceptions of the nuances of color, and the pace of change in different sorts of trees, hedges, bushes, she inscribes the process in time. She recreates, in writing, the phenomenon of the coming of spring and thus duplicates, textually, the creative dynamic of nature. Her text constitutes, itself, a spring and presents itself in the same gratuitous way for the pleasure of the observer/reader.

In taking the credit for the successful accomplishment of spring, citing all of her efforts rewarded ("J'ai si bien fait que le printemps est achevé"), Sévigné lightheartedly casts herself as the causal Mother Nature in the same way that she identified earlier with La Fontaine's Dame Mouche,[25] repeating the same humorous folly of mistaking sequence for cause, and thus poking fun at her own self-importance. At the same time, it is she who saw attentively in her text to the minutiae spelling out spring's arrival and the change of season. This act of representation grounds a rivalrous relation with nature ("en cas de besoin je saurais fort bien faire un printemps"). Her expertise, gained through patient application of her leisure time to observation of detail, instates her as authority in the domain of nature as well as that of motherhood. And she lays claim to that authority through this, her "creative" writing.

If a coherent figure of Sévigné's maternity can be construed from these fragmented readings of her relations with her son-in-law, with her married daughter, and with nature, it is of a mother already socially encoded as superfluous, who reproduces that encodement in her own discourse of excess, while at the same time contesting it, and who seeks in ratified roles at once to fulfill and to explode the definition her culture has constructed for her. In subscribing to their prescribed roles, she and her daughter, while ostensibly devoted to each other, are divided against each other and, in their alienation, lend support to the ideology that oppresses them. In embracing a privileged relationship with nature, and entertaining an image of herself as "Mother Nature," Sévigné reproduces the anthropomorphizing mania of an androcentric culture, a cult intent on extending dominion over all that exceeds its understanding, summarized in the conflation of mother and nature. She offers herself up to that culture, always already contained and encoded, as model of the fiction of maternity so necessary to its continuance.

EIGHT

"The Reproduction of Mothering"

Women mother daughters who, when they become women, mother.
NANCY CHODOROW [1]

Nancy Chodorow's analysis of the reproduction of mothering has been justly taken to task as not sufficiently attentive to the historical, class, ethnic, and sexual differences that produce multiple inflections of "mothering." Her theorizing assumes a norm that in fact mainly mirrors the particular condition of white, generally middle-class, heterosexual, and most likely Anglo-European women who have been trained by example to a particular sociohistorical pattern of mothering, and who have embraced it. Attempts to theorize inevitably generalize at the expense of the exceptional, and the exceptional most often proves to be whatever the theorist is not.[2] For purposes of this study, however, Chodorow's analysis is useful. Her focus privileges a female profile with which Sévigné and her daughter can be identified, and her theory offers a useful framework for considering the problematic of their relationship. Indeed, Sévigné and her daughter can be read as exemplary precursors in every sense of the mother-daughter dynamic Chodorow investigates in contemporary society. As if to perpetuate what was (until recently) held up as an ideal paragon of maternity, and to proffer a model of normative comportment, selections of the Sévigné letters featured regularly in reading lists for young Catholic girls as they were trained in convent schools for their expected life roles.

Sévigné's epistolary enactment of maternity encoded a structuring of mother-daughter relations that was to extend beyond the immediate couple

A version of this chapter previously appeared in *Stanford French Review* 11, 2 (1987).

and to participate in the structuring of family relations, both genderically and generationally. It is in her capacity as grandmother that the impact of her mothering is relayed through the greater family circuit. And it is in the daughter's accession to and performance of the mothering role (as inscribed by her mother) that her own filial experience can be apprehended. Both of these positions, mother and daughter, appear to defer their respective identities ceaselessly back and forth onto each other. However, something of a pattern of identity transmission is discernible once the relational positions are expanded to read grandmother/mother - daughter/mother - daughter/granddaughter. By reading the construction backward, by examining the ways in which the grandchildren figure in the grandmother's letters, one is afforded glimpses of the implicit if elusive third term, the doubled mother. A seemingly rebellious daughter has internalized and now mirrors, as mother herself, the mothering she has known as daughter.

But, none of these perspectives is to be neatly found in the *Correspondance*. Indeed, accounts of experience in any case have to be understood as fictions of self-structuring by self-inventing narrators; both the tale and its teller are suspect—neither mother, daughter, nor granddaughter can tell the whole story. Each can only tell her own. There is no whole story to be told.

Little is known of Françoise-Marguerite's childhood. Sévigné retrospectively claims to have adored her daughter from birth, but their early relationship is nowhere documented as in any way remarkable. Duchêne's research concludes: "Avec des intervalles, Mademoiselle de Sévigné fut, comme tout le monde, élevée au couvent par une mère qui l'aimait sans l'adorer." [3] [With intervals, Mademoiselle de Sévigné was, like everyone, brought up in a convent by a mother who loved her without adoring her]. Her childhood was in no way different, as far as can be known, from that of any other girl of her station and her generation. On the surface at least, it resembles the conventional upbringing she in turn, despite the grandmother's protests, gave her own daughter, Pauline. The mother-daughter relationship between Sévigné and Françoise-Marguerite, as has already been mentioned, is not articulated until the daughter's departure, at the age of twenty-five, when she is married and already mother of a daughter herself, to join her husband in Provence.

It should be remembered that Françoise-Marguerite grew up without an immediate paternal figure in the family. The son, Charles, two years younger than his sister, was not expected to, nor did he, assume that position. This void can be presumed to have intensified relations between herself and her mother. The widow performed both paternal and maternal roles, and the daughter fixated on this sole parental figure as a major organizing principle in her psychic and social world.

This family configuration is not reproduced in the daughter's marriage. Her husband was a constant presence with a distinguished career entailing myriad social obligations that required his wife's frequent participation and support. She shared in his identity. The demands of their social standing both competed with and contributed to shape her maternal role, dividing her attention while at the same time augmenting her concern for her children's honorable continuation of their father's lineage. Accordingly, a great deal of attention was given to their placement, taking into account family finances as well as prestige, and particular ambition was focused on the only son, Louis-Provence.

Despite these differences in the Sévigné and the Grignan family configurations, in the way that Mme de Grignan brought up her children, and in the way their grandmother Sévigné participated in their shaping, as inscribed in the letters, patterns of maternal attitudes are discernible in the two women that afford a fairly detailed tableau of a seventeenth-century transmission of mothering practices within a privileged milieu.

Within this frame, the mother-daughter relationship can be read as a generational power struggle, wherein dominance transfers through the female family continuum by virtue of the simple passage of time and the assumption of motherhood by the daughter, next in line. As widowed mother, Sévigné has exercised significant power over her daughter, deciding the nature of her education, arranging her marriage, binding her to and training her through the epistolary exchange. Her maternal authority, rather than bond the two women in healthy affection for each other, produces tension and conflict instead: desperate pursuit on the part of the needy mother, uneasy flight on the part of the oppressed but dutiful daughter.[4] The ever recurrent hope for mutual appeasement and resolution, which the two women so fiercely desire from each other, and which is so regularly frustrated, perpetuates the struggle, sustaining, all the while, the epistolary exchange.

The introduction of grandchildren to the familial affective economy reproduces the triangulation of the two women's relationship to M. de Grignan, the husband/son-in-law (see chapter 7). At the same time, it promises to ease tensions in that the two women recognize in these children/grandchildren a common cause. Ultimately, however, the mutual attempts at healing the mother-daughter relationship through concerted interest in the grandchildren are not effective, since the premise of the cure remains that of reproducing and repeating the power dynamic that had exacerbated the relationship in the first place. Sévigné may have tried to correct what she came to perceive as her mistakes with Françoise-Marguerite in her relations with her grandchildren. In her old age, with the wisdom of experience, the values she had held in her prime may have lost their hold. Apparently, however, the lessons in question were ones Sévigné had learned but could not teach.[5] Sévigné recommends parenting practices to her daughter, passing on to her the outline of personal therapy and social accomplishment that she herself had followed, positioning the child as primarily instrumental to the mother's fulfillment; and her daughter, estranged if not individuated from her mother, never bonds with her first daughter and alienates her second.[6] The tragedy reproduces itself.

Sévigné's rubric of the maternal is tellingly revealed in her inscribed role of grandmother. It is in the articulation of prescriptions for raising her grandchildren, her seeking of validation through repetition, that one finds reliable traces of her maternal code. Sévigné's mode of relating to her grandchildren, as represented in the letters to her daughter, introduces a literary paradigm for the family generational configuration, particularly the female continuum of mother-daughter-granddaughter, that extends both beyond the seventeenth century and the text, finding corroboration in contemporary studies of family dynamics.[7] As grandmother, Sévigné seeks an alliance with the grandchildren. Her need of such a coalition indicates a subtextual acknowledgment of vulnerability vis-à-vis the daughter, now in maternal ascendancy herself.

Another archetypal literary parent-figure, Victor Hugo, later spells out and romanticizes, he in paternal perspective, the generational interplay that characterizes the enduring patriarchal family structure. In the poem "*Jeanne était au pain sec*," under the pertinent heading of the section, "Grand Age et bas âge mêlés" from *L'Art d'être grand-père*,[8] the poet-grandfather-je outlines, at once succinctly and sentimentally, the balance of power that obtains in the traditional extended family. Enfeebled and dethroned grandparent allies with as yet weak and subservient grandchild against the children/parents now in authority, demonstrating the tension that stabilizes the triangular relationship. The legalistic terms deployed throughout the poem—"crime," "devoir," "proscrite," "forfaiture," "lois," "gouvernement," "ordre," "pouvoir," "règle," "autorité,"—suggest a coy tactic of reductio ad absurdum by overstatement of a trivial family dispute but indicate just as persuasively the political struggle vexing the core of domestic relations.

Sévigné's discourse, in its grandmotherly mode, relates less wittingly the same triangular pattern of alliances and reverberates with similar tensions. Nor is it inappropriate to measure the widow Sévigné's rhetoric against that of a nineteenth-century self-poeticized patriarch. In spite of the centuries that separate Sévigné and Hugo, the modern family structure was articulating itself and crystallizing conservatively into its gender-codified shape throughout the span of time that encompasses their writings. As in Hugo's poem, where the grandparent allies with the grandchild, serving as buffer, mediator, defender, thus undermining current parental authority, challenging his successors, and assuring his affective future, so also does Sévigné seek her constituency in the grandchildren. Her campaign is particularly forceful because of the authoritative dimension accruing to her voice as widow. She incorporates paternal authority into her performance as both mother and grandmother. Where the Sévigné letters differ in interest from the Hugo poem is in the access they afford to a view of women's relations within the patriarchal social system.

The *Correspondance* offers access to scenes of everyday family intimacy[9] and provides running commentary relating to the grandchildren. There were three: Marie-Blanche, Louis-Provence, and Pauline. The history of their mother's tribulations in childbearing is typical of the experience of women in general at that time; Mme de Grignan bore six infants, but only three children survived, and her own strength was drained as well.[10] Sévigné's epistolary advice for raising the children, along with her daughter's extrapolated reception of such counsel, illustrates the way certain practices of mothering are transmitted and prevail and, by implication, standard experiences of childhood as well.

In the seventeenth century, boys and girls are assigned different values, in keeping with their anticipated roles in life, and entrusted accordingly to those who are to serve as their models and teachers. As de Grenaille pronounces: "C'est à faire aux pères de cultiver le naturel de leurs héritiers, et . . . les mères ne doivent avoir proprement soin que des filles."[11] [It is the fathers' responsibility to cultivate the nature of their heirs, and . . . mothers must properly take care only of the daughters]. Daughters, according to Sévigné and the wisdom of her day, are encoded to function as decorative and engaging toys;[12] they are considered worthy projects that can serve to set off the status and virtue of their parents, their mothers in particular. The greater importance assigned to male children as heirs of the family name, reputation, and fortune translates in the letters as a set of concerns and methods for bringing up the Grignan son quite distinct from those suggested for the daughters.[13] Sévigné shows a certain deference toward her grandson and the men charged with his education and offers advice concerning him in more indirect ways than with regard to her granddaughters. Her instructions, interventions, and comments on her grandchildren provide striking examples of the common tensions that underlie female intergenerational dynamics and relate to the issue of male privilege in the family, as well as illustrating discreet ways women develop to maneuver and wield familial power from a position of marginal authority.

Although the grandchildren motif frequently provides, by displacement, a source of relief for mother and daughter in their strained exchange, its introduction arouses ambivalent feelings in Sévigné as well. The advent of grandchildren forces her to reassess and reaffirm her familial role—she fears being superseded as maternal figure by her daughter and thus losing her constructed social identity. Thus she will occasionally distance herself from the grandchildren and even disparage the relationship:

Vous savez combien je suis loin de la radoterie qui fait passer violemment l'amour maternelle aux petits enfants; la mienne est demeurée tout court au premier étage, et je n'aime ce petit peuple que pour l'amour de vous. (II, L. 417, p. 77)

You know how far I am from the nonsense that makes maternal love pass violently on to the granchildren; mine has simply remained at the first stage, and I love these little people only for the love of you.

She reassures her insecure daughter of her primary devotion here but also reasserts her privilege of monopoly in the maternal domain: she can share her understanding of maternal love with no one, especially not her own daughter, its ostensible object and cause. She has not identified and cultivated the maternal role only to see it diffuse and pass on, with the advent of grandchildren, to their mother, her daughter.

In 1675, Sévigné persists in claiming to enjoy a greater understanding of maternal love than her daughter (mother of three herself by then) by reason of that same daughter, but she suggests that it is an understanding Françoise-Marguerite would do well to spare herself:

Vous ne comprenez point encore trop bien l'amour maternel; tant mieux, ma fille. Il est violent, mais à moins que d'avoir des raisons comme moi, ce qui ne se rencontre pas souvent, on peut à merveille se dispenser de cet excès. (II, L. 445, p. 149–50)

You still don't understand maternal love too well; all the better, daughter. It is violent, but unless one has reasons like mine, which one doesn't often find, one can do quite well without this excess.

As much as Sévigné fears being displaced by her daughter as mother, she fears being displaced in her daughter's affections by the Grignan children. Ever conscious of her superfluity in the familial affective economy, she seeks to encode and assign that excess elsewhere, now visiting it on her son-in-law, now on her daughter, and even, as the above passage suggests, on her grandchildren.

The arrival and assimilation of the little ones into the family does, however, contribute to relax the tension between the two women as they attempt to make of them a common cause. Sévigné comes to diffuse her dependence on her daughter, to visit her relational needs and her energetic concerns, in a seemingly healthier focus, upon the grandchildren. Increasingly, the lives and significance of the two women as mothers converge, confront one another, and result not only in rivalry and compassion, often enough, but, significantly, in repetition. A certain female profile, role, and function in society is being perpetuated.

Grandmothering in the letters seems to fall into familiar patterns as well. Sévigné relates actively to her grandchildren in much the same affectionately detached way that she relates to nature (see chapter 7). She writes faithfully to her daughter expressions and models of relaxed and generous nurturing. She observes the children's behavior and development in a candid but committed way, expressing genuine pleasure in their company, offering a steady stream of advice on their upbringing, and voicing thoughtful concern for their future. Her relationship to them is not as fraught as it has been with her daughter. Less personally invested in them, less dependent on them for her own construction of self, she enjoys a healthier distance from them that enables her to appreciate them as people in their own right.

As Sévigné shows interest and delight in her grandchildren, she also frequently finds herself mediating between them and their mother, intervening especially, as socially sanctioned, on behalf of her granddaughters. She often requests that Mme de Grignan show more leniency and kindness to them, while she generally defers to "greater" wisdom with regard to her grandson. She seeks to soothe mother and children, she assists in easing tensions, and she defuses domestic crises but contributes thereby, it must be added, to ensuring the continuance of the microcosmic paternal order at Grignan.

Marie-Blanche, the elder daughter, spent her infancy with her grandmother alone in Paris. Mme de Grignan expressed disappointment that her firstborn was not a male. Her apologetic announcement of the birth to her departed husband in Provence, echoed in the same letter by Sévigné, indicates to what extent they had both internalized patriarchal values:

Si ma bonne santé peut vous consoler de n'avoir qu'une fille, je ne vous demanderai point pardon de ne vous avoir pas donné un fils. (I, L. 115, p. 132)

If my good health can console you for only having a daughter, I will not ask your forgiveness for not having given you a son.

Sévigné, for her part, lightly casts the blame on the father for having produced a daughter rather than the desired son, she bemoans all the votive candles they (she and her daughter together) had lit throughout the pregnancy in prayer for a male child, and she adds: "Rien ne console que la parfaite santé de ma fille" (I, L. 115, p. 133) [Nothing consoles but the perfect health of my daughter]. This was no small consolation, however, given that the count had already lost two wives and did not yet have an heir. This concern to produce a male child rather than a daughter, on the part of both grandmother and mother, should be understood not merely as an indication of the degree of their ready assimilation of prevailing social values,[14] but also as a wish to dispatch the taxing labor of childbearing by promptly ensuring continuance of the family line and putting that tacit conjugal obligation to rest.

The disappointed mother remained indifferent to Marie-Blanche and left her in Sévigné's keeping at the age of two-and-a-half months. The grandmother, however, became quite attached to her; she captured in her writing the animated two-year-old and sent representations of the child to her departed mother:

Elle fait cent petites choses, elle parle, elle caresse, elle bat, elle fait le signe de la croix, elle demande pardon, elle fait la révérence, elle baise la main, elle hausse les épaules, elle danse, elle flatte, elle lève le menton; enfin elle est jolie de tout point. Je m'y amuse des heures entières. Je ne veux point que cela meure. Je vous le disais l'autre jour, je ne sais pas comme l'on fait pour ne pas aimer sa fille. (I, L. 174, p. 515)

She does a hundred little things, she speaks, she caresses, she hits, she makes the sign of the cross, she asks for forgiveness, she curtseys, she kisses the hand, she shrugs her shoulders, she dances, she flatters, she raises her chin; in a word, she is pretty in every way. I have fun with her for hours on end. I do not want this to die. I was telling you the other day, I do not know how someone could manage not to love her daughter.

Sévigné revels in the diversion afforded her by Marie-Blanche's antics, she acknowledges her still precarious hold on life, and she already thinks ahead to the time when this amusing phase of mimetic development and joyful self-discovery will be behind the child. Her recognition of the stages of infancy and her careful notation of her grandchild's behavior indicate attentive observation. Such a display of competence entitles her to continued distinction as maternal authority. She is already mediating here between her daughter and her grandchild, appealing indirectly to Mme de Grignan, via her claim to incomprehension of any other behavior, to follow her own example and love her daughter in turn. At the same time, she challenges, in offering her own epistolary model of maternal prowess, the daughter's scriptoral and affective ability to do so. The subliminal invitation to imitation implies a consequent relationship of rivalry between the two writing mothers.

Sévigné attempts to correct her daughter's harshness toward the child, but to no avail. When Mme de Grignan commits the five-year-old Marie-Blanche to the same convent education to which her mother had confided her, the grandmother expresses concern and wonders how she could have made such a cruel decision herself years ago:

J'ai le coeur serré de ma petite-fille; elle sera au désespoir de vous avoir quittée et d'être, comme vous dites, en prison. J'admire comme j'eus le courage de vous y mettre; la pensée de vous voir souvent et de vous en retirer me fit résoudre à cette barbarie, qui était trouvée alors une bonne conduite et une chose nécessaire à votre éducation. (II, L. 506, p. 283)

I pity my grandaughter; she will be in despair over leaving you and being, as you say, in prison. I wonder how I had the courage to put you there; the thought of seeing you often and taking you out of there made me resolve myself to this bar-barousness, which was then found to be proper behavior and necessary to your education.

In order to lend force to her disapproval, Sévigné must express doubts about the decision she herself once made. She offers as justification her conformity to the social conventions for raising daughters that prevailed at the time. The effect, however, is simply to point up the simultaneously conflictual aspects and repetitious history of mothering and its perpetua-tion of self-rejection—daughters doing regretfully as their mothers did regretfully before them.

At the age of eight, Marie-Blanche's claim to have a religious voca-tion conveniently relieved her parents of the eventual obligation to pro-vide the more financially painful marriage dowry. On this occasion, the grandmother demonstrated her awareness of children's impressionability in their struggle for identity. Sévigné took up the cause of Marie-Blanche and urged that her feelings be investigated:

Ayez quelque pitié de la pauvre petite d'Aix. Songez à elle et ne craignez point de répandre l'espérance de sa vocation en la remuant; si elle est bien appelée, elle ne s'évaporera pas. (II, L. 790, p. 1030) [15]

Have some pity on the poor little one at Aix. Take care of her and do not fear to scatter the hope of her vocation by stirring it up; if she has the calling, it will not disappear.

Marie-Blanche spent the rest of her life in the convent. Her grandmother's later letters indicate that she is happy, but there is a suggestion of over-statement, motivated perhaps by Sévigné's need to make the best of the situation, to assuage her daughter's feelings of guilt about Marie-Blanche's fate and her own role in overdetermining it:

Vous me représentez fort bien votre fille aînée; je la vois. Je vous prie de l'embrasser pour moi; je suis ravie qu'elle soit contente. (III, L. 2032, p. 410–11)

You portray your elder daughter to me quite well; I see her. I beg you to kiss her for me; I am delighted she is happy.

The compliment is double: not only does Sévigné express pleasure at the reported happiness of her grandchild, which redounds on Mme de Grignan as mother; she approves of the scriptoral representation of the daughter by the mother, thus flattering Mme de Grignan as writer. Her own activities as mother and writer are validated by their repetition in the daughter's life, so that it is not sure, in fact, whether the compliment transfers or simply extends in projection to include Mme de Grignan as self-confirming double.

The second child, Louis-Provence, had a radically different introduction to life: he was welcomed even before his arrival because of the determined conviction that he was to be a male. Sévigné writes to her daughter in her fourth month of pregnancy: "Vous êtes grosse assurément d'un garçon" (I, L. 171, p. 264) [You are surely pregnant with a boy]. In her sixth month, when Mme de Grignan has some physical complaints, Sévigné interprets this as a portent that she is carrying a girl, and indulges in a cruel jest:

Mais qu'est-ce que vous me dites d'avoir mal à la hanche? Votre petit garçon serait-il devenu fille? Ne vous embarrassez pas; je vous aiderai à l'exposer sur le Rhône dans un petit panier de jonc. (I, L. 190, p. 317)

But what are you telling me, that your hip hurts? Could your little boy have become a girl? Don't worry; I will help you expose her on the Rhône in a small reed basket.

The self-denigrating misogyny inherent in such an allusion to female infanticide is mitigated only by the resemblance of the proposal to the story of Moses, which conveys implicitly its own eventual triumphal resolution. Sévigné's artful and complicitous remark articulates the proposed abandonment rather than the recuperation of a hypothetical infant daughter. She fantasizes further a fairy-tale resolution of a happy ending for the unborn but already victimized child: "et puis elle abordera dans quelque royaume où sa beauté sera le sujet d'un roman" (I, L. 190, p. 317) [and then she will land in some kingdom where her beauty will be the subject of a novel]. Not in this world—but in another, vaguer one; not she herself, as subject—but her beauty, as esthetic object of another's gaze; not in reality—but in fiction: such is the empty apotheosis that Sévigné envisions for an infant granddaughter. General pressure on Mme de Grignan to produce a male child, an heir, even motivated by concern for her health, represents an attitude of subordination to the patriarchal order and implies the female self as first victim. Such attitudes are, of course, not atypical for the period.[16] However, it should be remembered, and particularly as Louis-Provence's upbringing is considered, that if this order was manifestly problematic for most women, it also less obviously but just as powerfully taxed some men.

Unlike Marie-Blanche, Louis-Provence was tended in infancy at his mother's side. During this period, Sévigné, still keeping the firstborn (perhaps to be understood as a consolation gift from her departed daughter, intended, at some level, as her replacement), sings Marie-Blanche's praises frequently, as if to attempt to maintain a hold for her in her mother's affections (I, L. 269, p. 502), but also suggesting a certain rivalry between the two women in the parallel favoring of their respective little charges: "Vous me parlez de votre dauphin. Je vous plains de l'aimer si tendrement . . . Je n'aime que trop la petite de Grignan" (I, L. 292, p. 554) [You speak to me of your dauphin. I pity you for loving him so tenderly . . . I love the little de Grignan girl only too much]. Sévigné understood her daughter's affections for her son to be at the cost of those she might have for Marie-Blanche, and, implicitly, for her mother and herself.

From the age of four, Louis-Provence's education was a matter of great concern to his family as they sought to shape and groom him for his role as Grignan scion and heir. At five, he began instruction in German, and when he was six, Sévigné voiced concern that he begin schooling with a regular tutor (II, L. 493, p. 589). There was a great deal of worry about his social timidity (II, L. 385, p. 480), and efforts were made to build his confidence. His body was subjected to corrective tortures from infancy to rectify a twisted back and consequent limp. By the age of seven, he was being successfully launched in Paris, and presented at court, under the tutelage of his paternal uncle, the chevalier de Grignan. He was thus removed from the female domestic sphere and introduced into the male public realm, entrusted mainly to his father's side of the family for initiation into society. His observant grandmother found him reasonably handsome, modest, and truthful; he was not, she reports to her daughter from Paris, at all sufficiently interested in books but was adequately versed in etiquette (III, L. 1060, p. 482). The boy is a family project: uncles, cousins, and grandmother all look out for his interests, knowing that henceforth the family name and fortune will be carried on by him.

Sévigné enthusiastically takes up Louis-Provence's cause in Paris and transforms it into her vocation, as she had her daughter's previously, and Marie-Blanche's briefly, but she does not participate as directly in the actual molding of the boy. As she basks in the refracted glory of her well-received progeny, she is pleased to report to Mme de Grignan:

Ce marquis a été à Versaille; il s'y est fort bien comporté. Enfin, le voilà dans le monde. Il y a fait fort bien; il est à la mode . . . je ne finirais point si je voulais vous nommer tous ceux qui en disent du bien. (III, L. 1046, p. 443)

This marquis has been to Versailles; he behaved himself quite well there. Finally, he is launched in society. He has done quite well there; he is in fashion . . . I would not finish if I wanted to name to you all who speak well of him.

As much as Sévigné enjoys Louis-Provence's success for its own merits, she takes satisfaction in the attention she receives as immediate addressee for compliments on her grandson. She identifies her social justification in promoting his interests as he makes his way at court; it is through him that she feels herself alive, vital to the world around her: "C'est ce [cet enfant] qui m'occupe, et qui m'entretient, et qui m'émeut, et qui me fait sentir que je suis encore trop en vie" (III, L. 1146, p. 690) [It is this child who occupies me, and who entertains me, and who moves me, and who makes me feel I am still very much alive]. It is consistently through others, and particularly through the members of her family, that Sévigné seeks and finds fulfillment in her life.

In the Grignan family hierarchy, Pauline, the third child, the second daughter, is subordinate to her brother Louis-Provence. Sévigné approves this ranking, while suggesting, by way of compensation for Pauline, that her mother make in the young girl her emotional investment. She uses the argument of the patronym borne by Pauline as sign of her entitlement to decent treatment, after the needs of the son, "la chose principale," have been met, subscribing thus consistently to patriarchal family order:

Vous faites fort bien de donner un habit et une cornette à cette jolie Pauline; il est impossible de s'en passer. Mais, en attendant, je ne laisserais pas de l'avoir auprès de moi. Elle ne saurait être mieux, et je ne vois rien qui mérite que vous la lâchiez et l'envoyiez au grenier; c'est toujours Mlle de Grignan, ce nom est une parure. Et dans la dépense que vous fait votre fils et sa compagnie, toute économie vous sied bien, et à cette petite personne et à votre table et à votre train. Suivez sur cela, ma bonne, vos justes résolutions, et croyez qu'il y a plus de grandeur d'en user ainsi que de manquer à la chose principale, qui est votre petit capitaine, qui fait encore cinq cavaliers. (III, L. 1047, p. 445)

You do quite well to give an outfit and a bonnet to this pretty Pauline; it is impossible to do without them. But, meanwhile, I would not cease to have her near me. She couldn't be better off, and I see nothing that warrants you letting her go and sending her to the attic; she is always Mlle de Grignan—this name is an ornament. And with the expense that your son and his company cost you, all thrift suits you well, for this small person, as well as for your home economy and your life style. Follow in this, *ma bonne*, your wise resolutions, and believe that there is more greatness in behaving this way than in missing the principal thing, which is your little captain, who is equal to five knights.

In fact, the Grignan child to receive the greatest amount of epistolary attention is Pauline. She is first named in her grandmother's letters when she is almost one, and she and her mother have left Paris for Grignan: "J'espère que Pauline se porte bien puisque vous n'en parlez point" (I, L. 390, p. 727) [I hope Pauline is well since you do not speak of her]. If much was not made of Pauline in the early years, it was probably because of general reluctance to invest emotionally in an as yet unassured life, but also because, as a daughter, she represented the same dilemma of dowry as had her older sister, Marie-Blanche. The male heir apparent had already been produced, and, further, Pauline was superseded in infancy by the birth of yet another son, Jean-Baptiste, who survived for sixteen months (1676–77).[17]

Sévigné noted early on that Pauline would have to rely on her own talents and graces if she were to find a position in life (II, L. 766, p. 942). To Mme de Grignan's repeated threats to commit her second daughter to a convent, as she had the first, Sévigné opposes pleas that she keep Pauline with her. She writes: "Divertissez-vous en. Pourquoi craindre de se trop amuser de ses enfants?" (II, L. 592, p. 505) [Enjoy yourself with her. Why fear having too much fun with one's children?]. In the interest of her retention in the Grignan household, Pauline is reduced by her grandmother to the status of a diversionary but worthy project: "Pauline me paraît digne d'être votre jouet" (II, L. 584, p. 478) [Pauline seems worthy to me of being your toy].

Her recommendations for Pauline's upbringing are based not only on observation of the child but also on an idea of how the eventual product should function privately and socially and, further, on the therapeutic value for the mother of contributing to the formation of that person. As Locke encodes the child's mind as a tabula rasa, with vast implications for the philosophy of education,[18] so Sévigné conceives and writes of the girlchild as what might be termed a quintessential *tabula amans;* this notion carries its own set of consequences for the education of young girls, reflecting a complete ideology of womanhood, the premise being the relational nature of women.[19]

Sévigné was hardly alone in her interest. In the later part of the seventeenth century, the "querelle des femmes"[20] had been displaced into various attempts at asserting, on the one hand, women's equality, on the other, at least their virtue.[21] Traces of medieval rancor were deflected and protracted into heated debates concerning the intellectual ambitions of the *précieuses,*[22] and anxiety about the social order in general was channeled through discourse that both interrogated and upheld a rigorous system of gender relations. Attention was focused on the issue of women's status and "proper place" in spite or perhaps because of their significant advances in the realms of knowledge and power, where, hitherto, masculine privilege had exercised eminent domain.[23] The appropriateness and aims of education for women became increasingly lively concerns (as witness the various behavior and epistolary manuals already cited, Mme de Maintenon's project for schooling an impoverished feminine elite at Saint-Cyr [1686], Fènelon's treatise on the education of young girls [1687], to mention only a few examples). These themes are dramatized in *L'Ecole des femmes* (1662), where Arnolphe, keeper, guardian, and wooer, outlines his proposed education for Agnès. His ambition to retain the youthful and innocent girl in a "childlike" state (i.e., one of ignorance), to fashion her to his liking, that is, to meet his whims and needs exclusively, represents an extreme interpretation of the exercise of power in the conservative educational relationship:

> Ainsi que je voudrai, je tournerai cette âme:
> Comme *un morceau de cire* entre mes mains elle est,
> Et je lui puis donner la forme qui me plaît.[24]

> Just as I like, I will shape this soul:
> Like *a bit of wax* in my hands she is,
> And I can give her the form that pleases me.

How significant is the difference between his project to subjugate Agnès, his "bit of wax" to suit his own purposes, and the grandmother Sévigné's advice to her daughter here on educating the granddaughter? As she says:

On juge par ses réponses [celles de Pauline] qu'elle a beaucoup d'esprit et de vivacité. Joignez à cela beaucoup d'envie de vous plaire, et vous ferez une merveille de *cette petite cire molle*. Vous la tournerez comme vous voudrez et cela vous fera un grand amusement et une occupation digne de vous, et selon Dieu et selon le monde. (III, L. 1016, p. 380; my emphasis)

One judges by Pauline's responses that she has much wit and vivacity. Add to that a great desire to please you, and you will do wonders with *this soft little ball of wax*. You will mold her as you wish and this will provide you with great amusement and an occupation worthy of you, according to God and the world.

Once again structuring her discourse out of those in circulation, Sévigné uses the same metaphor as does Arnolphe to allude to Pauline, and she proposes as well the same sort of self-interested motivation for shaping the ball of wax. It is not for Agnès's and Pauline's own good that their education is proposed, but for the gratification of their respective educators.

Arnolphe's experiment fails: if the social system empowers him, nature, in the form of Agnès's desire for Horace, prevails and defeats him. Agnès is not bound to Arnolphe by any family loyalty, in spite of the paternal role he has played in her life. She is an emotionally free agent, and Arnolphe consequently cannot shape her, in spite of the obsessively controlled condition of isolation in which he keeps her. Mme de Grignan's experiment is more likely to succeed: as Sévigné points out, the most useful tool she has at hand to mold Pauline to her will is the child's love for her. She returns again and again to this theme:

Ma chère bonne, cette enfant ne songe qu'à vous plaîre. Ménagez bien ce désir; vous en ferez une personne toute parfaite, et avec douceur. Elle vous adore; faut-il autre chose pour se corriger de ce qui vous déplaît? (III, L. 1108, p. 596)

Ma chère bonne, this child thinks only of pleasing you. Humor this desire well; you will make of her a completely perfect person, and a gentle one. She adores you; what else is needed to correct in her what displeases you?

Female filial devotion thus features as a malleability to be exploited by the maternal power, and the maternal project is to develop a worthy and amusing object, securing thereby not only personal pleasure but public approbation as well. Sévigné's advice, as a mother, to her daughter, reflects Sévigné's own performance as mother and suggests Mme de Grignan's own experience as daughter.

The grandmother appears to attempt to make the role of motherhood seem appealing in order to seduce the daughter into caring for her own child. The perception of Pauline as diversion for the mother, as, in fact, the mother's privileged sphere of control in an otherwise relatively powerless situation, is articulated and encouraged by the grandmother. Where the son, Louis-Provence would be removed from the mother's world and assimilated within the male domain, Pauline could remain with her mother under her domestic jurisdiction until marriage. Sévigné's pleas for motherhood of an engaged sort with the available daughter represent an invitation to repeat the solution she invented through her maternal letters for giving meaning and visibility to her own life.

Sévigné regularly voices concern for Pauline's state and her mother's apparent lack of compassion. She repeats warnings against alienating, ironically, to her own fitfully estranged daughter. She recommends correction by seduction and may even be reminding Mme de Grignan of her own moodiness in pointing out that Pauline is not exceptional in this regard. Pauline's is perhaps a conditioned trait, inherited from the mother-model:

Au reste, ma fille, pensiez-vous que Pauline dût être parfaite? Elle n'est pas douce dans sa chambre;[25] il y a bien des gens fort aimés, fort estimés qui ont eu ce défaut. Je crois qu'il vous sera aise de l'en corriger, mais gardez-vous surtout de vous accoutumer à la gronder et à l'humilier. (III, L. 1037, p. 424)

Moreover, my daughter, were you thinking Pauline had to be perfect? She is not gentle in her room; there are many well-loved, well-respected people who have had this flaw. I believe it will be easy for you to correct her of it, but beware above all of getting into the habit of scolding and humiliating her.

She frequently plays the role of protector and defender for Pauline. She warns against treating her harshly, stressing the efficacy of a strategy of affection:

Pauline n'est donc pas parfaite; tant mieux, vous vous divertirez à la repétrir. Menez-la doucement. L'envie de vous plaîre fera plus que toutes les gronderies. (III, L. 1035, p. 419)

Pauline is, then, not perfect; so much the better—you will amuse yourself in re-forming her. Lead her gently. The desire to please you will do more than all the scoldings.

A little later, Sévigné goes so far as to accuse her daughter concerning her treatment of Pauline: "Vous n'êtes point juste" (III, L. 1074, p. 510). She suggests that she might even side with Pauline occasionally in arguments with the mother: "Il me semble que dans plusieurs petits procès qu'elle a contre vous, je lui serais favorable" (III, L. 1104, p. 587) [It seems to me that in several little cases she has against you, I would be on her side]. In pleading her granddaughter's case, Sévigné is in a sense pleading her own. She appears to sense that Mme de Grignan is visiting her anger toward her own mother and her own unhappiness on her daughter. The grand-mother is irremediably implicated in the relationship obtaining between mother and daughter. If Mme de Grignan were to cultivate her relation-ship with Pauline as her mother portrays herself as having done with her, such a repetition would validate the prior mother-daughter relationship in the continuum. Sévigné seeks just such an affective affirmation, one that reflects and projects, one that blurs the boundaries of self and perpetuates the identity confusion discussed earlier:

Aimez, aimez votre fille, c'est la plus raisonnable et la plus jolie chose du monde, mais aimez aussi toujours votre chère maman, qui est plus à vous qu'à elle-même. (III, L. 1026, p. 400)

Love, love your daughter; this is the most reasonable and the prettiest thing in the world, but always love your dear mother as well, who belongs more to you than to herself.

As she matures, Pauline shows signs of some of the same precocious ques-tioning of gender characterization that her grandmother has occasionally voiced (see above, introduction to part II):

Pauline est bien plaisante de se faire une tristesse de ce verset du Miserere ["Oui, je suis né dans l'iniquité, et dans le péché ma mère m'a conçu"].[26] C'est en effet une

chose fâcheuse à dire, que *sa mère l'a conçue dans le péché;* l'affaire est digne de
réflexion et tire à de grandes conséquences. Je vois que cette petite imagination a
bientôt fait ses rapports, et bien juste. (III, L. 1194, p. 832–33)

Pauline is quite amusing in being saddened over this verse from the Miserere [Yes, I
was born in iniquity, and in sin my mother conceived me]. It is indeed a distressing
thing to say, that *her mother conceived her in sin;* the matter is worthy of reflection
and has important consequences. I see that this little imagination has soon made
its connections, and quite rightly.

Her ability to think independently and to question authority pleases
Sévigné. As far as can be deduced from the text of the letters, such intellectual prowess only served, though, to make Pauline aware and resentful of
the injustices visited upon her rather than ideologically opposed to them.

In the epistolary education of Pauline, her grandmother proposes and
outlines a maternally useful and exemplary relationship: Pauline, as privileged secretary, will take dictation of her mother's filial letters and share
the burden of the correspondence while learning from it. The two roles of
mother's daughter and mother's secretary coincide in their functions: each
of them entails honorable education and distinguished servitude for the
daughter-scribe and comforting relief for the dictating mistress and her
correspondent.[27] In the putative mutual beneficiality of this arrangement,
the triangle pattern resurfaces and displays its potential for producing
confusion among the three women: the daughter will learn what to say
and how by absorbing the mother-model as the mother in turn molds her
discourse to meet her mother's:

Pauline est trop heureuse, ma chère enfant, d'être votre secrétaire. Elle apprend à
penser, à tourner ses pensées en voyant comme vous lui faites tourner les vôtres.
Elle apprend la langue française, que la plupart des femmes ne savent pas . . .
L'ennui de dicter n'est point comparable à la contrainte d'écrire. Continuez donc
une si bonne instruction pour votre fille, et un si grand soulagement pour nous. (III,
L. 1114, p. 607)

Pauline is too lucky, my dear child, to be your secretary. She learns to think, to
shape her thoughts by seeing how you make her shape yours. She learns the French
language, which most women don't know . . . The boredom of dictating is not
comparable to the strain of writing. So continue such a good training for your
daughter, and such a great relief for us.

Such an arrangement seeks to repeat and mirror the epistolary relationship Sévigné has cultivated with Mme de Grignan. Sévigné remains firmly
instated in the governing position with regard to her daughter's writing
obligations, and so her recommendations on instruction for Pauline are
offered perhaps as a palliative for Mme de Grignan's continued honor of

epistolary servitude. Pauline's apprenticeship will coincide with the period of her filial subordination and will constitute a source of compensatory satisfaction for her still filially dutiful mother. In theory, her turn to dictate will come, but only with her passage to generational ascendancy.

As Sévigné and her daughter, Françoise-Marguerite, had a difficult relationship, so then did Mme de Grignan and her daughter Pauline. The mother-daughter dissension perpetuates itself, feeding on the prior model. Pauline is inscribed as reacting against her general condition in temperamental moodiness without being able to articulate the source of her frustration. She expresses some of the same rebellious misgivings on the institutionalization of misogyny as had her grandmother, but she does not succeed in allaying them in her own life. In spite of her demonstrated understanding of some of the tensions proper to the female condition in a patriarchal society, she rejects, and thereby embraces, her own rejecting mother as model.

We do not know how Pauline brought up her own three daughters. The *Correspondance* does not extend to include traces of that generation. We do know that she, as executrix, directed the initial publication of Sévigné's letters. She exacted a promise from the editor, the chevalier Perrin, that he would destroy the original manuscripts after they had been prepared in a form acceptable to her for publication. He kept his word. Pauline herself, as far as one can tell, destroyed her own mother's letters (I, p. 765).[28] Pauline then, is responsible for the *Correspondance* as it is read today— only the grandmother's half of the exchange, and not entirely reliable at that.

The concluding promise of the innocently complicitous granddaughter, invented and exacted by the political and seductive grandfather of Hugo's poem, issuing from her space of exclusion, comes to mind. The pact of self-subverting feminine subscription to the paternal order is sealed. Herself condemned to a regime of dry bread,

> ... Jeanne alors, dans son coin noir,
> M'a dit tout bas, levant ses yeux si beaux à voir,
> Pleins de l'autorité des douces créatures:
> —Eh bien, moi, je t'irai porter des confitures.

> ... Jeanne then, from her dark corner,
> Told me softly, raising her eyes so beautiful to see,
> Full of the authority of gentle creatures:
> —Very well, as for me, I will bring you jam.

In the case of the *Correspondance*, the "art" of enacting prescribed roles of mother and grandmother, as played out in intergenerational family politics, reveals itself as counterproductive and self-defeating—relaying unhappiness through the mirror continuum. Invitations to imitation, rivalrous needs, and confusions of identity in the performance of maternity contribute to the coloration of a feminine heritage as transmitted through the institution of daughterhood, ever abetting the solidarity of paternal power. Readers of the *Correspondance* who would take up the cause of the speechless daughter, Françoise-Marguerite, and who would attempt to assign stable meaning to the mother's letters from the vantage of that void, do well to remember that she was silenced by her own daughter. The venerated grandmother's surviving text, this testament to maternal devotion, is compromised and challenged by the textual void that permanently confronts it.

Such difficult relations among the women read here can be seen as a direct consequence of their common marginality within the patriarchal framework, intent on maintaining paternal order. Their powerlessness in the larger society stimulates them to internalize its predominant values in search of integration, to seek and to invent spheres of influence within their assigned milieu. Relegated to the domestic sphere, women exercise power over children as allowed, and, in forming daughters, transmit and perpetuate some of the same abuses of which they in their time have been victims. Thus pain among women is seen to be continually soothed and aggravated, as long as their attempts at healing one another and themselves occur in the margins of a social order that devalues and divides them. This is perhaps particularly evident at historical junctures of contradiction when tensions between progress and conservatism polarize and expose generational positions that much more radically.

The above tracings of relations are the product of a reading of Sévigné's letters structured in the nature of a quest. I was actively seeking an articulation of intergenerational relations in the temporal continuum of the four women represented (Sévigné, her daughter Françoise-Marguerite, and the two granddaughters, Marie-Blanche and Pauline). I expected this would enable me to illustrate how women live in consequence (in its varied meanings) of one another within an already circumscribed world. Just as eloquent as the signals I found, however, were the silences that surround the "voice" of the correspondence. Another sort of quest would document from other sources, foreground, and flesh out the lives of Françoise-Marguerite and her daughters.[29] But, within Sévigné's discourse, these figures are subordinated to the imperative of maternal self-inscription, and their mediated presence therein attests to their haunting absence. They are available today through the subjectivity of another's discourse, and I read back through them only instead to confront my own and to find them, in a sense, already there.

Envoi

"Lives do not serve as models; only stories do that . . . We can only retell and live by the stories we have read or heard. We live our lives through texts . . . these stories have formed us all; they are what we must use to make new fictions, new narratives."   CAROLYN HEILBRUN [1]

It is tempting to read closure into Sévigné's last letters, to use her words to punctuate this study. Indeed, such a rhetorical gesture is eloquently provided for. She imparts an evaluative sense of finality when she states in one of her last letters (10 January 1696): "Pour moi, je ne suis plus bonne à rien; j'ai fait mon rôle et, par mon goût, je ne souhaiterais jamais une si longue vie" (III, L. 1361, p. 1135) [As for me, I am no longer good for anything; I have played my part, and, for my own taste, I would never want such a long life]. With a sense of the completion of her own history, she wrote out her exit cue and died four months later. She had had her entrance, played her role, and sensed that the show was over. Reunited at Grignan with her daughter, who was about to become a grandmother herself, Sévigné saw the female cycle about to reproduce itself and concluded that her time had come. She appears to bow before the greater performance of nature and the universe on the divine scale, proclaiming the superior talents of God as dramatist and producer. In a last gesture of humility, she submits to Providence:[2]

Mais nous sommes heureux que ce soit la volonté de Dieu qui la [la vie] règle, comme toutes les choses de ce monde: tout est mieux entre ses mains qu'entre les nôtres. (III, L. 1361, p. 1135)

But we are lucky that it's God's will that orders life, like all things in this world: everything is better in his hands than in ours.

In this act of submission and renouncement, she reinscribes her innocent rebellion of maternal writing within the paternal order and yields her *author*-ity in retreating to her assigned place of silence in the great scheme of things.

However, it is at this juncture that the *Correspondance* takes on a life of its own through its transformation into text, its publication and circulation, its canonization, and the readings that are produced from it. It generates new readings that take the form of writings on, around, or about the letters. At the close of this study, it seems important to emphasize that endings and beginnings are ceaselessly interchangeable in the world of text, to go back into the text and seek a point of departure from it that at once moves out of it and back into it, that grounds in a gesture of self-reflexivity the text that my reading has produced. The particular reading/writing act that is represented here calls for a scrutiny of the dynamics of such activity in the *Correspondance* and broadens into an investigation of how reading models are encoded and polarized into mother-daughter profiles and played out in the institutionalized drama of maternity that marks the world of feminist theory today, merely another instantiation of Adrienne Rich's understanding of the institution of motherhood. From there, then, perhaps we can begin to make the "new fictions, new narratives" that Carolyn Heilbrun calls for.

Mme de Sévigné filtered her world through textuality and texts through her experience. Easy allusions to plots, characters, settings, lessons, lines, verses, absorbed through her ceaseless reading, mark her constant recourse to the world of the text at once to understand and to explain—to write out—her own take on life. And confidence in her ability to read the world around her as text is evidenced by her readiness to translate experience through paradigms and words absorbed from the comforting world of letters. Thus her writing is permeated with that of others, as merely a glance at her letters shows. Such regular intertextuality attests to the fluidity of boundaries between acts of reading and writing, between notions of imagined and actual experience, between concepts of other and self.

Virginia Woolf enshrined Sévigné in her canon not only as a talented writer, but as an avid reader as well. She wrote of her: "She has a natural dwelling place in books, so that Josephus or Pascal or the absurd long romances of the time are not read by her so much as embedded in her mind. Their verses, their stories rise to her lips along with her own thoughts."[3] While such remarks occur in a laudatory appraisal of Sévigné's contributions to the field of writing, they raise certain questions: 1) what does it mean to have "a natural dwelling place in books"; and 2) what are the implications for a writing woman of being steeped in an androcentric literature that mirrors the world as men order it in relation to themselves?[4] Add the observation that "you are or become what you read,"[5] and the question opens out to be: how does one make oneself "at home" with

other people's texts and still have one's own thoughts? How is one to distinguish in a voracious reader between what she reads and what she thinks
and writes? In what ways does the tradition she inhabits inhibit or enable
her own coming to writing?

Today concepts of "immasculation" and "resistance"[6] signal two poles
of reading behavior typical of women's relations to an androcentric canon,
the one submitting unwittingly to, the other deliberately challenging the
indoctrination in second-class citizenry for women implicit in the traditional masculine narrative. I tend to locate Sévigné's discourse between
these two poles, in a space of understanding she invented for herself by
filtering her reading through her immediate concern of relation, by mobilizing the texts of others, rerouting and incorporating them to her own
purpose in her immediate project of correspondence with her daughter.

We have seen examples of the way in which Sévigné's self-inscription
was complicated by her intimacy with other texts ("Il y a aujourd'hui bien
des années, ma chère bonne, qu'il vint au monde une créature destinée à
vous aimer préférablement à toutes choses; je prie votre imagination de
n'aller ni à droite ni à gauche: *Ce monsieur-là, Sire, c'était moi même.*"
[see chapter 3]). We have also seen how, at the same time, such expression represents an attempt at another sort of bonding, through cultural
commonality. It produces a new story—at once familiar and strange.

A cursory glance at the index of the Duchêne edition of the *Correspondance* affords a reliable inventory of Sévigné's preferred authors and works
and even suggests certain of her predilections as well as her strong dis-
likes through the number of references cited. What interests me primarily,
though, is to consider not *what* Sévigné read, but *how* she read; under
what circumstances, how that reading experience informed her own writing project, and how it contributes to explain some of the tensions of taste
between mother and daughter. What I maintain is that, even while evincing discreet and troubling signs of immasculation, dependent as she was
on the dominant discourse in circulation for modes of expression, Sévigné
resisted the greater message of androcentrism by vigorously devoting her
writing energy to the construction of a new plot, neither the traditional
feminine marriage nor its counterpart, the masculine quest plot (although
not without elements of these).[7] Instead she ventured to cultivate in writing
a relation with another woman, her daughter, and to begin the articulation as well as the public enactment of what has since come to be known
as the deep-structure story in women's lives: the mother-daughter story.
In so doing, she valorized a relation as well as a way of relating through
the epistolary genre, and she readdressed an androcentric world of letters,
transforming it within her writing into a gynocentric plot.

One writing figure in particular was invested with charged meaning for the reading-writing mother-daughter couple: Descartes's place in seventeenth-century discourse engendered eloquent differences of opinion between the two women. Sévigné deployed strategies for at once incorporating and countering this influential figure in her letters; they invite speculation on her discreet opposition to his work. Although René Descartes did not yet enjoy firm canonical status, his writings were circulating among the learned and the literati. They were considered heretical by certain elements and were censured by the Jesuits in particular (II, L. 661, p. 633). Nevertheless, they aroused great interest and attracted enthusiasts. These converts to Cartesian reasoning were themselves lightly referred to as heretical, "cartésiens à brûler" [Cartesians to burn] (I, L. 197, p. 337). Françoise-Marguerite was one of these, while her mother ostensibly clung to the teachings of Aristotle (I, L. 154, p. 217). Descartes's writings became a pivotal issue in the mother-daughter exchange, as intent for its continuance on differentiation as on correspondence.

Sévigné expressed profound skepticism regarding Descartes's method and the privileging of reason, while Mme de Grignan subscribed fervently to the new cult. The daughter replied seriously to Bussy, who had written, facetiously labeling her a heretic:

Je vois bien qu'elle [Mme de Coligny] me croit fort engagée dans la secte de M. Descartes, à qui vous donnez l'honneur de ma perte. Je ne veux point pourtant encore l'abjurer; il arrive des révolutions dans toutes les opinions et j'espère que les siennes triompheront un jour et couronneront ma persévérance (II, L. 663, p. 636).

I can see that Mme de Coligny thinks I am quite involved in the sect of M. Descartes, to whom you attribute the honor of my fall. I do not, however, want to recant just yet; revolutions occur in all opinions and I hope that his will triumph one day and reward my perseverance.

Sévigné did not counter Descartes's influence over her daughter with arguments. Rather, she incorporated the figure of the philosopher and fragments of Cartesian discourse into her own and framed them in a way not so much to dispute them, but to suggest their inadequacies for explaining the world as she apprehended it. The Descartes motif served as a vehicle for the articulation of her own repeated refusal of method, coherent enough to constitute itself a system of valuation. She consistently, but always obliquely, opposed her sociability, her affectivity, her imagination and spontaneity to his reclusiveness, his intellectualness, his reason, and his cautious analyses.

She set up a quiet polarity between herself and Descartes and competed with him for her daughter's adjuration. Insisting on her own maternal identity, she referred facetiously time and again in correspondence with her daughter to Descartes as "votre père" [II, L. 515, p. 307; L. 526, p. 339; L. 796, p. 1047; L. 803, p. 1067] [your father] and charged the daughter with an implicit decision to make between "l'humeur de la mère" [the mother's mood] and "la loi du père" [the law of the father]. She recognized the dangers of paternalism attendant in the enthusiastic subscription to the thinking of any one individual (II, L. 785, p. 1011) and warned against substituting any particular system for the invention of one's own. An "esprit de système" [a methodical mind], she cautioned, would interfere with the daughter's own way of experiencing the world and arriving at her own truth (II, L. 780, p. 998). In so doing, she competed discretely with the philosopher for a position of influence over her daughter, vaunting the virtues of her own system as being precisely antisystem.

She further insisted on representing Descartes in her letters not as a disembodied and exalted oracle, but simply as a member of the Descartes family, with nieces and nephews in Brittany, a normal human being with conventional attachments and common concerns. She thus sought discreetly to remove the aura of authority under which she felt her daughter had fallen sway. The difference of opinion between mother and daughter around the figure of Descartes generates a tension that exceeds one of personal tastes, temperamental proclivities, generational differences; it characterizes a continuing debate on ways of making meaning in and of the world, a debate that is reflected in their ways of reading.

Sévigné lived, read, and wrote among writers, writers of a leisure class, friends who wrote. The cultural elite of seventeenth-century salon society participated collectively, both creatively and critically, in the shaping of a worldly literature. In this atmosphere of lettered sociability, conversation was as important an art as writing. Even reading was not exclusively the solitary activity we have come to consider it to be. People read aloud to one another for amusement, undertook projects of collective edification, and bonded through books. Instantaneous commentary and interpretation accompanied such séances and spilled into the texts these readers were simultaneously producing themselves, especially letters, whose open form accommodated all matter for and manner of reflection.

Mme de Sévigné safely assumed and contributed to assure participation in the world of text for her correspondents. Works just off the press, as well as clandestinely pirated, circulated among the more extended elite and made their way to the provinces, often accompanied by critiques from the very friends who were sending them. All of these readers shared a common frame of reference, a worldview shaped by and reflected in their common literary heritage, such that they could allude gracefully and succinctly to complicated ideas with the mere mention of a particular author or the citation of a single verse. Thus many of Sévigné's opinions on the works she read can be understood to be not so much individual insights as consensual gleanings. As much attention is given in her letters to the communal act of producing meaning through the sharing of the reading performance as to the actual content of the text in question. Texts for reading feature frequently as mere pretexts for conversation.

In a typical passage, to her daughter, in 1677, Sévigné reported on her reading scene:

Le Baron (Charles de Sévigné) est ici, qui ne me laisse pas mettre le pied à terre, tant il me mène rapidement dans les lectures que nous entreprenons; ce n'est toutefois qu'après avoir fait honneur à la conversation. *Dom Quichotte*, Lucien, *les Petites Lettres*, voilà ce qui nous occupe. Je voudrais de tout mon coeur, ma fille, que vous eussiez vu de quel air et de quel ton il s'acquitte de cette dernière lecture. Elles ont pris un tour particulier quand elles ont passé par ses mains; c'est une chose entièrement divine, et pour le sérieux et pour la parfaite raillerie. Elles me sont toujours nouvelles, et je crois que cette sorte de divertissement vous amuserait bien autant que l'indéfectibilité de la matière. Je travaille pendant que l'on lit. (II, L. 591, p. 498)

The Baron (Charles) is here, who does not let me alight for a moment, so quickly does he lead me through the readings we undertake; but it's only after doing honor to conversation. *Don Quixote*, Lucien, *les Petites Lettres*, this is what occupies us. I would truly like, my daughter, for you to have seen the manner and tone in which he carried out this last reading. They [Pascal's letters] took on a particular style when they passed through his hands; it's an absolutely divine thing, both for the seriousness and for the perfect humor of it. They are always new to me, and I think that this kind of diversion would amuse you just as much as the perfection of the reading material. I sew while he reads.

and she acknowledged in the same letter her daughter's report on her current reading:

Je m'assure pourtant que vous vous accommoderez de Virgile. Corbinelli me l'a fait admirer; il faudrait quelqu'un comme lui pour vous accompagner dans ce voyage. Je m'en vais tâter du *Schisme des Grecs*; on en dit du bien. Je conseillerai à La Garde de vous le porter. (II, L. 591, pp. 499–500)

I am sure, however, that you will get used to Virgil. Corbinelli made me admire him; you would need someone like him to accompany you on this voyage. I am going to attempt the *Schism of the Greeks*; it is highly recommended. I will advise La Garde to bring it to you.

Several features of Sévigné's reading profile are evident here: (1) the eclecticism of her taste; (2) the extent to which the reading experience was a shared one, the written text savored aurally and the critique of content displaced onto the style of delivery; (3) the contrast of this collective activity with the serious, abstract, and more purposeful nature of the daughter's preferred reading, gestured in the inflationary term "l'indéfectibilité de la matière"; (4) the circulation of texts among friends; and (5) Sévigné's divided attention as she listened and did needlework at once.

The above passages might suggest that Sévigné deferred to her co-readers, her son "le Baron" and Corbinelli, as animators and guides, subordinating her own opinion to theirs, allowing her judgment to be shaped by their rendering of texts. But, in fact, the very plurality of these reading partners ensured against the too great influence of any one of them. She was saddened when she found her circle of readers reduced:

Mes maîtres de philosophie m'ont un peu abandonnée. La Mousse est allé en Poitou avec Mme de Sanzei . . . Nous lisons tristement ensemble le petit livre des *Passions*. (II, l. 537, p. 374)

My philosophy teachers have abandoned me a bit. La Mousse went to Poitou with Mme de Sanzei . . . We are sadly reading together the little book of the *Passions*.

Essential to a felicitous reading experience for Sévigné was not one guiding voice, but a multiplicity of them producing competing interpretations, thus enabling her both to participate in the making of meaning and to add her own voice to the conversation. Note that, above, Descartes's "livre des Passions" is framed in Sévigné's text by feelings of abandonment and sadness. Although these are commentary on the context of the reading, they also frame the title itself and perform an oblique act of valuation not simply on the situation but on the named text as well.

Books, for Sévigné, featured as diversions, objects to be consumed indiscriminately along with others—pastimes:

Nous sommes loin de nous ennuyer: beaucoup de promenades, de causeries; des échecs, un trictrac, des cartes en cas de besoin; les *Petites Lettres* de Pascal, des comédies, *La Princesse de Clèves*, que je fais lire à ces prêtres qui en sont ravis, une très bonne chère et [sic] de campagne et des perdrix et poulardes qui viennent de Bretagne à Monsieur de Rennes. (II, L. 742, p. 860)

We are far from getting bored; many walks, talks; chess, backgammon, cards in case we need them; Pascal's *Petites Lettres*, comedies, *La Princesse de Clèves*, which I have read to these priests, who are delighted by it, very good country food and partridge and fowl that come from Britanny to Monsieur de Rennes.

Here she does impose reading of her choice on her côterie, promoting her friend's novel, but primarily her simple listing of these varied activities points up their shared purpose: a defense against boredom and monotony for this leisure group, committed to justifying and maintaining its social status by applying itself to the cultivation of exquisite taste in all things.

Contrasted with the maternal equation of reading and sociability, the daughter projects another sort of reading profile. More often than not, she is portrayed as reading alone, in her study, engaging in a solitary activity. Sévigné mirrors her daughter's self-portrait back to her, gesturing knowingly at the influence she discerns in the background:

Vous vous vantez d'être *Agnès* et de ne rien faire dans votre cabinet. Il me semble pourtant que vous êtes une substance qui pensez beaucoup; que ce soit au moins, ma bonne, d'une couleur à ne vous point noircir l'imagination. J'essaie d'éclaircir mes entre chien et loup autant qu'il m'est possible. (II, L. 780, p. 998)

You boast of being *Agnes* and of doing nothing in your study. It seems to me however that you are a substance that thinks a great deal; let it be at least, *ma bonne,* of a shade that does not darken your imagination. I try to enlighten my crepuscules as much as I can.

How Mme de Grignan reads is determined by what she reads. A committed Cartesian, she followed through on the conditions of the philosopher's practice, secluding herself in her study, applying herself to following his prescriptions for arriving at certainty by the methodical exercise of her intellectual faculties.

For, understated but necessary to Descartes's project of determining what he might know was a decision to seal himself off from contact with others; to create a social void that would ensure that any ideas he entertained were his own. He portrayed himself as "un homme qui marche seul et dans les ténèbres" [a man who walks alone in the darkness][8] and, from his position of self-imposed exile in Amsterdam, prided himself in having succeeded at establishing a living arrangement propitious to his project:

Parmi la foule d'un grand peuple fort actif, et plus soigneux de ses propres affaires que curieux de celles d'autrui . . . j'ai pu vivre aussi solitaire et retiré que dans les déserts les plus écartés.[9]

In the midst of the crowd of a great and active people, more caring about their own concerns than curious about those of other people . . . I was able to live as solitary and withdrawn as in the most remote deserts.

In spite or perhaps because of incessant demands on her as daughter, wife, mother, mistress of Grignan, Mme de Grignan attempted to replicate in her study the condition of isolation necessary to the pursuit of truth à la Descartes. Her mother objected to this negation of reading as a social act and consistently opposed the lessons of Cartesian philosophy not so much out of concern for their truth value as out of conviction that the valorization of reason was at the expense of sociability, of relation.

Sévigné believed the cultivation of the intellect to be at the cost of community and shared commonsense wisdom, therefore unsalutary; and she faulted Cartesianism for her daughter's poor health. To her friend Guitaut, she wrote with concern as well as chagrin:

Elle est toujours aussi maigre et aussi faible . . . Elle se gouverne un peu à sa fan-
taisie, et sous ombre de la philosophie de M. Descartes, qui lui apprend l'anatomie,
elle se moque un peu des régimes et des remèdes communs; enfin on ne mène pas
une cartésienne comme une autre personne. (II, L. 672, p. 652)

She is still just as thin and just as weak . . . She conducts herself more or less
according to her whims, and in the shadow of M. Descartes's philosophy, which
teaches her anatomy, she mocks diets and common cures a bit; well, one does not
persuade a Cartesian like just anybody.

Sévigné's skepticism was not an uncomplicated valuation: it was shaped
as much by class bias eschewing the notion of work, application, patience,
purpose, "la crasse de la philosophie" (III, L. 1121, p. 625) [the squalor of
philosophy], as it was a considered position on the nature of truth. In accordance with the elitist esthetic of her milieu, she rejected all that smacked
of pedantry and compromised the wit and spontaneity in which she and
her circle of friends prided themselves ("Il faut tout savoir sans avoir
jamais rien appris" [One must know everything without ever having had
to learn it]). But her cautions did suggest more substantially that people as
social beings could only arrive at meaningful understandings of the world
through community, and that it was in community that the subject was apt
to experience herself and flourish as such.

The seventeenth-century world Sévigné and her daughter shared was
undergoing a profound transformation: traces of a rupture of general
understanding are particularly evident in the two models of reading represented in the correspondence. The married daughter, variously occupied,
had to be selective because of her limited reading time and thus ended up
privileging certain texts over others, whereas the widowed mother, given
her availability to the pursuit of reading, could pride herself in her indis-
criminate taste. The purpose of reading appears to be quite different for the
two: the mother reads expansively for enjoyment, improvement, and self-
confirmation through active participation in and reinscription of a shared
worldview, while the daughter economically privileges the search for a
more abstract "Truth." Mme de Grignan sought an efficient framework
in her reading for making sense of her world and found in the theories of
Descartes more worthwhile reading than in the less explicitly purposeful
pleasures of fiction and the lessons of an apparently no longer relevant past.
If Sévigné concerned herself with matters of verity, they were primarily of a
contingent, anthropological, and occasionally theological nature, and only
of interest to the extent that she could relate directly to them, incorporate
them into the textual world that she was in the process of constructing
through her letters. Her daughter, on the other hand, was of the first generation of modernists and a fervent subscriber to the rise of an impersonal
science.

The era of modernism was taking hold; the facts that Descartes had written his *Treatise on Method* in the French vernacular rather than the more erudite Latin and that he postulated by example the accessibility of truth for all those prepared to apply his method of reasoning (and endowed with a modicum of intelligence) promised an era of equity, a great leveling whereby women's understanding of their own experience would no longer be mediated. Instead, they would be able to confirm for themselves their own existence and the veracity of their thoughts. It is understandable that such a tool of self-confirmation and affirmation should have appealed to Mme de Grignan. However, to Descartes's reasoned "cogito," Sévigné the mother consistently opposed her own, privileging affectivity and relations:

Ainsi, ma bonne, *je pense, donc je suis;* je pense avec tendresse, donc je vous aime; je pense uniquement à vous de cette manière, donc je vous aime uniquement. (II, L. 763, p. 924)

Thus, *ma bonne, I think, therefore I am;* I think with affection, therefore I love you; I think only of you in this way, therefore I love only you.

—the "cogito sensible" analyzed by Guenoun, or the "relational cogito": "Ma belle fille a dit fort joliment: 'Ah, voilà la vraie mère!' Je suis donc la vraie mère!" (III, L. 1113, p. 604–5).[10] She rerouted Descartes' causal argument through her own sensibility and reinscribed his formula on her own terms.

The immediate question, then, is whether the reading and writing proclivities of the two women constitute actual reflections of the different temperaments and tastes of two individuals or are generated oppositionally in relation to each other, at once affirming and challenging the biological ties that bind a mother and her daughter. Was Mme de Grignan enabled to explore philosophy, the rational world, driven and sustained by the ceaseless assurance of her mother's devotion, rooted in the irrational? And was Mme de Sévigné's inability to appreciate her daughter's passion for reason a function of her own investment in the imaginary? More broadly, to what extent was the tension expressed around reading tastes a consequence of a more englobing phenomenon of generational differences such that, while inhabiting the same world and the same milieu, their tastes were shaped at different moments and informed by different vogues, and perhaps, although different, not so very individual at all?

Does this sort of tension between generations of readers (exemplified in this particular mother-daughter couple) suggest a sequential pattern implying notions of progress as the comfortable world of a classically oriented mindset is challenged and supplanted (as literary history bears out) by the cult of reason? Or rather, does it imply merely an alternating one, an almost predictable oscillation, lending credence to theories of reactionary generation patterns? And what might that say about where we are today as readers?

Finally, I would venture generally, this tension of taste between mother and daughter instantiates a moment of significant ideological rupture. It marks a historical moment of conflict in the ongoing tension between two competing approaches to constructing meaning in the world: opinion (*doxa*) and scientific knowledge (*episteme*). The first, as represented by Sévigné, privileges intuition, imagination, spontaneity, relation—in short, it valorizes the subject at play with itself and the world, intertextuality; it challenges the second, isolated and imprisoned in its own concatenated discourse, intent on constructing order and imposing meaning by subordinating the world to the rational hierarchizing self-sufficient "cogito." In at least the elitist academies today, a mood of intellectual sociability is loosening the grip of reason on the collective imagination, to the dismay of some, to the delight of others. Interdisciplinary conversation is at intertextual work, perhaps not discovering as much as remembering other ways of producing meaning. As Mme de Grignan said, in defense of Descartes: "Il arrive des révolutions dans toutes les opinions." And indeed it is, perhaps, simply a matter of opinion. Meanwhile, there is much to be said in favor of open doors and acknowledging the multiple discourses that inform our own.[11]

For women readers in particular, the two models of reading, enfigured in the mother-daughter debate around Descartes, gesture to a dilemma that regularly besets and vexes feminist studies—will we be mothers or daughters? The mother's daughter or the father's? Can we be both at once? Mothers of daughters, of sons? Indeed, how many permutations of these positions are possible? And what is politically at stake in each? Can they be altogether avoided? What does mother mean? What does daughter mean? Is there a paradigm other than the familial one from which we can more productively or at least comfortably speak and write, live? One woman, a professor of French, approached me when I first aired these ideas and questions (MLA, New Orleans, 1988), expressed gratitude, and stated: "I really identify with Mme de Sévigné and don't know what to do with these feminists so enamoured of theory—we need to get back to the mother." Immediately after, I got a reaction to the same presentation from a younger, prominent feminist theorist: "Mme de Sévigné reminds me of my mother! Upper-middle-class, with her reading groups, completely baffled at my work on Lacan!" I like to think of this work as a gesture of bridge building between these two women, between the encoded mothers and daughters in all of us, and to the foundations of a new story.

Notes

Introduction (pp. 1–23)

1. This problem was enacted in the mixed reception of Sandra Gilbert and Susan Gubar, eds., *The Norton Anthology of Literature by Women: The English Tradition* (New York: W. W. Norton, 1985).

2. This wording is borrowed from Barbara Herrnstein Smith, *Contingencies of Value: Alternative Perspectives for Critical Theory* (Cambridge, Mass.: Harvard University Press, 1988).

3. The relative silence of feminist critics on Madame de Sévigné's writings contrasts with the lively conversations that have recently been focused on such of her contemporaries as Mlle de Gournay, Mlle de Scudéry, Mme de Villedieu, Mme de La Fayette.

4. For examples of these approaches, see Joan DeJean, "Lafayette's Ellipses: The Privileges of Anonymity," *PMLA* 99, 5 (1984): 884–901; Peggy Kamuf, *Fictions of Feminine Desire* (Lincoln: University of Nebraska Press, 1982), chaps. 2 and 3 in particular; Nancy K. Miller, "Emphasis Added: Plots and Plausibilities in Women's Fiction," *PMLA* 96, 1 (1981): 36–48; Domna C. Stanton, "Woman as Object and Subject of Exchange: Marie de Gournay's *Le Proumenoir* (1594)," *L'Esprit Créateur* 23, 2 (1983): 9–25; Gabrielle Verdier, "Gender and Rhetoric in Some Seventeenth-Century Love Letters," *L'Esprit Créateur* 23, 2 (1983): 45–57.

5. *Lettres de Madame de Sévigné, de sa famille et de ses amis*, Recueillies et annotées par M. Monmerqué, 14 vols. (Paris: Hachette, Les Grands Ecrivains de la France, 1862–68); Sévigné, *Lettres*, ed. Emile Gérard-Gailly, 3 vols. (Paris: Editions Gallimard, Bibliothèque de la Pléiade, 1953–57); Sévigné, *Correspondance*, ed. Roger Duchêne, 3 vols. (Paris: Editions Gallimard, Bibliothèque de la Pléiade, 1972–78). I follow Duchêne's edition throughout, and references are included in the text (volume, letter, page).

These repeated editions also attest to the difficulty of putting together a definitive edition of a collection of letters dispersed over the centuries, some copied and then destroyed, some hidden away and then discovered; but, just as persuasively, they underscore their enduring fascination (see Duchêne's edition, I, pp. 755–833 for a history of the editions and the letter manuscripts).

See Duchêne's bibliography for a listing of editions of and works on the Sévigné *Correspondance*.

6. For a most helpful discussion of plausibility (*la vraisemblance*) and propriety (*la bienséance*), see Miller, "Emphasis Added," 36–48.

7. By *patriarchal* I am alluding to twentieth-century theoretical constructs that are useful for bringing facets of the seventeenth century into focus, but which are not reality: they serve to illuminate the marginalization of women, but the forces they foreground affect men also, and not always to men's benefit, as I think my argument and in particular my discussions of Charles de Sévigné and Louis-Provence de Grignan make obvious.

8. Jean Cordelier, *Madame de Sévigné par elle-même* (Paris: Editions du Seuil, 1973), 40, 55.

9. Harriet Ray Allentuch, Bernard Bray, Jean Cordelier, Roger Duchêne, Solange Guénoun, Louise K. Horowitz, Domna Stanton, Marie-Odile Sweetser, and Gabrielle Verdier have recently contributed studies that illuminate features of the maternal Sévigné; see bibliography.

10. Elisabeth Badinter, *L'Amour en plus: Histoire de l'amour maternel (XVIIe–XXe siècle)* (Paris: Flammarion, 1980); Adrienne Rich, *Of Woman Born: Motherhood as Experience and Institution* (New York: W. W. Norton, 1976).

11. If she did have a significant relationship with a maternal figure during her formative years, not surprisingly it eluded documentation, and it does not surface in her own letters—it is part of the unwritten story.

12. Virginia Woolf, *A Room of One's Own* (New York: Harcourt, Brace & World, 1929), 47.

13. Jean-Marie Apostolides, *Le Roi-Machine: Spectacle et politique au temps de Louis XIV* (Paris: Editions de Minuit, 1981).

14. For a more detailed analysis of court life, see Norbert Elias, *The Court Society*, trans. Edmund Jephcott (New York: Pantheon Books, 1983). For a fuller study of elite women's status in the seventeenth century, see: Carolyn C. Lougee, *Le Paradis des femmes: Women, Salons, and Social Stratification in Seventeenth-Century France* (Princeton, N.J.: Princeton University Press, 1976); Ian Maclean, *Woman Triumphant: Feminism in French Literature (1610–1652)* (Oxford: Clarendon Press, 1977).

15. She also traveled to Vichy to take the waters for her rheumatism (May–June 1676, August–October 1677), and to Bourbon as well for the same purpose (September–October 1687).

16. Lougee, 142; the descending hierarchy in the French titular system is: prince, duke, marquis, count, viscount, baron (200). Also see Marcel Marion, *Dictionnaire des institutions de la France aux XVIIe et XVIIIe siècles* (Paris: Editions A. & J. Picard, 1989 reprint of the original 1923 edition), which asserts in the "baron" entry, 38, that the hierarchy was theoretical but not followed in practice.

17. Cette affligée ne l'est point du tout; elle dit qu'elle ne le [son mari] connaissait point et qu'elle avait toujours souhaité d'être veuve. Il lui laisse tout son bien de sorte que cette femme aura quinze ou seize mille livres de rente. Elle aimerait bien à vivre réglément et à dîner à midi comme les autres, mais l'attachement que son père a pour elle la fera toujours déjeuner à quatre heures du soir. (II, L. 526, p. 336)

This afflicted one isn't so in the least; she says she didn't know him [her husband] at all and that she had always wished to be a widow. He leaves her all his assets so that this woman will have a sixteen- or seventeen-thousand-pound pension. She would quite like to live regularly and dine at noon as others do, but the fondness her father has for her will always make her lunch at four o'clock in the afternoon.

18. Je plains aussi les pauvres mères comme Mme de Soyecourt et Mme de Cauvisson. Pour les jeunes veuves, elles ne sont guère à plaindre; elles seront bien heureuses d'être leurs maîtresses ou de changer de maîtres. (III, L. 1220, p. 914)

I also pity the poor mothers like Mme de Soyecourt and Mme de Cauvisson. As for the young widows, they are scarcely to be pitied; they will be quite happy either to be their own mistresses or to change masters.

19. Maclean, 17, 94.

20. Marianne Hirsch, "A Mother's Discourse: Incorporation and Repetition in *La Princesse de Clèves*," *Yale French Studies* 62 (1981): 67–87; and also see her illuminating review essay, "Mothers and Daughters," *Signs: Journal of Women in Culture and Society* 7 (autumn 1981): 200–22.

21. Cordelier, 65–69.

22. Roger Duchêne, *Réalité vécue et art épistolaire: Mme de Sévigné et la lettre d'amour* (Paris: Bordas, 1970), 154.

23. Roger de Bussy-Rabutin, *Histoire amoureuse des Gaules par Bussy-Rabutin*, revue et annotée par P. Boiteau, 4 vols. (Paris, 1856), 1:307.

24. The translations provided in the text are not intended to serve as poetic equivalents but as tools to assist the reader; I thank my research assistant Susan Weiner for her work on them.

25. Jean Laplanche et J. B. Pontalis, *Vocabulaire de la psychanalyse* (Paris: Presses Universitaires de France, 1967), 65–66. This reading has been explored by Harriet Ray Allentuch, "My Daughter/Myself: Emotional Roots of Madame de Sévigné's Art," *Modern Language Quarterly* 43 (June 1982): 121–37.

26. This is further elaborated in chap. 4, "The Daughter's Apprenticeship," below. See David Hunt, *Parents and Children in History: The Psychology of Family Life in Early Modern France* (New York: Basic Books, 1970); he emphasizes the central mothering role of nurses and governesses for the offspring of the elite (100–109) and points to the conflation of child and servant in adult attitudes toward children (149).

27. Jean de La Fontaine, *Oeuvres complètes* (Mayenne: Editions Gallimard, Bibliothèque de la Pléiade, 1954), tome 1, livre quatrième, fable première: "Le Lion amoureux," dédiée à Mlle de Sévigné.

28. Mme de Sévigné was not altogether oblivious to the advantages of securing a son-in-law. Later in her letters, she comments explicitly on the self-interest of another mother-in-law as she speculates on the consequences of the marriage of Mlle de Ferté:

La duchesse de Ferté leur tombera sur les bras; elle l'a bien compté ainsi. Elle dit qu'elle s'est épuisée, qu'elle n'a plus que dix mille livres de rente, qu'elle a voulu un gendre pour elle, qu'elle s'est mariée à son gendre, et ne finit point de parler sur ce ton . . . Tout cela fait prévoir la douceur de cette alliance. (III, L. 1058, p. 478)

The duchess of Ferté will put herself in their hands; she has quite counted on it. She says she is insolvent, that she has no more than a ten thousand pound pension, that she wanted a son-in-law for herself, that she married her son-in-law, and never stops talking like this . . . It all makes us foresee the sweetness of this alliance.

29. The performance is multidimensional. The basic activity frequently takes place in the drawing room, where Mme de Sévigné enacts the role of the mother writing to her daughter before witnesses. In the following passage, Mme de Sévigné is in the process of moving into the Hôtel de Carnavalet (October 1677), which

will be henceforth her Paris address; but, ever the devoted mother, she persists in writing to the end, even as the furniture is removed from under her:

> Adieu, ma bonne, adieu tous mes chers Grignan et *Grignanes*. Je vous aime et vous honore; aimez-moi un peu. On m'ôte mon écritoire, mon papier, ma table, mon siège. Oh! déménage tant que tu voudras, me voilà debout . . . Mon écriture est méchante, mais ma plume est enragée; elle criaille, et ne fait que des filets: la voilà jetée et déménagée. (II, L. 620, p. 576)

> Goodbye, *ma bonne*, goodbye all my dear Grignans and Grignanes. I love and honor you; love me a bit. They're taking away my inkwell, my paper, my table, my seat. Oh! move as much as you like, now I'm on my feet . . . My writing is bad, but my pen is enraged; it squeals, and makes only streaks: now it is flung and moved.

There are in this passage signs of a double public witnessing the epistolary performance (a scene set up by Mme de Sévigné herself, since she is the one who has ordered the move and decided to write in the midst of it): 1) there is the *on*, an immediate public of movers, disrupting, disturbing, thus implicated as participatory and causative at once, then addressed familiarly as *tu*, increasingly involved in the act being inscribed and held responsible for the dénouement of the scene; and 2) there is the public of addressees ("Adieu, ma bonne, adieu, tous mes chers Grignan et Grignanes") for whose communal pleasure the scene is being inscribed. The orchestrating *je* presents herself to her immediate and to her eventual audience as a protesting victim; the persona has been invented to convey to both her immediate entourage and her eventual addressees her attachment to her daughter and her daughter's family, encoded behaviorally and scripturally as her determination to write.

The messy handwriting serves as concrete evidence of her interrupted commitment to writing. An element of feint informs Mme de Sévigné's endeavor to render a firsthand account of her move. Though she attempts to inscribe its reality, it becomes apparent that her version is indeed a dramatizing fiction, that she is performing a mimesis of sincerity. For how can this pen, textually "déménagée," inscribe its own absence?

30. Louis Marin, *Le Portrait du roi* (Paris: Editions de Minuit, 1981), 80; and Apostolides.

31. Erving Goffman, *The Presentation of Self in Everyday Life* (London: Pelican Books, 1971), 244–45.

32. Ibid., 245, *pace* with regard to the gender changes.

33. Cordelier, 35.

34. Aristotle, *The "Art" of Rhetoric*, trans. J. H. Freese (Cambridge, Mass.: Harvard University Press, Loeb Classical Library, 1959), 17.

35. Charles E. Kany, *The Beginnings of the Epistolary Novel in France, Italy, and Spain*, University of California Publications in Modern Philology, vol. 21, no. 1 (Berkeley: University of California, 1939), 1.

36. Aristotle, *"Art" of Rhetoric*, 353.

37. François de Grenaille, *L'Honneste fille*, 3 vols. (Paris: chez Antoine de Sommauille et Toussainct Quinet, 1639–40), 1:136.

38. Cordelier, 35, as much as suggests this, but retains the *vous*, and thus persists in understanding her writing as strictly other-related.

39. Catherine MacKinnon quoting from Hélène Cixous's "Laugh of the Medusa," in "Feminism, Marxism, Method, and the State: An Agenda for Theory," in *The Signs Reader: Women, Gender, and Scholarship*, ed. Elizabeth Abel and

Emily K. Abel (Chicago: University of Chicago Press, 1983), 227–56, 242. This same contention that the mirror stage theory is not a gender-neutral construction is made by Naomi Schor, *Breaking the Chain: Women, Theory, and French Realist Fiction* (New York: Columbia University Press, 1985), 96.

40. See, for example, Nancy Chodorow, *The Reproduction of Mothering: Psychoanalysis and the Sociology of Gender* (Berkeley and Los Angeles: University of California Press, 1978); Dorothy Dinnerstein, *The Mermaid and the Minotaur: Sexual Arrangements and Human Malaise* (New York: Harper & Row, 1977).

41. Marianne Hirsch, "Mothers and Daughters," *Signs: Journal of Women in Culture and Society* 7 (autumn 1981): 214.

42. Roger Duchêne's edition of the *Correspondance* has done a great deal to provide information that assists in understanding allusions in the letters, but still there are obscure areas that cannot be decoded by any reader today.

43. Bernard Bray, "L'Epistolier et son public en France au dix-septième siècle," *Travaux de linguistique et de littérature* 11 (1973): 17:

Dans les lettres imprimées, le lecteur s'établit en substitut du destinataire. Happé par le *vous*, il accueille pour lui-même les confidences qui ont été d'abord écrites pour un autre. Il s'identifie à cet autre, il prend à son propre compte la polarisation qui liait le scripteur au destinataire.

In printed letters, the reader takes his place as the substitute for the addressee. Caught up by the *vous*, he assumes for himself the confidences that were first written for someone else. He identifies with this other, he takes for his own the polarization that linked the writer to the addressee.

44. Jacqueline Duchêne also has been intent on restoring a place to the daughter; see her *Françoise de Grignan ou le mal d'amour* (Paris: Librairie Arthème Fayard, 1985). Very few of the daughter's writings survived; these are, for the most part, letters to individuals other than her mother, or messages penned by her in her mother's letters to others. No letters addressed by the daughter to her mother appear to have survived.

45. Simone de Beauvoir, *Mémoires d'une jeune fille rangée* (Paris: Gallimard, 1958); Marie Cardinal, *Les Mots pour le dire* (Paris: Bernard Grasset, 1975); Marguerite Duras, *L'Amant* (Paris: Editions de Minuit, 1984); Luce Irigary, *Et l'une ne bouge pas sans l'autre* (Paris: Editions de Minuit, 1979); Violette Leduc, *L'Asphyxie* (Paris: Gallimard, 1946); Nathalie Sarraute, *Enfance* (Paris: Gallimard, 1983).

46. I thank Michael Fischer for pointing out this useful term from Joyce's *The Wake* to me.

47. Nicole Bonvalet suggests as much in her study, "Etudes parallèles: Lorsque les femmes lisent Madame de Sévigné," *Oeuvres et critiques* 5, 1 (automne 1980): 121–41.

48. See Diana Fuss, *Essentially Speaking: Feminism, Nature, and Difference* (New York: Routledge, 1989). While I agree with Fuss that, upon investigation, essentialism and constructionism prove to be mutually interdependent terms, the one more useful than the other depending on the circumstances, it seems in this instance that a specific daughterhood experience grounded in a history of mother-daughter relations would find certain resonances with another such experience, this without my wanting to privilege essentialism over constructionism.

49. For a summary explanation of the term *différance*, spelled with an *a*, which designates Jacques Derrida's master-concept, combining reference to "difference"

and "deferment" simultaneously, see the translator's preface to his *Of Grammatology*, trans. Gayatri Chakravorty Spivak (Baltimore: Johns Hopkins University Press, 1976), especially xliii.

50. Indeed, it is this very virtuosity of narrative perspective that is refined and exploited in the eighteenth-century novel, the standard example of which is Choderlos de Laclos's *Les Liaisons dangereuses.*

51. J. L. Austin, *How to Do Things with Words* (Cambridge, Mass.: Harvard University Press, 1962); John R. Searle, *Speech Acts: An Essay in the Philosophy of Language* (Cambridge: Cambridge University Press), 1969.

1. Women and the Epistolary Domain in Seventeenth-Century France (pp. 27–56)

1. Jean de La Bruyère, "Des Ouvrages de l'esprit 37," *Les Caractères ou les moeurs de ce siècle* (Paris: Editions Garnier Frères, 1962), 79–80.

2. Julia Kristeva, "Women's Time," *Signs: Journal of Women in Culture and Society* 7 (1981): 24.

3. Molière, *Les Précieuses ridicules*, sc. 9, ll. 176–77, *Oeuvres complètes*, ed. Georges Couton (Paris: Editions Gallimard, Bibliothèque de la Pléiade, 1971), tome 1.

4. For a fuller analysis of seventeenth-century social stratification, hierarchization, and interdependence under Louis XIV and the importance of etiquette in a prestige or status economy, see Norbert Elias, *The Court Society*, trans. Edmund Jephcott (New York: Pantheon Books, 1983).

5. François Poullain de la Barre, *De l'égalité des deux sexes* (Paris: Fayard, 1984), 34.

6. To give an example of the onomastic situation surrounding the La Bruyère text in question, on the pages facing the text cited as an epigraph to this chapter (see n. 1), the following authors are specifically named: Térence, Molière, Malherbe, Théophile, Ronsard, Marot, Belleau, Jodelle, du Bartas, Racan—all male.

7. La Bruyère, 79.

8. This passage is regularly cited as evidence of the high esteem in which *épistolières* were held. See Gabrielle Verdier, "Gender and Rhetoric, in Some Seventeenth Century Love Letters," *L'Esprit Créateur* 232 (1983): 47; Bernard Bray, Introduction to *Lettres portugaises, Lettres d'une péruvienne et autres romans d'amour par lettres*, textes etablis, présentés et annotés par Bernard Bray et Isabelle Landy-Houillon (Paris: Garnier Flammarion, 1983), 19.

9. The gender-coded nature-culture opposition is spelled out in Sherry B. Ortner, "Is Female to Male as Nature Is to Culture?" in *Woman, Culture, and Society*, ed. Michelle Zimbalist Rosaldo and Louise Lamphere (Stanford, Calif.: Stanford University Press, 1974), 67–87.

10. This position finds resonance with Kristeva's words in the epigraph to this chapter. Her own stand is equally elusive, if differently so. Her "we" defies alignment and coincides neither with "women" nor with "they."

11. "Sentiment" is here understood according to the definition offered by Louis Marin: "sentiment, ou idée, apparaissant dans l'âme à l'occasion des impressions faites sur nos corps par les choses extérieures . . . indépendant de la volonté" [sentiment, or idea, appearing in the mind upon the occasion of impressions made on our bodies by external things . . . independent of the will]. Marin, *La Critique du discours* (Paris: Editions de Minuit, 1975), 199.

12. Antoine Furetière, in his *Dictionnaire universel contenant généralement tous les mots français tant vieux que modernes et les termes de toutes les sciences et des arts* (Geneva: Slatkine Reprints, 1970), offers eight different definitions of the term; rather than attempt to assign one of them to the word as it is used here, it appears more appropriate to leave it at play in the full semantic field, because, in fact, the connotative impact of the term (combining both feeling and judgment) is significant here as it attaches particularly to a mode of discourse conventionally associated with "women."

13. Madeleine de Scudéry was subjected to ridicule by Boileau; Mme de La Fayette favored anonymity over the hazards of public authorship at least for her novel *La Princesse de Clèves*; Molière made it quite clear through *Les Femmes savantes* and *Les Précieuses ridicules* that there were social dangers for women who took themselves seriously; of course, the aristocratic esthetic of *négligence* also had its part in influencing the nonserious tenor of many of Sévigné's reflections on her writing.

14. Letters penned by various women would have been known primarily from the salons where they circulated both at inception and at reception often enough, or from individual published collections such as that of Madame de Villedieu, *Recueil de quelques lettres ou relations galantes, dédié à Mlle de Sévigné* (Paris: Barbin, 1668), or again from collections and manuals such as that of François de Grenaille, *Nouveau recueil de lettres des dames tant anciennes que modernes* (Paris: chez Toussainct Quinet, 1642); for a complete discussion of women's published correspondences, see Janet Gurkin Altman, "The Letter Book as a Literary Institution 1539–1789: Toward a Cultural History of Published Correspondences in France," *Yale French Studies* 71 (1986): 17–62.

15. In his review of Duchêne's edition, Georges Couton at once praises it and laments the apparent impossibility of getting any closer to the original unless a hitherto unknown manuscript should surface. *Studi francesi* 18 (1974): 505.

Des sources, Roger Duchêne a tiré tout ce qu'on pouvait tirer. Son édition est, hélas! définitive, parfaite en l'état actuel de notre information.

From the sources, Roger Duchêne has gotten all one could get. His edition is, alas! definitive, perfect in the current state of our information.

16. Altman, "Letter Book," 54–56.

17. In perspective, however, it is unlikely that La Bruyère was more than grudging in his praise since his chapter "Des femmes" evinces a strong dose of misogyny; as Barthes reads him, women constitute a race apart: "une classe anthropologique: les femmes (c'est une race particulière, alors que l'homme est général: on dit: *de l'homme*, mais *des femmes*)" [an anthropological class: women (they are a separate race, while man is general: one says *of man*, but *of women*)]. Roland Barthes, "La Bruyère," *Essais Critiques* (Paris: Editions du Seuil, 1964), 223.

18. For a more detailed study of the state of the mails at this time, see Eugène Vaillé, *Histoire générale des Postes Françaises: Louvois, Surintendant général des Postes (1668–1691)*, vol. 4 (Paris: Presses Universitaires de France, 1951).

19. Roger Duchêne provides a most useful overview of the status of the epistolary genre in seventeenth-century France in *Réalité vécue et art épistolaire: Madame de Sévigné et la lettre d'amour* (Paris: Bordas, 1970), chaps. 1 and 2; and Altman, "Letter Book," provides an excellent study of the publication of letter books at that time.

20. For a complete list, see Roger Duchêne, *Réalité vécue*, 391–94.

21. "Il faut écrire ses lettres proprement, sans aucunes effaceures, sur du fin papier (doré et musqué si one veut) et avec de belles marges" [One must write letters properly, without any erasings, on fine paper (gilded and scented if one wants) and with fair margins]. Jean Puget de La Serre, *Le Secrétaire à la mode* (Amsterdam: Jean Janssen, 1655), 55–56.

22. Charles du Boscq, *Nouveau recueil de lettres des dames de ce temps avec leurs réponses*, 3e éd. (Paris: A. Courbé, 1642), advertissement.

23. Whereas Du Bosq insists on anonymity of author (propriety) and, as a consequence, has to insist at length on authenticity of text (plausibility), François de Grenaille, less cavalierly and more high-handedly, parades both the deceptive and the inventive nature of his own collection:

> Si vous lisez ici des Lettres Capitales pour les surnoms, c'est que je n'en sais pas les uns, et que j'affecte d'ignorer les autres . . . Après tout, si j'ai supposé quelques lettres, ce n'est pas pour mieux faire que celles que je sers, mais pour tâcher de les imiter.

> If you read here Capital Letters for last names, it is because I do not know some of them, and I pretend not to know the others . . . After all, if I have assumed some letters as my own, it is not to do better than those I serve, but to try to imitate them.

Grenaille, *Nouveau recueil*, advertissement.

24. Ibid., 69–70.

25. Pierre d'Ortigue de Vaumorière, *Lettres sur toutes sortes de sujets avec des avis sur la manière de les écrire* (Paris: Jean Guignard, 1690), 13.

26. Du Plaisir, *Sentimens sur les lettres et sur l'histoire avec des scrupules sur le stile* (Paris: C. Blageart, 1683).

27. Charles Sorel, *Oeuvres diverses, ou discours mêlés* (Paris: La Compagnie des Libraires, 1663), 466.

28. Vaumorière, *Lettres*, 34–35.

29. Pierre d'Ortigue de Vaumorière, *L'Art de plaire dans la conversation*, 2e éd. (Paris: Jean Guignard, 1691), 16.

30. Vaumorière, *Lettres*, 52.

31. Ibid., 6.

32. André Louis Personne, *Lettres et billets en tous les genres d'écrire* (Paris: L. Raveneau, 1662), i–ii.

33. Vaumorière, *Lettres*, 10.

34. But, as Vaumorière proceeds to elaborate his distinction between the spoken and the written word, he locates the difference simply in frequency of practice. Because of less regular experience with writing than with talking, inevitably fewer people write well than speak well, he claims. And, because of the permanence of writing as opposed to the transitory nature of speech, it is important, he states, to be more exact when writing than when speaking, since the oral word is subject to the vagaries of human memory, whereas the written word endures; but this distinction regards only practice (*Lettres*, 3).

35. Ibid., 17.

36. Ibid., 25.

37. La Serre, 14.

38. La Serre, 11, discusses appropriate tones for offering advice to one's social inferior:

> Si on écrit à son inférieur, ou à quelqu'un avec qui on soit fort familier, on le peut exhorter à suivre le conseil qu'on lui donne, et même le presser, en lui remonstrant que s'il le méprise il est à craindre qu'il ne lui en arrive du mal.

If one writes to one's inferior, or to someone with whom one is quite familiar, one can exhort him to follow the advice one gives, and even press him, by threatening that if he scorns it, it is to be feared that evil may befall him.

39. Vaumorière, *Lettres*, 40.

40. Ibid., 26, 28–29.

41. Pierre Richelet, *Les plus belles lettres des meilleurs auteurs français* (Lyon: Benoit-Bailly, 1689).

42. Vaumorière, *Lettres*, 59.

43. This is pure speculation, but, given Sévigné's complete absorption in this generic activity, and their ready availability, it is not difficult to imagine that her curiosity would have led her at least to leaf through manuals that came her way; such reading, of course, is not the sort one readily admits to, then or now.

44. Vaumorière, *Lettres*, 24.

45. Ibid., 16.

46. Carolyn C. Lougee, *Le Paradis des femmes: Women, Salons, and Social Stratification in Seventeenth-Century France* (Princeton, N.J.: Princeton University Press, 1976), 52.

47. Emile Magne, *Voiture et l'Hôtel de Rambouillet: Les Années de gloire, 1635–1648* (Paris: Editions Emile-Paul Frères, 1930), 11; Magne, *Voiture et les origines de l'Hôtel de Rambouillet, 1597–1635* (Paris: Mercure de France, 1911); M. A. Ubicini, *Oeuvres de Voiture: Lettres et poésies* (Geneva: Slatkine Reprints, 1967), viii.

48. For an interesting discussion of the significance of the term *voiture* in the *Correspondance*, see Bernard Bray, "Les 'Voitures' de Mme de Sévigné," *Romanische Forschungen* 83 (1971): 596–602.

49. Antoine Adam, *Histoire de la litterature française au XVIIe siècle* (Paris: Editions Domat Montchrestien, 1948), 1:243.

50. Ibid., 254.

51. Ibid., 256.

52. Guez de Balzac, *Les Premières Lettres de Guez de Balzac (1618–1627)*, ed. H. Bibas and K.-T. Butler (Paris: Librairie Droz, 1933), vol. 1, lettre L, p. 202.

53. Ibid., p. 204.

54. Adam, 151.

55. Monsieur l'Abé***, *Essais de lettres familières sur toute sorte de sujets avec un discours sur l'Art Epistolaire et quelques remarques nouvelles sur la langue française* (Paris: Jacques LeFebvre, 1690), 216.

56. Domna Stanton, *The Aristocrat as Art: A Study of the Honnête Homme and the Dandy in 17th and 19th Century Literature* (New York: Columbia University Press, 1980), discusses the Méré-Voiture conflict. She points out that Méré attempted to ostracize Voiture from the elite circle of *honnêteté* [virtue] because of what he perceived as a tendency to lapse into *préciosité* [preciosity] (30). In an extended footnote (229–30, n. 33), Stanton states that the dissension suggests social rivalry as much as any more esthetically grounded differences but points out that Méré took specific exception to Voiture's "consistent disregard for correct usage."

57. Adam, 4:166.

58. Ibid., 1:389.

59. Social arbitration in the guise of literary appreciation is evident in such statements as the following:

La qualité propre de la poésie de Voiture est liée au type des rapports qui l'ont unie à la réalité de son temps. Voiture a certes été pour beaucoup dans le climat irréel et précieux de la vie des salons et de la galanterie; mais en retour sa poésie s'est ouverte au monde réel, en dépit des apparences qu'il a voulu conserver.

The unique quality of Voiture's poetry is linked to the type of relations that joined it to the reality of his time. Voiture was certainly marked by the unreal and precious climate of salon life and gallantry; but his poetry was open to the real world, in spite of the appearences he wanted to maintain.

Vincent Voiture: Poésies, éd. critique de Henri Lafay (Paris: Librairie Marcel Didier, 1971), ciii.

60. Vincent de Voiture, *Oeuvres: lettres et poésies*, ed. M. A. Ubicini (Paris: Charpentier, 1855), 1:ii.

61. Ibid., Lettre 71, p. 217.

62. Personne, Lettre LVIII à Monsieur Quillet.

2. Sévigné's Apprenticeship (pp. 57–82)

1. Cordelier discounts all of the letters that precede those addressed to her daughter as so many examples of "correspondance précieuse." He marks the date of the birth of the writer as the date of her daughter's departure, just as R. Duchêne and Solange Guénoun view that as the date of the birth of the mother. I do not think that Sévigné's sustained and formative correspondence with her cousin Bussy can be dismissed so lightly. See Jean Cordelier, *Madame de Sévigné par elle-même* (Paris: Editions du Seuil, 1973), 5.

2. Thanks to Alice Kaplan and Philip Stewart for drawing this point out when I presented this chapter as a paper at Duke University in 1987.

3. As had been the case for Marie de Gournay or Mlle de Scudéry, for example, ridiculed and dismissed by many of Sévigné's male contemporaries.

4. John C. Lapp, *The Esthetics of Negligence: La Fontaine's "Contes"* (Cambridge: Cambridge University Press, 1971), 31, describes *négligence* thus:

He [La Fontaine] adopts as his basic structure an informal conversation between friends, one which rejects "les conversations réglées et tout ce qui sent la conférence académique." Chance alone will dictate the subjects these friends discuss, and to describe their manner of treating them he uses the well-worn Platonic metaphor that Montaigne had applied to Ariosto: the bees as they fly from flower to flower. Indeed La Fontaine's remarks on his friends' discourse remind us of "De l'art de conférer" when Montaigne emphasizes that conversation should aim at "l'exercice des âmes sans autre fruit," and not only shun all practical goals but follow "pour la plupart la conduicte du hasard."

5. In *The Aristocrat as Art: A Study of the Honnête Homme and the Dandy in 17th and 19th Century French Literature* (New York: Columbia University Press, 1980), 178, Stanton recognizes the tenet of *négligence* as paramount in seventeenth-century aspirations to *honnêteté*: "To avoid such ridicule—the ungainly, unesthetic bumbling that seventeenth-century comedy exposes—the artist calls upon yet another 'dissimulated artifice' (I, 143), that 'pleasant deception' (II, 34) known as négligence: with the help of 'a certain negligence which conceals artifice and confirms that we give no thought to what we do' (188:20), the Sender can display the kind of naturalness which is the mark of great art." Also see: Roger Duchêne, "Madame de Sévigné et le style négligé," *Oeuvres et critiques*, 1, 2 (été 1976): 113–27.

6. Fritz Nies, *Gattungspoëtik und Publikumsstruktur, Zur Geschichte der Sevignebriefe* (Munich: Wilhelm Fink Verlag, 1972).

7. Alain Viala, *La Naissance de l'écrivain: Sociologie de la littérature à l'âge classique* (Paris: Editions de Minuit, 1985), 150.

8. Ibid., 150.

9. Viala, 142, writes:

"Le palmarès constitué par les premiers ouvrages d'enseignement de la littérature retient quarante-quatre auteurs. Le XVIIe siècle qui se taille la part du lion, est ainsi hiérarchisé: premier, Corneille; deuxième, Racine; troisièmes ex-aequo, Boileau, Bossuet, et Molière; au rang suivant: Malherbe, Racan, Vaugelas, La Fontaine; puis Voiture, etc. Même Mme de Sévigné prend place parmi les classiques dès 1740."

The prize list established by the first teaching texts for literature features forty-four authors. The seventeenth century, which provides the lion's share, is hierarchized in the following way: first, Corneille; second, Racine; sharing third place, Boileau, Bossuet, and Molière; in the next rank: Malherbe, Racan, Vaugelas, La Fontaine; then Voiture, etc. Even Mme de Sévigné takes her place among the classics from 1740.

10. This section is very much influenced by Barbara Herrnstein Smith's distinction between a material and a social economy in her book *Contingencies of Value: Alternative Perspectives for Critical Theory* (Cambridge, Mass.: Harvard University Press, 1988), 30–31.

11. In September 1661, Fouquet, minister of finances under Mazarin, was arrested by order of Louis XIV, tried, and imprisoned for life. He had amassed great wealth during his tenure of office and was a generous patron of the arts. His disgrace was brought on by the suspicious ostentation of a splendid party he gave in August 1661 in honor of the king, at his newly completed Château de Vaux. Shortly after his disgrace, Louis XIV hired Fouquet's architects and gardeners and set about creating Versailles. All those who were friendly with Fouquet were potentially implicated in his fall from favor and were as concerned for their own fates as for his during the trial. It was said that a collection of letters from his various lady friends had been found, and that it included letters from Sévigné. She admitted only to having corresponded with Fouquet on behalf of her cousin M. de La Trousse, regarding his marriage. But gossip preferred livelier speculation, and it is still not clear whether the acknowledged La Trousse letters were cited to cover as alibis for other sorts of messages from Sévigné to Fouquet. See letters dated October 1661–January 1662, I, L. 50–L. 72, pp. 48–83, addressed mainly to Pomponne, and accompanying notes.

12. Sévigné's interest in eventual publication and, as a consequence, what can be known of her through her letters might be compared to La Fontaine's intentions in *Voyage en Limousin*, described by E. B. O. Borgerhoff, *The Freedom of French Classicism* (Princeton, N.J.: Princeton University Press, 1950), 134: "He [La Fontaine] wrote to his wife the series of letters which is called the *Voyage en Limousin*. They were a mixture of prose and verse and, as was the custom, only semi-private. They would be read aloud or passed around. They could not be expected then to expose any side of La Fontaine which he would not willingly show the world. But then, as I have said, it seems there was no side to hide, no secret. Yet I think these letters do reveal a La Fontaine of whom perhaps he himself was not conscious."

13. See III, n. 5, p. 1258, for Duchêne's concurrence.

3. The Moment of Separation (pp. 83–95)

1. Roland Barthes, *Fragments d'un discours amoureux* (Paris: Editions du Seuil, 1977), 52.

2. In I, n. 4, p. 951, Duchêne points briefly to the introduction of these themes in this first letter.

3. As Janet Gurkin Altman points out, there was one earlier instance of a mother-daughter correspondence: Mesdames des Roches published their missives to each other in 1586, but these were largely formulaic, occasional markers, and are not mentioned in Sévigné's letters. See Altman, "The Letter Book as a Literary Institution 1539–1789: Toward a Cultural History of Published Correspondences in France," *Yale French Studies* 71 (1986): 26.

4. Duchêne identifies these verses in I, p. 950, n. 1.

5. To push the symbolism perhaps to its furthest is to bear in mind that *box* is encoded in western culture as standing in for the female genitals; in this sense, Mme de Grignan, although already married and mother of one, only claims herself in the fullest sense, including her sexuality, at the moment of her departure from her mother's house, and her mother denigrates that filial sexuality by referring to it as "petite." Further, the gift of a diamond ring, of any sort of ring, has a ceremonial implication to it, which, in this context, might be seen to replicate the marriage ceremony, putting the daughter in a clearly double bind.

6. For a broader discussion of the nature of the gift, see Marcel Mauss, *The Gift: Forms and Functions of Exchange in Archaic Societies*, trans. Ian Cunnison (New York: W. W. Norton, 1967), especially p. 63.

7. For an illuminating discussion of the significance of these dates, see Susan H. Léger, "Reading in (the) Place of the Daughter: The Letters of Madame de Sévigné," Special Session, "Feminist Readings, Filial Pieties: Daughters in/and/of Texts," MLA convention, New York, 1986.

8. This reading is at variance with one offered by Harriet Allentuch, *Madame de Sévigné: A Portrait in Letters* (Baltimore: Johns Hopkins Press, 1963), 188: "From the beginning, Madame de Sévigné shunned society to recover from a depression. After separating from her daughter, she wanted to be alone. Grief and, in particular, excessive grief, was not to be paraded in public, especially in salon and court circles, where people observed one another with hungry curiosity."

9. Louise Horowitz analyzes Sévigné's favoring of those friends who second her in her maternal obsession in "The Correspondence of Madame de Sévigné: Lettres ou Belles-Lettres?" *French Forum* 6 (1981): 13–27:

> Within this group [the intimate inner circle of friends and family which allows the letter to mirror perfectly the closed social circle at its base], those who Mme de Sévigné *claims* are most deeply involved with Mme de Grignan's welfare receive the greatest attention, as if all shared collectively her passion for her daughter. The world is named and described within the confines of the mother's preoccupation. . . . The letter-writer's efforts to extend her own feelings to a whole social circle suggest either self-delusion or, more likely, a wish to "seduce" her daughter by rendering her a *universal* "princesse lointaine." (23–24)

10. Mme de La Fayette had two younger sisters who were both nuns; little is known about them. See I, L. 131, n. 2, p. 981–82.

4. The Daughter's Apprenticeship (pp. 96–134)

1. François de Grenaille, *L'Honneste fille* (Paris: chez Antoine de Sommauille et Toussainc Quinet, 1639–40), 1:101, 137.

2. Ibid., 136.

3. Ibid., 136–37.

4. As was already discussed regarding Sévigné's writing relationship with Bussy, chap. 2.

5. Grenaille, 1:97.

6. For a more detailed analysis of the time-lag phenomenon as significant in the epistolary situation, see Janet G. Altman, *Epistolarity: Approaches to a Form* (Columbus: Ohio State University Press, 1982), 140.

7. The rhetoric of intuitive "entente" is not unique to the Sévigné correspondence. It is interesting to compare the seventeenth-century passage of "petits esprits" above with a twentieth-century "invisible message" transmitted between mother and daughter and noted in the mother's letter: "You say I called at just the right moment as though a message had been sent that you were in trouble, and I can only say that your letter came as if YOU had been sent an invisible message that you needed me and that gave a sense of meaning to my life that had absolutely melted" (21 February, 1974 from Anne Sexton to her daughter, Joy). Karen Payne, ed., *Between Ourselves: Letters between Mothers and Daughters, 1750–1982* (Boston: Houghton Mifflin Company, 1983), 15.

8. Just a few seventeenth-century examples of these are: Nicolas Faret, *L'Honneste homme ou l'art de plaire à la cour*, ed. Maurice Magendie (Paris: Presses Universitaires de France, 1925); Antoine Gombaud, chevalier de Méré, *Oeuvres complètes*, tome 1, "Les Conversations," tome 2, "De la conversation," texte établi et présenté par Charles-H. Boudhours (Paris: Editions Fernand Roches, 1930); Pierre d'Ortigue de Vaumorière, *L'Art de plaire dans la conversation*, 2d edition (Paris: Jean Guignard, 1691).

9. See Jean Laplanche and J.-B. Pontalis, "Choix d'objet narcissique," and "Narcissisme," *Vocabulaire de la Psychanalyse* (Paris: Presses Universitaires de France, 1967), 64–66, 261–65.

10. Thus mirroring microcosmically the figuration Norbert Elias describes as representative of the interdependent relations of the king, the nobility, and the bourgeoisie, the world in which Sévigné and her daughter correspond; see Elias, *The Court Society* (New York: Pantheon, 1983), 142.

11. Patricia Meyer Spacks offers a most helpful analysis of the analogies between letters and conversation, *Gossip* (New York: Alfred A. Knopf, 1985), chap. 4, "Borderlands."

12. Grenaille, 1:89; it is interesting that the metaphor of painter is applied to the mother's role in the formation of the daughter here as it was earlier applied in the Le Brun-Titian comparisons, by Bussy, and then relayed by Sévigné to her daughter, to manners of writing; the daughter, like writing, is represented as an artifact.

13. Pomponne was the member of a distinguished religiously oriented family: nephew of the "Grand Arnauld," a defender of Jansenism, who upheld the controversial cause of Port-Royal against the Jesuits; the son of a *solitaire* of Port Royal; and nephew and brother to prominent abbesses as well. Pomponne himself was minister for foreign affairs under Louis XIV (1671–79) and was in and out of favor as the tide of family fortune followed the fate of the Jansenist movement.

14. In her discussion of Walpole's letters and his admiration for Sévigné, Spacks, 81–82, dwells on the criteria of appropriateness and grace, summarized in the term *manner,* and correlating, in my view, with categories of behavior and language.

15. Retz was a politically ambitious cardinal who fell from favor as a consequence of his involvement in the Fronde, plotting against Mazarin in particular; he was reduced to maneuvering and observing from the sidelines, and to vindicating his point of view in the writing of his *Mémoires*; Sévigné remained a faithful friend to him, but Françoise-Marguerite did not share her mother's affection for him.

16. Censorship was a given condition of seventeenth-century correspondence. Codes were established, elaborated, and changed regularly in order to disguise meanings of messages to third parties; letters were addressed to fictitious people in order not to attract attention, or they were sent by means other than the conventional channels. Michel LeTellier, Marquis de Louvois, was officially responsible for the Surintendance Générale des Postes from 1668, a date that coincides with the flourishing of the *Correspondance*. Although he personally believed in the confidentiality of letters, he was not his own master:

> Louvois tenait essentiellement au respect du secret des lettres . . . Mais si Louvois était intransigeant pour la violation des correspondances par son personnel, il obéissait lui-même à des obligations politiques qui lui imposaient moins de discretion. Boislisle nous a informés de l'existence du Cabinet Noir sous Louis XIV et Louvois était partie.

> Louvois essentially believed in the confidentiality of letters. . . . But if Louvois was intransigeant about the violation of correspondence by his personnel, he himself obeyed the political obligations that demanded less discretion of him. Boislisle has informed us of the existence of the Black Cabinet under Louis XIV and Louvois was a party to this.

Eugène Vaillé, *Histoire générale des Postes (1668–1691)* (Paris: Presses Universitaires de France, 1951), 4:123–24.

For a more recent discussion of censorship under Louis XIV, with particular reference to surveillance of the mails, see Joseph Klaits, *Printed Propaganda under Louis XIV: Absolute Monarchy and Public Opinion* (Princeton, N.J.: Princeton University Press, 1976), 50; and for specific treatment of Sévigné and the mail system, see Henri-René Lafon, "Les Grands Écrivains et la poste: Madame de Sévigné et la poste," *Revue des P.T.T. de France*, XIe année (mai–juin 1956): 38–42.

17. She made a point of cultivating the courier Dubois who handled the mail between herself and her daughter when she resided at Les Rochers, and she sought, through this personalization of the bureaucratic system, to ensure a further guarantee of its reliability; see, for instance, I, L. 175, p. 277.

18. Bernard Bray, "Quelques Aspects du système épistolaire de Madame de Sévigné," *Revue d'histoire littéraire de la France* 69 (1969): 491–505. Bray emphasizes the difference between the letters written from Paris and those from the country; the further Sévigné finds herself from court, the less news and gossip she has to relate; thus the spirit of invention and self-reflection is more marked in the letters from Les Rochers.

19. As was seen in chap. 2; and in I, L. 146, p. 187; L. 167, p. 258.

20. The term *Pierrot* has a history of usage in the letters alluding intertextually to the sleazy amorous overtures of the hypocrite *Tartuffe*; it conveys the desire to establish a more intimate relationship, alluding to the inappropriate advances made by a gentleman to a young girl not of his class, exploiting the authority of his social standing to command her to familiarity with him. For a sense of the context, see I, L. 230, n. 2, p. 1208; and I, L. 64, n. 5, p. 903, wherein:

> Le chancelier, dit une note du chansonnier Maurepas, «étant un jour enfermé avec une garce, qui l'appelait toujours Monseigneur, il lui dit, dans l'emportement du plaisir, de la nommer plutôt Pierrot»."

> The chancellor, says a note from the songwriter Maurepas, «being one day shut up with a girl, who always called him Monseigneur, told her, in the transport of pleasure, to call him rather Pierrot».

And for a study of Sévigné's humor, see Jo Ann Marie Recker, *Appelle-moi Pierrot: Wit and Irony in the Letters of Madame de Sévigné* (Amsterdam: Benjamins, 1986).

21. These anecdotal letters tend to be those most readily anthologized and presented as most representative of Sévigné's finest writing.

22. Both Bernard Bray and Elizabeth Goldsmith offer interpretations of Sévigné's tendency to rewrite letters from her daughter: Bray states that such passages represent the mother's lessons to the daughter, aimed at improving her style or reminding her of her lack thereof, whereas Goldsmith sees this echo effect as evidence of the kind of response necessary to maintain the dynamic of the correspondence. See Bray, "Quelques Aspects," 504; Elizabeth Goldsmith, "Bridging Distances: Writing as Displacement and Location in the Letters of Madame de Sévigné," diss., Cornell, 1978.

23. Jacques Lacan, Ecrits, A Selection, trans. Alan Sheridan (New York: W. W. Norton, 1977), 1.

24. Duchêne, Correspondance, I, L. 132, n. 8, p. 985, notes that use of the expression "ma bonne" seems to be unique to Sévigné, and that if others use it, it is to mirror back to Sévigné her own term (and only one example is given of this); Sévigné refers only to her daughter as "ma bonne"; Mme de Lafayette will be "ma belle" "ma pauvre petite," "ma très chère"; and Mme de Lafayette likewise will address Sévigné as "ma belle," "ma chère amie," "ma très chère."

25. Harriet Ray Allentuch, in "My Daughter/My Self: Emotional Roots of Madame de Sévigné's Art," Modern Language Quarterly 43, 2 (June 1982): 121–37, sees Sévigné substituting her daughter for her own long-deceased mother in a role reversal similar to the one I am pointing to, but I see it as less nostalgic, and as patterned on another relationship, that of the aristocratic child to the nursemaid, which is probably a more complicated but equally charged tie as that to a seventeenth-century biological mother.

26. The only instance I find where the expression is used other than by the mother to address her daughter is in a footnote, where, in a letter to Mme de Flamarens, Chapelain alludes to Sévigné as "notre bonne," suggesting that, in so doing, he is borrowing her own words in affectionate mimicry of the way she addresses her daughter (I, L. 50, p. 49, n. 1, p. 881).

27. The abbé de Coulanges, Sévigné's maternal uncle, served as her material mentor, assisting her in administering her possessions, guiding her in her immediate worldly concerns. So it is not surprising that his appelation, "le bien bon," should be tinged with the same connotations of at once patronizing and childish affection for one who is of service as those in play with her daughter.

28. Julia Kristeva, "Stabat Mater," trans. Arthur Goldhammer, in The Female Body in Western Culture: Contemporary Perspectives," ed. Susan Rubin Suleiman (Cambridge, Mass.: Harvard University Press, 1986), 116.

29. David Hunt, Parents and Children in History: The Psychology of Family Life in Early Modern France (New York: Basic Books, 1970), 70.

30. Solange Guénoun analyzes this beautifully in "La Correspondance de Madame de Sévigné et de Madame de Grignan: Une Séparation littéraire," diss. Princeton, 1980, 46.

31. Grenaille, 1:86.

5. Private and Public—The Space Between (pp. 135–51)

1. Michel de Montaigne, Oeuvres complètes, ed. Albert Thibaudet et Maurice Rat (Paris: Bibliothèque de la Pléiade, Gallimard, 1962), Essais, bk. 1, chap. 40, "Consideration sur Ciceron," 246.

2. Virginia Woolf, "Madame de Sévigné," *Collected Essays* (New York: Harcourt, Brace, & World, 1967), 66.

3. Floyd Gray, *Le Style de Montaigne* (Paris: Librairie Nizet, 1958), 131–32, highlights the comparability of the writing energies behind the *Correspondance* and the *Essais*, speculating that if La Boétie had lived, Montaigne would have written letters, and that if Sévigné had been a man, she would have written essays.

4. Here I am very much in agreement with Bernard Bray:

Elles [Mme de Sévigné et Mme de Grignan] tentent implicitement de transformer ce manuscrit privé et discutable, qu'elles élaborent ensemble, en un ouvrage public et indiscutable.

They [Mme de Sévigné and Mme de Grignan] implicitly attempt to transform this private and debatable manuscript, which they elaborate together, into a public and indisputable work.

Bray, "Quelques Aspects du système épistolaire de Mme de Sévigné," *Revue d'histoire littéraire de la France* 69 (1969): 504–5. In this article, Bray contests the myth of Sévigné as accidental author and attempts to present her as a writer well aware of her talent, cultivating her art, with an eye to eventual publication (491–505). In a later article, he further theorizes on the act of writing and insists that it implies a will to publish as he draws out Michel Butor's pronouncement:

Dans l'acte même d'écrire il y a un public impliqué. Nous serions en droit de généraliser la formule en l'appliquant à la littérature épistolaire: Dans l'acte même d'écrire une lettre tous les publics sont impliqués.

In the act of writing there is an implied public. We would have the right to generalize the formula in applying it to epistolary literature: In the very act of writing a letter all publics are implied.

Bernard Bray, "L'Epistolier et son public en France au XVIIe siècle," *Travaux de linguistique et de littérature* 2, 11 (1973): 12.

5. See both Patricia Meyer Spacks, *Gossip* (New York: Alfred A. Knopf, 1985), 6, and the chapter "Borderlands," where she analyzes this nebulous area of literary production; and Norbert Elias, *The Court Society*, trans. Edmund Jephcott (New York: Pantheon Books, 1983), 74, where he explains the public nature of all behavior in the court context.

6. Woolf, "Madame de Sévigné," 41.

7. Jean Cordelier, *Madame de Sévigné par elle-même* (Paris: Editions du Seuil, 1973), 35.

8. Louise K. Horowitz, "The Correspondence of Madame de Sévigné: Lettres ou Belles-Lettres?" *French Forum* 6 (1981): 24.

9. Louise K. Horowitz, "Madame de Sévigné," *Love and Language: A Study of the Classical French Moralist Writers* (Columbus: Ohio State University Press, 1977), 97.

10. As Roger Duchêne sees it, "Texte public, texte privé: Le Cas des lettres de Madame de Sévigné," *Papers on French Seventeenth Century Literature* 8, 15, 2 (1981): 46–47.

11. The pronoun *on* derives its power precisely from its imprecision, invoking what Louis Marin refers to as the "doxa vaga," or "sapience collective," this anonymous consensus, guardian of propriety. *Le Récit est un piège* (Paris: Les Editions de Minuit, 1978), 32.

12. Roger Duchêne, "Texte public," 62.

13. Roger Duchêne tends to dismiss this interpretation as implausible and to

count allusions to publication in the *Correspondance* as mere instances of hyperbolic flattery. See I, L. 152, n. 7, p. 1046.

14. Bray discusses the private/public nature of personal correspondences in Jean Chapelain, *Soixante-dix-sept Lettres inédites à Nicolas Heinsius (1649–1658)*, intro. Bernard Alain Bray (The Hague: Martinus Nijhoff, 1965), 60.

15. Nicole is frequently cited in the *Correspondance* for his persuasive style, but his pairing here with Voiture is an aberration (and the daughter's, not the mother's, who merely echos it) of the more usual Voiture-Balzac pairing.

16. In his Introduction to the *Correspondance*, Roger Duchêne speculates:

> Si la marquise s'est souciée de voir de ses lettres à son cousin lues par un "tiers," fût-il un roi dont elle admirait la grandeur, l'esprit et le bon goût, combien se serait-elle émue de voir tomber dans les mains du public tout ce qu'on a conservé d'elle. (I, p. viii)

> If the marquise worried about seeing her letters to her cousin read by a "third party," be it even a king whose greatness, wit and good taste she admired, how disturbed she would have been to see all that remained of her fall into the hands of the public.

6. Constructs of Maternity (pp. 155–86)

1. Simone de Beauvoir, *Le Deuxième Sexe: Livre II. L'Expérience vécue*, pt. 4, chap. 12, "Enfance" (Paris: Gallimard, 1949), 13; the English translation is from *The Second Sex*, trans. and ed. H. M. Parschley (New York: Vintage Books, 1974), 301.

2. See Nicole Bonvalet, "Etudes parallèles: Lorsque les femmes lisent Madame de Sévigné," *Oeuvres et critiques* 5, 1 (automne 1980): 121–42, for an extensive bibliography of women's writings on Sévigné, some of them pedagogical tools written explicitly for the edification of young women students.

3. Carolyn G. Heilbrun, *Writing a Woman's Life* (New York: W. W. Norton, 1988), 130.

4. See chap. 4 and references especially to François de Grenaille, *L'Honneste fille* (Paris: chez Antoine de Sommauille et Toussainct Quinet, 1639–40).

5. See Carolyn C. Lougee, *Le Paradis des femmes: Women, Salons, and Social Stratification in Seventeenth-Century France* (Princeton, N.J.: Princeton University Press, 1976), pt. 1: "Feminism," 11–55; pt. 2: "Antifeminism," 59–110.

6. Luce Irigaray, *Et l'une ne bouge pas sans l'autre* (Paris: Editions de Minuit, 1979), 18–19.

7. Carol Gilligan, *In a Different Voice: Psychological Theory and Women's Development* (Cambridge, Mass.: Harvard University Press, 1982).

8. Jean de La Fontaine, *Oeuvres complètes*, vol. 1, *Fables, Contes et Nouvelles* (Mayenne: Bibliothèque de la Pléiade, 1954), 167–68.

9. *Correspondance*, III, Index, p. 1830, "fables, La Fontaine, II: 242, 472, 473, 758, 772, 773."

10. Molière, *L'Ecole des femmes*, act 5, sc. 9, l. 1764, *Oeuvres complètes*, ed. Georges Couton (Paris: Editions Gallimard, Bibliothèque de la Pléiade, 1971), tome 1.

11. Some readers of the *Correspondance*, such as Eva Avigdor, emphasize the quality of intertextuality in the Sévigné letters and read the literary allusions as ample evidence of a cultivated mind. Others, such as Roger Duchêne, see foremost in the letters the documentation of an obsessive and authentic maternal love.

Another group, best represented by Bernard Bray, sees the letters as conscious attempts to cultivate the art of writing and produce literature. Yet other critics, in particular Robert Nicolich, concentrate on the writer's tendency to dramatize daily life around her, and they comment on her frequent recourse to a lexicon of theatre, signaling these as signs of her will to reinvent and rewrite life. Still others, most especially Guénoun, recognize the therapeutic value for Sévigné of writing out her obsessions. See Eva Avigdor, *Mme de Sévigné: Un Portrait intellectuel et moral* (Paris: Nizet, 1974), 111–51; Roger Duchêne, *Réalité vécue et art épistolaire: Mme de Sévigné et la lettre d'amour* (Paris: Bordas, 1970), 307; Bernard Bray, "Quelques Aspects du système épistolaire de Madame de Sévigné," *Revue d'histoire littéraire de la France* 69 (1969): 491–505; Bray, "L'Epistolière au miroir: Réciprocité, réponse et rivalité dans les lettres de Mme de Sévigné à sa fille," *Marseille* 95, 4e trimestre (1973): 23–29; Robert Nicolich, "Life as Theatre in the Letters of Madame de Sévigné," *Romance Notes* 16 (1975): 376–82; Solange Guénoun, "Correspondance et paradoxe," *Papers on French Seventeenth Century Literature* 8, 15, 2 (1981): 137–52.

12. Marianne Hirsch, "Mothers and Daughters," *Signs: Journal of Women in Culture and Society* 7 (1981), 218, alerts readers to the problematic nature of the *I* or the *je* when the referent is a female subject:

Female identity in fiction can no longer be studied in the context of traditional ego psychology that fails to take into account women's fluid ego boundaries. As Jean Baker Miller states, "The ego, the 'I' of psychoanalysis may not be at all appropriate when talking about women. Women have different organizing principles around which their psyches are structured." Literary critics are discovering these differences in women's literature and are beginning to study not separate and autonomous female characters but relationships between characters. Relationships between women emerge as important, alternate, often submerged plots.

13. Jane Flax, "The Conflict between Nurturance and Autonomy in Mother-Daughter Relationships and within Feminism," *Feminist Studies* 4 (1978): 174.

14. Hirsch, 211.

15. Irigaray, 22.

16. Théophile de Viau, *Pyrame et Thisbé*, act 4, sc. 1, ll. 765–68; my emphasis.

17. Such a distinction brings to mind Aristotle's equation of man with active form, of woman with receptive matter and emotion, and therefore of woman's consequent inferiority. See, for example, Aristotle, *Politics*, trans. Ernest Barker (Oxford: Clarendon Press, 1946), bk. 1, chap. 12.

18. Nancy Chodorow, *The Reproduction of Mothering: Psychoanalysis and the Sociology of Gender* (Berkeley and Los Angeles: University of California Press, 1978), 169.

19. As Goffman states it, "the 'self' as a performed character . . . is a dramatic effect, arising diffusely from a scene that is presented, and the characteristic issue, the crucial concern is whether it will be credited or discredited." Erving Goffman, *The Presentation of Self in Everyday Life* (London: Pelican Books, 1971), 244–45.

20. Louise K. Horowitz, "The Correspondence of Madame de Sévigné: Lettres ou Belles-Lettres?" *French Forum* 6, 1 (January 1981): 13–27, also interrogates the sociability of the mother's letters.

21. Meredith Skura, *The Literary Uses of the Psychoanalytic Process* (New Haven, Conn.: Yale University Press, 1981), 90.

22. On the "essentialism"-"constructionism" debate generally, see Diana Fuss, *Essentially Speaking: Feminism, Nature, and Difference* (New York: Routledge, 1989).

23. Julia Kristeva, "Stabat Mater," *Histoires d'amour* (Paris: Editions Denoël, 1983), 244. Although it is not in the scope of this study to explore, it is intriguing that three years later, in the English translation of this essay, this passage is missing: see Kristeva, "Stabat Mater," trans. Arthur Goldhammer, in *The Female Body in Western Culture: Contemporary Perspectives*, ed. Susan Rubin Suleiman (Cambridge, Mass.: Harvard University Press, 1986), 114.

24. Helen Longino, in "The Ideology of Competition," *Competition: A Feminist Taboo?* ed. Valerie Miner and Helen Longino (New York: Feminist Press, 1987), 248–58.

25. Sévigné's *Correspondance* is in fact one of the very first evidences we have of an interest in child rearing at all, unless the child also happens to be a future king, as is the case in Héroard's journal recording the childhood of Louis XIII.

26. Bernard Bray, "L'Epistolière au miroir," touches on the theme of the dynamic of scriptoral rivalry generated between mother and daughter in the letter exchange, but he does not extend his analysis to a consideration of the implications for the relationship between the two women.

27. Domna Stanton, "On Female Portraiture in Sévigné's Letters," *Papers on French Seventeenth-Century Literature* 8, 15, 2 (1981): 92.

28. Flax, 183, offers an interesting subtext to this discussion on reason versus feeling: "She [the woman] confirms the split between irrationality (mother) and rationality (father) experienced in early childhood. She thus recreates the patriarchal ideology present in many cultures, including our own, which splits thought from feeling in order to maintain male dominance."

29. Elisabeth Badinter, *L'Amour en plus: Histoire de l'amour maternel (XVIIe siècle–XXe siècle)* (Paris: Flammarion, 1980), 11.

30. Roland Barthes, *Mythologies* (Paris: Éditions du Seuil, 1957), 194.

31. Pierre Albouy, *Mythes et mythologies dans la littérature française* (Paris: Armand Colin, Collections U2, 1969), 40, points to the readiness of the elite of seventeenth-century France, and of Louis XIV as paragon, to fashion themselves and to be received in mythic mode:

> Dans cette civilisation aristocratique, le monarque et les grands sont . . . effectivement considérés comme des êtres d'élection, prêts à devenir des personnages, en quelque mesure, mythiques.

> In this aristocratic civilization, the monarch and the nobility are . . . effectively considered to be select creatures, ready to become, to some extent, mythic characters.

32. In Jean-Baptiste Lulli and Philippe Quinault, *Proserpine*, in *Collection des théâtres français: Suite du répertoire* (Paris: Senlis et Tremblay, 1829), vol. 13, *Grands Opéras, I*, the libretto in fact interprets the mother-daughter tie as wholly subordinated to the Jupiter-Ceres relationship that produced Persephone in the first place, and never, in the course of the entire opera, do mother and daughter exchange a word or share a scene alone as a duo:

> Hélas! qu'un tendre amour accroit l'empressement
> De la tendresse maternelle!
> Proserpine est pour moi le gage précieux
> De l'amour du plus grand des dieux:
> C'est Jupiter que j'aime en elle.   (act 3, sc. 5)

> Alas! how a tender love increases the eagerness
> Of maternal tenderness!
> Persephone is for me the precious token
> Of the love of the greatest of the gods:
> It is Jupiter I love in her.

33. This reading of the Ceres-Persephone relationship questions the idealizing of the mother-daughter relationship that feminists have celebrated in their continued citing of this particular myth (see Gilligan, 22–23; Adrienne Rich, *Of Woman Born: Motherhood as Experience and Institution* [New York: W. W. Norton, 1976] 240–43). Although it might point to a distant other history, by the seventeenth century the myth is recuperated by the dominant ideology and serves its purposes, and so the myth must be considered not as message in itself, but as vehicle for messages.

34. Barthes, *Mythologies* 207, points to the association between myth and memory:

Le concept [du mythe] . . . se donne d'une figure globale, il est une sorte de nébuleuse, la condensation plus ou moins floue d'un savoir. Ses éléments sont noués par des rapports associatifs: il est supporté non par une étendue, mais par une épaisseur . . . son mode de présence est mémoriel.

The concept [of the myth] passes as a global figure, it is a sort of Nebula, the more or less vague condensation of a body of knowledge. Its elements are tied by associative rapports: it is sustained not by a dimension, but by a density . . . its mode of presence is memorial.

35. Ibid., 215.

36. Ibid., 218.

37. Ibid., 216.

38. Julia Kristeva, "Maternité selon Giovanni Bellini," *Polylogue* (Paris: Editions du Seuil, 1977), 409–35; Kristeva, "Stabat Mater," *Histoires d'amour*, 225–47.

39. Julia Kristeva, "Women's Time," *Signs: Journal of Women in Culture and Society* 7 (1981), 29; in French: "Le Temps des femmes," *34/44: Cahiers de recherche de sciences des textes et documents* 5 (hiver 1979): 5–19.

40. Solange Guénoun, "Correspondance et paradoxe," 137, and n. 3, also reflects on the nature of Sévigné's *cogito* but integrates it with Derrida's reflections on Rousseau's "cogito sensible." Nancy K. Miller, "Women's Autobiography in France: For a Dialectics of Identification," in *Women and Language in Literature and Society*, eds. Sally McConnell-Ginet, Ruth Borker and Nelly Furman (New York: Praeger, 1980), 258–73, locates yet another *cogito* for women writing: "The cogito for Sand, Stern and Beauvoir would thus seem to be: I write, therefore I am" (266).

7. Complementary Constructions (pp. 187–231)

1. Jean de La Bruyère, "De la Société #45," *Les Caractères ou les moeurs de ce siècle* (Paris: Editions Garnier Frères, 1962), 166. La Bruyère's aphorism suggests that seventeenth-century familial relations preclude positive relations among women and are premised on affective arrangements favoring male bonding and men.

2. Auguste Bailly, *Madame de Sévigné* (Paris: Librairie Arthème Fayard, 1955). Bailly notes, 103, that from the moment of Françoise-Marguerite's marriage, Sévigné sought to make of her rival, the new husband, an accomplice:

Il faut se l'attacher, ce rival trop puissant, il faut se faire aimer de lui; il faut l'enchaîner par des liens si forts et si tendres qu'il ne puisse séparer la mère et la fille sans se déchirer lui-même. Dans le cercle de famille, il incarne désormais le personnage redoutable dont tout l'avenir dépend: le trésor est entre ses mains! Et de sa plume la plus souple, de son style le plus enveloppant, Madame de Sévigné entreprend de le séduire.

She had to attach herself to him, this too powerful rival, she must make herself loved by him; she must chain him by links so strong and tender that he could not separate the mother and the daughter without tearing himself apart as well. In the family circle, he incarnates henceforth the fearful character upon whom all the future depends; the treasure is in his hands! And with her most supple pen, with her most engaging style, Madame de Sévigné undertakes to seduce him.

3. Elisabeth Badinter, *L'Amour en plus: Histoire de l'amour maternel (XVIIe–XXe siècle)* (Paris: Flammarion, 1980), 30.

4. Jean Laplanche and J.-B. Pontalis, *Vocabulaire de la psychanalyse* (Paris: Presses Universitaires de France, 1967), 310, under "Phallique (femme ou mère)."

5. Nor should it be forgotten that Sévigné was only six years older than her son-in-law, while he was fourteen years older than Françoise-Marguerite; she was a widow, he was twice a widower; the mother-in-law and son-in-law did in fact share more of a generational worldview than the married couple.

6. His first wife, Angélique-Clarisse d'Angennes (daughter of Mme de Rambouillet) died in 1664 after the birth of her second child in 1663; his second wife, Marie-Angélique du Puy-du-Fou, died in 1667, and her infant son died in the next year.

7. Roger Duchêne, *Réalité vécue et art épistolaire: Madame de Sévigné et la lettre d'amour* (Paris: Bordas, 1970), 122.

8. Norbert Elias, *The Court Society*, trans. Edmund Jephcott (New York: Pantheon Books, 1983). Elias describes succinctly the economic bind in which the aristocracy found itself: "High rank entails the duty to own and display an appropriate house. What appears as extravagance from the standpoint of the bourgeois economic ethic—'if he was running into debt why did he not reduce his expenses?'—is in reality the expression of the seigneurial ethos of rank. This ethos grows out of the structure and activity of court society, and is at the same time a precondition for the continuance of this activity. It is not freely chosen" (53).

9. Ibid., chaps. 3, 4, 5.

10. Carolyn C. Lougee, *Le Paradis des femmes: Women, Salons, and Social Stratification in Seventeenth-Century France* (Princeton, N.J.: Princeton University Press, 1976), 48–51.

11. Lougee, 49, summarizes the gender organization of the practice: "The roturier lady gained ennoblement from the match, and the noble man the money."

12. François de Grenaille, *L'honneste fille* (Paris: chez Antoine de Sommauille et Toussainct Quinet, 1639–40), 1:137.

13. Pierre Charron, *De la sagesse* (1601), as cited in David Hunt, *Parents and Children in History: The Psychology of Family Life in France* (New York: Basic Books, 1970), 70.

14. In fact, the maternal mother-in-law does not even figure as subject in Simone de Beauvoir's reflections on that relationship: she discusses the disappointment and frustration of the married son's mother as she is displaced by his new wife (652) and dwells on the well-documented tradition of the son-in-law's misogynous feelings visited on the figure of his mother-in-law (196), but she does not attempt to enter into an understanding of that figure from the perspective of her particular position in the social configuration of the family. Simone de Beauvoir, *The Second Sex*, trans. H. M. Parschley (New York: Vintage Books, 1974).

15. Adrienne Rich, *Of Woman Born: Motherhood as Experience and Institution* (New York: W. W. Norton, 1976), 226.

16. This is not to suggest that an actual living father would have enjoyed a nec-

essarily intimate relationship with either his wife or his daughter in the seventeenth century—indeed, evidence is to the contrary; but it is to claim that passions and roles would have been distributed differently, and that they would not have been concentrated as they were in the widow-mother figure.

17. Simone de Beauvoir, *Le Deuxième Sexe* (Paris: Gallimard, 1949), bk. 2, pt. 2, "Situation"; Nancy Chodorow, *The Reproduction of Mothering: Psychoanalysis and the Sociology of Gender* (Berkeley and Los Angeles: University of California Press, 1978), chap. 7; Rich, chap. 9.

18. My calculation of the number of separations is slightly at variance with Roger Duchêne's (I, pp. xxi–xxx): in his chronology, he counts eight explicitly but documents nine; I include that between 5 October 1673, when Sévigné left her daughter in Provence, and February 1674, when Mme de Grignan joined her in Paris.

19. Jane Flax, "The Conflict between Nurturance and Autonomy in Mother-Daughter Relationships and within Feminism," *Feminist Studies* 4, (1978): 186, comments on the negative influence that mothers and women can unwittingly exert on themselves and each other: "Women become the instruments of their own oppression, just as mothers unconsciously deny or repress their daughters' moves toward autonomy. 'Love' is put into the service of oppression and the perpetuation of powerlessness. The life-giver becomes the life-denier."

20. The first letter penned by Sévigné in the entire collection is dated 1648; the last, 1696.

21. Grenaille, *L'Honneste fille*, 1:221–22.

22. Dorothy Dinnerstein, *The Mermaid and the Minotaur: Sexual Arrangements and Social Malaise* (New York: Harper & Row, 1977), chap. 6.

23. In his youth, Charles de Sévigné regularly cut down the forests of the family property of Le Buron and sold the wood for ready income.

24. See "Patterns of Excellence," chap. 6.

25. "J'ai tant fait que nos gens sont enfin dans la plaine"; see "The Art of Vicarious Living," chap. 6.

8. "The Reproduction of Mothering" (pp. 232–50)

1. Nancy Chodorow, *The Reproduction of Mothering: Psychoanalysis and the Sociology of Gender* (Berkeley and Los Angeles: University of California Press, 1978), 209. This is not an unproblematic statement: not all daughters become mothers upon reaching female adulthood, yet they do all become "women." The distinction between "woman" and "mother" needs to be respected and explored beyond the internalization of the mother in the daughter implied. However, here, Sévigné does produce a daughter who becomes a mother in turn, and Chodorow's study is useful in studying the transmission of "mothering" in this continuum. I focus, though, on the relaying of the sociocultural construction of "mothering" and problematize rather than explain or valorize this female-identified role as the locus of gender difference.

2. Elizabeth V. Spelman, *Inessential Woman: Problems of Exclusion in Feminist Thought* (Boston: Beacon Press, 1988).

3. Roger Duchêne, *Réalité vécue et art épistolaire: Madame de Sévigné et la lettre d'amour* (Paris: Bordas, 1970), 195.

4. In *Madame de Sévigné par elle-même* (Paris: Editions du Seuil, 1973), 77,

Jean Cordelier offers a Proustian interpretation of the relationship, casting Mme de Grignan as "un de ces êtres de fuite" [one of these creatures in flight].

5. Thanks to English Showalter for pointing out the difference that age brings to perspective, and how this might help to explain the difference between Sévigné's own parenting practices and those she recommends to her daughter.

6. Other reasons contribute as well to explain the lack of bonding between Mme de Grignan and her first child: disappointment in having produced a daughter rather than a son; the high infant mortality rate that discouraged parents from becoming attached to children until their lives were more securely assured; and the common practice in certain classes of entrusting infants to wet nurses and governesses in their first years of life; thus relationships between mothers and their infants cannot be explained in purely psychological terms but must be understood in the sociohistoric context of the moment of their enactment.

7. Nancy Chodorow's general argument; and Jane Flax, "The Conflict between Nurturance and Autonomy in Mother-Daughter Relationships and within Feminism," *Feminist Studies* 4 (1978): 171–89.

8. Victor Hugo, *Oeuvres complètes*, XVI–XVII/1, ed. Jean Massin (Paris: Le Club Français du Livre, 1970), 910.

9. Philippe Ariès, *L'Enfant et la vie familiale sous l'ancien régime* (Paris: Editions du Seuil, 1973). Ariès, sensitive to Sévigné's talent for rendering the behavior and appearance of children in her letters, compares her representations of her grandchildren to le Nain's genre paintings and Basse's engravings (73).

10. Elisabeth Badinter, *L'Amour en plus: Histoire de l'amour maternel (XVIIe–XXe siècle)* (Paris: Flammarion, 1980), 129. Here she points out that, in the seventeenth century, infant mortality was over 25 percent for children under a year old.

11. François de Grenaille, *L'Honneste fille* (Paris: chez Antoine de Sommauille et Toussainct Quinet, 1639–40), 1:84. It is worth noting that, although de Grenaille postulated distinct paternal and maternal spheres of influence, he himself not only wrote authoritatively on *L'Honneste garçon* (1642) but also felt free to pronounce first on *L'Honneste fille*, and whereas in the former he simply exercised the authority he had arrogated to himself, in the latter he prescribed behavior not only for daughters but for their mothers as well.

12. Ariès, 180. This documentation is somewhat circular since Ariès draws heavily from Sévigné's letters in his study.

13. Ian Maclean, *Woman Triumphant: Feminism in French Literature: 1610–1652* (Oxford: Clarendon Press, 1977). Maclean notes: "While in the second half of the seventeenth century women were able to acquire learning and culture in adult life, little action was taken to provide for girls the same education as their brothers" (154).

14. Patrocinio P. Schweickart, "Reading Ourselves: Toward a Feminist Theory of Reading," in *Gender and Reading: Essays on Readers, Texts and Contexts*, ed. E. A. Flynn and P. P. Schweickart (Baltimore: Johns Hopkins University Press, 1986), 42.

15. In François de Grenaille's *Nouveau recueil de lettres des dames tant anciennes que modernes* (Paris: chez Toussainct Quinet, 1642), two model letters (both probably fictions by the author of the "collection") are included on the subject of committing young girls to life in the convent: L. IX from Mme de Gongy to her daughter is encapsulated thus: "Sur le fait qu'elle doit aller au couvent puisqu'elle n'a et n'aura jamais d'argent" (p. 391) [On the fact that she must go to a convent

since she doesn't and will never have any money]; L. XII features a friend's advice to Mme de Gongy that she test her young daughter's vocation before agreeing to her decision. Both Sévigné and her daughter, then, are perhaps simply enacting attitudes that are already culturally encoded, textually circulated, and presumably in practice.

16. Badinter, 79–83.

17. See I, Chronologie, p. xxviii. Sévigné may also have realized that her own attentions to the grandchild might only alienate the mother from her. She may have deliberately minimized her interest in order not to jeopardize the mother-daughter relationship, as had perhaps happened in the case of Marie-Blanche.

18. And this notion was already prevalent in seventeenth-century treatises on the education of children: see Carolyn C. Lougee, *Le Paradis des femmes: Women, Salons, and Social Stratification in Seventeenth-Century France* (Princeton, N.J.: Princeton University Press, 1976), 68.

19. For analyses of the relational nature of women, as a consequence of roles assigned them in patriarchal society, see Chodorow; Carol Gilligan, *In a Different Voice: Psychological Theory and Women's Development* (Cambridge, Mass.: Harvard University Press, 1982). For documentation of the actual pedagogic use to which the Sévigné letters were put, see Fritz Nies, "La Fortune des lettres," *Papers on French Seventeenth-Century Literature* 8, 15, 2(1981): 129–35; Nies, *Gattungspoetik und Publikumsstruktur zur Geschichte der Sévignébriefe* (Munich: Wilhelm Fink Verlag, 1972).

20. An ongoing dispute, dating from the Middle Ages and having its roots in the misogynist teachings of the Church, that pitted defenders of women against their detractors and found voice in various literary works produced through the seventeenth century.

21. Poullain de la Barre, *De l'égalité des deux sexes* (Paris: Fayard, 1984), originally appeared in 1673; Charles Perrault, *Apologie des femmes* (Paris: Editions Gibert Jeune, Librairie d'Amateurs, 1694).

22. Nicolas Boileau-Despréaux, Satire X, "Contre les femmes," *Oeuvres complètes*, ed. Charles-H. Boudhors (Paris: Société des Belles Lettres, 1960); Maclean, 35–38.

23. Maïté Albistur and Daniel Armogathe, *Histoire du féminisme français du moyen âge à nos jours*, t.1. (Paris: des femmes, 1977), 174–247.

24. Molière, *L'Ecole des femmes*, act 3, sc. 3, 11. 810–12, *Oeuvres complètes* ed. Georges Couton (Paris: Editions Gallimard, Bibliothèque de la Pléiade, 1971), tome 1. Bernard Magne, "L'Ecole des femmes ou la conquête de la parole," *Revue des sciences humaines* 37, 145 (January–March 1972): 127, n. 11, emphasizes the direct articulation of the will to power that this passage represents.

25. At the time of this letter (December 1688), Pauline was fourteen years old; another letter, dated barely a month later (24 January 1689), has Sévigné reporting on her grandson's social life in Paris: "Votre enfant fut hier au bal chez M. de Chartres. Il était fort joli; il vous mandera de ses prospérités" (III, L. 1060, p. 482) [Your child was at the ball at M. de Chartres's yesterday. He was very handsome; he will send you word of his success]; while a difference in age must be kept in mind (her brother was then eighteen), the semantic field that encodes Pauline and her older sister, Marie-Blanche, consistently features images of enclosure, "prison," "chambre," while their brother circulates and enjoys freedom of movement; although he was being literally, that is physically, disciplined for his role in life as well, it was obviously to be a differently circumscribed one from that of his sisters.

26. See Duchêne's helpful note, III, L. 1194, n. 8, p. 1546, in which he identifies the textual allusion as being to one of the psalms recited during Holy Week.

27. Nathaniel Adam, secrétaire de Madame de Mortemart, *Le Secrétaire français* (Paris: Anthoine du Breuil, 1616), (7–8), takes pains to valorize his own profession:

> Entre tous les offices qui defpendent [*sic*] d'un royaume, d'une République ou d'une grande maison bien régie, il semble qu'il n'y en ayt point de plus celebre ny de plus honnorable que celuy du Secrétaire.

> Of all the functions that depend on a kingdom, a Republic, or a well-governed great house, it seems that there is none more celebrated or more honorable than that of Secretary.

and then goes on to describe the privileged relationship:

> ... un tel officier est plus familier et plus proche de son maistre que nul autre, participant ordinairement en ses conseils et plus importantes affaires, le servant non seulement és [*sic*] choses du corps, mais davantage en celles de l'esprit, dont le soulagement est inestimable.

> ... such an officer is more familiar with and closer to his master than anyone else, usually participating in his decisions and his most important concerns, serving him not only materially, but especially intellectually, the comfort of which is invaluable.

and so, here again, Sévigné is proposing a relationship that is already in place, if borrowed from another sphere, the terms of which ("familier," "servant," "soulagement") are recognizable in her own discourse.

28. Bernard Bray, "Quelques Aspects du système épistolaire de Mme de Sévigné," *Revue d'histoire littéraire de la France* 69 (1969). Bray goes into slightly greater detail than Roger Duchêne in pointing to this troublesome fact, and in inculpating Pauline:

> Il est vrai que Mme de Grignan avait probablement en vue une édition dans laquelle sa propre contribution fût conservée: Mme de Simiane [Pauline], par la destruction dont elle se rendit coupable en 1734, amputa une oeuvre amébée de l'une de ses parties constituantes. (505)

> It is true that Mme de Grignan probably had in mind an edition in which her own contribution would be conserved: Mme de Simiane [Pauline], by the destruction of which she was guilty in 1734, amputated a nascent work of one of its constitutive parts.

29. This is roughly the project of Jacqueline Duchêne, *Françoise de Grignan, ou le mal d'amour* (Paris: Fayard, 1985).

Envoi (pp. 251–61)

1. Carolyn Heilbrun, *Writing A Woman's Life* (New York: W. W. Norton, 1988), 37. I am not totally persuaded by the statement that the story of a woman's life is more powerful than the living example of a woman's life, except to the extent that even that example is transformed by the observer into narrative in the very process of perception, that the point of the story is always furnished from outside the story itself.

2. This passage is reminiscent of Sara Ruddick's work on "Maternal Thinking," *Feminist Studies* 6, 2 (Summer 1980): 342–67. As she puts it: "Humility which emerges from maternal practices . . . is not a peculiar habit of self-effacement, rather like having an inaudible voice, it is selfless respect for reality and one of the most difficult and central of virtues."

3. Virginia Woolf, "Madame de Sévigné," *Collected Essays* (New York: Harcourt, Brace, & World, 1967), 3:66–67.

4. When I state that the woman writer was "steeped in an androcentric litera-

ture that mirrors the world as men order it," I should specify that I am alluding more precisely to Sévigné, referring to the authors and works she cites in her letters (readily available through the index of the Duchêne edition), that these are, by an overwhelming majority, works penned by male authors. I do not believe she is an exceptional seventeenth-century reader in this regard, but I would wager that research on other women writers would bear out the same conclusion; although a female-authored book might have attracted more attention by virtue of its exceptionality and its novel perspective, and although there was a significant increase in the production of such texts during Sévigné's time, this does not alter the fact that most of the books circulated and read then were written and arbitrated by men; I think it important to distinguish between wanting to recover the heritage of a female literary tradition as an enabling twentieth-century tool for feminist theorists, critics, and women writers and idealizing that heritage into a model that, for all its glory, is ultimately both less accurate and less pragmatically useful in the negotiating of contemporary experience, that would romanticize a "separate spheres" construction of women's writing.

5. Annette Kolodny, "A Map for Rereading: Gender and the Interpretation of Literary Texts," in *The New Feminist Criticism*, ed. Elaine Showalter (New York: Pantheon, 1985), 59.

6. Patrocinio P. Schweickart, "Reading Ourselves: Toward a Feminist Theory of Reading," in *Gender and Reading: Essays on Readers, Texts, and Contexts*, ed. Elizabeth A. Flynn and Patrocinio P. Schweickart (Baltimore: Johns Hopkins University Press, 1986), 41–42.

7. Heilbrun, 121. I do not agree with the implicit valorizing of "quest plot" in Heilbrun's argument but see it rather as yet another problematic pole.

8. René Descartes, *Discours de la Méthode* (Paris: Garnier-Flammarion, 1966), 45. It is tempting to wander a bit here, to consider to what extent the construction of meaning in isolation contributes to the conceptualization of knowledge as a commodity and of the thinker/writer as author/possessor/negotiator of this commodity. Now in interdisciplinary work where sharing and exchange are taking place, and at an ever increased velocity, given the technology of communication, the author is no longer viewed as originary, is no longer privileged; ideas are simply put into circulation; hence the crises around plagiarism—as it becomes an obsolete concept—the logical consequence of the reintroduction of the conversational model into scholarly discourse.

9. Ibid., 57.

10. See "Patterns of Excellence," chap. 6.

11. I thank, among many others, Jane Gallop and Elizabeth Long in particular for helpful conversations on early versions of this chapter, and Elizabeth for a careful reading.

Bibliography

Adam, Antoine. *Histoire de la littérature française.* Vols. 1, 2, and 4. Paris: Editions Domat Montchrestien, 1948.

Adam, Nathaniel. *Le Secrétaire français.* Paris: Anthoine du Breuil, 1616.

Albistur, Maïté, and Daniel Armogathe. *Histoire du féminisme français: Du moyen âge à nos jours.* Tome 1. Paris: des femmes, 1977.

Albouy, Pierre. *Mythes et mythologies dans la littérature française.* Paris: Armand Colin, Collections U2, 1969.

Allentuch, Harriet Ray. *Madame de Sévigné: A Portrait in Letters.* Baltimore: Johns Hopkins Press, 1963.

———. "My Daughter/Myself: Emotional Roots of Madame de Sévigné's Art." *Modern Language Quarterly* 43, 2 (June 1982): 121–37.

Altman, Janet Gurkin. *Epistolarity: Approaches to a Form.* Columbus: Ohio State University Press, 1982.

———. "The Letter Book as a Literary Institution 1539–1789: Toward a Cultural History of Published Correspondences in France." *Yale French Studies* 71 (1986): 17–62.

Apostolides, Jean-Marie. *Le Roi-Machine: Spectacle et politique au temps de Louis XIV.* Paris: Editions de Minuit, 1981.

Ariès, Philippe. *L'Enfant et la vie familiale sous l'ancien régime.* Paris: Editions du Seuil, 1973.

Aristotle. *The "Art" of Rhetoric.* Translated by J. H. Freese. Cambridge, Mass.: Harvard University Press, Loeb Classical Library, 1959.

———. *Politics.* Translated by Ernest Barker. Oxford: Clarendon Press, 1946.

Austin, J. L. *How to Do Things with Words.* Cambridge, Mass.: Harvard University Press, 1962.

Avigdor, Eva. *Madame de Sévigné: Un Portrait intellectuel et moral.* Paris: Nizet, 1974.

Badinter, Elisabeth. *L'Amour en plus: Histoire de l'amour maternel (XVIIe–XXe siècle).* Paris: Flammarion, 1980.

Bailly, Auguste. *Madame de Sévigné.* Paris: Librairie Arthème Fayard, 1955.

Balzac, Guez de. *Les Premières Lettres de Guez de Balzac, 1618–1627.* Edited by H. Bibas and K.-T. Butler. Tome 1. Paris: Librairie Droz, 1933.

Barthes, Roland. *Fragments d'un discours amoureux.* Paris: Editions du Seuil, 1977.

————. *Mythologies*. Paris: Editions du Seuil, 1957.

————. "La Bruyère." *Essais Critiques*. Paris: Editions du Seuil, 1964.

Beauvoir, Simone de. *Le Deuxième Sexe*. Paris: Editions Gallimard, 1949. Translated as *The Second Sex* by H. M. Parschley. New York: Vintage Books, 1974.

————. *Mémoires d'une jeune fille rangée*. Paris: Gallimard, 1958. Translated as *Memoirs of a Dutiful Daughter* by James Kirkup. New York: Harper Torchbooks, 1958.

Beugnot, Bernard. "Débats autour du genre épistolaire: Réalité et écriture." *Revue d'histoire littéraire de la France* 74 (1974): 195–202.

Boileau-Despréaux, Nicolas. "Réflexions critiques sur quelques passages du Rhéteur Longin," and Satire X: "Contre les femmes." *Oeuvres complètes de Boileau*. Edited by Charles-H. Boudhors. Paris: Société des Belles Lettres, 1960.

Bonvalet, Nicole. "Etudes parallèles: Lorsque les femmes lisent Mme de Sévigné." *Oeuvres et critiques* 5, 1 (automne 1980): 121–42.

Borgerhoff, E. B. O. *The Freedom of French Classicism*. Princeton, N.J.: Princeton University Press, 1950.

Boscq, Charles Du. *Nouveau Recueil de lettres des dames de ce temps avec leurs réponses*. 3d ed. Paris: A. Courbé, 1642.

Bray, Bernard. "L'Epistolier et son public en France au XVIIe siècle." *Travaux de linguistique et de littérature* 2, 11 (1973): 7–17.

————. "L'Epistolière au miroir: Réciprocité, réponse et rivalité dans les lettres de Madame de Sévigné à sa fille." *Marseille* 95, 4e trimestre (1973): 23–29.

————. "Quelques Aspects du système épistolaire de Madame de Sévigné." *Revue d'histoire littéraire de la France* 69 (1969): 491–505.

————. "Les 'Voitures' de Mme de Sévigné." *Romanische Forschungen* 83 (1971): 596–602.

Bussy-Rabutin, Roger de. *Histoire amoureuse des Gaules par Bussy-Rabutin*. Revue et annotée par P. Boiteau. 4 vols. Paris, 1856.

Cardinal, Marie. *Les Mots pour le dire*. Paris: Bernard Grasset, 1975.

Chapelain, Jean. *Soixante-dix-sept Lettres inédites à Nicolas Heinsius (1649–1658)*. Introduction by Bernard Alain Bray. The Hague: Martinus Nijhoff, 1965.

Chodorow, Nancy. *The Reproduction of Mothering: Psychoanalysis and the Sociology of Gender*. Berkeley and Los Angeles: University of California Press, 1978.

Cordelier, Jean. *Madame de Sévigné par elle-même*. Paris: Editions du Seuil, 1973.

Couton, Georges. Review of Madame de Sévigné, *Correspondance*, ed. Duchêne. *Studi francesi* 18 (1974): 505.

DeJean, Joan. "Lafayette's Ellipses: The Privileges of Anonymity." *PMLA* 99, 5 (1984): 884–901.

Derrida, Jacques. *Of Grammatology*. Trans. Gayatri Chakravorty Spivak. Baltimore: Johns Hopkins University Press, 1976.

Descartes, René. *Discours de la méthode*. Paris: Garnier-Flammarion, 1966.

Dinnerstein, Dorothy. *The Mermaid and the Minotaur: Sexual Arrangements and Human Malaise*. New York: Harper & Row, 1977.

Duchêne, Jacqueline. *Françoise de Grignan ou le mal d'amour*. Paris: Librairie Arthème Fayard, 1985.

Duchêne, Roger. *Réalité vécue et art épistolaire: Madame de Sévigné et la lettre d'amour*. Paris: Bordas, 1970.

————. "Madame de Sévigné et le style négligé." *Oeuvres et critiques* 1, 2 (été 1976): 113–27.

————. *Madame de Sévigné ou la chance d'être femme*. Paris: Fayard, 1982.

————. "Texte public, texte privé: Le Cas des lettres de Madame de Sévigné." *Papers on French Seventeenth Century Literature* 8, 15, 2 (1981): 31–69.

Du Plaisir, *Sentimens sur les lettres et sur l'histoire avec des scrupules sur le stile.* Paris: C. Blageart, 1683.

Duras, Marguerite. *L'Amant*. Paris: Editions de Minuit, 1984.

Elias, Norbert. *The Court Society*. Translated by Edmund Jephcott. New York: Pantheon Books, 1983.

Faret, Nicolas. *L'Honneste Homme ou l'art de plaire à la cour*. Edited by Maurice Magendie. Paris: Presses Universitaires de la France, 1925.

Flax, Jane. "The Conflict between Nurturance and Autonomy in Mother-Daughter Relationships and within Feminism." *Feminist Studies* 4 (1978): 171–89.

Furetière, Antoine. *Dictionnaire universel contenant généralement tous les mots français tant vieux que modernes et les termes de touts les sciences et des arts.* Geneva: Slatkine Reprints, 1970.

Fuss, Diana. *Essentially Speaking: Feminism, Nature, and Difference*. New York: Routledge, 1989.

Gilbert, Sandra, and Susan Gubar, eds. *The Norton Anthology of Literature by Women: The English Tradition*. New York: W. W. Norton, 1985.

Gilligan, Carol. *In a Different Voice: Psychological Theory and Women's Development*. Cambridge, Mass.: Harvard University Press, 1982.

Goffman, Erving. *The Presentation of Self in Everyday Life*. London: Pelican Books, 1971.

Goldsmith, Elizabeth. "Bridging Distances: Writing as Displacement and Location in the Letters of Madame de Sévigné." *Dissertation Abstracts* 41:1 (1980): 273A (Cornell).

————. "Proust on Madame de Sévigné's Letters: Some Aspects of Epistolary Writing." *Papers on French Seventeenth Century Literature* 8, 15, 2 (1981): 117–27.

Gombaud, Antoine, chevalier de Méré. *Oeuvres complètes*. Texte établi et présenté par Charles-H. Boudhors. Paris: Editions Fernand Roches, 1930.

Gray, Floyd. *Le Style de Montaigne*. Paris: Librairie Nizet, 1958.

Grenaille, François de. *L'Honneste fille*. 3 vols. Paris: chez Antoine de Sommauille et Toussainct Quinet, 1639–40.

————. *Nouveau recueil de lettres des dames tant anciennes que modernes*. Paris: chez Toussainct Quinet, 1642.

Guénoun, Solange. "La Correspondance de Madame de Sévigné: Une Séparation littéraire." *Dissertation Abstracts* 41:10 (1981): 4412A (Princeton).

————. "Correspondance et paradoxe." *Papers on French Seventeenth Century Literature* 8, 15, 2 (1981): 31–69.

Guilleragues, Gabriel de Lavergne, sieur de. *Lettres portugaises. Lettres portugaises, Lettres d'une péruvienne, et autres romans d'amour par lettres*. Textes établis, présentés et annotés par Bernard Bray et Isabelle Landy-Houillon. Paris: Garnier Flammarion, 1983.

Heilbrun, Carolyn. *Writing A Woman's Life*. New York: W. W. Norton, 1988.

Hirsch, Marianne. "Mothers and Daughters." *Signs: Journal of Women in Culture and Society* 7 (autumn 1981): 200–22.

————. "A Mother's Discourse: Incorporation and Repetition in *La Princesse de Clèves*." *Yale French Studies* 62 (1981): 67–87.

Horowitz, Louise K. *Love and Language: A Study of the Classical French Moralist Writers*. Columbus: Ohio State University Press, 1977.

———. "The Correspondence of Madame de Sévigné: Lettres ou Belles-Lettres?" *French Forum* 6 (1981): 13–27.

Hugo, Victor. *Oeuvres complètes*. XVI–XVII/1. Edited by Jean Massin. Paris: Le Club Français du Livre, 1970.

Hunt, David. *Parents and Children in History: The Psychology of Family Life in Early Modern France*. New York: Basic Books, 1970.

Irigaray, Luce. *Et l'une ne bouge pas sans l'autre*. Paris: Editions de Minuit, 1979.

Kamuf, Peggy. *Fictions of Feminine Desire*. Lincoln: University of Nebraska Press, 1982.

Kany, Charles E. *The Beginnings of the Epistolary Novel in France, Italy, and Spain*. University of California Publications in Modern Philology, vol. 21, no. 1. Berkeley: University of California, 1939.

Klaits, Joseph. *Printed Propaganda under Louis XIV: Absolute Monarchy and Public Opinion*. Princeton, N.J.: Princeton University Press, 1976.

Kolodny, Annette. "A Map for Rereading: Gender and the Interpretation of Literary Texts." In *The New Feminist Criticism*, edited by Elaine Showalter, 46–62. New York: Pantheon, 1985.

Kristeva, Julia. "Maternité selon Giovanni Bellini." *Polylogue*. Paris: Editions du Seuil, 1977.

———. "Stabat Mater." *Histoires d'amour*. Paris: Editions Denoël, 1983; and translated by Arthur Goldhammer in *The Female Body in Western Culture: Contemporary Perspectives*, edited by Susan Rubin Suleiman, 99–118. Cambridge, Mass.: Harvard University Press, 1986.

———. "Women's Time." *Signs: Journal of Women in Culture and Society* 7 (1981): 13–35; in French: "Le Temps des femmes." *34/44: Cahiers de recherche de sciences des textes et documents* 5 (hiver 1979): 5–19.

La Bruyère, Jean de. *Les Caractères ou les moeurs de ce siècle*. Paris: Garnier Frères, 1962.

La Fontaine, Jean de. *Oeuvres complètes*. Edited by Pierre Clarac, René Groos, and Jacques Schiffrin. Mayenne: Gallimard, Bibliothèque de la Pléiade, 1954.

Lacan, Jacques. *Ecrits, A Selection*. Translated by Alan Sheridan. New York: W. W. Norton, 1977.

Lafon, Henri René. "Les Grands Écrivains et la poste: Madame de Sévigné et la poste." *Revue des P.T.T. de France* XIe année (mai–juin 1956): 38–42.

Laplanche, Jean, and J. B. Pontalis. *Vocabulaire de la psychanalyse*. Paris: Presses Universitaires de la France, 1967.

Lapp, John C. *The Esthetics of Negligence: La Fontaine's Contes*. Cambridge: Cambridge University Press, 1971.

La Serre, Jean Puget de. *Le Secrétaire à la mode*. Amsterdam: Jean Janssen, 1655.

Leduc, Violette. *L'Asphyxie*. Paris: Gallimard, 1946.

Léger, Susan. "Reading in (the) Place of the Daughter: The Letters of Madame de Sévigné." Special Session, "Feminist Readings, Filial Pieties: Daughters in/and/ of Texts." MLA convention, New York, 1986.

Longino, Helen. "The Ideology of Competition." In *Competition: A Feminist Taboo?* edited by Valerie Miner and Helen Longino, 248–58. New York: Feminist Press, 1987.

Lougee, Carolyn C. *Le Paradis des femmes: Women, Salons, and Social Strati-*

fication in Seventeenth-Century France. Princeton, N.J.: Princeton University Press, 1976.

Lulli, Jean-Baptiste, and Thomas Quinault. *Proserpine.* In *Collection des théâtres français: Suite du répertoire,* vol. 13. Paris: Senlis et Tremblay, 1829.

MacKinnon, Catherine. "Feminism, Marxism, Method, and the State: An Agenda for Theory." In *The Signs Reader: Women, Gender, and Scholarship,* edited by Elizabeth Abel and Emily K. Abel, 227–56. Chicago: University of Chicago Press, 1983.

Maclean, Ian. *Woman Triumphant: Feminism in French Literature (1610–1652).* Oxford: Clarendon Press, 1977.

Magne, Emile. "L'Ecole des femmes ou la conquête de la parole." *Revue des sciences humaines* 37, 145 (January–March 1972): 125–40.

———. *Voiture et les origines de l'hôtel de Rambouillet, 1597–1635.* Paris: Mercure de France, 1911.

———. *Voiture et l'Hôtel de Rambouillet: Les Années de gloire, 1635–1648.* Paris: Editions Emile-Paul Frères, 1930.

Marin, Louis. *La Critique du discours.* Paris: Editions de Minuit, 1975.

———. *Le Récit est un piège.* Paris: Editions de Minuit, 1978.

———. *Le Portrait du roi.* Paris: Editions de Minuit, 1981.

Marion, Marcel. *Dictionnaire des institutions de la France aux XVIIe et XVIIIe siècles.* Reprint of the original 1923 edition. Paris: Picard, 1989.

Mauss, Marcel. *The Gift: Forms and Functions of Exchange in Archaic Societies.* Translated by Ian Cunnison. New York: W. W. Norton, 1967.

Miller, Nancy K. "Emphasis Added: Plots and Plausibilities in Women's Fiction." *PMLA* 96, 1 (1981): 36–48.

———. "Women's Autobiography in France: For a Dialectics of Identification." In *Women and Language in Literature and Society,* edited by Sally McConnell-Ginet, Ruth Borker and Nelly Furman, 258–73. New York: Praeger, 1980.

Molière [Jean-Baptiste Poquelin]. *L'Ecole des femmes. Oeuvres complètes.* Edited by Georges Couton. Tome 1. Paris: Editions Gallimard, Bibliothèque de la Pléiade, 1971.

———. *Les Précieuses ridicules. Oeuvres complètes.* Edited by Georges Couton. Tome 1. Paris: Editions Gallimard, Bibliothèque de la Pléiade, 1971.

Monsieur l'Abé***. *Essais de lettres familières sur toute sorte de sujets avec un discours sur l'Art Epistolaire et quelques remarques nouvelles sur la langue française.* Paris: Jacques LeFebvre, 1690.

Montaigne, Michel de. *Oeuvres complètes.* Edited by Albert Thibaudet and Maurice Rat. Paris: Editions Gallimard, Bibliothèque de la Pléiade, 1962.

Nicolich, Robert N. "Life as Theatre in the Letters of Madame de Sévigné." *Romance Notes* 16 (1975): 376–82.

Nies, Fritz. "La Fortune des *Lettres.*" *Papers on French Seventeenth Century Literature* 8, 15, 2 (1981): 129–35.

———. *Gattungspoëtik und Publikumsstruktur. Zur Geschichte der Sevigne-briefe.* Munich: Wilhelm Fink Verlag, 1972.

Ortner, Sherry. "Is Female to Male as Nature is to Culture?" In *Woman, Culture, and Society,* edited by Michelle Zimbalist Rosaldo and Louise Lamphere, 67–87. Stanford, Calif.: Stanford University Press, 1974.

Payne, Karen, ed. *Between Ourselves: Letters between Mothers and Daughters, 1750–1982.* Boston: Houghton Mifflin Company, 1983.

Perrault, Charles. *Apologie des femmes*. Paris: Editions Gibert Jeune, Librairie D'Amateurs, 1694.

Personne, André Louis. *Lettres et billets en tous les genres d'écrire*. Paris: L. Raveneau, 1662.

Poullain de la Barre, François. *De l'égalité des deux sexes*. Paris: Fayard, 1984.

Recker, Jo Anne Marie. *Appelle-moi Pierrot: Wit and Irony in the Letters of Madame de Sévigné*. Amsterdam: Benjamins, 1986.

Rich, Adrienne. *Of Woman Born: Motherhood as Experience and Institution*. New York: W. W. Norton, 1976.

Richelet, Pierre. *Les plus belles lettres des meilleurs auteurs français*. Lyon: Nenoit-Bailly, 1689.

Ruddick, Sara. "Maternal Thinking." *Feminist Studies* 6, 2 (Summer 1980): 342–67.

Sarraute, Nathalie. *Enfance*. Paris: Gallimard, 1983.

Schor, Naomi. *Breaking the Chain: Women, Theory, and French Realist Fiction*. New York: Columbia University Press, 1985.

Schweickart, Patrocinio P. "Reading Ourselves: Toward a Feminist Theory of Reading." In *Gender and Reading: Essays on Readers, Texts, and Contexts*, edited by E. A. Flynn and P. P. Schweickart, 31–62. Baltimore: Johns Hopkins University Press, 1986.

Searle, John R. *Speech Acts: An Essay in the Philosophy of Language*. Cambridge: Cambridge University Press, 1969.

Sévigné, Marie de Rabutin-Chantal, Mme de. *Correspondance*. Edited by Roger Duchêne. 3 vols. Paris: Editions Gallimard, Bibliothèque de la Pléiade, 1972–78.

———. *Lettres*. Edited by Emile Gérard-Gailly. 3 vols. Paris: Editions Gallimard, Bibliothèque de la Pléiade, 1953–57.

———. *Lettres de Madame de Sévigné, de sa famille et de ses amis*. Recueillies et annotées par M. Monmerqué. 14 vols. Paris: Hachette, Les Grands Ecrivains de la France, 1862–68.

Skura, Meredith. *The Literary Uses of the Psychoanalytic Process*. New Haven, Conn.: Yale University Press, 1981.

Smith, Barbara Herrnstein. *Contingencies of Value: Alternative Perspectives for Critical Theory*. Cambridge, Mass.: Harvard University Press, 1988.

Sorel, Charles. *Oeuvres diverses ou discours mêlés*. Paris: La Compagnie des Librairies, 1663.

Spacks, Patricia Meyer. *Gossip*. New York: Alfred A. Knopf, 1985.

Spelman, Elizabeth V. *Inessential Woman: Problems of Exclusion in Feminist Thought*. Boston: Beacon Press, 1988.

Stanton, Domna C. *The Aristocrat as Art: A Study of the Honnête Homme and the Dandy in 17th and 19th Century French Literature*. New York: Columbia University Press, 1980.

———. "On Female Portraiture in Sévigné's Letters." *Papers on French Seventeenth Century Literature*, 8, 15, 2 (1981): 89–94.

———. "Woman as Object and Subject of Exchange: Marie de Gournay's *Le Proumenoir* (1594)." *L'Esprit Créateur* 23, 2 (1983): 9–25.

Sweetser, Marie-Odile. "Madame de Sévigné: Ecrivain sans le savoir?" *Cahiers de l'Association Internationale des Etudes Françaises* 39 (mai 1987): 141–55.

Vaillé, Eugène. *Histoire générale des Postes Françaises: Louvois, Surintendant général des Postes (1668–1691).* Vol. 4. Paris: Presses Universitaires de la France, 1951.

Vaumorière, Pierre d'Ortigue de. *L'Art de plaire dans la conversation.* 2d ed. Paris: Jean Guignard, 1691.

———. *Lettres sur toutes sortes de sujets avec des avis sur la manière de les écrire.* Paris: Jean Guignard, 1690.

Verdier, Gabrielle, "Gender and Rhetoric in Some Seventeenth-Century Love Letters." *L'Esprit Créateur* 23, 2 (1983): 45–57.

Viala, Alain. *La Naissance de l'écrivain: Sociologie de la littérature à l'âge classique.* Paris: Editions de Minuit, 1985.

Villedieu, Madame de. *Recueil de quelques lettres ou relations galantes, dédié à Mlle de Sévigné.* Paris: Barbin, 1668.

Voiture, Vincent de. *Oeuvres: Lettres et poésies.* Edited by M. A. Ubicini. Paris: Charpentier, 1855; and Geneva: Slatkine Reprints, 1967.

———. *Poésies.* Critical edition by Henri Lafay. Paris: Librairie Marcel Didier, 1971.

Woolf, Virginia. "Madame de Sévigné." *Collected Essays,* 3:66–70. New York: Harcourt, Brace & World, 1967.

———. *A Room of One's Own.* New York: Harcourt, Brace & World, 1929.

Index

UNIVERSITY PRESS OF NEW ENGLAND publishes books under its own imprint and is the publisher for Brandeis University Press, Brown University Press, Clark University Press, University of Connecticut, Dartmouth College, Middlebury College Press, University of New Hampshire, University of Rhode Island, Tufts University, University of Vermont, and Wesleyan University Press.

Library of Congress Cataloging-in-Publication Data

Farrell, Michèle Longino.
  Performing motherhood : the Sévigné correspondence / Michèle Longino Farrell.
    p.   cm.
Includes bibliographical references and index.
ISBN 0–87451–536–X. — ISBN 0–87451–537–8 (pbk.)
    1. Sévigné, Marie de Rabutin-Chantal, marquise de, 1626–1696—Criticism and inter-
pretation. 2. Mothers and daughters—France—History—17th century. 3. Women and lit-
erature—France—History—17th century. 4. Authors, French—17th century—Correspon-
dence. 5. French letters—History and criticism.
I. Title.
PQ1925.F37   1991
846'.4—dc20   91–13244   ⊗